The 4 Sons Haggadah

הגדה של פסח - -

MOSAICA PRESS

THE YOUNG ISRAEL EDITION

The 4 Sons Haggadah

הגדה של פסח -

RABBI ALLEN SCHWARTZ

Published by:
Mosaica Press, Inc.
www.mosaicapress.com
info@mosaicapress.com

לזכר נשמת

אמי מורתי

חיה שרה ז"ל

בת ר' משה שניידער

ויבדל בין חיים לחיים

לכבוד אבי מורי

צבי מנחם מענדל שווארץ

שיהיה אלטע אלטע זיידע בעזה"י

משפחת שווארץ

In loving memory of

Elizabeth Kent

פיגא בת אהרון ז"ל

Steve Kent

ישראל יעקב בן קאפל הלוי ז"ל

Linda Kent

רבקה מאטל בת ישראל יעקב ז"ל

Sarah Schwartz

חיה שרה בת ר' משה ז"ל

*Michael and Michelle Schwartz
and family*

~

In memory of

Mort Kaufman

משה בן יעקב ז"ל

Rabbi Allen Schwartz is a nationally known rabbi, and we are fortunate to have this opportunity to benefit from his wisdom in this innovative Haggadah.

Jessica and I met outside Rabbi Schwartz's shul, Ohab Tzedek, as I noticed my wife coming down the steps after Friday night services, smiling. Rabbi Schwartz's shul provided a comfortable place for singles to meet, and we would never have met in this way without this opportunity.

We have always appreciated our friendship with Rabbi Schwartz and are thrilled to support this important project. We thank the Board of the National Council of Young Israel for supporting this important Haggadah to help educate the youth of our Young Israel synagogues.

Dedicated in memory of my parents
Mordecai ben Moshe (Harry Max Weiss)
and Yehudit bat Yaakov (Judge Irene Weiss)
and Jessica's father
Shaul ben Moshe (Saul Rubin)

And in honor of our children

Benjamin, Aliza, Daniella, Aryeh, Yosef, and Leora

May they learn and grow
from this tremendous Haggadah.

Jessica and Farley Weiss

Dedicated in memory of
our beloved mother on her 27th yahrzeit

Mollie (Stern) Frager
Malka bas Zalman Yehuda z"l

Dedicated in memory of
our beloved father on his 14th yahrzeit

Max Frager
Mordechai Avraham ben Shmuel z"l

Dedicated in memory of our beloved

Louis Goldstein
Leib Yehuda ben Shlomo z"l

We should all go m'chayil el chayil.
Wishing the
National Council of Young Israel
tremendous success.

Dr. David and Adena Frager

Arnon and Blimie Frager

Seena Rubenstein

Dr. Zvi and Sharon Blaustein

Jay and Rebecca Goldstein

Dr. Joseph and Karen Frager

Sherman and Susan Frager

Rabbi Eli and Chavi Alpert

ישיבת פוניבז'
ע"ר 580028286
מפעלי חתורה והחסד של מרן גאון ישראל חגרי"ש כהנמן מפוניבז' זצלל"ה
חגאון חרב אברחם כתנמן זצ"ל תשכ"יו-תשס"ט
גבעת זכרון-מאיר, קרית חישיבה, בני-ברק, ת.ד. 26
PONEVEZ YESHIVA
The Torah and Chessed Institutions of Rabbi J. Kahaneman, the Ponevez Rav'zal
Rabbi Abraham Kahaneman זצ"ל תשכ"יו-תשס"ט
KIRYAT HAYESHIVA, BNEI-BRAK, ISRAEL, P.O.B. 26
Tel. 03-6183111 טל. 111 ponevezy@gmail.com

בנשיאות ובהנהלת הרב אליעזר כהנמן
Rabbi Eliezer Kahaneman, President

בס"ד

ט' אלול תשע"ט

הובא לפני ספר הגדש"פ עם ביאור בשפת אנגלית מעשה ידי הרה"ג ר'
אליעזר שווארץ שליט"א מחשובי הרבנים באמריקא.

והנה ידוע אשר עיקר מצות סיפור יצי"מ בליל הסדר הוא להבין ולהסביר
לבני הבית ולהבנים את אשר הפליא ד' לעשות עם אבותינו ועמנו בלילה
הזה.

והדברים מפורשים ברמ"א סי' תע"ג סעיף ו' וז"ל ויאמר בלשון שמבינים
הנשים והקטנים או יפרש להם הענין וכן עשה ר"י מלונדרי כל ההגדה
בלשון לע"ז כדי שיבינו הנשים והקטנים עכ"ל.

אכן הרי מפורש בהגדה "ואפילו כולנו חכמים כולנו נבונים כולנו יודעים
את התורה מצוה עלינו לספר ביציאת מצרים", ובודאי הדברים
הנפלאים אשר הרב הגאון המחבר הנודע בשערים אשר פיו מפיק
מרגליות מביא לפנינו היום ראוים הם לבוא לפני שולחנם של חכמים
ונבונים ויודעים את התורה וימצאו בהם כדי מדתם.

ואברך את הרב הגאון המחבר שליט"א שיזכה להרבות תורה ואמונה
בישראל וחפץ ד' בידו יצלח אכי"ר.

בברכת כהנים באהבה

הרב אליעזר כהנמן

The Haggadah itself declares, "Even if we are all wise, understanding, and learned of the Torah, it is nonetheless incumbent upon us to tell the story of our departure from Egypt." The wondrous words of this commentary are worthy to be placed before the tables of wise and understanding people, steeped in Torah learning, that they may find Torah according to their own measure.

Rabbi Yehudah Aryeh Halevi Dunner

Rav, "Divrei Shir" Zeirei Agudas Israel
37 Ha'admor Migur Street, Bnei Brak 51527, Israel
Tel: 03-6181981

הרב יהודה אריה הלוי דיינר,

רב ביהכנ"ס צא"י "דברי שיר"
רח' האדמו"ר מגור 37, בני ברק 51527
טל. 03-6181981

With these lines, I would like to say how I enjoyed to see the wonderful explanations on the Haggadah of Pesach written by Rabbi Allen Schwartz, *shlita*. Every point is clear and interesting. Whoever looks inside will see *gevaldiger* thoughts. May Rabbi Schwartz continue to spread Torah and *chessed* in Eretz Yisroel and the world and be blessed from Heaven with health and wealth.

מאד שמחתי לעבור על הביאורים הנפלאים על ענייני הגדה של פסח שנכתב ע"י ידידי החשוב והנכבד רב מעש, הרב אליעזר שווארץ שליט"א, רב קהילת אוהב צדק נו יורק. הכל נכתב בבהירות ומתיקות דבר מתוקן השוה לכל נפש. והרב המחבר שליט"א כבר נודע בשערים של תורה, שהוא מרביץ תורה בארץ ישראל ובחוץ לארץ וגם מופלא בענייני חסד והחלקת תורה. ולא נשאר אלא לברך הרב המחבר שליט"א שימשיך להרביץ תורה ויראה מתוך בריאות גופא ונהורא מעליא עד ביאת המבשר במהרה בימינו אמן. ממני החתום למען כבוד התורה ולומדיה.

בכבוד רב ובידידות,

יהודה אריה הלוי דונר

AZRIELI GRADUATE SCHOOL
YESHIVA UNIVERSITY

2520 AMSTERDAM AVENUE   NEW YORK, NY 10033
(212) 960-0186
David Pelcovitz, Ph.D.,

Gwendolyn and Joseph Straus Chair in
Psychology and Education

The 4 Sons Haggadah by Rabbi Allen Schwartz provides a valuable and thought provoking perspective on the haggadah that strikes a balance between carefully presented and explained Jewish wisdom on approaching children with different cognitive and behavioral styles and current thinking in educational psychology.

Psychological research shows that the longer siblings are living under the same roof the more different they become from one another. In an effort to develop their uniqueness – siblings often develop different personalities and approaches to learning, requiring parents to meet the challenge of differentiating their strategies in teaching and inspiring each of their children. Rabbi Schwartz does a masterful job of using the haggadah's approach to the four sons as a guide helping our children to learn and connect in different ways. Using this framework one can understand the Torah's approach to the "evil" child, reframed as a cynic, as an effort to relate to a challenging family member, who by showing up to the seder, manifests a desire to continue to connect to family and Judaism. Similarly, recasting the child who doesn't even know how to ask as withdrawn allows for a novel reinterpretation of the approach to such children that is consistent with current psychological practices aimed at motivating, engaging and drawing out children with this personality.

Rabbi Schwartz has provided us with a creative, practical and inspiring approach to meeting the unique needs of our children. I strongly recommend this haggadah to anybody looking to enhance their seder experience as well as a thought provoking guide to connecting to the diverse needs of our children regardless of temperament and personality.

Contents

PREFACE

The Pesach Seder is very child-centric and I have hundreds of memories over the decades of my own children's enthusiastic participation in the Seder proceedings. Their comments, experiences, and insights have contributed to many of the thoughts included in this work and I recognize here the incredible *nachas* that we have derived over the years from Shonnie, Chani, Moshe, Ellie, Esti, and Mindy.

This work would never have seen the light of day if not for the comments and significant technical contributions made by my life partner, Alisa. This Haggadah is hers as much as it is mine. I would also like to thank my parents for bequeathing to me the most wonderful memories of our Sedarim so many years ago. This work is dedicated in part, to the memory of my mother, Chaya Sara bas Rav Moshe, a"h, and להבדיל בין חיים לחיים, to my father, he should be well, Mr. Milton Schwartz. They built their lives from the ashes and taught us the value of self-sacrifice, the moral underpinnings and love of Torah and Jewish observance. Their generation served as a crucial bridge of Jewish continuity at a very critical time for our people.

My Pesach thoughts have also been molded by my thirty-plus years at Congregation Ohab Zedek. We ran many a Seder for the community at the shul, and those experiences have created many long-term memories for me and my family. I have spent more than half my life at this wonderful shul and it too has played a significant role since the middle of the nineteenth century in assuring Jewish continuity through very challenging times.

Of course, I would like to thank the students I have taught at Yeshiva University, Manhattan Day School, Ma'ayanot High School, Ramaz High School, Camp Morasha, and Camp Mesorah over the last thirty-five years. The Rabbinic claim that our students teach us more than anyone is an appropriate dictum for this work.

Finally, my *hakaras hatov* goes out to the staff at Mosaica Press for their professional handling of this work and the expert guidance extended along every step of the way to take this book to its final stages. I thank Rabbi Yaacov Haber, Rabbi Reuven Butler, Doron Kornbluth, Sherie Gross, Rayzel Broyde, and Brocha Mirel Strizower for all their efforts.

INTRODUCTION

We call this book the "Haggadah" on the basis of the verse, "והגדת לבנך ביום ההוא — You shall **relate** to your son on that day."[1] The history that the Haggadah recounts tells us our first story as a people. The Torah could have used several words to describe the sharing of our history. The Hebrew phraseology could have been "ואמרת לבנך — You shall **say** to your son," or "ודברת לבנך — You shall **speak** to your son," or perhaps even "וספרת לבנך — You shall **recount** to your son." None of these, however, capture the essence of the word "והגדת — You shall **relate**."

The Midrash[2] expounds the use of the same root in the verse "ותגיד לבני ישראל — **Relate** to the People of Israel,"[3] at the Revelation at Sinai as follows: "הגד להם ותדקדק עמהם — Relate to them and be precise with them." The Talmud[4] expounds this verse in three additional ways, on the verse, "ויגד משה את דברי העם אל ה' — Moshe **related** the people's words to God,"[5] also in the context of the Revelation at Sinai. One, that Moshe spoke to the Israelites in a way that was as tough as sinews.[6] Additionally, the Talmud relates that Moshe spoke in a way that imparted, "דברים שמשיבין דעתו של אדם — words **that appease** the minds of man." This is derived from a similar expression of Moshe declaring the words of the people to God; "וישב משה את דברי העם אל ה' — Moshe **brought back** the people's words to God."[7] Finally, the Talmud

---

1   *Shemos* 13:8.

2   *Mechilta, Shemos* 19:3; ותגיד לבני ישראל.

3   *Shemos* 19:3.

4   *Talmud Bavli, Shabbos* 87a.

5   *Shemos* 19:9.

6   *Rashi* translates גידים as a bitter plant, as does *Aruch* (גד). Others translate the word as "sinews." See *Torah Sheleimah, Shemos* 19:3, ד"ה נאות, where attention is drawn to the spelling of the word ותגיד. It is the only place in the Torah where this root has a י between the letters ג and ד, which hints at גידים. This may be why *Rashi* cites this explanation to *Shemos* 19:3, whereas the Talmud connects this exposition to *Shemos* 19:9, cited above.

7   This exposition stems from *Shemos* 19:8, which is part of the same dialogue between God and the Israelites. Only, instead of ויגד, the verb is וישב, which hints to an expression of ישוב, or appeasement.

expounds that Moshe imparted דברים שמושכין את לבו של אדם כאגדה, that he spoke in a way that would draw their hearts as *Aggadah* does.[8]

These four expositions demonstrate that we must impart Torah in a way that is tailored specifically to the minds and imaginations of those listening.

The Haggadah itself is aware of four different types of children and requires us to relate to each on his own level. This is expressed in the most basic Biblical verse defining educational theory: "חנוך לנער על פי דרכו — Educate the child according to his own way."[9] We can apply these four expositions stemming from the revelation at Sinai to the four sons of the Haggadah.

1. הגד להם ותדקדק עמהם — **Relate to them and be precise with them**. This would apply to the *chacham*, the wise son who scrupulously categorizes everything he sees as he precisely formulates his question about the testimonies, statutes, and judgments before him. He deserves a scrupulously detailed answer.

2. קשין לאדם כגידים — **As tough to a person as sinews**. This approach prefers not to beat around the bush. This child, called the *rasha*, is being cynical and needs a direct approach. Sinews connect tendons. They strengthen limbs. A chain is only as strong as its weakest link. This has often been said to justify extra care and concern for the *she'eino yodei'a lishol* type of child who is withdrawn, but the cynical child requires the same care on our part. It is incumbent upon us to know how to reach him.[10]

3. דברים שמשיבין דעתו של אדם — **Words that appease the minds of man**. We are bidden to teach this child in a way that will appease his spirit. He is תם, simple and pure. He is a blank page. Educators must rise to the challenge to assure that the spirit of this child is settled and ready to absorb the lessons of the Torah and the redemption from Egypt.

4. דברים שמושכים את לבו של אדם כאגדה — **Words that draw the hearts of man as Aggadah does**. We must open up to him in a way that excites him as a good story can. The name Haggadah stems from the verse that relates to this child, the שאינו יודע לשאול. "והגדת לבנך — you shall relate to your son" is the only one of the verses that is not preceded by a question, because this child did not ask one, and he may not ever ask unless we draw it out of him.[11]

---

8   *Aggadah*, which stems from the same word as Haggadah, draws the attention of people. It is a collection of the moral and ethical expositions of the commandments and Biblical narratives. See below *Baruch HaMakom* (Maggid section 6), at the end of the *chacham*'s answer of why the Haggadah says, כנגד ארבעה בנים, **opposite** four sons.

9   *Mishlei* 22:6.

10 See *Chazon Ish*, *Yoreh Deah* 2:16, where he suggests that the mitzvah to hate the sinner in light of *Talmud Bavli, Bava Metzia* 32b, no longer applies today because we have lost the art of reaching such people.

11 See *Ibn Ezra*, *Shemos* 19:9, ומלת הגיד לעולם על דבר חדש שלא הזכירו. The word הגיד always refers to something new that had not been previously mentioned. This also bespeaks the necessary creativity to draw out the withdrawn child.

Each of these children presents the educator or parent with a unique challenge, and the message of the Haggadah is to approach each one from his own direction — על פי דרכו.[12]

The thesis of this work is to present the *inquisitive* learner with three different approaches to each paragraph of the Maggid Section of the Haggadah, and a fourth approach, to present to a withdrawn child who is not yet inquisitive. In all, four different approaches to each section of Maggid will be presented.

A few final notes: The exposition of four Torah verses to relate to four sons is found, besides in the Haggadah, in the *Mechilta*[13] as well as the *Talmud Yerushalmi*.[14] There are some minor and some significant differences between these three sources, and we will address them in Maggid Section 7. However, one difference must be addressed at this early stage of this work. The Haggadah's categorization of the four children seems incongruous. Three sons are described by intellect — the wise son, the simpleton, and the son with no capacity to inquire — while only one is described by morality, the wicked son.

Perhaps we can settle this incongruity if we describe the *tam* as a pure son rather than as a simpleton.[15] With this new interpretation, the pure son stands in contrast to the wicked son on moral grounds, while the wise son stands in contrast

---

12 Rav Shimshon Raphael Hirsch in his commentary to *Bereishis* 25:27, ד"ה ויגדלו הנערים, makes this point with respect to the upbringing of Yaakov and Eisav.

Our Sages, who never objected to drawing attention to the small and great mistakes and weaknesses in the history of our great forefathers, thereby making them all the more instructive for us (see remarks to *Bereishis* 12:10), here, too, on ויגדלו הנערים, make a remark which is indeed a "signpost" for all of us. They point out that the striking contrast in the grandchildren of Avraham may have been due not so much to a difference in their temperaments as to mistakes in the way they were brought up. As long as they were little, no attention was paid to the slumbering differences in their natures (see *Rashi*, verse 24), both had exactly the same teaching and educational treatment, and the great law of education "חנוך לנער על פי דרכו וגו' — Bring up each child in accordance with his own way" was forgotten; that each child must be treated differently, with an eye to the dormant tendencies of his nature, and out of them, be educated to develop his special characteristics for the one pure human and Jewish life. The great Jewish task in life is basically simple, one and the same for all, but in its realization is as complicated and varied as human natures and tendencies are varied, and the manifold varieties of life that result from them.

Had Yitzchak and Rivkah studied Eisav's nature and character early enough, and asked themselves how all the strength and energy, agility, and courage that lay slumbering in this child be won over to be used in the service of God, and the future גבור be trained to become not a גבור ציד but in truth a גבור לפני ה', then Yaakov and Eisav, with their totally different natures, could still have remained twin brothers in spirit and life; quite early in life, Eisav's "sword" and Yaakov's "spirit" could have worked hand in hand, and who can say what a different aspect the whole history of the ages might have presented. But, as it was, ויגדלו הנערים, only when the boys had grown into men, one was surprised to see that, out of one and the selfsame womb, having had exactly the same care, training, and schooling, two such contrasting persons emerge.

13 *Mechilta, Bo* §125 (*Shemos* 13:14).

14 *Talmud Yerushalmi, Pesachim* 10:4.

15 This would appear to be the Sages' view of the description of Yaakov in *Bereishis* 25:27 and it would surely appear to be the way *Rashi*'s grandson Rav Yaakov — Rabbeinu Tam — understood the word, and is indeed the interpretation of the *Vilna Gaon*.

to the son without capacity to inquire on intellectual grounds.[16] We will prefer the designation of the word "תם" for this child, found in the Haggadah and the *Mechilta*, to the *Yerushalmi's* designation, "טפש," a stupid child.[17] With this designation, the incongruity falls away. Therefore "תם" will be translated as "the pure son." As such, the answers to the question in this work will be addressed to people who are wise, cynical, pure, and withdrawn.

Additionally, not every question in this work will have answers for all four sons. When there is no compelling explanation of a particular question for one son over another, a generic answer will be offered.

Finally, in some instances, the questions are interspersed as to require one long answer to each child for all the questions. In other paragraphs of the Haggadah, each question is answered separately for all four sons.

The Structure of Maggid

The *Seder* is called as such because of its systematic order. The Sections of Maggid are as follows.

1. הא לחמא עניא — *Ha Lachma Anya*
2. מה נשתנה — *Mah Nishtanah*
3. עבדים היינו — *Avadim Hayinu*
4. מעשה ברבי אליעזר —*Maaseh B'Rabbi Eliezer*
5. אמר רבי אלעזר בן עזריה — *Amar Rabbi Elazar ben Azaryah*
6. ברוך המקום — *Baruch HaMakom*
7. ארבעה בנים — *K'Neged Arbah Banim*
7a. חכם — *Chacham*
7b. רשע — *Rasha*
7c. תם — *Tam*
7d. שאינו יודע לשאול — *V'She'Eino Yodei'a Lishol*
8. יכול מראש חדש — *Yachol MeiRosh Chodesh*
9. מתחילה עובדי עבודה זרה — *MiTchilah Ovedei Avodah Zarah*
10. ברוך שומר הבטחתו — *Baruch Shomer Havtachaso L'Yisrael*

---

16   See Rav Aharon Soloveitchik, *Logic of the Heart, Logic of the Mind* (Genesis Jerusalem Press; 1991), pp. 23–29; See also *Iyov* 9:22 where תם is contrasted with רשע.

17   *Yalkut Shimoni, Bo* §225, also refers to this child as טיפש, as does *Rashi, Shemos* 13:14, ד"ה מה זאת, who says זה תינוק טפש שאינו יודע להעמיק שאלתו וסותם ושואל מה זאת ובמקום אחר הוא אומר מה העדות והחקים והמשפטים וגו' הרי זאת שאלת בן חכם. דברה תורה כנגד ארבעה בנים תם רשע ושאינו יודע לשאול והשואל דרך חכמה. *Rashi* is clearly not sensitive to the question of dichotomy posed here. *Rambam*, in *Hilchos Chametz U'Matzah* 7:2, also refers to this child as a טיפש.

   See below, *Arbah Banim — Tam* (Maggid Section 7c), where more evidence of the intellectual purity of this child is presented.

11. והיא שעמדה — *V'Hee She'Amdah*

12. צא ולמד — *Tzei U'Lemad*

13. מקרא ביכורים — *Mikra Bikkurim*

13a. וירד מצרימה — *Va'yeired Mitzraimah*

13b. ויגר שם — *VaYagar Sham*

13c. במתי מעט — *Bimsei M'at*

13d. ויהי שם לגוי — *VaYehi Sham*

13e. גדול ועצום — *Gadol V'Atzum*

13f. ורב — *VaRav*

13g. וירעו אותנו המצרים — *VaYarei'u*

13h. ויענונו — *VaYe'anunu*

13i. ויתנו עלינו עבודה קשה — *VaYitnu Aleinu*

13j. ונצעק אל ה' אלוקי אבותינו — *VaNitzak El Hashem*

13k. וישמע ה' את קולנו — *VaYishma Hashem*

13l. וירא את ענינו — *VaYar Es Anyeinu*

13m. ואת עמלינו — *V'Es Amaleinu*

13n. ואת לחצינו — *V'Es Lachatzeinu*

13o. ויוציאנו ה' ממצרים — *VaYotzienu Hashem*

13p. ביד חזקה — *B'Yad Chazakah*

13q. ובזרוע נטויה — *U'Vizro'a Netuyah*

13r. ובמורא גדול — *U'Vemora Gadol*

13s. ובאותות — *U'Ve'Osos*

13t. ובמופתים — *U'Vemofsim*

14a. דבר אחר — *Davar Acher*

14b. אלו עשר מכות — *Eilu Eser Makkos*

14c. רבי יוסי הגלילי — *Rabbi Yosi HaGelili*

15a. כמה מעלות — *Kamah Maalos Tovos/Dayeinu*

15b. על אחת כמה וכמה — *Al Achas Kamah V'Kamah*

16. רבן גמליאל היה אומר — *Rabban Gamliel Hayah Omer*

16a. פסח — *Pesach*

16b. מצה — *Matzah*

16c. מרור — *Maror*

17. בכל דור ודור — *Bechol Dor VaDor*

18. לפיכך — *Lefichach*

19. תהלים קיג-קיד — *Hallel: Tehillim 113–114*

20. ברכת הגאולה — *Birchas HeGeulah*

A series of questions follow regarding the order and inclusion of certain paragraphs in *Maggid*.[18] Since the basis of the mitzvah of *sippur yetzias Mitzrayim* is the Torah verse that speaks to the שאינו יודע לשאול, the withdrawn child, these questions heavily favor pedagogical methods directed to such a participant at the *Seder*. It is likely that the one for whom we need to be most prepared at the *Seder* is just such a participant. Surely we need to have answers ready for a broad spectrum of questions, but we need to be most prepared to present material to those who don't know how to ask or perhaps even more so for those who *do* know, but aren't interested in participating (that would be שאינו רוצה לשאול). It is incumbent upon us to be ready for all types of discussions, and if necessary, educe information from participants, the best form of education.

- *Avadim Hayinu* and *Mitchilah Ovedei Avodah Zarah* (Maggid Sections 3 and 9) both fulfill the Talmudic requirement of telling the story of the Exodus from Egypt by first referring to the shameful and disparaging part of our history and then moving on to the praiseworthy elements. This is known as מתחיל בגנות ומסיים בשבח.[19] Rav and Shmuel argue whether this is fulfilled by *Avadim Hayinu* or *Mitchilah Ovedei Avodah Zarah*, so we include both, but why is *Avadim Hayinu* recited first? Surely *Mitchilah Ovedei Avodah Zarah*, which references Terach and Avraham, precedes *Avadim Hayinu* chronologically. The perfect place for *Avadim Hayinu* should have been right *after Mitchilah Ovedei Avodah Zarah*, since this passage ends with, "ויעקב ובניו ירדו מצרים — Yaakov and his sons descended to Egypt."

- On a night of storytelling and inspiring children to ask questions, what is the significance of *Amar Rabbi Elazar ben Azaryah* (Maggid Section 5), which refers to the daily mitzvah to remember the Exodus from Egypt (Mishnah, *Berachos* 1:5)? If remembering the Exodus from Egypt is a mitzvah every night, what is so special about Pesach night?

- What is the significance of *Yachol MeiRosh Chodesh* (Maggid Section 8)? Why should the Haggadah consider other possible times for telling the story of the Exodus, and what connection does it have to the Four Sons, after which this passage is placed?

- Why is the main source of exposition of Maggid the Rabbinic *derash* of the *Sifri* to *Devarim* 26:5–8, discussing *Mikra Bikkurim*, that is said in Maggid Section 13? Wouldn't it be better to expound verses in *Shemos* where the story takes place?

---

18 Some of these questions are asked by *Malbim* and his answers divide Maggid into six sections, based on the verse "והגדת לבנך ביום ההוא לאמר בעבור זה עשה ה' לי בצאתי ממצרים — You shall relate to your son on that day, saying: It is because of what God did for me when I left Egypt."

19 *Talmud Bavli, Pesachim* 116a.

- *Rabban Gamliel Hayah Omer* (Maggid Section 16) seems to be out of place. It is a Mishnah at the end of *Maseches Pesachim*,[20] and requires the recitation of specific statements to assure participants of the *Seder* know why we are performing the mitzvos of the evening. Perhaps a better place for it would have been right after *Yachol MeiRosh Chodesh* (Maggid Section 8), when we say, "לא אמרתי בעבור זה אלא בשעה שיש מצה ומרור מונחים לפניך — I only said 'for the sake of *this*' to state that this mitzvah only applies when we have matzah and maror before us."[21] Moreover, this passage interrupts Maggid Sections 15 and 17 — *Dayeinu* and *Bechol Dor VaDor* — which seem to be very well connected. *Dayeinu* refers to all of God's kindnesses throughout our early history and *Bechol Dor VaDor* refers to the obligation of every generation to feel as if these kindnesses were replicated in our own day. Why interrupt these two thematically connected passages with Rabban Gamliel's obligation?
- Why is *Bechol Dor VaDor* the end of Maggid? We have already established that every generation must feel the personal effects of the Exodus from Egypt, and that we and our descendants would still be enslaved if not for God's intervention. Surely this is the main point of *Avadim Hayinu*, said above in Maggid Section 3. Why repeat it here?
- Why do we begin *Hallel* where we do? If it is to be completed after the meal, why not simply say the full *Hallel* after the meal?
- The name of the book we read at the *Seder* is the Haggadah. This stems from the command to relate the Egyptian Exodus to our children, even if they fail to ask about it. Perhaps a better name of the book would have been סיפור, which is the root of storytelling. The verb is used in the Torah[22] in the context of the redemption, as well as the Haggadah itself.[23]

The *Malbim* explains that the Haggadah is based on this Torah verse "והגדת לבנך ביום ההוא לאמר בעבור זה עשה יהוה לי בצאתי ממצרים — And you shall relate to your son on that day, saying, 'It is because of this that God acted for me when I left Egypt'" (*Shemos* 13:8), and that Maggid is based on breaking down the verse into the following six sections.

1. והגדת לבנך — **And you shall relate to your son:** Maggid Sections 1–7.

---

20   Ibid.

21   Rabban Gamliel's passage refers to the *matzah* that our ancestors ate. The *Yachol MeiRosh Chodesh* section of Maggid refers to what *we* are doing, and, at the time the Haggadah was codified, we were no longer offering the *korban Pesach*.

22   See *Shemos* 10:2; "ולמען תספר באזני בנך ובן בנך — And that **you may recount** in the hearing of your sons and your son's sons."

23   See the *Maaseh B'Rabbi Eliezer* section of Maggid (Maggid Section 4); "שהיו מספרים ביציאת מצרים כל אותו הלילה — They were **recounting** the story of the Exodus from Egypt that entire night."

2. ביום ההוא — **On that day**: Maggid Section 8.

3. לאמר — **Saying**: Maggid Sections 9–15.

4. בעבור זה — **It is because of this**: Maggid Section 16 (a–c).

5. עשה ה' לי — **That God acted for me**: Maggid Section 17.

6. צאתי ממצרים — **When I left Egypt**: Maggid Sections 18–20.

1. והגדת לבנך — **And you shall relate to your son** (Maggid Sections 1–7): This section does not yet tell any story or narrative. It is an introduction to tell us *why* we are obligated to recount the story. This is not merely an intellectual endeavor. If that were the case, elders would perform the mitzvah very quickly, largely aided by what they already know. Such a brief reference may suffice for the rest of the year's daily obligation to remember the redemption. The night of Pesach however, is different. This is the night when we preserve Jewish continuity. This is the night that we point to more than just wisdom, but to actual experience. These passages assure that our children will also teach these concepts to their children as the process continues, בכל דור ודור, in every generation. The Sages mentioned in this section indicate that while the rest of the year, we remember something, tonight we tell it to someone else and share our experiences. As such, *Avadim Hayinu* is not out of place. It is perfectly situated to begin Maggid with an explanation of *why* we have the *Seder* on Pesach. (This answers questions 1 and 2.)

2. ביום ההוא — **On that day** (Maggid Section 8): The obligation to tell the story of our redemption is tied to a particular day. The mitzvah of *sippur yetzias Mitzrayim* must be experiential. It is for this reason that we fulfill this mitzvah while eating matzah and maror. *Yachol MeiRosh Chodesh* (Maggid Section 8) is perfectly placed as an addendum to the parents' message to the withdrawn child who doesn't ask questions. The statement to him includes the word "זה — this." זה is said when we see something, or when we point to something.[24] This is an important pedagogical method for teaching withdrawn children. We must pique their interest with clarity and point directly to what they can understand. בעבור זה connects *Arbah Banim* and *Yachol MeiRosh Chodesh* (Maggid Sections 7 and 8) with the first two sections of Maggid, and explains the importance of יכול מראש חודש. (This answers question 3.)

3. לאמר — **Saying** (Maggid Sections 9–15): This section begins to tell our history and connects the experience in Egypt to subsequent subjugations and

---

24 See *Talmud Bavli, Menachos* 29a and its exposition of the verses of "זה מעשה המנורה — **this** is how the Menorah is made" (*Bamidbar* 8:4), "החודש הזה לכם — **This** month is for you" (*Shemos* 12:2), "זה לכם הטמא — **This** is unclean to you" (*Vayikra* 11:29), and "זה אשר תעשה על המזבח — **This** is what you shall offer on the Altar" (*Shemos* 29:37). See also *Talmud Bavli, Taanis* 31a, "זה ה' קוינו לו — **This** is God to whom we had hoped" (*Yeshayahu* 25:9), and *Talmud Yerushalmi, Moed Katan* 18a, "כי זה אלוקים אלוקינו — For **this** is God, our God" (*Tehillim* 48:15).

salvations. The main section is an exposition of *Devarim* 26:5–8 and the word-by-word or phrase-by-phrase *derash* of *Sifri*, to paint a picture of the details of slavery and redemption culminating in the Ten Plagues and our entry into the Land of Israel. Since entry into Israel is the culmination of our redemption, we don't expound verses in *Shemos* where the story actually unfolds, but from *Sefer Devarim* as we prepare to enter the Promised Land. These verses were recited by one who delivers his first fruits to the Temple and are also a connection to the ongoing redemption. (This answers question 4.)

4. בעבור זה — **It is because of this** (Maggid Section 16): Rabban Gamliel did not mean that one must recite three paragraphs in order to fulfill the various mitzvos of Pesach, matzah, and maror. The Talmud[25] states that even if a Jew was force-fed matzah he would fulfill his obligation, ostensibly even without reciting these paragraphs. Rather, Rabban Gamliel means that one does not fulfill the mitzvah of *sippur yetzias Mitzrayim* without pointing to these mitzvos. Once again, the word זה is operative in the verse to the child as well as to Rabban Gamliel. *Rabban Gamliel Hayah Omer* (Maggid Section 16) is thus not out of place. It is recited near the actual eating of the matzah and maror to connect these mitzvos to the mitzvah of Maggid. *Kamah Maalos Tovos/Dayeinu* (Maggid Section 15) is still part of לאמר because a component of Maggid is to feel thankful. (This answers question 5.)

5. עשה ה' לי — **That God acted for me** (Maggid Section 17) — These words are the source of the obligation for each person to consider the personal effect of the redemption. The key word is לי, and this is why this verse is also told to the cynical son, who removes himself from the proceedings. The *Seder* is meant to be inclusive, where we inculcate a sense of belonging and personal experience. It is only after all the detail of the previous paragraphs that we can truly feel the personal experience. (This answers question 6.)

6. בצאתי ממצרים — **When I left Egypt** (Maggid Sections 18–20) — This section of Maggid assures that we translate all our experiences of the evening beyond faith, to include gratitude. We do so with expressions of praises and thanksgiving, which explains why we begin *Hallel* at this juncture of the *Seder*[26] to paraphrase these very words as we do in *Tehillim* 114. (This answers question 7.)

7. The answer to question 8 is now also clear. The main section of the Haggadah, called Maggid, is fundamentally based on the verse which begins והגדת לבנך, so the perfect name of the book to fulfill the mitzvah of *sippur yetzias Mitzrayim* is the Haggadah.

---

25 *Talmud Bavli, Rosh Hashanah* 28a.

26 See first question in *Lefichach* (Maggid Section 18) for why we say two chapters of *Hallel* before the meal and the rest of *Hallel* after the meal.

בְּדִיקַת חָמֵץ

On the night of the fourteenth of Nisan, a search for chametz is conducted by the light of a candle. Before the search, the following blessing is recited:

בָּרוּךְ אַתָּה יהוה אֱלֹהֵינוּ מֶלֶךְ הָעוֹלָם, אֲשֶׁר קִדְּשָׁנוּ בְּמִצְוֹתָיו וְצִוָּנוּ עַל בִּעוּר חָמֵץ:

Blessed are You, Hashem, our God, King of the universe, Who has sanctified us with His commandments and commanded us concerning the removal of chametz.

Conversation not relating to the search should be avoided until the search is completed. After the search, the following declaration of nullification is made:

כָּל חֲמִירָא וַחֲמִיעָא דְּאִכָּא בִרְשׁוּתִי, דְּלָא חֲמִתֵּהּ, וּדְלָא בְעַרְתֵּהּ, וּדְלָא יְדַעְנָא לֵיהּ, לִבָּטֵל וְלֶהֱוֵי הֶפְקֵר כְּעַפְרָא דְאַרְעָא:

בִּעוּר חָמֵץ

The chametz is burned on the morning of the fourteenth of Nisan, before the end of the fifth hour of daylight. After burning the chametz, the following declaration is made:

כָּל חֲמִירָא וַחֲמִיעָא דְּאִכָּא בִרְשׁוּתִי, דַּחֲזִתֵּהּ וּדְלָא חֲזִתֵּהּ, דַּחֲמִתֵּהּ וּדְלָא חֲמִתֵּהּ, דְּבַעַרְתֵּהּ וּדְלָא בַעַרְתֵּהּ, לִבָּטֵל וְלֶהֱוֵי הֶפְקֵר כְּעַפְרָא דְאַרְעָא:

All leavening and chametz that is in my possession, which I have not seen nor disposed of and about which I am unaware, is hereby nullified and shall be ownerless as the dust of the earth.

סדר אמירת קרבן פסח

Following *Minchah*, many people have the custom to recite the verses which relate to the bringing of the Pesach offering.

רִבּוֹן הָעוֹלָמִים, אַתָּה צִוִּיתָנוּ לְהַקְרִיב קָרְבַּן הַפֶּסַח בְּמוֹעֲדוֹ בְּאַרְבָּעָה עָשָׂר יוֹם לַחֹדֶשׁ הָרִאשׁוֹן, וְלִהְיוֹת כֹּהֲנִים בַּעֲבוֹדָתָם וּלְוִיִּם בְּדוּכָנָם וְיִשְׂרָאֵל בְּמַעֲמָדָם קוֹרְאִים אֶת הַהַלֵּל. וְעַתָּה בַּעֲוֹנוֹתֵינוּ חָרַב בֵּית הַמִּקְדָּשׁ וּבָטַל קָרְבַּן הַפֶּסַח, וְאֵין לָנוּ לֹא כֹהֵן בַּעֲבוֹדָתוֹ וְלֹא לֵוִי בְּדוּכָנוֹ וְלֹא יִשְׂרָאֵל בְּמַעֲמָדוֹ, וְלֹא נוּכַל לְהַקְרִיב הַיּוֹם קָרְבַּן פָּסַח. אֲבָל אַתָּה אָמַרְתָּ וּנְשַׁלְּמָה פָרִים שְׂפָתֵינוּ. לָכֵן יְהִי רָצוֹן מִלְּפָנֶיךָ יְיָ אֱלֹהֵינוּ וֵאלֹהֵי אֲבוֹתֵינוּ שֶׁיִּהְיֶה שִׂיחַ שִׂפְתוֹתֵינוּ חָשׁוּב לְפָנֶיךָ כְּאִלּוּ הִקְרַבְנוּ אֶת הַפֶּסַח בְּמוֹעֲדוֹ וְעָמַדְנוּ עַל מַעֲמָדוֹ, וְדִבְּרוּ הַלְוִיִּם בְּשִׁיר וְהַלֵּל לְהוֹדוֹת לַיָי. וְאַתָּה תִכּוֹן מִקְדָּשְׁךָ עַל מְכוֹנוֹ, וְנַעֲשֶׂה וְנַקְרִיב לְפָנֶיךָ אֶת הַפֶּסַח בְּמוֹעֲדוֹ, כְּמוֹ שֶׁכָּתַבְתָּ עָלֵינוּ בְּתוֹרָתֶךָ עַל יְדֵי מֹשֶׁה עַבְדֶּךָ כָּאָמוּר:

שמות יב:א-יא

וַיֹּאמֶר יְהֹוָה אֶל מֹשֶׁה וְאֶל אַהֲרֹן בְּאֶרֶץ מִצְרַיִם לֵאמֹר: הַחֹדֶשׁ הַזֶּה לָכֶם רֹאשׁ חֳדָשִׁים רִאשׁוֹן הוּא לָכֶם לְחָדְשֵׁי הַשָּׁנָה: דַּבְּרוּ אֶל כָּל עֲדַת יִשְׂרָאֵל לֵאמֹר בֶּעָשֹׂר לַחֹדֶשׁ הַזֶּה וְיִקְחוּ לָהֶם אִישׁ שֶׂה לְבֵית אָבֹת שֶׂה לַבָּיִת: וְאִם יִמְעַט הַבַּיִת מִהְיוֹת מִשֶּׂה וְלָקַח הוּא וּשְׁכֵנוֹ הַקָּרֹב אֶל בֵּיתוֹ בְּמִכְסַת נְפָשֹׁת אִישׁ לְפִי אָכְלוֹ תָּכֹסּוּ עַל הַשֶּׂה: שֶׂה תָמִים זָכָר בֶּן שָׁנָה יִהְיֶה לָכֶם מִן הַכְּבָשִׂים וּמִן הָעִזִּים תִּקָּחוּ: וְהָיָה לָכֶם לְמִשְׁמֶרֶת עַד אַרְבָּעָה עָשָׂר יוֹם לַחֹדֶשׁ הַזֶּה וְשָׁחֲטוּ אֹתוֹ כֹּל קְהַל עֲדַת יִשְׂרָאֵל בֵּין הָעַרְבָּיִם: וְלָקְחוּ מִן הַדָּם וְנָתְנוּ עַל שְׁתֵּי הַמְּזוּזֹת וְעַל הַמַּשְׁקוֹף עַל הַבָּתִּים אֲשֶׁר יֹאכְלוּ אֹתוֹ בָּהֶם: וְאָכְלוּ אֶת הַבָּשָׂר בַּלַּיְלָה הַזֶּה צְלִי אֵשׁ וּמַצּוֹת עַל מְרֹרִים יֹאכְלֻהוּ: אַל תֹּאכְלוּ מִמֶּנּוּ נָא וּבָשֵׁל מְבֻשָּׁל בַּמָּיִם כִּי אִם צְלִי אֵשׁ רֹאשׁוֹ עַל כְּרָעָיו וְעַל קִרְבּוֹ: וְלֹא תוֹתִירוּ מִמֶּנּוּ עַד בֹּקֶר וְהַנֹּתָר מִמֶּנּוּ עַד בֹּקֶר בָּאֵשׁ תִּשְׂרֹפוּ: וְכָכָה תֹּאכְלוּ אֹתוֹ מָתְנֵיכֶם חֲגֻרִים נַעֲלֵיכֶם בְּרַגְלֵיכֶם וּמַקֶּלְכֶם בְּיֶדְכֶם וַאֲכַלְתֶּם אֹתוֹ בְּחִפָּזוֹן פֶּסַח הוּא לַיָי:

שמות יב:כא-כח

וַיִּקְרָא מֹשֶׁה לְכָל זִקְנֵי יִשְׂרָאֵל וַיֹּאמֶר אֲלֵהֶם מִשְׁכוּ וּקְחוּ לָכֶם צֹאן לְמִשְׁפְּחֹתֵיכֶם וְשַׁחֲטוּ הַפָּסַח: וּלְקַחְתֶּם אֲגֻדַּת אֵזוֹב וּטְבַלְתֶּם בַּדָּם אֲשֶׁר בַּסַּף וְהִגַּעְתֶּם אֶל הַמַּשְׁקוֹף וְאֶל שְׁתֵּי הַמְּזוּזֹת מִן הַדָּם אֲשֶׁר בַּסָּף וְאַתֶּם לֹא תֵצְאוּ אִישׁ מִפֶּתַח בֵּיתוֹ עַד בֹּקֶר: וְעָבַר יְהֹוָה לִנְגֹּף אֶת מִצְרַיִם וְרָאָה אֶת הַדָּם עַל הַמַּשְׁקוֹף וְעַל שְׁתֵּי הַמְּזוּזֹת וּפָסַח יְהֹוָה עַל הַפֶּתַח וְלֹא יִתֵּן הַמַּשְׁחִית לָבֹא אֶל בָּתֵּיכֶם לִנְגֹּף: וּשְׁמַרְתֶּם אֶת הַדָּבָר הַזֶּה לְחָק לְךָ וּלְבָנֶיךָ עַד

עוֹלָם: וְהָיָה כִּי תָבֹאוּ אֶל הָאָרֶץ אֲשֶׁר יִתֵּן יְהֹוָה לָכֶם כַּאֲשֶׁר דִּבֵּר וּשְׁמַרְתֶּם אֶת הָעֲבֹדָה הַזֹּאת: וְהָיָה כִּי יֹאמְרוּ אֲלֵיכֶם בְּנֵיכֶם מָה הָעֲבֹדָה הַזֹּאת לָכֶם: וַאֲמַרְתֶּם זֶבַח פֶּסַח הוּא לַיְהֹוָה אֲשֶׁר פָּסַח עַל בָּתֵּי בְנֵי יִשְׂרָאֵל בְּמִצְרַיִם בְּנָגְפּוֹ אֶת מִצְרַיִם וְאֶת בָּתֵּינוּ הִצִּיל וַיִּקֹּד הָעָם וַיִּשְׁתַּחֲווּ: וַיֵּלְכוּ וַיַּעֲשׂוּ בְּנֵי יִשְׂרָאֵל כַּאֲשֶׁר צִוָּה יְהֹוָה אֶת מֹשֶׁה וְאַהֲרֹן כֵּן עָשׂוּ:

שמות יב:מג-נ

וַיֹּאמֶר יְהֹוָה אֶל מֹשֶׁה וְאַהֲרֹן זֹאת חֻקַּת הַפָּסַח כָּל בֶּן נֵכָר לֹא יֹאכַל בּוֹ: וְכָל עֶבֶד אִישׁ מִקְנַת כָּסֶף וּמַלְתָּה אֹתוֹ אָז יֹאכַל בּוֹ: תּוֹשָׁב וְשָׂכִיר לֹא יֹאכַל בּוֹ: בְּבַיִת אֶחָד יֵאָכֵל לֹא תוֹצִיא מִן הַבַּיִת מִן הַבָּשָׂר חוּצָה וְעֶצֶם לֹא תִשְׁבְּרוּ בוֹ: כָּל עֲדַת יִשְׂרָאֵל יַעֲשׂוּ אֹתוֹ: וְכִי יָגוּר אִתְּךָ גֵּר וְעָשָׂה פֶסַח לַיְהֹוָה הִמּוֹל לוֹ כָל זָכָר וְאָז יִקְרַב לַעֲשֹׂתוֹ וְהָיָה כְּאֶזְרַח הָאָרֶץ וְכָל עָרֵל לֹא יֹאכַל בּוֹ: תּוֹרָה אַחַת יִהְיֶה לָאֶזְרָח וְלַגֵּר הַגָּר בְּתוֹכְכֶם: וַיַּעֲשׂוּ כָּל בְּנֵי יִשְׂרָאֵל כַּאֲשֶׁר צִוָּה יְהֹוָה אֶת מֹשֶׁה וְאֶת אַהֲרֹן כֵּן עָשׂוּ:

ויקרא כג:ד-ה

אֵלֶּה מוֹעֲדֵי יְהֹוָה מִקְרָאֵי קֹדֶשׁ אֲשֶׁר תִּקְרְאוּ אֹתָם בְּמוֹעֲדָם: בַּחֹדֶשׁ הָרִאשׁוֹן בְּאַרְבָּעָה עָשָׂר לַחֹדֶשׁ בֵּין הָעַרְבַּיִם פֶּסַח לַיהֹוָה:

במדבר ט:א-יד

וַיְדַבֵּר יְהֹוָה אֶל מֹשֶׁה בְמִדְבַּר סִינַי בַּשָּׁנָה הַשֵּׁנִית לְצֵאתָם מֵאֶרֶץ מִצְרַיִם בַּחֹדֶשׁ הָרִאשׁוֹן לֵאמֹר: וְיַעֲשׂוּ בְנֵי יִשְׂרָאֵל אֶת הַפֶּסַח בְּמוֹעֲדוֹ: בְּאַרְבָּעָה עָשָׂר יוֹם בַּחֹדֶשׁ הַזֶּה בֵּין הָעַרְבַּיִם תַּעֲשׂוּ אֹתוֹ בְּמוֹעֲדוֹ כְּכָל חֻקֹּתָיו וּכְכָל מִשְׁפָּטָיו תַּעֲשׂוּ אֹתוֹ: וַיְדַבֵּר מֹשֶׁה אֶל בְּנֵי יִשְׂרָאֵל לַעֲשֹׂת הַפָּסַח: וַיַּעֲשׂוּ אֶת הַפֶּסַח בָּרִאשׁוֹן בְּאַרְבָּעָה עָשָׂר יוֹם לַחֹדֶשׁ בֵּין הָעַרְבַּיִם בְּמִדְבַּר סִינַי כְּכֹל אֲשֶׁר צִוָּה יְהֹוָה אֶת מֹשֶׁה כֵּן עָשׂוּ בְּנֵי יִשְׂרָאֵל: וַיְהִי אֲנָשִׁים אֲשֶׁר הָיוּ טְמֵאִים לְנֶפֶשׁ אָדָם וְלֹא יָכְלוּ לַעֲשֹׂת הַפֶּסַח בַּיּוֹם הַהוּא וַיִּקְרְבוּ לִפְנֵי מֹשֶׁה וְלִפְנֵי אַהֲרֹן בַּיּוֹם הַהוּא: וַיֹּאמְרוּ הָאֲנָשִׁים הָהֵמָּה אֵלָיו אֲנַחְנוּ טְמֵאִים לְנֶפֶשׁ אָדָם לָמָּה נִגָּרַע לְבִלְתִּי הַקְרִיב אֶת קָרְבַּן יְהֹוָה בְּמֹעֲדוֹ בְּתוֹךְ בְּנֵי יִשְׂרָאֵל: וַיֹּאמֶר אֲלֵהֶם מֹשֶׁה עִמְדוּ וְאֶשְׁמְעָה מַה יְצַוֶּה יְהֹוָה לָכֶם: וַיְדַבֵּר יְהֹוָה אֶל מֹשֶׁה לֵּאמֹר: דַּבֵּר אֶל בְּנֵי יִשְׂרָאֵל לֵאמֹר אִישׁ אִישׁ כִּי יִהְיֶה טָמֵא לָנֶפֶשׁ אוֹ בְדֶרֶךְ רְחֹקָה לָכֶם אוֹ לְדֹרֹתֵיכֶם וְעָשָׂה פֶסַח לַיהֹוָה: בַּחֹדֶשׁ הַשֵּׁנִי בְּאַרְבָּעָה עָשָׂר יוֹם בֵּין הָעַרְבַּיִם יַעֲשׂוּ אֹתוֹ עַל מַצּוֹת וּמְרֹרִים יֹאכְלֻהוּ: לֹא יַשְׁאִירוּ

ממנו עד בקר וְעֶצֶם לֹא יִשְׁבְּרוּ בוֹ כְּכָל חֻקַּת הַפֶּסַח יַעֲשׂוּ אֹתוֹ: וְהָאִישׁ אֲשֶׁר הוּא טָהוֹר וּבְדֶרֶךְ לֹא הָיָה וְחָדַל לַעֲשׂוֹת הַפֶּסַח וְנִכְרְתָה הַנֶּפֶשׁ הַהִוא מֵעַמֶּיהָ כִּי קָרְבַּן יְהוָה לֹא הִקְרִיב בְּמֹעֲדוֹ חֶטְאוֹ יִשָּׂא הָאִישׁ הַהוּא: וְכִי יָגוּר אִתְּכֶם גֵּר וְעָשָׂה פֶסַח לַיהוָה כְּחֻקַּת הַפֶּסַח וּכְמִשְׁפָּטוֹ כֵּן יַעֲשֶׂה חֻקָּה אַחַת יִהְיֶה לָכֶם וְלַגֵּר וּלְאֶזְרַח הָאָרֶץ:

במדבר כח:טז
וּבַחֹדֶשׁ הָרִאשׁוֹן בְּאַרְבָּעָה עָשָׂר יוֹם לַחֹדֶשׁ פֶּסַח לַיהוָה:

דברים טז:א-ח
שָׁמוֹר אֶת חֹדֶשׁ הָאָבִיב וְעָשִׂיתָ פֶּסַח לַיהוָה אֱלֹהֶיךָ כִּי בְּחֹדֶשׁ הָאָבִיב הוֹצִיאֲךָ יְהוָה אֱלֹהֶיךָ מִמִּצְרַיִם לָיְלָה: וְזָבַחְתָּ פֶּסַח לַיהוָה אֱלֹהֶיךָ צֹאן וּבָקָר בַּמָּקוֹם אֲשֶׁר יִבְחַר יְהוָה לְשַׁכֵּן שְׁמוֹ שָׁם: לֹא תֹאכַל עָלָיו חָמֵץ שִׁבְעַת יָמִים תֹּאכַל עָלָיו מַצּוֹת לֶחֶם עֹנִי כִּי בְחִפָּזוֹן יָצָאתָ מֵאֶרֶץ מִצְרַיִם לְמַעַן תִּזְכֹּר אֶת יוֹם צֵאתְךָ מֵאֶרֶץ מִצְרַיִם כֹּל יְמֵי חַיֶּיךָ: וְלֹא יֵרָאֶה לְךָ שְׂאֹר בְּכָל גְּבֻלְךָ שִׁבְעַת יָמִים וְלֹא יָלִין מִן הַבָּשָׂר אֲשֶׁר תִּזְבַּח בָּעֶרֶב בַּיּוֹם הָרִאשׁוֹן לַבֹּקֶר: לֹא תוּכַל לִזְבֹּחַ אֶת הַפָּסַח בְּאַחַד שְׁעָרֶיךָ אֲשֶׁר יְהוָה אֱלֹהֶיךָ נֹתֵן לָךְ: כִּי אִם אֶל הַמָּקוֹם אֲשֶׁר יִבְחַר יְהוָה אֱלֹהֶיךָ לְשַׁכֵּן שְׁמוֹ שָׁם תִּזְבַּח אֶת הַפֶּסַח בָּעָרֶב כְּבוֹא הַשֶּׁמֶשׁ מוֹעֵד צֵאתְךָ מִמִּצְרָיִם: וּבִשַּׁלְתָּ וְאָכַלְתָּ בַּמָּקוֹם אֲשֶׁר יִבְחַר יְהוָה אֱלֹהֶיךָ בּוֹ וּפָנִיתָ בַבֹּקֶר וְהָלַכְתָּ לְאֹהָלֶיךָ: שֵׁשֶׁת יָמִים תֹּאכַל מַצּוֹת וּבַיּוֹם הַשְּׁבִיעִי עֲצֶרֶת לַיהוָה אֱלֹהֶיךָ לֹא תַעֲשֶׂה מְלָאכָה:

יהושע ה: י-יא
וַיַּחֲנוּ בְנֵי יִשְׂרָאֵל בַּגִּלְגָּל וַיַּעֲשׂוּ אֶת הַפֶּסַח בְּאַרְבָּעָה עָשָׂר יוֹם לַחֹדֶשׁ בָּעֶרֶב בְּעַרְבוֹת יְרִיחוֹ: וַיֹּאכְלוּ מֵעֲבוּר הָאָרֶץ מִמָּחֳרַת הַפֶּסַח מַצּוֹת וְקָלוּי בְּעֶצֶם הַיּוֹם הַזֶּה:

מלכים ב כג:כא-כג
וַיְצַו הַמֶּלֶךְ אֶת כָּל הָעָם לֵאמֹר עֲשׂוּ פֶסַח לַיהוָה אֱלֹהֵיכֶם כַּכָּתוּב עַל סֵפֶר הַבְּרִית הַזֶּה: כִּי לֹא נַעֲשָׂה כַּפֶּסַח הַזֶּה מִימֵי הַשֹּׁפְטִים אֲשֶׁר שָׁפְטוּ אֶת יִשְׂרָאֵל וְכֹל יְמֵי מַלְכֵי יִשְׂרָאֵל וּמַלְכֵי יְהוּדָה: כִּי אִם בִּשְׁמֹנֶה עֶשְׂרֵה שָׁנָה לַמֶּלֶךְ יֹאשִׁיָּהוּ נַעֲשָׂה הַפֶּסַח הַזֶּה לַיהוָה בִּירוּשָׁלָם:

דברי הימים ב ל:א-כ
וַיִּשְׁלַח יְחִזְקִיָּהוּ עַל כָּל יִשְׂרָאֵל וִיהוּדָה וְגַם אִגְּרוֹת כָּתַב עַל אֶפְרַיִם וּמְנַשֶּׁה לָבוֹא לְבֵית יְהוָה בִּירוּשָׁלַם לַעֲשׂוֹת פֶּסַח לַיהוָה אֱלֹהֵי יִשְׂרָאֵל: וַיִּוָּעַץ הַמֶּלֶךְ וְשָׂרָיו וְכָל הַקָּהָל בִּירוּשָׁלַם לַעֲשׂוֹת הַפֶּסַח בַּחֹדֶשׁ הַשֵּׁנִי: כִּי לֹא יָכְלוּ לַעֲשֹׂתוֹ בָּעֵת הַהִיא כִּי הַכֹּהֲנִים לֹא הִתְקַדְּשׁוּ לְמַדַּי וְהָעָם לֹא נֶאֶסְפוּ לִירוּשָׁלָם: וַיִּישַׁר הַדָּבָר בְּעֵינֵי הַמֶּלֶךְ וּבְעֵינֵי כָּל הַקָּהָל: וַיַּעֲמִידוּ דָבָר

להַעֲבִיר קוֹל בְּכָל יִשְׂרָאֵל מִבְּאֵר שֶׁבַע וְעַד דָּן לָבוֹא לַעֲשׂוֹת פֶּסַח לַיהוָה אֱלֹהֵי יִשְׂרָאֵל בִּירוּשָׁלָם כִּי לֹא לָרֹב עָשׂוּ כַּכָּתוּב: וַיֵּלְכוּ הָרָצִים בָּאִגְּרוֹת מִיַּד הַמֶּלֶךְ וְשָׂרָיו בְּכָל יִשְׂרָאֵל וִיהוּדָה וּכְמִצְוַת הַמֶּלֶךְ לֵאמֹר בְּנֵי יִשְׂרָאֵל שׁוּבוּ אֶל יְהוָה אֱלֹהֵי אַבְרָהָם יִצְחָק וְיִשְׂרָאֵל וְיָשֹׁב אֶל הַפְּלֵיטָה הַנִּשְׁאֶרֶת לָכֶם מִכַּף מַלְכֵי אַשּׁוּר: וְאַל תִּהְיוּ כַּאֲבוֹתֵיכֶם וְכַאֲחֵיכֶם אֲשֶׁר מָעֲלוּ בַּיהוָה אֱלֹהֵי אֲבוֹתֵיהֶם וַיִּתְּנֵם לְשַׁמָּה כַּאֲשֶׁר אַתֶּם רֹאִים: עַתָּה אַל תַּקְשׁוּ עָרְפְּכֶם כַּאֲבוֹתֵיכֶם תְּנוּ יָד לַיהוָה וּבֹאוּ לְמִקְדָּשׁוֹ אֲשֶׁר הִקְדִּישׁ לְעוֹלָם וְעִבְדוּ אֶת יְהוָה אֱלֹהֵיכֶם וְיָשֹׁב מִכֶּם חֲרוֹן אַפּוֹ: כִּי בְשׁוּבְכֶם עַל יְהוָה אֲחֵיכֶם וּבְנֵיכֶם לְרַחֲמִים לִפְנֵי שׁוֹבֵיהֶם וְלָשׁוּב לָאָרֶץ הַזֹּאת כִּי חַנּוּן וְרַחוּם יְהוָה אֱלֹהֵיכֶם וְלֹא יָסִיר פָּנִים מִכֶּם אִם תָּשׁוּבוּ אֵלָיו: וַיִּהְיוּ הָרָצִים עֹבְרִים מֵעִיר לָעִיר בְּאֶרֶץ אֶפְרַיִם וּמְנַשֶּׁה וְעַד זְבֻלוּן וַיִּהְיוּ מַשְׂחִיקִים עֲלֵיהֶם וּמַלְעִגִים בָּם: אַךְ אֲנָשִׁים מֵאָשֵׁר וּמְנַשֶּׁה וּמִזְּבֻלוּן נִכְנְעוּ וַיָּבֹאוּ לִירוּשָׁלָם: גַּם בִּיהוּדָה הָיְתָה יַד הָאֱלֹהִים לָתֵת לָהֶם לֵב אֶחָד לַעֲשׂוֹת מִצְוַת הַמֶּלֶךְ וְהַשָּׂרִים בִּדְבַר יְהוָה: וַיֵּאָסְפוּ יְרוּשָׁלַם עַם רָב לַעֲשׂוֹת אֶת חַג הַמַּצּוֹת בַּחֹדֶשׁ הַשֵּׁנִי קָהָל לָרֹב מְאֹד: וַיָּקֻמוּ וַיָּסִירוּ אֶת הַמִּזְבְּחוֹת אֲשֶׁר בִּירוּשָׁלָם וְאֵת כָּל הַמְקַטְּרוֹת הֵסִירוּ וַיַּשְׁלִיכוּ לְנַחַל קִדְרוֹן: וַיִּשְׁחֲטוּ הַפֶּסַח בְּאַרְבָּעָה עָשָׂר לַחֹדֶשׁ הַשֵּׁנִי וְהַכֹּהֲנִים וְהַלְוִיִּם נִכְלְמוּ וַיִּתְקַדְּשׁוּ וַיָּבִיאוּ עֹלוֹת בֵּית יְהוָה: וַיַּעַמְדוּ עַל עָמְדָם כְּמִשְׁפָּטָם כְּתוֹרַת מֹשֶׁה אִישׁ הָאֱלֹהִים הַכֹּהֲנִים זֹרְקִים אֶת הַדָּם מִיַּד הַלְוִיִּם: כִּי רַבַּת בַּקָּהָל אֲשֶׁר לֹא הִתְקַדָּשׁוּ וְהַלְוִיִּם עַל שְׁחִיטַת הַפְּסָחִים לְכֹל לֹא טָהוֹר לְהַקְדִּישׁ לַיהוָה: כִּי מַרְבִּית הָעָם רַבַּת מֵאֶפְרַיִם וּמְנַשֶּׁה יִשָּׂשכָר וּזְבֻלוּן לֹא הִטֶּהָרוּ כִּי אָכְלוּ אֶת הַפֶּסַח בְּלֹא כַכָּתוּב כִּי הִתְפַּלֵּל יְחִזְקִיָּהוּ עֲלֵיהֶם לֵאמֹר יְהוָה הַטּוֹב יְכַפֵּר בְּעַד: כָּל לְבָבוֹ הֵכִין לִדְרוֹשׁ הָאֱלֹהִים יְהוָה אֱלֹהֵי אֲבֹתָיו וְלֹא כְּטָהֳרַת הַקֹּדֶשׁ: וַיִּשְׁמַע יְהוָה אֶל יְחִזְקִיָּהוּ וַיִּרְפָּא אֶת הָעָם:

דברי הימים ב לה:א-יט
וַיַּעַשׂ יֹאשִׁיָּהוּ בִירוּשָׁלַם פֶּסַח לַיהוָה וַיִּשְׁחֲטוּ הַפֶּסַח בְּאַרְבָּעָה עָשָׂר לַחֹדֶשׁ הָרִאשׁוֹן: וַיַּעֲמֵד הַכֹּהֲנִים עַל מִשְׁמְרוֹתָם וַיְחַזְּקֵם לַעֲבוֹדַת בֵּית יְהוָה: וַיֹּאמֶר לַלְוִיִּם הַמְּבִינִים לְכָל יִשְׂרָאֵל הַקְּדוֹשִׁים לַיהוָה תְּנוּ אֶת אֲרוֹן הַקֹּדֶשׁ בַּבַּיִת אֲשֶׁר בָּנָה שְׁלֹמֹה בֶן דָּוִיד מֶלֶךְ יִשְׂרָאֵל אֵין לָכֶם מַשָּׂא בַּכָּתֵף עַתָּה עִבְדוּ אֶת יְהוָה אֱלֹהֵיכֶם וְאֵת עַמּוֹ יִשְׂרָאֵל: וְהָכִינוּ לְבֵית אֲבוֹתֵיכֶם כְּמַחְלְקוֹתֵיכֶם בִּכְתָב דָּוִיד מֶלֶךְ יִשְׂרָאֵל וּבְמִכְתַּב שְׁלֹמֹה בְנוֹ: וְעִמְדוּ בַקֹּדֶשׁ לִפְלֻגּוֹת בֵּית הָאָבוֹת לַאֲחֵיכֶם בְּנֵי הָעָם וַחֲלֻקַּת בֵּית אָב לַלְוִיִּם: וְשַׁחֲטוּ הַפָּסַח וְהִתְקַדְּשׁוּ וְהָכִינוּ לַאֲחֵיכֶם לַעֲשׂוֹת כִּדְבַר יְהוָה בְּיַד מֹשֶׁה: וַיָּרֶם יֹאשִׁיָּהוּ לִבְנֵי הָעָם צֹאן כְּבָשִׂים וּבְנֵי עִזִּים הַכֹּל לַפְּסָחִים לְכָל הַנִּמְצָא לְמִסְפַּר שְׁלֹשִׁים אֶלֶף וּבָקָר שְׁלֹשֶׁת אֲלָפִים אֵלֶּה מֵרְכוּשׁ הַמֶּלֶךְ: וְשָׂרָיו לִנְדָבָה לָעָם לַכֹּהֲנִים וְלַלְוִיִּם הֵרִימוּ חִלְקִיָּה וּזְכַרְיָהוּ וִיחִיאֵל נְגִידֵי בֵּית הָאֱלֹהִים לַכֹּהֲנִים נָתְנוּ לַפְּסָחִים אַלְפַּיִם וְשֵׁשׁ מֵאוֹת וּבָקָר שְׁלֹשׁ מֵאוֹת: וְכָנַנְיָהוּ וּשְׁמַעְיָהוּ וּנְתַנְאֵל אֶחָיו וַחֲשַׁבְיָהוּ וִיעִיאֵל

הַמֶּלֶךְ וְהַשֹּׁעֲרִים לְשַׁעַר וָשַׁעַר אֵין לָהֶם לָסוּר מֵעַל עֲבֹדָתָם כִּי אֲחֵיהֶם הַלְוִיִּם הֵכִינוּ לָהֶם: וַתִּכּוֹן כָּל עֲבוֹדַת יְהֹוָה בַּיּוֹם הַהוּא לַעֲשׂוֹת הַפֶּסַח וְהַעֲלוֹת עֹלוֹת עַל מִזְבַּח יְהֹוָה כְּמִצְוַת הַמֶּלֶךְ יֹאשִׁיָּהוּ: וַיַּעֲשׂוּ בְנֵי יִשְׂרָאֵל הַנִּמְצְאִים אֶת הַפֶּסַח בָּעֵת הַהִיא וְאֶת חַג הַמַּצּוֹת שִׁבְעַת יָמִים: וְלֹא נַעֲשָׂה פֶסַח כָּמֹהוּ בְּיִשְׂרָאֵל מִימֵי שְׁמוּאֵל הַנָּבִיא וְכָל מַלְכֵי יִשְׂרָאֵל לֹא עָשׂוּ כַּפֶּסַח אֲשֶׁר עָשָׂה יֹאשִׁיָּהוּ וְהַכֹּהֲנִים וְהַלְוִיִּם וְכָל יְהוּדָה וְיִשְׂרָאֵל הַנִּמְצָא וְיוֹשְׁבֵי יְרוּשָׁלָ͏ִם: בִּשְׁמוֹנֶה עֶשְׂרֵה שָׁנָה לְמַלְכוּת יֹאשִׁיָּהוּ נַעֲשָׂה הַפֶּסַח הַזֶּה:

וַיּוֹזֶב שָׂרֵי הַלְוִיִּם הֵרִימוּ לַלְוִיִּם לַפְּסָחִים חֲמֵשֶׁת אֲלָפִים וּבָקָר חֲמֵשׁ מֵאוֹת: וַתִּכּוֹן הָעֲבוֹדָה וַיַּעַמְדוּ הַכֹּהֲנִים עַל עָמְדָם וְהַלְוִיִּם עַל מַחְלְקוֹתָם כְּמִצְוַת הַמֶּלֶךְ: וַיִּשְׁחֲטוּ הַפָּסַח וַיִּזְרְקוּ הַכֹּהֲנִים מִיָּדָם וְהַלְוִיִּם מַפְשִׁיטִים: וַיָּסִירוּ הָעֹלָה לְתִתָּם לְמִפְלַגּוֹת לְבֵית אָבוֹת לִבְנֵי הָעָם לְהַקְרִיב לַיהֹוָה כַּכָּתוּב בְּסֵפֶר מֹשֶׁה וְכֵן לַבָּקָר: וַיְבַשְּׁלוּ הַפֶּסַח בָּאֵשׁ כַּמִּשְׁפָּט וְהַקֳּדָשִׁים בִּשְּׁלוּ בַּסִּירוֹת וּבַדְּוָדִים וּבַצֵּלָחוֹת וַיָּרִיצוּ לְכָל בְּנֵי הָעָם: וְאַחַר הֵכִינוּ לָהֶם וְלַכֹּהֲנִים כִּי הַכֹּהֲנִים בְּנֵי אַהֲרֹן בְּהַעֲלוֹת הָעוֹלָה וְהַחֲלָבִים עַד לָיְלָה וְהַלְוִיִּם הֵכִינוּ לָהֶם וְלַכֹּהֲנִים בְּנֵי אַהֲרֹן: וְהַמְשֹׁרֲרִים בְּנֵי אָסָף עַל מַעֲמָדָם כְּמִצְוַת דָּוִיד וְאָסָף וְהֵימָן וִידֻתוּן חוֹזֵה

עירוב תבשילין

When Pesach (or any festival) occurs on a Friday, an *eruv tavshilin* must be made in order to allow cooking (and other preparations) for Shabbos on that Friday. The *eruv* consists of a whole piece of matzah and at least a *k'zayis* (approximately the volume of half an egg) of a cooked food, which are set aside (before the festival begins) and kept intact until Shabbos preparations are completed. The *eruv* is held in the hand, and the following blessing is recited:

בָּרוּךְ אַתָּה יהוה אֱלֹהֵינוּ מֶלֶךְ הָעוֹלָם, אֲשֶׁר קִדְּשָׁנוּ בְּמִצְוֹתָיו וְצִוָּנוּ עַל מִצְוַת עֵרוּב:

Blessed are You, Hashem, our God, King of the universe, Who has sanctified us through His commandments and commanded us concerning the precept of the *eruv*.

Declaration of intent:

בַּהֲדֵין עֵירוּבָא יְהֵא שָׁרֵא לָנָא לַאֲפוּיֵי וּלְבַשּׁוּלֵי וּלְאַטְמוּנֵי וּלְאַדְלוּקֵי שְׁרָגָא וּלְאַפּוּקֵי וּלְמֶעְבַּד כָּל צָרְכָנָא מִיּוֹמָא טָבָא לְשַׁבַּתָּא:

By this *eruv*, it shall be permitted for us to bake, to cook, to insulate pots of hot food, to light candles, and to do all [permissible acts] that are necessary on the festival in preparation for the Sabbath.

הַדְלָקַת הַנֵּרוֹת

The following are the blessings over the lighting of the holiday candles. On Shabbos, the words in parentheses are added.

בָּרוּךְ אַתָּה יהוה אֱלֹהֵינוּ מֶלֶךְ הָעוֹלָם, אֲשֶׁר קִדְּשָׁנוּ בְּמִצְוֹתָיו וְצִוָּנוּ לְהַדְלִיק נֵר שֶׁל (שַׁבָּת וְשֶׁל) יוֹם טוֹב:

Blessed are You, Hashem, our God, King of the universe, Who has sanctified us through His commandments and commanded us to kindle the candle of (the Sabbath and) the festival.

בָּרוּךְ אַתָּה יהוה אֱלֹהֵינוּ מֶלֶךְ הָעוֹלָם, שֶׁהֶחֱיָנוּ וְקִיְּמָנוּ וְהִגִּיעָנוּ לַזְּמַן הַזֶּה:

Blessed are You, Hashem, our God, King of the universe, Who has granted us life and sustained us and allowed us to reach this occasion.

קַדֵּשׁ	וּרְחַץ
כַּרְפַּס	יַחַץ
מַגִּיד	רָחְצָה
מוֹצִיא	מַצָּה
מָרוֹר	כּוֹרֵךְ
שֻׁלְחָן	עוֹרֵךְ
צָפוּן	בָּרֵךְ
הַלֵּל	נִרְצָה

קַדֵּשׁ

The first of the four cups of wine is poured. The leader should have another person pour the wine for him, as a gesture of aristocracy and freedom. As he is about to recite Kiddush, he should bear in mind that he is about to fulfill the mitzvah of Kiddush and the mitzvah of the first of the four cups of wine. On Friday night, the words in parentheses are added.

(וַיְהִי עֶרֶב וַיְהִי בֹקֶר יוֹם הַשִּׁשִּׁי: וַיְכֻלּוּ הַשָּׁמַיִם וְהָאָרֶץ וְכָל צְבָאָם: וַיְכַל אֱלֹהִים בַּיּוֹם הַשְּׁבִיעִי מְלַאכְתּוֹ אֲשֶׁר עָשָׂה, וַיִּשְׁבֹּת בַּיּוֹם הַשְּׁבִיעִי מִכָּל מְלַאכְתּוֹ אֲשֶׁר עָשָׂה: וַיְבָרֶךְ אֱלֹהִים אֶת יוֹם הַשְּׁבִיעִי וַיְקַדֵּשׁ אֹתוֹ, כִּי בוֹ שָׁבַת מִכָּל מְלַאכְתּוֹ אֲשֶׁר בָּרָא אֱלֹהִים לַעֲשׂוֹת:)

(And it was evening and it was morning, the sixth day. The heavens and the earth and all their hosts were completed. God completed on the seventh day His work that He had done, and He rested on the seventh day from all His work that He had done. God blessed the seventh day and sanctified it, for on it He rested from all His work that God had created to make.)

סַבְרִי מָרָנָן וְרַבָּנָן וְרַבּוֹתַי:

בָּרוּךְ אַתָּה יהוה אֱלֹהֵינוּ מֶלֶךְ הָעוֹלָם, בּוֹרֵא פְּרִי הַגָּפֶן:

בָּרוּךְ אַתָּה יהוה אֱלֹהֵינוּ מֶלֶךְ הָעוֹלָם, אֲשֶׁר בָּחַר בָּנוּ מִכָּל עָם, וְרוֹמְמָנוּ מִכָּל לָשׁוֹן, וְקִדְּשָׁנוּ בְּמִצְוֹתָיו, וַתִּתֶּן לָנוּ יהוה אֱלֹהֵינוּ בְּאַהֲבָה (שַׁבָּתוֹת לִמְנוּחָה וּ) מוֹעֲדִים לְשִׂמְחָה, חַגִּים וּזְמַנִּים לְשָׂשׂוֹן (אֶת יוֹם הַשַּׁבָּת הַזֶּה וְ) אֶת יוֹם חַג הַמַּצּוֹת הַזֶּה זְמַן חֵרוּתֵנוּ (בְּאַהֲבָה) מִקְרָא קֹדֶשׁ, זֵכֶר לִיצִיאַת מִצְרָיִם. כִּי בָנוּ

With your permission, my masters:

Blessed are You, Hashem, our God, King of the universe, Who creates the fruit of the vine.

Blessed are You, Hashem, our God, King of the universe, Who has chosen us from all the nations, raised us above all nationalities, and made us holy through His commandments. You, Hashem, our God, gave us, with love (Sabbaths for rest and) holidays for rejoicing, festivals and festive seasons for gladness, (this Sabbath

בָּחַרְתָּ וְאוֹתָנוּ קִדַּשְׁתָּ מִכָּל הָעַמִּים, (וְשַׁבָּת)
וּמוֹעֲדֵי קָדְשֶׁךָ (בְּאַהֲבָה וּבְרָצוֹן) בְּשִׂמְחָה
וּבְשָׂשׂוֹן הִנְחַלְתָּנוּ. בָּרוּךְ אַתָּה יהוה, מְקַדֵּשׁ
(הַשַּׁבָּת וְ) יִשְׂרָאֵל וְהַזְּמַנִּים:

day and) this day of the Festival of Matzos, the time of our freedom (with love), a holy convocation, in commemoration of the Exodus from Egypt. For You have chosen us and sanctified us from all the nations, and You have bestowed upon us Your holy (Sabbath and) festivals (with love and favor), with happiness and joy. Blessed are You, Hashem, Who sanctifies (the Sabbath and) Israel and the festive seasons.

On Saturday night, the following section in parentheses is added. One examines their fingernails by the light of a candle after the first blessing is said.

(בָּרוּךְ אַתָּה יהוה אֱלֹהֵינוּ מֶלֶךְ הָעוֹלָם, בּוֹרֵא
מְאוֹרֵי הָאֵשׁ: בָּרוּךְ אַתָּה יהוה אֱלֹהֵינוּ מֶלֶךְ
הָעוֹלָם, הַמַּבְדִּיל בֵּין קוֹדֶשׁ לְחוֹל, בֵּין אוֹר
לְחוֹשֶׁךְ, בֵּין יִשְׂרָאֵל לָעַמִּים, בֵּין יוֹם הַשְּׁבִיעִי
לְשֵׁשֶׁת יְמֵי הַמַּעֲשֶׂה, בֵּין קְדֻשַּׁת שַׁבָּת לִקְדֻשַּׁת
יוֹם טוֹב הִבְדַּלְתָּ, וְאֶת יוֹם הַשְּׁבִיעִי מִשֵּׁשֶׁת יְמֵי
הַמַּעֲשֶׂה קִדַּשְׁתָּ, הִבְדַּלְתָּ וְקִדַּשְׁתָּ אֶת עַמְּךָ
יִשְׂרָאֵל בִּקְדֻשָּׁתֶךָ: בָּרוּךְ אַתָּה יהוה, הַמַּבְדִּיל
בֵּין קוֹדֶשׁ לְקוֹדֶשׁ:)

(Blessed are You, Hashem, our God, King of the universe, Who creates the radiances of fire. Blessed are You, Hashem, our God, King of the universe, Who distinguishes between the sacred and the profane, between light and darkness, between Israel and the nations, and between the seventh day and the six workdays. You distinguished between the holiness of the Sabbath and the holiness of the festivals, and You have sanctified the seventh day above the six workdays. You have distinguished and sanctified Your people Israel through Your holiness. Blessed are You, Hashem, Who distinguishes between [one level of] holiness and [another level of] holiness.)

בָּרוּךְ אַתָּה יהוה אֱלֹהֵינוּ מֶלֶךְ הָעוֹלָם,
שֶׁהֶחֱיָנוּ וְקִיְּמָנוּ וְהִגִּיעָנוּ לַזְּמַן הַזֶּה:

Blessed are You, Hashem, our God, King of the universe, who has granted us life, sustained us, and allowed us to reach this occasion.

The entire cup of wine (or at least a majority of it) is now drunk. Men recline on the left side while drinking the wine.

ורחץ

The hands are washed with a cup of water. No blessing is recited.

כרפס

A small piece of vegetable (commonly used are celery, potatoes, or cucumbers) is dipped in salt water or vinegar, and the following blessing is recited. While reciting this blessing, one should bear in mind that it also includes the maror, which will be eaten later at the Seder.

בָּרוּךְ אַתָּה יהוה אֱלֹהֵינוּ מֶלֶךְ הָעוֹלָם, בּוֹרֵא פְּרִי הָאֲדָמָה:

Blessed are You, Hashem, our God, King of the universe, Who creates the produce of the ground.

The vegetable is eaten without reclining.

יחץ

The middle matzah is broken in two, in such a manner that one piece is larger than the other. The larger piece is set aside to be eaten later as the Afikoman. The smaller half is placed back between the other two, and the Haggadah is recited over it.

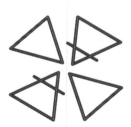

מַגִּיד

1. Why does Maggid begin in Aramaic and why does it switch to Hebrew at the end?
2. "This is the bread of affliction that our forefathers ate in the Land of Egypt." How does this opening statement fit the Torah's reason for eating matzah (*Shemos* 12:39), which appears later in the Haggadah, in *Rabban Gamliel Hayah Omer* (Maggid Section 16b)?
3. Why do we introduce the *Seder* with an invitation for others to attend?
4. Why do we invite all who are hungry as well as all who are in need?

Throughout the Maggid section, the matzah should be uncovered, in plain view, in fulfillment of the description of matzah as "bread over which much discussion [of the Exodus] is held" (*Pesachim* 36a). The plate with the matzos is raised as the following paragraph is recited:

הָא לַחְמָא עַנְיָא דִּי אֲכַלוּ אַבְהָתָנָא בְּאַרְעָא דְמִצְרָיִם. כָּל דִּכְפִין יֵיתֵי וְיֵכֻל. כָּל דִּצְרִיךְ יֵיתֵי וְיִפְסַח. הָשַׁתָּא הָכָא, לְשָׁנָה הַבָּאָה בְּאַרְעָא דְיִשְׂרָאֵל. הָשַׁתָּא עַבְדֵי, לְשָׁנָה הַבָּאָה בְּנֵי חוֹרִין:

This is the bread of affliction that our fathers ate in the land of Egypt. Whoever is hungry, let him come and eat; whoever is in need, let him come and celebrate Pesach. This year [we are] here, next year in the land of Israel! This year [we are] slaves, next year freed men!

The Wise Son

The point of *Ha Lachma Anya* is to inculcate a sense of hope for redemption. We *now* eat the bread of affliction just as our ancestors did in Egypt.[1] Maggid begins in Aramaic as a sign that at the time of its formulation, most Jews lived outside of Israel and Aramaic was their spoken

The Cynical Son

The purpose of *Ha Lachma Anya* is to set a mood for the proceedings of the evening. Aramaic was the spoken language of the masses at the time the Haggadah was being established and we want to be sure the invitations will be understood by all. The *Seder* is meant to be inclusive and we

The Pure Son

Midrash Eichah to the verse "גלתה יהודה מעוני – Yehudah is exiled of afflictions"[1] expounds the word מעוני. It says "לא גלו ישראל עד שאכלו חמץ בפסח, שנאמר גלתה יהודה מעוני," that Yisrael was not exiled until they ate chametz on Pesach, as the verse says, "Yehudah is exiled because of עוני." This is a hint to

The Withdrawn Son

We begin with a language accessible to all and conclude in Hebrew, the language we hope to speak when we return to Israel.[1] Our Sages teach that one of the reasons we merited redemption from Egypt was because, in addition to not changing our dress and names, we didn't change language. For this reason, the Talmud, and common documents such as *kesubos* or prayers such as *Kaddish* are also in Aramaic. It is also a reminder to incorporate Talmudic teachings when telling the story (such is the implied understanding of the Haggadah's answer to the Wise Son. See *Arbah Banim*; Maggid Section 7). *Ha Lachma Anya* ends in Hebrew though, so that the gentile authorities among whom we live, who also speak Aramaic but not Hebrew, will not accuse us of rebellion as we express our redemptive aspirations.

Maggid begins with an invitation to others to join our meal. The purpose of the *Seder* is to remind us of our desperately impoverished state in Egypt. What better way to do this than to invite others to our table?[2]

We invite two different groups to our table as a memory of the Temple service. כל דכפין refers to those who are hungry. They are invited to come in and eat. In addition, we invite כל דצריך – not to be translated as "all who are needy." The needy are included in כל דכפין. כל דצריך refers to those who *need* to perform the mitzvos of the evening. Let them join us so they can ויפסח – eat the *korban Pesach*, or nowadays, join us for all the other mitzvos, such as wine for the four cups, matzah, and maror. It is for this reason that we have special funds for Pesach known as *Maos Chittim*, because the mitzvos all involve eating. We don't establish a name for such funds for any other holiday, with the exception of Purim, because the mitzvos of that day also involve eating.[3] This is why we have two separate phrases, one for food in general and one for the food (and drink) comprising the mitzvos of the evening.

therefore begin in the language understood by most people. The proceedings of the evening are also meant to instill in us a sense of longing for redemption, and to improve our lot and the lot of those around us. The concluding lines are a petitionary prayer for redemption and freedom, and in general such supplications are in Hebrew.[1] The *Ha Lachma Anya* passage says that we ate the bread of affliction *in* Egypt. This does not contradict the reason given in the Torah for eating matzah. Had we not been rushed out of Egypt, we would have had time for our dough to rise to take provisions with us into the desert. We therefore commemorate this rush by eating the food we took with us. In addition to this, we did eat such a bread product in our years in Egypt. Many interpretations are suggested for לחמא עניא or לחם עוני.[2] The word עוני can describe the bread because matzah has the bare minimum of ingredients – flour and water, and it can also describe the one eating it. A poor man would prefer to make matzah from the little flour he has. It is harder to digest the bread and therefore will remain longer in the stomach and forestall hunger.[3] Eating matzah at the *Seder* reminds of both these reasons. On this night we *all* eat the bread of the impoverished to foster a sense of inclusiveness and equality. A function of this inclusiveness is a series of invitations we make for the hungry and those in need. It comes as an obvious adjunct to our celebration of Pesach to invite the less fortunate to celebrate with us.[4] We so badly want to be inclusive that we open our doors to everyone, whether they want to join us because they feel a need to, or because they are simply hungry. If anyone feels cynical of the way we conduct a Seder, we recite a text that fosters inclusiveness and equality at the very outset. This should make everyone feel part of the proceedings. As above, we therefore frame the invitation in a language understood by all.[5]

the matzah, called לחם עוני. The Haggadah attempts to end affliction in order to realize redemption. The first step in this direction is to recognize what needs to be mended. Such mending must be open for all, and is introduced in the language that everyone understands. The most effective way to bring people under the protective wing of God's Divine Presence is to assist with their physical and material struggles. Rav Yisrael Salanter taught that we should place our own spiritual pursuits ahead of our own material and physical pursuits. A function of this is that we pray in the morning before we eat. But the material pursuits of others should be considered a spiritual pursuit of ours. In other words, "Did I eat?" is a material question, while "Did I pray?" is a spiritual question. However, the question, "Did you eat?" is for me a spiritual question. This is why the Haggadah connects the poverty of eating matzah with the concern for others who are lacking. The main reason for eating matzah on Pesach surely is connected to the day we left Egypt. We stress, however, that such food was ingested in Egypt to connect to the next part of the passage and the connection can be understood in light of the following:

The redemption from Egypt came at an appointed time – after four hundred years – that was revealed to Avraham at the Bris Bein HaBesarim.[2] We can only know when an appointed time is finished if we know when it starts. We see from the backdrop of Shemos 12:40–41, which states that the exile lasted four hundred and thirty years, that there was some confusion as to when to begin counting these years. In fact, our Sages relate that members of the tribe of Ephraim miscalculated these years to a tragic end. They left Egypt thirty years early and were killed before they made it to Eretz Yisrael.[3] "Rushing the redemption" is not an option for an appointed date. Similarly, when Yirmiyahu announced a seventy-year exile, this was not a time to be manipulated. Others, such as Chananya ben

Azur, who predicted a much shorter exile, also met a tragic end.[4] A predetermined time cannot be rushed.

In our times we are not necessarily awaiting an announced time. Rather, the redemption can come sooner, because of our deeds. Every mitzvah, every act of kindness, every invitation to a hungry person in need, brings us that much closer to being free and enjoying the blessing of peace in Israel. We announce here that we are searching for opportunities to spread good will and thereby gain God's favor.

Those in need are specifically invited to ויפסח, to eat the korban Pesach. The problem is that at this late time, after we have already made kiddush and have started the Seder, it's too late to invite a guest for the korban Pesach. Such an inclusion must have been made earlier that day, at the time of the offering of the korban. This may connect to the invitation of those who are hungry. The two statements can be seen as invitations for two different groups of people. כל דכפין refers to gentiles who may simply be hungry,[5] and כל דצריך refers to Jews who need to perform the mitzvos of the evening.

There may be a way to connect these two invitations by reassigning their announcements to a different time. Inviting guests to eat the korban Pesach at a time when no one can join is disingenuous. Rather, let us consider that such an announcement was made earlier in the day when the invitation had a practical meaning. Early in the day on Erev Pesach is also the perfect time to ask hungry gentiles to come and eat. We have all this chametz and no one to eat it. Surely it's preferable to offer it to gentiles than to burn it. Every one of us should find a place to deliver such chametz. It will enhance goodwill and bring us closer to the time when we will, with God's help be eating the korban Pesach.

In this way the three parts of הא לחמא עניא are intertwined. The matzah reminds us of poverty, which drives us to help others, which will hopefully lead to our redemption. When we want something very much, the best language to ask for it is in Hebrew.[6] This is why our fervent prayer for redemption, the theme of the evening, is in Hebrew.

our language. After all those years in Egypt, we still gave Hebrew names, which demonstrates the hope and expectation to soon be back in our homeland again. This hope is the driving force behind the proceedings at the *Seder*.

The *Chidah* explains that the Egyptians kept us at such a constant rush at all times to produce the requisite number of bricks[2] that we *never* had time for our dough to rise. We see in Biblical narratives that whenever someone pressed for time is serving bread, they serve matzah.[3] God's plan, therefore, was for our redemption to parallel this aspect of our slavery. The Egyptians rushed us through all our labors and would continue to rush us right out of their land.

The *Seder* is a time to remember – as we will say later in Maggid – that in every generation, there have been attempts to destroy and obliterate us and we've survived them all with the help of God. The invitations at the beginning of Maggid remind us that we are never alone. Right now we are on the giving end of כל דכפין and כל דצריך, but it is a comfort to know that if we are ever on the receiving end, there will be those who say the same words. We invite the hungry for a full meal, and we invite those who need to fulfill the requirement of eating the *korban Pesach*. Regardless of the reason for joining, all are invited.[4]

MAGGID SECTION 2 – MAH NISHTANAH

This paragraph is known as the "Four Questions." In actuality, it appears as one question with four answers. The question, "How is this night different from all other nights?" is answered in four ways. Here are four ways that this night differs from all other nights. This is indeed what appears to us, but consistent with the modes of questions and answers in ancient rhetoric, the "four answers" are actually all part of the original question. Otherwise we wouldn't need the letter ש before each "answer." Each of the four lines beginning with שבכל הלילות is another example of what confuses a child about how different this night is. In other words, we should consider that the question מה נשתנה should be repeated before each line to constitute four separate questions, not four answers to the same question. The above point may also be resolved if we translate מה נשתנה not "*How* is this night different?," but "*Why* is this night different?" We can perhaps also understand מה as a term of amazement, at how engaging and endearing this night is. מה therefore would read like "מה אהבתי תורתך כל היום היא שיחתי – O! How I love Your Torah! – It is my speech throughout the day."[1]

1. Why do we ask מה נשתנה on Pesach as opposed to any other holiday when things are done differently?

2. Why do we specifically ask about these four things, while omitting other unusual customs for the evening, such as four cups, washing but not for bread, or not immediately starting our meal after *kiddush*, etc.?

3. How can we be sure *every* child will be inspired to ask these four questions? If there are four types of children at the *Seder*, why don't we teach each child to ask a question on his own level?

4. In the event that there are no children at the table, the Talmud tells that even wise adults ask each other these questions. What is the point of such an exercise?

All Jewish holidays have unique characteristics. On Sukkos, a child may be inspired to ask, "On all other nights we eat meals at the table in our house, but tonight we eat in the *sukkah*." On Yom Kippur the child may ask, "On all other holidays, we make *kiddush* and eat after evening prayers, but tonight we ate beforehand." This can be replicated again and again. The sheer number of unusual activities at the *Seder*, however, draws the attention of children. Indeed, many of the activities at the *Seder* are specifically meant to pique the interest of the child to stay awake to the very end. This is hopefully true of every child.

The plate with the matzos is temporarily removed to the far end of the table. The second cup of wine is poured, after which a child asks the following four questions:

מַה נִּשְׁתַּנָּה הַלַּיְלָה הַזֶּה מִכָּל הַלֵּילוֹת:

Why is this night different from all other nights?

שֶׁבְּכָל הַלֵּילוֹת אָנוּ אוֹכְלִין חָמֵץ וּמַצָּה, הַלַּיְלָה הַזֶּה כֻּלּוֹ מַצָּה:

For on all nights we eat chametz and matzah, but on this night only matzah!

שֶׁבְּכָל הַלֵּילוֹת אָנוּ אוֹכְלִין שְׁאָר יְרָקוֹת, הַלַּיְלָה הַזֶּה מָרוֹר:

For on all nights we eat other vegetables, and on this night bitter herbs!

שֶׁבְּכָל הַלֵּילוֹת אֵין אָנוּ מַטְבִּילִין אֲפִילוּ פַּעַם אֶחָת, הַלַּיְלָה הַזֶּה שְׁתֵּי פְעָמִים:

For on all nights we do not dip our food even once, on this night we do it twice!

שֶׁבְּכָל הַלֵּילוֹת אָנוּ אוֹכְלִין בֵּין יוֹשְׁבִין וּבֵין מְסוּבִּין, הַלַּיְלָה הַזֶּה כֻּלָּנוּ מְסוּבִּין:

For on all nights we eat either sitting upright or reclining, and on this night we all recline!

The Wise Son

The *Seder* starts like any other Shabbos or *Yom Tov* meal with *kiddush* and the washing of the hands. From there, a perceptive and inquisitive child begins to notice unusual behavior. For one thing, there is no blessing on the washing, and we don't follow the washing with the customary blessing of *Hamotzi*. Three elements of difference arouse the child's attention: firstly, the eating of karpas; secondly, the breaking of the matzah into two pieces; and thirdly, the pouring of the second cup of wine. Normally at this time we would begin to eat a meal. Additionally, the child's interest is piqued by the covering and uncovering of the *Seder* plate.[4] Some of the unusual things, the child has seen already, such as the matzah and the reclining. He has already seen one act of dipping – the karpas in salt water. He has not yet seen the dipping of maror in *charoses*. As the Mishnah indicates, the child is taught to ask these questions. The children are certainly

The Cynical Son

We consciously seek to do things differently on Pesach more than on any other holiday. The purpose of these exercises is to fully appreciate how we became a nation. The fact that we began our peoplehood as slaves was meant to imbue within us an appreciation for freedom. The remembrance of the consumption of matzah and maror (the subjects of the first two questions) will assure us that when we are fortunate enough to dip and recline (the subjects of the last two questions) we will always be thankful for our freedoms and take nothing for granted. This sentiment, though, goes one step further. The recollection of our collective origins would assure that we would always be sensitive to the deprivations and suffering of others. It is for this reason that the Torah stresses the fair treatment of the stranger more often than any other mitzvah. No less than thirty-six times are we reminded to care for the stranger.[6] In terms

The Pure Son

The general question "How is this night different from all other nights?" can be understood on multiple levels. "This night" can refer to our exile,[7] and we note the difference between this "night" and other "nights." Our first exile, in Egypt, was timed for four hundred years.[8] Any attempt to shorten this appointed time would be doomed to failure. Our Sages relate that members of the tribe of Ephraim were mistaken by thirty years and left Egypt early to disastrous results, as they were all killed by Philistines.[9] Our second exile to Babylonia was also timed for seventy years.[10] Any attempt to shorten this appointed time would also be doomed to failure. A false prophet, Chananya ben Azur, predicted a two-year exile[11] with disastrous ends for himself. He didn't even live long enough to see his prediction disproven.[12] Our present exile is different from all other exiles in that it has not been timed. No prediction for its end has ever been made. This exile can be hastened.

The Withdrawn Son

מה נשתנה represents an amazement of how different things are this night. This is likened unto witnessing God's works and saying "מה רבו מעשיך ה' כולם בחכמה עשית – How great are your works O Lord, You have made them all with wisdom."[5] Or Yaakov's recognition of the holiness of the place upon which he slept, when he said "מה נורא המקום הזה – How awesome is this place,"[6] or Bilaam observing the camp of Israel, and in amazement saying, "מה טובו אהליך יעקב משכנתיך ישראל – How good are your tents O Yaakov, your dwellings O Yisrael."[7] This is especially poignant in *Tehillim* chapter 66, which is dedicated to the wonders of *yetzias Mitzrayim*. Verse 3 reads "מה נורא מעשיך ברב עוזך יכחשו לך אויביך – How awesome are Your deeds, Your enemies cower at Your great strength." The first word of this passage is meant to drive us to assure the children are amazed. Our actions are meant to create a doorway for all children to ask questions. (See below *Arbah Banim – She'eino*

The Wise Son – continued

not limited to asking these four questions,[5] and not every child will realize to ask these four on his own. Rather, these four questions represent a theme for the entire evening and this is a point that is crucial for young and old, wise and withdrawn, pure and cynical. What is so confounding to the eye of the child at the *Seder* is not simply the sheer number of unusual or unprecedented customs at the *Seder*, but that there doesn't seem to be a unified theme behind the customs. The first two questions regarding matzah and maror bespeak the bitterness of our slavery and the deprivation of our daily lives. The last two questions regarding dipping and reclining bespeak our redemption, salvation, and freedom.[6] The child may wonder what the point is of these conflicting themes. These themes will be manifest in a number of ways in subsequent paragraphs.[7]

The Cynical Son – continued

of repetition, this makes such a concern more pressing than idolatry, Shabbos, or any particular belief system. It is why Jews have largely backed every liberating and redemptive movement and have been behind the emancipation of others throughout history.

We need not teach any of these questions to any specific child, but everyone attending the *Seder* must be appraised of how the experience of Pesach characterizes us as people. The Jew is constantly stepping back and changing behavior, and in each case these changes help us evaluate who we are as individuals. On Shabbos we step back from creative activity. On Yom Kippur we step back from physical pleasures. On Sukkos we step back from our regular residence. In observance of *kashrus* we step back from unbridled consumption. In observance of ritual family purity we step back from the physicality of human love.

In each of these we have the opportunity to evaluate ourselves. Experts today tell us how important it is to refrain from the use of technology for twenty-four hours once a week. Most people find it difficult to do so for one hour. But Shabbos observers do it all the time, as we evaluate our creative energies and renew them weekly. Physical pleasures become so much more meaningful when they are not taken for granted, and we refrain from them by intention. The kosher consumer must be assured of so many things before tossing food into the mouth. Is it kosher? Is it dairy? Is it a meat product? Was this fruit properly tithed? And then we must be sure of the proper blessing before the simple and natural act of eating. By the end of Sukkos, we are hopefully more attuned to the plight of the homeless, to the point of actually doing something for them. The observance of *taharas hamishpachah* attunes us as well to the many facets of human connections and assures that marriage stays fresh and is constantly renewed.

These themes, exemplified by the ebb and flow of the Four Questions, comprise the essence of the *Seder*, and our experience as a people.

The Pure Son – continued

It can come sooner if we deserve it. Our Sages expound the words, "בעתה אחישנו – I will hasten (the redemption) in its time" (*Yeshayahu* 60:22), to teach this very message. Our salvation will either be hastened, or it will come on time. How can it be both? The Gemara answers that if we deserve it, our salvation will be hastened. If we don't, it will come at an appointed, albeit unannounced, time.[13] Indeed, the prophet Yeshayahu seems to support just such a reading of *Mah Nishtanah*, in the following prophecy.[14]

The Pure Son — continued

שומר מה מלילה, שומר מה מליל? אמר שומר אתא בקר וגם לילה, אם תבעיון בעיו שבו אתיו

Watchman, what of the night? Watchman, what of the night? The watchman replied: Morning came and so did the night. If you would inquire, inquire; come back again.

The ending of the exile is in *our* hands and this is how this "night" is different from all other "nights."

We also take note of how this night is really treated like a day. Usually, positive commandments, especially those that have the word יום applied to

them,[15] are performed by day and not by night. The mitzvah of *sippur yetzias Mitzrayim* also has the word יום applied to it; והגדת לבנך ביום ההוא לאמר. The passage in the Haggadah beginning *Yachol MeiRosh Chodesh* considers that this mitzvah should perhaps also be performed by day, if not for the inextricable connection between the telling of the story of redemption, and the mitzvos of the evening, such as matzah and maror. These mitzvos are performed at night with the eating of the *korban Pesach*.[16] Therefore, *sippur yetzias Mitzrayim* is also at night.[17] So this night is different from all other nights in that it acts like a day.

The Withdrawn Son — continued

Yodei'a Lishol, Maggid Section 7, in the approach to the withdrawn child, of את פתח לו, which literally means to "open up to him," but in this context, can mean to create openings for him. Let there always be a door into which every child feels comfortable entering). If the child doesn't ask questions, we teach him at least these four.

These four questions show how the *Seder* encapsulates an element of our festive holy days, and what each represents, all in one night of remembering our origins as a people.

Our *Baalei Mussar* explain the thin nature of the matzah and sheer simplicity of its ingredients, enable us to embrace the characteristics of humility and forbearance. On Shavuos, we celebrate the

giving of Torah, whose acquisition is better facilitated by these characteristics. Yet we don't eat matzah on Shavuos. Maror may be the perfect food for Rosh Hashanah because the symbol it bespeaks is submission and obedience, yet we don't eat maror on Rosh Hashanah. Dipping may have been just the thing to do to enhance the delight of every Shabbos, yet there is no custom of doing so. And the holiday of our rejoicing, Sukkos, may have been the best time for reclining, to demonstrate our comfort with the protection of God's cover. Yet we don't recline on Sukkos. All four of these may have been more appropriate for other holidays. Yet we do all of them on Pesach. These messages are for young and old and may be redirected and remolded to fit each child on his own level.

MAGGID SECTION 3 – AVADIM HAYINU

1. How is this section of Maggid a proper response to the questions of מה נשתנה?
2. This part of Maggid has several verbosities. A simplification will outline these extraneous words and phrases. What can explain these elaborations? (See table on following page.)
3. Why switch from first person היינו and ויציאנו to third person את אבותינו, and why switch from משעבדים to עבדים?
4. Why is *sippur yetzias Mitzrayim* first called a mitzvah and then called praiseworthy?

Proposed Simplified Text	Haggadah Text
עבדים היינו במצרים	עבדים היינו לפרעה במצרים
We were slaves in Egypt	We were slaves to Pharaoh in Egypt
ויוציאנו ה' משם	ויוציאנו ה' אלוקינו משם ביד חזקה ובזרוע נטויה
And God took us out from there	And God, our Lord, took us out from there with a mighty hand and an outstretched arm
ואילו לא עשה כן	ואילו לא הוציא הקדוש ברוך הוא את אבותינו ממצרים
And if He had not done so	And if the Holy One, Blessed be He, had not taken our forefathers from Egypt
הרי אנו נשארנו עבדים שם	הרי אנו ובנינו ובני בנינו משעבדים היינו לפרעה במצרים
We would have remained slaves there	Indeed, we, and our children, and our children's children, would remain enslaved to Pharaoh in Egypt
ואפילו כלנו חכמים	ואפילו כלנו חכמים כלנו נבונים כלנו זקנים כלנו יודעים את התורה
Even if we are all wise men	And even if we were all wise men, we were all sages, we would all know the Torah
מצוה עלינו לספר ביציאת מצרים	מצוה עלינו לספר ביציאת מצרים
We must tell the story of our leaving Egypt	We must tell the story of our leaving Egypt
וכל המרבה	וכל המרבה לספר ביציאת מצרים
And the more we do so	And the more that we discuss leaving Egypt
הרי זה משבח	הרי זה משבח
This is more praiseworthy.	This is more praiseworthy.

The plate with the matzos is returned to the table, and the matzos are uncovered.

עֲבָדִים הָיִינוּ לְפַרְעֹה בְּמִצְרָיִם, וַיּוֹצִיאֵנוּ יהוה אֱלֹהֵינוּ מִשָּׁם בְּיָד חֲזָקָה וּבִזְרֹעַ נְטוּיָה. וְאִילּוּ לֹא הוֹצִיא הַקָּדוֹשׁ

We were slaves to Pharaoh in Egypt, and Hashem, our God, took us out from there with a strong hand and with an outstretched arm. And if the Holy One, blessed is He, had not

בָּרוּךְ הוּא אֶת אֲבוֹתֵינוּ מִמִּצְרַיִם, הֲרֵי אָנוּ וּבָנֵינוּ וּבְנֵי בָנֵינוּ מְשֻׁעְבָּדִים הָיִינוּ לְפַרְעֹה בְּמִצְרָיִם: וַאֲפִילוּ כֻּלָּנוּ חֲכָמִים, כֻּלָּנוּ נְבוֹנִים, כֻּלָּנוּ זְקֵנִים, כֻּלָּנוּ יוֹדְעִים אֶת הַתּוֹרָה, מִצְוָה עָלֵינוּ לְסַפֵּר בִּיצִיאַת מִצְרָיִם. וְכָל הַמַּרְבֶּה לְסַפֵּר בִּיצִיאַת מִצְרַיִם, הֲרֵי זֶה מְשׁוּבָּח:

taken our ancestors out of Egypt, then we, our children, and our children's children would still be subservient to Pharaoh in Egypt. Even if we were all wise, or we were all full of understanding, or we were all elders, or we were all knowledgeable in the Torah, it would still be incumbent upon us to recount the story of the Exodus from Egypt – and whoever expands upon the recounting of the story of the Exodus from Egypt is praiseworthy.

The Wise Son

An important theme of the *Seder* is מתחיל בגנות ומסיים בשבח.[8] We begin the evening with a description of our shameful past and we conclude with praise of how far we have come. Rav and Shmuel dispute what the גנות refers to. Rav considers Maggid Section 9 – *Mitchilah Ovedei Avodah Zarah* – to fulfill this requirement and Shmuel considers our section of Maggid to fulfill it. In practice, we fulfill the Mishnah's directive by reciting both.[9] This answer precisely addresses the two types of questions of מה נשתנה. On one hand we eat foods that remind us of slavery, yet on the other hand we behave

The Cynical Son

The reason for all the elaborations and references to mitzvos and praiseworthy actions is to assure that we enhance our sense of gratitude for how far we have come as a nation. However, gratitude alone is not enough of a lesson for us in this redemption story. The prophet, Amos, whose moral compass drove him to leave his home in the Judean city of Tekoa to rebuke the corrupt residents of the Northern Tribes of Israel, delivered an astonishing diatribe at his audience, with respect to *yetzias Mitzrayim*.

The Pure Son

The redemption from Egypt transformed us from a nation of slaves to human whim to slaves of the Divine Will, as the Torah indicates: "כי עבדי הם אשר הוצאתי אותם מארץ מצרים – For they are my slaves when I freed them from the land of Egypt."[18]

This is an ongoing process from our ancestors to this very day. For this reason, we introduce our morning and evening *Amidah* with a reference to God as גאל ישראל in the past tense, the One Who redeemed us. Then, in the *Amidah* itself, as we petition God for our daily needs, we refer to Him as גואל ישראל, in the present tense. In Temple times,

The Withdrawn Son

Although we read from a Haggadah to fulfill the mitzvah of והגדת לבנך, the name of the mitzvah is ספור יציאת מצרים, and our Maggid Section bids us וכל המרבה לספר ביציאת מצרים. We are not simply relating, we are recounting, we are telling a story, and that story requires us to stress every aspect of our subjugation to Pharaoh and to Egypt. We must reiterate every aspect of our recognition of God's redemption, and how indebted we are to Him. Had God not redeemed us when He did we would have had a cultural indebtedness to Egyptian society. We left the slavery of Egypt so that we like wealthy people by dipping and reclining. This transformation is a remembrance of our humble beginnings and how far God has taken us.

All the elaborations in this section of Maggid are meant to drive home the idea that nothing short of a series of miracles could free us from the Egyptian bondage. This is why we stress פרעה in addition to מצרים, why we stress what the Lord *our God* did for us and then we stress again that this was done by הקדוש ברוך הוא, for with redemption we began to feel holy and blessed. This is to say that one who aspires to be *kadosh* and *baruch*, can truly appreciate calling Hashem ויוציאנו הקב"ה. at first refers to the actual generation that left Egypt. (This first line is actually the Torah's immediate response to the Wise Son's question.[10] This answer hints at the fact that we would like to consider all inquisitive children wise.) Then, in retrospect, we consider that if God had not taken our ancestors out of Egypt we would still be subjugated to Pharaoh. What God did so many years ago still has an impact on us to this very day. The doubled expression, of ביד חזקה as well as בזרוע נטויה, needs explanation. In the Torah's response to the Wise Son's question, only ביד חזקה appears. In the context of this section of Maggid, we can explain that ביד חזקה refers to God's actions in destroying Egypt,[11] while בזרוע נטויה refers to how God impressed upon us the need for gratitude.

But how can we say that if not for this we would still be subjugated to Pharaoh? By the time the Haggadah was written, that dynasty was long gone. We can say that if not for our redemption from Egypt, that country would still be a world power and we would still be enslaved. Or perhaps we can say that even if we would no longer be slaves in Egypt (עבדים) we would in any case be beholden to Egypt (משעבדים). We would have devolved so far into their cultural milieu that we could never have emerged as a distinct nation to spread God's word.

There are some minimal requirements to fulfill the Torah law of *sippur yetzias Mitzrayim*. The rest of the year there is a mitzvah of *zechiras yetzias Mitzrayim*, remembering the redemption from Egypt with a daily reference.[12] This daily reference is a manifestation of our faith, and is why the mitzvah that commands our faith makes reference to *yetzias Mitzrayim*: "I am the Lord your God who took you out of Egypt."[13] On the night of Pesach we go one step further, from a mitzvah of *emunah*, faith, to a sentiment of *hoda'ah*, gratitude. We need not elaborate on our *emunah* in referring to *yetzias Mitzrayim*. We fulfill that with several references in our daily prayers.[14] However, when it comes to expressing gratitude, we do so to as great an extent as we can. For this reason, this section of Maggid ends with a call to add onto this mitzvah without limit. This is to be done by חכמים, נבונים, זקנים, and יודעים את התורה. This Maggid Section elaborates on all these types of knowledgeable people because it refers to four progressive levels of cognitive understanding.[15]

1. חכמים are familiar with the Torah's description of the slavery. They are steeped in the understanding of the Exodus narratives and their commentaries.

2. נבונים are aware of the implications of this slavery to our consciousness as a people. They are aware of the slave mentality that descended upon our people so that only a newcomer to the scene – Moshe, on his first day in the presence of his brethren – would even take notice of the Egyptian beating the Hebrew,[16] and consider that something was wrong.

3. זקנים will, through the experience of life, add meaning and depth to the proceedings of the evening.

4. יודעים את התורה are able to understand the Rabbinic expositions of the midrash to the description of our slavery, and expound upon them further. (This section of exposition begins with *Arami Oved Avi*, discussed in *Tzei U'Lemad*, Maggid Section 12).

הלא כבני כושיים אתם לי בני ישראל נאם ה' הלא את ישראל העלית מארץ מצרים ופלשתיים מכפתור וארם מקיר:

To Me Israelites, you are just like the Ethiopians, declares God. True, I brought Israel up from the land of Egypt, but also the Philistines from Kaftor and the Arameans from Kir.[7]

Other nations, including Ethiopians, Philistines, and Arameans also have their stories of redemption and salvation.[8] What makes the redemption from Egypt different is that we forged a covenant with God in its aftermath. It is our commitment to that covenant that is the ultimate expression of gratitude. The elaborations of this section of Maggid accentuate the source of this gratitude, which continues on to this day.

when we experienced that God had redeemed us from a life-threatening situation, we would bring a *korban todah*, a thanksgiving offering. Nowadays we thank Hashem with *Birchas HaGomel*,[19] a blessing that humbly acknowledges God's presence in all our lives and that His providence saved our lives. The Talmud,[20] based on *Tehillim* 107, states that *Birchas HaGomel* is said for four types of extenuating circumstances, those who

1. cross a desert;
2. leave incarceration;
3. survive a general threat to life (such as sickness or an accident);
4. cross a body of water.[21]

It emerges that those who *"bentch Gomel"* are replicating the events of *yetzias Mitzrayim*! When we left Egypt, we experienced every one of the four categories for reciting this blessing. We left what was a constant and ever-present threat to life, we left incarceration, we crossed into a desert, and we crossed a body of water.[22] In reality, we *all* have reason to bring a *korban todah* every day for things we may not even realize. It is for this reason that we recite *Tehillim* 100, *Mizmor L'Sodah*, every day as part of our prayer liturgy.[23]

Therefore, all our salvations are somewhat related to our original redemption from Egypt. It is for this reason that we at first say, "ויוציאנו – He took *us* out," and then we say, "הוציא את אבותינו – He took our ancestors." Every salvation reminds the Jew of our first salvation.[24] Every individual who is saved must internalize how this personal salvation fits in within the framework of the national experience. It is for this reason that we say מצוה עלינו in plural and then וכל המרבה in singular.

could turn our service to God in receiving and following the Torah. This is expressed as a charge to קובע עתים לתורה. This is usually translated as a directive to set aside time for Torah study. In the wake of our redemption we are bidden to apply an interpretation which bids us to set the cultural milieu of our times to a Torah directive and not vice versa. The times are always changing, but the Torah must be a constant inspiration in navigating those times. If the times direct the understanding of Torah, then before we know it, the Torah is diluted to an unrecognizable text. This is what our Sages meant when they said אין לך בן חורין אלא מי שעוסק בתורה.[8] The epitome of the emancipated Jew is the one who is engrossed in Torah and whose cultural mindset is not enslaved by the trends of the day, but by Torah values. Our mitzvah is to tell the story. The Haggadah itself will relate to the bare minimum to fulfill this obligation (See below, *Rabban Gamliel Hayah Omer*, Maggid Section 16). The maximum, however, knows no limit because it emerges from a sentiment of gratitude. Another mitzvah of the Torah whose core is the sentiment of gratitude is כבוד אב ואם, respect for parents. The mitzvah knows no limit as numerous Talmudic sources indicate,[9] because gratitude has no limit. Life becomes profoundly more meaningful when we see every day as a gift, and this section of Maggid with all its verbosities is meant to underscore this point.

The mitzvah of *sippur* is not only related to the word "story," but also to the word "book" or "*sefer*." The story of the Egyptian redemption must be indellibly written into our hearts the way a *sofer*, a scribe, writes words of Torah. At the two ends of our biblical history stand Moshe and Ezra. Ezra is well-known as Ezra HaSofer, the scribe (*Ezra* 7:11), and Moshe is referred to by Chazal as Moshe Safra Rabba, Moshe the great scribe (*Talmud Bavli, Sotah* 13b). These two leaders assured that the story of the Torah would be marked onto our consciousness forever, with the night of the Seder playing an essential role toward that end.

MAGGID SECTION 4 – MAASEH B'RABBI ELIEZER

1. What is the significance of this Maggid Section?
2. Is there something to be derived from this specific list of Sages?
3. Why are we told where they gathered?
4. What is the significance of the fact that they told the story all night until they had to be informed that the mitzvah of *Krias Shema* was upon them?

מַעֲשֶׂה בְּרַבִּי אֱלִיעֶזֶר וְרַבִּי יְהוֹשֻׁעַ וְרַבִּי אֶלְעָזָר בֶּן עֲזַרְיָה וְרַבִּי עֲקִיבָא וְרַבִּי טַרְפוֹן שֶׁהָיוּ מְסֻבִּין בִּבְנֵי בְרַק, וְהָיוּ מְסַפְּרִים בִּיצִיאַת מִצְרַיִם כָּל אוֹתוֹ הַלַּיְלָה, עַד שֶׁבָּאוּ תַלְמִידֵיהֶם וְאָמְרוּ לָהֶם, רַבּוֹתֵינוּ הִגִּיעַ זְמַן קְרִיאַת שְׁמַע שֶׁל שַׁחֲרִית:

An incident happened with Rabbi Eliezer, Rabbi Yehoshua, Rabbi Elazar ben Azaryah, Rabbi Akiva, and Rabbi Tarfon. They were reclining at the [Seder] table in B'nei Brak, and they were recounting the story of Exodus from Egypt all that night, until their students came in and told them: "Our rabbis! The time for reciting the morning Shema has arrived!"

The Wise Son

This section of Maggid is proof that even the wise Torah scholars and elders would in practice be מרבה לספר ביציאת מצרים, as the end of *Avadim Hayinu* (Maggid Section 3) indicates. This Maggid Section describes Sages reclining (מסובין) in B'nei Brak. This would seem to be extraneous information, but may be relevant considering some issues raised by our Sages. Rabbi Eliezer and Rabbi Yehoshua were the teachers of the other three and there is a Talmudic discussion whether or not a student may recline in the presence of his *rebbi*.[17] The fact, though, that they gathered in B'nei Brak may be a clue as to why they all reclined. B'nei Brak was the residence of Rabbi Akiva,[18] and thus, as the *"mara d'asra,"* the master of the place, and not their *rebbi*, the commentators agree that they could all recline.[19]

Rabbi Akiva and Rabbi Elazar ben Azariah dispute the final time for consumption of the *korban Pesach*. Rabbi Akiva holds that we have

The Cynical Son

This Maggid Section shows that the Sages didn't simply exhort others to be *marbeh* in *sippur yetzias Mitzrayim*, but that they did so themselves. All five of these Sages were descended from ancestors who were not enslaved. According to tradition, the tribe of Leivi was not enslaved.[9] Rabbi Tarfon,[10] Rabbi Elazar ben Azarya,[11] and Rabbi Eliezer[12] were Kohanim.[13] Rabbi Yehoshua was a Leivi and Rabbi Akiva was descended from converts.[14] Thus all five of these Sages were removed from the previous chapter's assertion that if God had not saved us we and our descendants would still be enslaved, because their ancestors were never slaves in the first place. Yet they related to those who *are* descended from slaves by including themselves in the full observance of the *avodah* of the evening.[15] (This may explain why Rabban Gamliel, who often appears with this group, is absent. He, from the tribe of Yehudah, *is* descended from slaves and thus wouldn't fit in).

The Pure Son

When Sages decide upon a worthy practice, a הלכה, it is most likely to take root if the practice is backed by a מעשה so that the practice becomes "הלכה למעשה." For this reason, our Maggid Section follows the exhortation to be מרבה ביציאת מצרים with the word מעשה. This group of Rabbis often associated together for various purposes. Rabban Gamliel, who often accompanied them, headed the Sanhedrin and needed to remain in Jerusalem. Rabbi Elazar's place in this group was questionable. He praised those who stayed home for the holiday and spoke against those who would leave home for Shabbos.[25] Some suggest that since Rabbi Elazar lived in Lud[26] his presence in B'nei Brak could only be justified for the fulfillment of some type of communal need.[27]

B'nei Brak was Rabbi Akiva's domain and he held that the mitzvos of the *Seder* could be performed all night. A parallel story appears[28] of a group of Sages joining Rabban Gamliel, and they were עוסקין

The Withdrawn Son

Everyone must expend themselves according to their own strengths and abilities in performing the mitzvah of *sippur yetzias Mitzrayim*, even to the level of doing so all night. The night of Pesach is known as "ליל שימורים – a night of protection."[10] There are a few normative practices in our time to underscore the point of this night as a *leil shimurim*. Although it was dangerous for Sages of their stature to gather together during the Roman persecutions, this group felt that the protection of the first night of Pesach afforded them safety. The Talmud[11] instituted a quasi-repetition of the *Amidah* for Friday night for the sake of latecomers so that they could rely on that for their *Amidah* and not have to walk home alone from shul.[12] This is known as *Magen Avos*, and normative halachah maintains that when the first night of Pesach falls on a Friday night, *Magen Avos* is not said. The protection it was meant to afford is not needed on *leil shimurim*.[13] Additionally, every night we recite the bedtime

The Wise Son—continued

until dawn, while Rabbi Elazar ben Azariah only allows it to be eaten until midnight. We will see (Maggid Sections 8 and 16) that the mitzvah of *sippur yetzias Mitzrayim* is tied to the mitzvos of the evening, such as the eating of *korban Pesach*, matzah, and maror. One may have thought that when time runs out on the mitzvos of the evening, time runs out on the mitzvah of *sippur yetzias Mitzrayim* as well. This Maggid Section indicates that the mitzvah of *sippur yetzias Mitzrayim* can and should be extended past the time of the other mitzvos. The time of *Krias Shema* (daybreak) is past the time of the mitzvos for both Rabbi Akiva and Rabbi Elazar ben Azariah, and both were telling the story beyond their own cutoff points.[20] The essence of this section of Maggid is to indicate the efforts these Sages expended in being מרבה לספר ביציאת מצרים. Even though we usually say העוסק במצוה פטור מן המצוה, someone involved in a mitzvah is exempt from other mitzvos,[21] they interrupted their mitzvah of *sippur yetzias Mitzrayim* because *Krias Shema* also makes reference to *yetzias Mitzrayim*.

And even regarding one for whom תורתו אומנותו, Torah study is his main occupation, we interrupt Torah study for *Krias Shema*.[22]

Usually Rabban Gamliel appears with this group, but not here, because he held a fundamentally different opinion from his colleagues regarding how to commemorate the *korban Pesach* when the Temple no longer stands.[23] Rabban Gamliel would eat גדי מקולס (literally, an "armored kid"), with its entrails alongside it, at the *Seder*. The *korban* was so tightly wrapped that it resembled a helmet, hence גדי מקולס.[24] His colleagues disagreed with this practice, saying it would resemble eating sacrificial meat outside the Temple.[25] This opinion separated Rabban Gamliel from the others. The stated practice of Rabbi Elazar ben Azaria, as well as Rabban Gamliel, is contradicted by the normative practice of the assembled rabbis in this section. This is a greater problem for Rabban Gamliel than for Rabbi Elazar and may explain Rabban Gamliel's absence. Also, Rabban Gamliel, as the head of the Sanhedrin, would rarely leave Jerusalem on a holiday.

The Cynical Son—continued

The fact that they gathered in B'nei Brak underscores the centrality of Rabbi Akiva to the proceedings. B'nei Brak was Rabbi Akiva's residence[16] and some historians state that these Sages were debating the virtues of rebelling against the Hadrianic persecutions.[17] Rabbi Akiva supported the Bar Kochba revolts,[18] and the claim here is that he was attempting to convince his colleagues and teachers of the need to join the revolt. In a previous generation, Rabban Yochanan ben Zachai felt that peace and submission was a preferable choice to revolt.[19] (This too may explain Rabban Gamliel's absence at this table. The presence of the *Nasi* might have drawn too much attention to these secretive

proceedings). By the time of this meeting, Rabbi Akiva felt a new approach to Roman persecution was necessary. The recitation of the Haggadah understandably raises nationalistic feelings as well as hopes and aspirations for freedom and redemption. As such, the Romans were wary about *Seder* observances, and many Jews had to turn to hiding. Jews would heroically do so throughout history, such as during the Inquisition, in the ghettos and in the former Soviet Union. Such "underground" *Seders* took their inspiration from these Sages, and perhaps it is for this reason that they did not realize that the sun had risen, and they had to be informed to turn to another mitzvah.

The Pure Son – continued

בהלכות פסח כל אותו הלילה, they stayed up all night studying the laws of Pesach. This story is cited as a source for the custom to remain awake all night after the *Seder* to learn the laws of Pesach.[29]

The Withdrawn Son – continued

Krias Shema, a collection of Torah chapters and verses meant to protect from disturbed sleep, bad dreams, and nighttime dangers.[14] The custom is not to recite these chapters and verses on *leil shimurim*, but only to say the chapter of *Shema* itself. We have all the protection we need for a safe night's sleep.[15]

The Midrash relates that the Israelites excitedly couldn't sleep the night before the redemption. Ironically, a separate Midrash notes that the Israelites did not demonstrate similar excitement the night before *Matan Torah*. Our custom is to switch these two events with B'nei Yisrael's behavior. On the night of Shavuos there is a widespread custom to learn all night, to compensate for the fact that B'nei Yisrael slept, known as *Tikkun Leil Shavuos*.[16] However, this is not a widespread custom for the night of Pesach. The fact that these five Sages remained awake all night is extraordinary, but has not been translated to normative practice to stay up all night, except for a notable few.[17]

MAGGID SECTION 5 – AMAR RABBI ELAZAR BEN AZARYAH

1. What is the purpose of this section at this point of the *Seder*?
2. What is the purpose of the background information of this section of Maggid? Why not simply state the dispute between Ben Zoma and the Sages?
3. Why is it important to recall the redemption from Egypt at night?
4. What is the nature of the two sides of this dispute and what is the halachah?

אָמַר רַבִּי אֶלְעָזָר בֶּן עֲזַרְיָה הֲרֵי אֲנִי כְּבֶן שִׁבְעִים שָׁנָה, וְלֹא זָכִיתִי שֶׁתֵּאָמֵר יְצִיאַת מִצְרַיִם בַּלֵּילוֹת עַד שֶׁדְּרָשָׁהּ בֶּן זוֹמָא, שֶׁנֶּאֱמַר לְמַעַן תִּזְכֹּר אֶת יוֹם צֵאתְךָ מֵאֶרֶץ מִצְרַיִם כֹּל יְמֵי חַיֶּיךָ. יְמֵי חַיֶּיךָ הַיָּמִים, כֹּל יְמֵי חַיֶּיךָ הַלֵּילוֹת. וַחֲכָמִים אוֹמְרִים יְמֵי חַיֶּיךָ הָעוֹלָם הַזֶּה, כֹּל יְמֵי חַיֶּיךָ לְהָבִיא לִימוֹת הַמָּשִׁיחַ:

Rabbi Elazar ben Azaryah said: I am like a seventy-year-old man, yet I did not merit [to demonstrate why] the Exodus from Egypt should be mentioned every night, until Ben Zoma explained it: It says (*Devarim* 16:3), "So that you remember the day you left Egypt all the days of your life." Just "the days of your life" would have referred to the days; "all the days of your life" therefore refers to the nights as well. But the other Sages say that just "the days of your life" would have referred to the present world; the addition of the word "all" comes to include the Messianic era as well.

The Wise Son

Maggid Section 5 is another proof of the length the Sages took to stress *zechiras yetzias Mitzrayim* not only at the *Seder* but at all times.[26] According to Rabbi Elazar ben Azariah, there is a mitzvah to remember *yetzias Mitzrayim* every night of the year. However, on all other nights the purpose of the mitzvah is to inculcate faith. On the night of the *Seder* the purpose of the remembrance is to inculcate *gratitude*.[27] The background of this section of Maggid stems from the Mishnah,[28] and relates to a story that caused Rabbi Elazar to age prematurely. Rabban Gamliel, the head of the Sanhedrin, had caused undue consternation to Rabbi Yehoshua on a number of occasions. The Sages decided to depose Rabban Gamliel and it was decided that the eighteen-year-old Rabbi Elazar ben Azariah should head the Sanhedrin. Before accepting such a life-changing position, he consulted his wife, who expressed concern of his youth and the daily burdens of the position. Rabbi Elazar seized the

The Pure Son

Children are starting to realize that the proceedings of the evening are not quite moving in the direction of any other Shabbos or *Yom Tov*. More and more, we recognize how different this night is from all other nights. Daytime is a time of clarity while nighttime is a time of confusion. In the Creation story, the evening darkness is called night and the morning light is called day. The word for morning – בוקר – bespeaks discernment and clarity.[30] The word for evening – ערב – bespeaks confusion and lack of clarity.[31] Perhaps we should only remember our redemption at a time of clarity, namely by day.[32] Rabbi Elazar ben Azariah insists that we need to do so at night. We need to stress our belief in a future redemption perhaps even more at night. It is for this reason that the halachah sides with Rabbi Elazar and that we do reference *yetzias Mitzrayim* not only by day, but by night as well, a sentiment that our Sages expound from a verse in *Tehillim*, "להגיד בבוקר חסדך ואמונתך

The Cynical Son

Our ongoing exile is likened unto a long night. Nighttime is an inconvenient time for activity. We would rather stay at home, or in bed, as the narrative of *Shir HaShirim* (5:2–6:1) indicates.

אֲנִי יְשֵׁנָה וְלִבִּי עֵר קוֹל דּוֹדִי דוֹפֵק פִּתְחִי לִי אֲחֹתִי רַעְיָתִי יוֹנָתִי תַמָּתִי שֶׁרֹאשִׁי נִמְלָא טָל קְוֻּצּוֹתַי רְסִיסֵי לָיְלָה. פָּשַׁטְתִּי אֶת כֻּתָּנְתִּי אֵיכָכָה אֶלְבָּשֶׁנָּה רָחַצְתִּי אֶת רַגְלַי אֵיכָכָה אֲטַנְּפֵם. דּוֹדִי שָׁלַח יָדוֹ מִן הַחֹר וּמֵעַי הָמוּ עָלָיו. קַמְתִּי אֲנִי לִפְתֹּחַ לְדוֹדִי וְיָדַי נָטְפוּ מוֹר וְאֶצְבְּעֹתַי מוֹר עֹבֵר עַל כַּפּוֹת הַמַּנְעוּל. פָּתַחְתִּי אֲנִי לְדוֹדִי וְדוֹדִי חָמַק עָבָר נַפְשִׁי יָצְאָה בְדַבְּרוֹ בִּקַּשְׁתִּיהוּ וְלֹא מְצָאתִיהוּ קְרָאתִיו וְלֹא עָנָנִי. מְצָאֻנִי הַשֹּׁמְרִים הַסֹּבְבִים בָּעִיר הִכּוּנִי פְצָעוּנִי נָשְׂאוּ אֶת רְדִידִי מֵעָלַי שֹׁמְרֵי הַחֹמוֹת. הִשְׁבַּעְתִּי אֶתְכֶם בְּנוֹת יְרוּשָׁלַ͏ִם אִם תִּמְצְאוּ אֶת דּוֹדִי מַה תַּגִּידוּ לוֹ שֶׁחוֹלַת אַהֲבָה אָנִי. מַה דּוֹדֵךְ מִדּוֹד הַיָּפָה בַּנָּשִׁים מַה דּוֹדֵךְ מִדּוֹד שֶׁכָּכָה הִשְׁבַּעְתָּנוּ. דּוֹדִי צַח וְאָדוֹם דָּגוּל מֵרְבָבָה. רֹאשׁוֹ כֶּתֶם פָּז קְוֻּצּוֹתָיו תַּלְתַּלִּים שְׁחֹרוֹת כָּעוֹרֵב. עֵינָיו כְּיוֹנִים עַל אֲפִיקֵי מָיִם רֹחֲצוֹת בֶּחָלָב יֹשְׁבוֹת עַל מִלֵּאת. לְחָיָו כַּעֲרוּגַת הַבֹּשֶׂם מִגְדְּלוֹת מֶרְקָחִים שִׂפְתוֹתָיו שׁוֹשַׁנִּים נֹטְפוֹת מוֹר עֹבֵר. יָדָיו גְּלִילֵי זָהָב מְמֻלָּאִים בַּתַּרְשִׁישׁ מֵעָיו עֶשֶׁת שֵׁן מְעֻלֶּפֶת סַפִּירִים. שׁוֹקָיו עַמּוּדֵי שֵׁשׁ מְיֻסָּדִים עַל אַדְנֵי פָז מַרְאֵהוּ כַּלְּבָנוֹן בָּחוּר כָּאֲרָזִים. חִכּוֹ מַמְתַקִּים וְכֻלּוֹ מַחֲמַדִּים זֶה דוֹדִי וְזֶה רֵעִי בְּנוֹת יְרוּשָׁלָ͏ִם. אָנָה הָלַךְ דּוֹדֵךְ הַיָּפָה בַּנָּשִׁים אָנָה פָּנָה דוֹדֵךְ וּנְבַקְשֶׁנּוּ עִמָּךְ.

The Withdrawn Son

Rabbi Elazar ben Azariah lived through a time of great upheaval. The Temple had just been destroyed. The Jewish People and its religious functionaries were about to undergo a seismic shift both internally as well as externally. One of our great leaders managed to carry our people through a similar seismic shift, at the period between the era of the *Shoftim* and the beginning of the monarchy. If not for the leadership of the prophet Shmuel, Israel may not have survived this drastic period. According to tradition, Rabbi Elazar ben Azariah was reincarnated from Shmuel and shared his ability, stamina, and enthusiasm to assure that his people would successfully navigate their transitions. Shmuel, like Rabbi Elazar, was chosen for his spiritual and religious mission at a young age. Our Sages say that Shmuel died at the age of fifty-two,[18] and the eighteen-year-old Rabbi Elazar ben Azariah added these fifty-two years to his own, bolstering his youth so he could take the moment and accepted the position, and perhaps the painstaking stress leading to this decision caused the miracle the Gemara refers to which left his hair streaked with white lines. Ironically, the straw that broke Rabban Gamliel's hold on the Sanhedrin was a question about whether the evening *Maariv* prayer service is obligatory or optional.[29] The debate in the Mishnah that this Maggid Section revolves around is whether the mitzvah of *zechiras yetzias Mitzrayim* is incumbent upon us by night as well as by day.[30] The question is, why would someone think not? For one, we left Egypt by day,[31] and the remembrance is referenced with the word day, כל ימי חייך.[32]

Rabbi Elazar ben Azariah, however, refers to the *derash* of Ben Zoma that the extraneous verbiage of כל ימי חייך points to a mitzvah that is to be performed by night as well as by day.[33] The Sages agree that the words כל ימי חייך deserve to be expounded to include more than just the day itself, but disagree with Ben Zoma's *derash*, since the Torah could have said כל חייך. The word ימי is superfluous, and is expounded to limit *zechiras yetzias Mitzrayim* to the daytime. כל then adds that *zechiras yetzias Mitzrayim* is incumbent upon us in the Messianic age as well as in our own time. In the ensuing discussion in the Gemara, Ben Zoma cites the prophet Yirmiyahu to argue his point:

הנה ימים באים נאום ה' ולא יאמרו עוד חי ה' אשר העלה את בני ישראל מארץ מצרים כי אם חי ה' אשר העלה ואשר הביא את זרע בית ישראל מארץ צפונה ומכל הארצות אשר הדחתים שם.

A time is coming, declares the Lord, when it shall no longer be said, "As the Lord lives who brought the Israelites out of the Land of Egypt," but rather, "As the Lord lives who brought out and led the offspring of the House of Israel from the northland and from all the lands to which I have banished them."[34]

Ben Zoma expounds this declaration to teach that some aspect of *zechiras yetzias Mitzrayim* will change in the Messianic age. He is quick to point out that it will be overshadowed and rendered secondary in scope, size, and nature to the Messianic redemption.[35] The fact that we *do* remember the Egyptian redemption by night would seem to indicate that the halachah sides with Rabbi Elazar ben Azariah. Indeed, the Mishnah (*Berachos* 12b) begins with the words מזכירין יציאת מצרים בלילות. We do reference the Egyptian exile at nighttime and this is codified accordingly by normative halachah.[36]

"I sleep, but my heart is awake. Hark! My beloved is knocking: Open for me, my sister, my beloved, my dove, my perfect one, for my head is full of dew, my locks with the drops of the night." "I have taken off my tunic; how can I put it on? I have bathed my feet; how can I soil them?" My beloved stretched forth his hand from the hole, and my insides stirred because of him. I arose to open for my beloved, and my hands dripped with myrrh, and my fingers with flowing myrrh, upon the handles of the lock. I opened for my beloved, but my beloved had hidden and was gone; my soul went out when he spoke; I sought him, but found him not; I called him, but he did not answer me. The watchmen who patrol the city found me; they smote me and wounded me; the watchmen of the walls took my jewelry off me. "I adjure you, O daughters of Jerusalem, if you find my beloved, what will you tell him? That I am lovesick." "What is your beloved more than another beloved, O fairest of women? What is your beloved more than another beloved, that you have so adjured us?" "My beloved is white and ruddy, surrounded by myriads. His head is as the finest gold; his locks are curled, [they are as] black as a raven. His eyes are like doves beside rivulets of water, bathing in milk, fitly set. His jaws are like a bed of spice, growths of aromatic plants; his lips are [like] roses, dripping with flowing myrrh. His hands are [like] wheels of gold, set with chrysolite; his abdomen is [as] a block of ivory, overlaid with sapphires. His legs are [as] pillars of marble, founded upon sockets of fine gold, his appearance is like the Lebanon, chosen as the cedars.

The Cynical Son – continued

His palate is sweet, and he is altogether desirable; this is my beloved, and this is my friend, O daughters of Jerusalem." "Where has your beloved gone, O fairest of women? Where has your beloved turned, that we may seek him with you?"

The call for redemption comes at night, but we would prefer to be bothered at a more convenient time. We answered the call too late, and our redemption as a result was not complete. These verses can refer to the return to Israel after the seventy-year Babylonian exile. The return was lethargic and encompassed a small minority of the Jewish population. By the time we took God's call seriously and pursued His message, there was no longer a knock on the door and we had to seek Him.[20] The search has caused us much abuse from the nations of the world, but through it all we have achieved an important goal, as is indicated at the very end of the narrative. We have taught the majority of the world's people to pursue a monotheistic rather than polytheistic ideal.

We might be inclined to consider God's mitzvos, especially those performed at night, to be inconvenient or burdensome, and wonder why we should bother with such "עבודה."

The Pesach story imbued into our people and into mankind a thirst for freedom and the idea that we can always change things for the better no matter how bad they currently seem. The Jew is always concerned with redemption and growth, and every day of our lives is consumed with that thirst. It is even more crucial to concentrate on this when we live in a proverbial nighttime of exile and suffering. Rabbi Elazar had risen to the heights of the Sanhedrin but still labored to convince his colleagues of this message. The youthful Rabbi Elazar, who was chosen to lead the Sanhedrin at the age of eighteen, exerted the youthful enthusiasm that would assure we would continue to fight for redemption even in our darkest days. It is for this reason that immediately following the first night of Pesach, we continue with another nighttime mitzvah, *Sefiras Ha'Omer*, to grow our redemption to a spiritual direction. This mitzvah counts forty-nine days from Pesach to Shavuos and is specifically performed at night, a time when it is all the more important to hear the knock on the door.[21]

The Pure Son – continued

בלילות – To proclaim Your kindness in the morning and Your faithfulness by nights."[33]

The Talmud[34] connects חסדך to the ויציב ונכון blessing following *Krias Shema* by day, and ואמונתך to the blessing following *Krias Shema* at night, ואמונה כל זאת. Both blessings stress *yetzias Mitzrayim*, and the nighttime blessing references our אמונה because we need to bolster our faith all the more in times of darkness and confusion.

Our Sages describe the blessings of the morning and nighttime *Krias Shema* as a confluence of the aspects of both day and night,[35] i.e., the forces of the world that seem to be suffused with clarity as well as those that seem confusing all stem from the same source. They are all part of God's world and God's plan. He chooses to walk before us in the darkness, as we are prohibited from quantifying Him in any physical way. It is perhaps most important for us when confronting God's mysterious ways, to ignite a candle of Torah and faith to shed light on the darkness before us.

The Withdrawn Son – continued

reins of leadership at his young age and thereby consider himself as if he were seventy years of age.

Although we left Egypt by day, since Pharaoh banished us and bid us to leave by night,[19] we remember the redemption by night as well as by day. Both the daily *Shacharis* as well as *Maariv* services make references to the Egyptian redemption and contain the blessing, "'ברוך אתה ה' גאל ישראל."

This approach is further supported by an additional Torah verse:

שמור את חודש האביב ועשית פסח לה' אלקיך כי בחודש האביב הוציאך ה' אלקיך מארץ מצרים לילה:

Observe the springtime month and offer the korban Pesach to the Lord your God, for in the springtime month at night the Lord your God delivered you from Egypt.[20]

Rashi cites the Talmud[21] that this refers to Pharaoh's actions and that since we were granted freedom at night, we remember the redemption at night as well as by day. Rav Saadya Gaon prefers another resolution to the verse referring to our ancestors leaving Egypt at night, when in reality, we left by day. After all, the verse says nothing of Pharaoh, and God told us not to leave our homes all that night. What deliverance took place at night? Rav Saadya Gaon answers that לילה refers to the night of the sixteenth. By the

time the last Israelite left Egypt, it was already the next night.

An additional resolution appears in *Targum Yonasan ben Uziel* to our verse. The Targum places the word לילה at the beginning of the verse, so that לילה refers to our observance of this springtime festival, not when we left Egypt. Add to this that the root שמר in Akkadian, an ancient Semitic language, refers to holding on to a grudge to the point of telling the reason for the grudge.[22] We now have a new meaning to ליל שימורים. It is a night of telling stories. If the Haggadah had been aware of Akkadian, it could have answered the question of יכול מבעוד יום, in *Yachol MeiRosh Chodesh* (Maggid Section 8) in a more direct way.

Rabbi Elazar ben Azariah wants *every* night to be suffused with the remembrance of our redemption and he uses the extraneous word כל to add night to day. The Sages conclude that the word כל means to add the Messianic age but between the lines exhorts us to act in a way in which כל ימי חייך להביא לימות המשיח, which can homiletically be translated to teach that: Every day of our lives we are to do what we can to bring about the days of Mashiach.

MAGGID SECTION 6 – BARUCH HAMAKOM

1. What is the point of this introduction to the Four Sons?
2. Why is God referred to as "המקום – Omnipresent" here?
3. Why is ברוך הוא mentioned twice?
4. Why does the Haggadah refer to "כנגד ארבעה בנים," and not "על אודות ארבעה בנים"? (אודות means concerning, while כנגד connotes some kind of contrast.)

בָּרוּךְ הַמָּקוֹם, בָּרוּךְ הוּא. בָּרוּךְ שֶׁנָּתַן תּוֹרָה לְעַמּוֹ יִשְׂרָאֵל, בָּרוּךְ הוּא:

Blessed be the Omnipresent! Blessed be He! Blessed be the One Who gave the Torah to His people Israel! Blessed be He!

The Wise Son

Each participant at the *Seder* is meant to relate to the proceedings on their own level. What makes a child wise is curiosity. We like to uncover the underlying meaning and causes of things. Within all the recreations of events we stress God's direct role in our redemption and that the observances of the evening fulfill His commandments. As such, this introduction acts as a ברכת המצוה, a blessing upon the mitzvah of *sippur yetzias Mitzrayim*, retelling the story of the Egyptian redemption. We usually don't say a blessing on a mitzvah that has no שיעור or limitations, so this introduction is a reminder to bear in mind the fulfillment of the Torah law of *sippur yetzias Mitzrayim*. We refer to God as "המקום" when we wish to stress His everlasting Presence, since מקום denotes place. It may appear anthropomorphic to refer to God as taking up space but it means to capture the essence of a comforting and caring God.[37] This is why we refer to God as המקום when comforting the mourner, with the words המקום ינחם אתכם.

The Pure Son

The Haggadah stresses God's direct role in the events we commemorate at the *Seder*. (See below, Maggid Section 13k.) God's Hand was readily observed in the redemption. A pure son will seek out God even when He is not so readily seen. Like God's ministering angels, he may wonder, "איה מקום כבודו – Where is the place of His Glory."[36] This curiosity may draw him to distant realms of wisdom, but his purity grounds him with the assurance that "מלא כל הארץ כבודו – The earth is filled with His Glory."[37] In fact, the angels only ask, "איה מקום כבודו," because they have already declared, "מלא כל הארץ כבודו."[38] The pure son knows that whatever he finds in the pursuit of these questions cannot weaken his resolve, and that he would never turn to the cynicism of others. This assurance to the pure son is the "מקום" that is blessed in the introduction to his question. The *tam*, despite his search, remains grounded.

There is a parallel source to this introduction of the Four Sons at the end of *Maseches Middos*. This is a tractate which outlines temple measurements and

The Cynical Son

This introduction is a quasi-blessing to prepare for the expositions of Biblical verses that will soon follow. This blessing is especially germane to prepare the four sons for the answers to their questions. The Haggadah is a learning experience and our learning starts with *birchas haTorah*, a blessing of the Torah.[22] The Talmud relates that the Israelites at the end of the First Temple period sinned in not saying *birchas haTorah* before learning.[23] Rabbeinu Nissim explains that the Israelites did not consider learning worthy of its own blessing.[24] We must remember that the section of Maggid fulfills not only a mitzvah of *sippur yetzias Mitzrayim*, but also of of connecting to Hashem through *limud haTorah*. The Talmud says we can, in the absence of prophetic communion with God, draw close to Him in wisdom and contemplation.[25] To the cynic, God is impersonal and just a pronoun (ברוך הוא). In fact, there are two sons like this because they have similar tendencies, and therefore the Haggadah addresses them similarly as we shall see shortly.

The Withdrawn Son

The withdrawn son is possibly a few short steps away from cynicism, and we must therefore open up to him. "ברוך המקום" refers to holy space. The entire universe is indeed encompassed by God's glory, but a withdrawn son needs to be shown the lines and boundaries of that holiness. Mount Sinai was a holy place. The Temple Mount in Jerusalem continues to be a holy place. The difference between the two is that the active participation of our people helped establish and build the Temple. At Mount Sinai, all we did was show up. For that reason, immediately after the blast of the shofar after *Matan Torah*, the holiness departed, whereas the holiness of the Temple remains. Our story begins with God telling Moses to remove his shoes because he stood on hallowed ground. Moshe would teach us the boundaries of holiness and a crucial message for all sons who show up at the *Seder*: Holiness will much more readily descend upon us if we actually participate. One who isn't asking questions must be drawn to doing so, as we are about to see in *Arbah Banim*; Maggid Section 7.

And when we pray for those in distress we pray that המקום ירחם עליהם, the Omnipresent should have mercy on them. It is crucial that wisdom be directed by morality and mercy. Wisdom is morally neutral and this reference assures that the wise child will be well grounded in morality.

The Haggadah refers to four verses, כנגד, opposite four sons, as if to say that the one addressing them can possibly speak to all four simultaneously. The *Shelah HaKadosh* describes *Erev Pesach* in Jerusalem where thousands of Jews stream to the same place to prepare their *korban Pesach*. Among them are doubtlessly all Jews of many stripes and we hope that they will all show up to ask their questions, and we must be ready with worthy answers no matter who is asking.

activities, and it tells of the process of validating the Kohanim as true descendants of Aharon, with no disqualification. The very last line reads:

ויום טוב היו עושים שלא נמצא פסול בזרעו של אהרן הכהן וכך היו אומרים: **ברוך המקום ברוך הוא** שלא נמצא פסול בזרעו של אהרן **וברוך הוא** שבחר באהרן ובניו לעמוד לשרת לפני ה׳ בבית קדשי הקדשים.

They would make a day of celebration that no disqualification was found in the descendants of Aharon the Kohen, and thus they would proclaim: Blessed is the Omnipresent, Blessed is He, for no disqualification was found in the descendants of Aharon. And Blessed is He Who chose Aharon and his sons to stand and minister before God in the chamber of the Holy of Holies.

There is reason to bless God for having children at the table. Their pedigree dictates that their potential is limitless and for this we bless Hashem. המקום connotes the ever-presence of God. We all know our own presence is fleeting and will draw to an end someday, but we gain a lasting presence through our children. For that reason, we refer to God this way when introducing the section of the Four Sons.

MAGGID SECTION 7 – K'NEGED ARBAH BANIM

1. Why is the reference to Four Sons at this point in the Haggadah?
2. What are the Torah sources of the Four Sons and what is each child being taught in those sources?
3. Why aren't the Four Sons in the order the Torah has them; first *rasha*, then *tam*, *she'eino yodei'a lishol*, and finally *chacham*?
4. Why are the Four Sons broken down in an incongruous manner; three by intellect (*chacham, tam, she'eino yodei'a lishol*), and one by morality (*rasha*)?

כְּנֶגֶד אַרְבָּעָה בָנִים דִּבְּרָה תוֹרָה: אֶחָד חָכָם, וְאֶחָד רָשָׁע, וְאֶחָד תָּם, וְאֶחָד שֶׁאֵינוֹ יוֹדֵעַ לִשְׁאוֹל:

The Torah speaks of four different kinds of sons: One who is wise, one who is cynical, one who is pure, and one who is withdrawn.

1. In essence, everything in the Haggadah until this point is an introduction to the section of Maggid, which is the Midrashic exposition of *Devarim* 26:5–8, beginning with *Arami Oved Avi*. We identify the food for which the seven-day holiday is named in *Ha Lachma Anya* (Maggid Section 1). Then we recite the Four Questions (Maggid Section 2) and our answer (Maggid Section 3). *Maaseh B'Rabbi Eliezer* and *Amar Rabbi Elazar ben Azaryah* (Maggid Sections 4 and 5) point to the fact that the experience of the evening is not necessarily an intellectual one. Our obligation is to *tell* a story and that is why we call this section of the Haggadah "Maggid." Even those who are as wise as the five Sages discussed in *Maaseh B'Rabbi Eliezer* (Maggid Section 4) must tell the story, and Rabbi Elazar ben Azariah teaches the constant nature of the remembrance of Egypt by day and by night. Such is the review of Maggid up to this point and we are now up to the part of the Haggadah which explains the nature of this book.

2. The list of the Four Sons can be found in the Haggadah, the Midrashic exposition to *Sefer Shemos* known as the *Mechilta*, as well as the *Talmud Yerushalmi*, and are lined up as follows:

ירושלמי פסחים פרק י הלכה ד	מכילתא בא מסכתא דפסחא פרשה יח	פסוקים בתורה	הגדה
תני ר' חייה כנגד ארבעה בנים דיברה תורה בן חכם בן רשע בן טיפש בן שאינו יודע לשאול.	ארבעה בנים הם אחד חכם ואחד רשע ואחד תם ואחד שאינו יודע לשאול.	כִּי יִשְׁאָלְךָ בִנְךָ מָחָר לֵאמֹר מָה הָעֵדֹת וְהַחֻקִּים וְהַמִּשְׁפָּטִים אֲשֶׁר צִוָּה ה' אֱלֹהֵינוּ אֶתְכֶם: וְאָמַרְתָּ לְבִנְךָ עֲבָדִים הָיִינוּ לְפַרְעֹה בְּמִצְרָיִם וַיּוֹצִיאֵנוּ ה' מִמִּצְרַיִם בְּיָד חֲזָקָה:	חָכָם מָה הוּא אוֹמֵר? מָה הָעֵדֹת וְהַחֻקִּים וְהַמִּשְׁפָּטִים אֲשֶׁר צִוָּה ה' אֱלֹהֵינוּ אֶתְכֶם? וְאַף אַתָּה אֱמָר לוֹ כְּהִלְכוֹת הַפֶּסַח: אֵין מַפְטִירִין אַחַר הַפֶּסַח אֲפִיקוֹמָן.
בן חכם מהו אומר [דברים ו כ] מה העדות והחקים והמשפטים אשר צוה ה' אלהינו אותם אף אתה אמור לו [שמות יג יד] בחוזק יד הוציאנו ה' ממצרים מבית עבדים.	חכם מה הוא אומר והעדות והחוקים והמשפטים אשר צוה ה' אלקינו אתכם אף אתה פתח לו כהלכות הפסח אין מפטירין אחר הפסח אפיקומן.	וַיִּתֵּן ה' אוֹתֹת וּמֹפְתִים גְּדֹלִים וְרָעִים בְּמִצְרַיִם בְּפַרְעֹה וּבְכָל בֵּיתוֹ לְעֵינֵינוּ: וְאוֹתָנוּ הוֹצִיא מִשָּׁם לְמַעַן הָבִיא אֹתָנוּ לָתֶת לָנוּ אֶת הָאָרֶץ אֲשֶׁר נִשְׁבַּע לַאֲבֹתֵינוּ: וַיְצַוֵּנוּ ה' לַעֲשׂוֹת אֶת כָּל הַחֻקִּים הָאֵלֶּה לְיִרְאָה אֶת ה' אֱלֹהֵינוּ לְטוֹב לָנוּ כָּל הַיָּמִים לְחַיֹּתֵנוּ כְּהַיּוֹם הַזֶּה: וּצְדָקָה תִּהְיֶה לָּנוּ כִּי נִשְׁמֹר לַעֲשׂוֹת אֶת כָּל הַמִּצְוָה הַזֹּאת לִפְנֵי ה' אֱלֹהֵינוּ כַּאֲשֶׁר צִוָּנוּ:	רָשָׁע מָה הוּא אוֹמֵר? מָה הָעֲבֹדָה הַזֹּאת לָכֶם? לָכֶם - וְלֹא לוֹ. וּלְפִי שֶׁהוֹצִיא אֶת עַצְמוֹ מִן הַכְּלָל כָּפַר בְּעִקָּר. וְאַף אַתָּה הַקְהֵה אֶת שִׁנָּיו וֶאֱמָר לוֹ: בַּעֲבוּר זֶה עָשָׂה ה' לִי בְּצֵאתִי מִמִּצְרָיִם. לִי - וְלֹא לוֹ. אִילּוּ הָיָה שָׁם, לֹא הָיָה נִגְאָל.
בן רשע מהו אומר [שם יב כו] מה העבודה הזאת לכם מה הטורח הזה שאתם מטריחין עלינו בכל שנה ושנה מכיון שהוציא את עצמו מן הכלל אף אתה אמור לו [שם יג ח] בעבור זה עשה ה' לי ולא לך אלו היית שם לא היית נגאל.	רשע מה הוא אומר מה העבודה הזאת לכם ולא לו ולפי שהוציא את עצמו מן הכלל וכפר בעיקר אף אתה הקהה את שיניו ואמור לו בעבור זה עשה ה' לי [שמות יג ח] לי ולא לך אלו היית שם לא היית נגאל.	וְהָיָה כִּי יֹאמְרוּ אֲלֵיכֶם בְּנֵיכֶם מָה הָעֲבֹדָה הַזֹּאת לָכֶם: וַאֲמַרְתֶּם זֶבַח פֶּסַח הוּא לַה' אֲשֶׁר פָּסַח עַל בָּתֵּי בְנֵי יִשְׂרָאֵל בְּמִצְרַיִם בְּנָגְפּוֹ אֶת מִצְרַיִם וְאֶת בָּתֵּינוּ הִצִּיל וַיִּקֹּד הָעָם וַיִּשְׁתַּחֲווּ: וַיֵּלְכוּ וַיַּעֲשׂוּ בְּנֵי יִשְׂרָאֵל כַּאֲשֶׁר צִוָּה ה' אֶת מֹשֶׁה וְאַהֲרֹן כֵּן עָשׂוּ:	תָּם מָה הוּא אוֹמֵר? מָה זֹּאת? וְאָמַרְתָּ אֵלָיו: בְּחֹזֶק יָד הוֹצִיאָנוּ יְיָ מִמִּצְרַיִם, מִבֵּית עֲבָדִים.
טיפש מה אומר [שמות יג יד] מה זאת אף את למדו הלכות הפסח שאין מפטירין אחר הפסח אפיקומן שלא יהא עומד מחבורה זו ונכנס לחבורה אחרת.	תם מה הוא אומר מה זאת ואמרת אליו בחזק יד הוציאנו ה' ממצרים מבית עבדים.	וְהָיָה כִּי יִשְׁאָלְךָ בִנְךָ מָחָר לֵאמֹר מָה זֹּאת וְאָמַרְתָּ אֵלָיו בְּחֹזֶק יָד הוֹצִיאָנוּ ה' מִמִּצְרַיִם מִבֵּית עֲבָדִים:	וְשֶׁאֵינוֹ יוֹדֵעַ לִשְׁאוֹל - אַתְּ פְּתַח לוֹ, שֶׁנֶּאֱמַר: וְהִגַּדְתָּ לְבִנְךָ בַּיּוֹם הַהוּא לֵאמֹר, בַּעֲבוּר זֶה עָשָׂה ה' לִי בְּצֵאתִי מִמִּצְרָיִם.
בן שאינו יודע לשאול את תחילה א"ר יוסה מתניתא אמרה בן אם אין דעת בבן אביו מלמדו:	ושאינו יודע לשאול את פתח לו הגד לבנך ביום ההוא שנא' והגדת לבנך ביום ההוא וגו'. ד"א מה העדות והחוקים ר' אליעזר אומר מנין אתה אומר שאם היתה חבורה של חכמים או תלמידים שצריכים לעסוק בהלכות פסח עד חצות לכך נאמר מה העדות וגו'.	שִׁבְעַת יָמִים תֹּאכַל מַצֹּת וּבַיּוֹם הַשְּׁבִיעִי חַג לַה': מַצֹּת יֵאָכֵל אֵת שִׁבְעַת הַיָּמִים וְלֹא יֵרָאֶה לְךָ חָמֵץ וְלֹא יֵרָאֶה לְךָ שְׂאֹר בְּכָל גְּבֻלֶךָ: וְהִגַּדְתָּ לְבִנְךָ בַּיּוֹם הַהוּא לֵאמֹר בַּעֲבוּר זֶה עָשָׂה ה' לִי בְּצֵאתִי מִמִּצְרָיִם:	

3. The order of the Torah verses places the *rasha's* question first, then that of the *she'eino yodei'a lishol*, followed by the *tam* and the *chacham*. The *chacham* is simply placed first in the Haggadah

because we don't want to begin with a *rasha*. Also, the *chacham* is juxtaposed to *Avadim Hayinu*, *Maaseh B'Rabbi Eliezer*, and *Amar Rabbi Elazar ben Azaryah* (Maggid Sections 3, 4, and 5) which speak of great Sages who made extraordinary efforts to experience the *Seder*, and the *chacham* continues this trend. The last one must be the *she'eino yodei'a lishol* since his answer points to mitzvos that commemorate the redemption, and this is directly related to *Yachol MeiRosh Chodesh* (Maggid Section 8), which immediately follows the Four Sons. The remaining two sons are indeed in the order of the Torah. The order may also be based on the apparent sophistication of the question. The highest level is the *chacham*'s

reference to *eidos, chukim u'mishpatim*, then the *rasha*'s reference to *avodah*, then the simple *mah zos*, followed by no question at all.

4. The question of the breakdown of the Four Sons is answered by the *Vilna Gaon* and is assumed above in the explanation of the *tam*. If we translate תם as simple-minded, then the question remains; the wise, simple, and withdrawn sons are classified by intellect, while the *rasha* alone is classified by morality. However, according to the *Vilna Gaon*, the *tam* is opposite the *rasha*. The *tam*'s sincere purity contrasts the *rasha*'s cynicism, while the *chacham*'s curiosity contrasts the *she'eino yodei'a lishol*'s withdrawn behavior.

The Wise Son

The *chacham*'s question is on the observance of Torah commandments in general. The answer to this general question connects to *yetzias Mitzrayim* in a way that is similar to the conversation Moshe had with God at the Burning Bush. Immediately upon informing him of his mission, God told Moshe that after the redemption, the Israelites would serve Him at Mount Horeb[38] (later to be called Mount Sinai). The freedom from Egyptian bondage allowed us to transform our energies from the service of Pharaoh to the service of God. The *chacham* understands this and wants clarification

The Cynical Son

The *rasha*'s question is the only one of the four which is directly related to the *korban Pesach*. As such the Torah's answer to his question is precisely what appears later in the Haggadah (in *Rabban Gamliel Hayah Omer*, Maggid Section 16a) as the explanation for the *korban Pesach*. Rabban Gamliel asserts that we do not fulfill the mitzvah of *sippur yetzias Mitzrayim* unless we render this explanation for the *korban Pesach*. When answering the *rasha*'s question we should not beat around the bush. We should tell it as straight as possible.

The Pure Son

The *tam*'s question is simple and pure: "מה זאת – What is this?" This covers anything and everything. While it can be understood as denoting the question of an immature or underdeveloped mind, this is not necessarily the case. To be sure, a number of sources[39] do indeed refer to this child as a טיפש, which can certainly be translated as a simpleton or slow thinker. However, I prefer to translate תם as pure. Surely our patriarch Yaakov, and Rashi's grandson, Rav Yaakov ben Meir, also known as Rabbeinu Tam, would agree with this translation. The Torah[40] refers to Yaakov as איש תם and *Onkelos* translates this as

The Withdrawn Son

The *she'eino yodei'a lishol* is withdrawn. He doesn't ask questions at all. He must be exposed to a significant change in what is happening around him to be prodded to think about what he sees. For this reason, our statement to him is juxtaposed to the matzah, which lends itself to the name of the holiday. The matzah is called לחם עוני for several reasons (see *Ha Lachma Anya*, Maggid Section 1), and one of those reasons is that matzah is a type of bread that leads to many a response, לחם שעונים עליו דברים הרבה. Matzah is a bread over which we answer many questions. The eating of the matzah is called מוציא מצה because of the different types of commandments he sees being performed. Some (עדות) are testimonies such as Shabbos, or *Shemittah*, which testify to God's creation and ownership of the land. Some (חקים) are statutes such as *kashrus*, which defy our logic and are decreed from above without a ready explanation, and some (משפטים) are readily understood, such as interpersonal laws. These classifications can also fit the observances at the *Seder* as we will shortly see. The Torah's answer to the *chacham* (עבדים היינו וכו') is the answer the Haggadah gives earlier to the Four Questions. This is to say that anyone who asks questions with a desire to learn about the mitzvos of the evening with genuine curiosity can be classified as wise.

We have refrained from referring to this son as wicked. There is no doubt the word bespeaks immorality but let us remember that he did show up at the *Seder*. A truly wicked person would not show up at all. I prefer to refer to him as cynical. He methodically doubts what is not readily clear to him and he will add mockery to doubt.

Our Sages[26] expound the words of Yeshayahu to shed light on the nature of this child. The prophet says, "אוי לרשע רע – Woe to the wicked for he shall fare ill."[27] The Talmud maintains that since the prophet reveals what is obvious, that the wicked come to fare ill, that there must also be a situation where a *rasha* will fare well. The Talmud differentiates between one who scrupulously follows the ritual laws but is not careful with interpersonal laws. This person is רע, evil. The one who defiantly violates the ritual laws but is good to others is called a good *rasha*. So too, our *rasha* may put emphasis on interpersonal relationships, so I refrain from referring to him as wicked, and prefer to call him cynical. *Rashi*, when referring to the reaction to this son's question in *Shemos* 12:27, notes that upon hearing the answer, the Israelites bowed and worshipped – ויקד העם וישתחוו – and he explains that their reaction came as a result of על

בשורת הבנים שיהיו להם. The people were so thrilled to learn that they would have sons asking these questions that they were moved to spontaneous worship. Although *Rashi* later[28] applies this verse to the בן רשע, the Israelites seem to have been unwavering in their gratitude over having such a child. As long as the child attends the *Seder*, we can impress upon him to act in a way which will result in ויקד העם וישתחוו. The cynical child often asks his questions to make a contrary point. This contrarian tendency sometimes borders on mischief. Perhaps "*rasha*" here is used similarly as in *Shmuel I* 14:47–48:

ושאול לכד המלוכה על ישראל וילחם סביב בכל אויביו במואב ובבני עמון ובאדום ובמלכי צובה ובפלשתים ובכל אשר יפנה **ירשיע**. ויעש חיל ויך את עמלק ויצל את ישראל מיד שסהו:

*After Shaul had secured his kingship over Israel, he waged war on every side against all his enemies: against the Moabites, Amonites, Edomites, the kings of Tzovah, the Philistines, and wherever he turned **he caused mischief**. He was triumphant, defeating the Amalekites and saving Israel from all who plundered it.*

The word ירשיע does not point to wickedness per se, but to mischief, even in a positive sense. This is how we will address the Haggadah's *rasha*.

גבר שלים, a completely perfected person. The purity of the תם is in his simplicity. Visitors to the *Chafetz Chaim* were amazed at the utter simplicity of his pure lifestyle. I had the privilege of studying with Rav Yosef Soloveitchik as well as Nechama Leibowitz in their apartments, and the profound simplicity of their lifestyle was a testament to the purity of their being and was a crown jewel upon their immense accomplishments and achievements.

The *tam*'s question is not directly related to *yetzias Mitzrayim*. It is tangentially related, as it is being asked in a section of mitzvos that are to commemorate the redemption, notably the mitzvos of *kedushas bechor*, the sanctity of the firstborn. There are three types of *kedushas bechor*:

1. Redemption of firstborn male babies from a Kohen
2. Sanctification of firstborn male sheep, goats, and calves
3. Redemption of firstborn male donkeys

The *tam*'s curiosity is piqued by this mitzvah. The answer to the question of *kedushas bechor* serves as an answer to explain the proceedings of the evening and also explains why our redemption is immediately followed by these mitzvos. Our answer takes us all back to the beginning of the story when Moshe is told to introduce his very words to Pharaoh with the phrase "בני בכורי ישראל – My son, My firstborn, is Israel," and in the very next verse, God skips to the end of the story with a threat to kill Pharaoh's firstborn. Why begin the story with these references to the firstborn? Our answer begins with the fact that many mitzvos require us to give the first of our resources and accomplishments to God or to his priestly representative, the *Kohen*. Examples include the first of our crops, the first of our shearing, and the first of our dough, in addition to *kedushas bechor*, our first mitzvah after leaving Egypt.

Until now, the best of our abilities, talents, and energies were spent building grand edifices to Pharaoh and working his fields. We had been turned to beasts of burden so that others could live off of our sweat and toil. With *yetzias Mitzrayim* we could give our best – notably the "בכור" of our talents – to much greater pursuits, such as learning Torah, pursuing justice, and building the *Mishkan* (the contents of the Torah portions immediately following our redemption). Hevel understood this message when he brought "מבכורות צאנו – from the first (choicest) of his flocks" to God, while Kayin only brought "מפרי האדמה – from his fruits."[41]

Netziv[42] cites another reason why *kedushas bechor* is mentioned in the immediate aftermath of *yetzias Mitzrayim*. A newly freed people would need religious guidance to assure that slavery to Egypt doesn't turn to slavery to desire. The antidote to this would be for the people to receive instruction from those appointed to teach. These teachers were originally to have been the firstborns. Their mission is therefore determined immediately upon our departure from Egypt.

two blessings are recited over it, one general blessing of המוציא as well as a *birchas hamitzvah* said before doing the mitzvah. These two words can also be understood within the context of how we need to relate to the *she'eino yodei'a lishol*. The matzah is meant to be "מוציא," to draw participation from a withdrawn child. It is the most glaring change at the table and constitutes the first of the Four Questions above in the *Mah Nishtanah* (Maggid Section 2).

A TIMELESS PEDAGOGICAL guide that underscores the Haggadah's purpose is the Biblical verse, "חנוך לנער על פי דרכו גם כי יזקין לא יסור ממנה – Train a child according to his own path and he will not swerve from it even in old age."[2]

The root of the word חנוך means to "put to use."[3] This is the purpose of education, to become a useful adult, contributing to the welfare of society. The Haggadah, and all things taught, must be directed to the level of the student. For this reason, the Haggadah classifies the children at the *Seder* based on four Torah references which explain our practices. All four answers are connected to *yetzias Mitzrayim*, but not all the questions are directly related.

MAGGID SECTION 7A – CHACHAM

1. Why does the Haggadah respond, "ואף אתה אמר לו"?
2. What is meant by "כהלכות הפסח, like the laws of Pesach"? What is being compared?
3. What kind of answer is "אין מפטירין אחר הפסח אפיקומן – after the Pesach offering is brought, no dessert is eaten"?
4. We will see that the *rasha* is criticized for excluding himself by saying "לכם." Why isn't the *chacham* similarly criticized for saying "אתכם"?

MAGGID SECTION 7B – RASHA

1. The Haggadah says the *rasha* is a "כופר בעיקר," someone who denies the fundamentals of his religion. How?
2. What does the Haggadah mean by "הקהה את שיניו – blunt (or clench) his teeth"?
3. How does the *rasha*'s answer relate to his question?
4. Why are we so sure that if he were in Egypt at the time of the redemption the *rasha* would not have been redeemed?

MAGGID SECTION 7C – TAM

1. What does the word "תם" mean?
2. Why are we so sure his question is asked sincerely?
3. Why do we connect the *tam* to the redemption of firstborn males?
4. What is the nature of the answer to the *tam*?

MAGGID SECTION 7D – V'SHE'EINO YODEI'A LISHOL

1. Why is the one who addresses the *she'eino yodei'a lishol* referred to as את, in feminine?
2. What is the meaning of "פתח לו"?
3. Why are we so sure that this child doesn't ask because he's withdrawn or unable to ask? Perhaps he is a non-believer like the *rasha*, and simply isn't up for confrontation?
4. What is the nature of the answer to this child?

חָכָם מַה הוּא אוֹמֵר: מָה הָעֵדֹת וְהַחֻקִּים וְהַמִּשְׁפָּטִים אֲשֶׁר צִוָּה יְהֹוָה אֱלֹהֵינוּ אֶתְכֶם. וְאַף אַתָּה אֱמָר לוֹ כְּהִלְכוֹת הַפֶּסַח, אֵין מַפְטִירִין אַחַר הַפֶּסַח אֲפִיקוֹמָן:

What does the wise son say? "What are the testimonies and the statutes and the laws that Hashem, our God, has commanded you?" (*Devarim* 6:20). You, in turn, should tell him all about the laws of the Pesach offering

[for instance]: "One may not eat any dessert after the meat of the Pesach offering."

רָשָׁע מַה הוּא אוֹמֵר: מָה הָעֲבֹדָה הַזֹּאת לָכֶם. לָכֶם וְלֹא לוֹ. וּלְפִי שֶׁהוֹצִיא אֶת עַצְמוֹ מִן הַכְּלָל כָּפַר בְּעִקָּר, וְאַף אַתָּה הַקְהֵה אֶת שִׁנָּיו וֶאֱמָר לוֹ, בַּעֲבוּר זֶה עָשָׂה יְהוה לִי בְּצֵאתִי מִמִּצְרָיִם: לִי וְלֹא לוֹ. אִלּוּ הָיָה שָׁם לֹא הָיָה נִגְאָל:

What does the cynical son say? "What is this service to you?" (*Shemos* 12:26) – implying "to you," but not "to him"! Because he excludes himself from the rest of the community, he has denied a fundamental principle. You, in turn, should blunt his teeth and tell him: "Because of this Hashem did for me when I left Egypt" (ibid. 13:8) – implying "for

me," but not "for him"! If he had been there then, he would not have been redeemed.

תָּם מַה הוּא אוֹמֵר: מַה זֹּאת. וְאָמַרְתָּ אֵלָיו בְּחֹזֶק יָד הוֹצִיאָנוּ יְהֹוָה מִמִּצְרַיִם מִבֵּית עֲבָדִים:

What does the pure son say? "What is this?" (ibid. 13:14). "And you shall say to him: With a strong hand Hashem took us out of Egypt, from the house of bondage" (ibid.).

וְשֶׁאֵינוֹ יוֹדֵעַ לִשְׁאוֹל אַתְּ פְּתַח לוֹ, שֶׁנֶּאֱמַר, וְהִגַּדְתָּ לְבִנְךָ בַּיּוֹם הַהוּא לֵאמֹר בַּעֲבוּר זֶה עָשָׂה יְהֹוָה לִי בְּצֵאתִי מִמִּצְרָיִם:

As for the one who is withdrawn – you must open for him, as it says, "You shall tell your child on that day: Because of this Hashem did for me when I left Egypt" (*Shemos* 13:8).

The Wise Son

7a. The Haggadah expects us to answer the questions first and foremost with the Torah's answers that immediately follow the questions. In addition to teaching the *chacham* what is written in the Torah, we are to teach him additional things, such as the laws of Pesach. This is what "אף אתה אמר לו – You should even tell him" refers to; not only do we tell the Torah's answers, but even this additional information, as well. This would explain the word "אף – even," that appears in the answer to the *rasha* as well, because the Haggadah's answer to the *rasha* is also not the same as the Torah's. The word אף does not appear in the answers to the *tam* or the *she'eino yodei'a lishol*, because they both receive the very answers that appear for them in the Torah. In the *Talmud Yerushalmi's* version of the Four Sons, אף appears at the *tam's* (טיפש) question as well, and is consistent with our approach here, for in the *Talmud Yerushalmi* he also doesn't receive the Torah's answer.

The Cynical Son

7b. The *rasha* contrasts the other sons in a number of ways.

1. The *tam* and the *chacham* both ask a question; "כי ישאלך בנך – When your son asks." The *rasha* doesn't ask, because he is really not interested in an answer. His words are introduced by "והיה כי יאמרו אליכם בניכם – when your sons *say*."

2. The *chacham* considers what he sees to be commanded from God. The absence of such connection for the *rasha* implies that he does not consider the mitzvos part of a Divine mission.[29]

3. The other three sons are all connected to a particular day.

   - חכם – כי ישאלך בנך מחר
   - תם – והיה כי ישאלך בנך מחר
   - שאינו יודע לשאול – והגדת לבנך **ביום ההוא**

The Pure Son

7c. The first and third questions are answered in the general introduction to the Four Sons. The fact that the *tam's* question connects to *kedushas bechor* adds significance to the inclusion of the word מחר to his question. By not asking his question in the day of actual *pidyon* of the firstborn, the *tam* shows his sincerity. He accepts the obligation to expend money to commemorate the redemption and now, *after* the performance of the mitzvah, he asks of its significance.[43]

The *tam's* answer in the Haggadah is the same as the Torah's answer. A simple question elicits a simple answer. Of all the Haggadah's answers it is the one which is meant to elicit the greatest sense of gratitude and, in reality, applies to all four sons. In fact, the *Yerushalmi* shows the versatility of this answer by extending it to the *chacham*! His sophisticated question elicits an answer that tries to assure that he remains emotionally as well as intellectually connected to the proceedings of the evening.

The Withdrawn Son

7d. The withdrawn child needs to be moved and inspired to ask questions. In fact, many of the things we do at the Seder are meant to elicit questions of unusual practices. The feminine את hints at the mother's involvement in working with such a child. Obviously, a mother connects with a child at a younger age.[23] "את" also hints at the way this child should be taught. Although our Sages generally preferred things to be taught as simply and as succinctly as possible,[24] when it comes to teaching a withdrawn child, it is better to teach in a verbose and elaborate manner, which is considered by our Sages to be the province of women.[25]

Tosafos[26] points to a contrast between two phrases that jump from masculine to feminine, that has relevance to this issue. There are two words for song used in Tanach: שיר and שירה. The word שיר is used more commonly (seventy-seven times) but שירה is used often enough (thirteen times)

In some versions of the Haggadah, the word is "בהלכות הפסח – **in** the laws of Pesach," which seems to be the *Mechilta*'s version as well. According to this, nothing is being compared.[39] The letter ב is just as extraneous as the letter כ and would require its own explanation. Some commentaries have the version, "כל הלכות הפסח – all the laws of Pesach,"[40] and finally the version that seems to encapsulate the overall message of all these versions is the one cited by the *Ritva*, "אף אתה אמר לו כל הלכות הפסח עד אין מפטירין אחר הפסח אפיקומן – Even tell him all the laws of Pesach until, 'After the Pesach offering is brought, no dessert is eaten,'" which leads to our question.

The answer to the *chacham* is the text of the Mishnah at the end of *Maseches Pesachim* and is the last instruction of the *Seder*. Basically, the *chacham* is being taught all the laws of Pesach to quench his thirst for explanations. *Midrash Sechel Tov*[41] suggests a novel explanation of this answer that maintains the text of the Haggadah as אף אתה אמר לו כהלכות הפסח, that is, that the last law of the *Seder* is that we don't eat anything after the *korban Pesach*.[42] This must be the last taste in our mouths. This is so that the essential experience of our transformation from slavery to freedom can be literally tasted. In fact, this is what all the laws of Pesach point to, namely replicating our experience of redemption to fulfill the obligation to relive the redemption, as our Sages say, "חייב אדם לראות את עצמו כאילו הוא יצא ממצרים – One is obligated to look upon himself as if he personally left Egypt."[43] We must assure that the intellectual child receives more than just an intellectual experience from the *Seder*. The Haggadah bids parents to inform the *chacham* that everything we teach him is כהלכות הפסח, that he can connect with God the way his ancestors did on the very night of the *Seder* over three thousand years before.

The use of אתכם is problematic. The Haggadah's reaction to the *rasha*'s לכם is harsh, yet the *chacham* gets a pass for using the similar word, אתכם.[44] Some of the commentaries[45] excuse the *chacham*'s use of the word אתכם because he has not yet attained the age of mitzvah obligation. As such, since he uses the words "אשר צוה ה' – that God commanded," he is not faulted for saying אתכם. *He* has not yet been commanded. The *rasha*, on the other hand, did not refer to אשר צוה and is therefore judged differently. Also, the *chacham* includes himself in the reference to ה' אלוקינו, *our* God.

A novel answer to the problem of אתכם is suggested by Rav David Tzvi Hoffman in his commentary to *Devarim* 6:20. He explains the verse through what is called סירום המקרא, whereby we reconfigure the order of the words in the verse (the verse begins in singular and concludes in plural, so this solution will enhance the incongruity of the verse). Rav Hoffman suggests that אתכם is not part of the child's question at all. It is a continuation of Moshe's statement to his parents. It begins in singular as if to say that the question may be put to the father, but the answer ought to come from both parents. According to this, the verse ought to read:

כי ישאלך בנך מחר לאמר (אתכם):

or

כי ישאלך בנך (אתכם) מחר לאמר מה העדות והחקים והמשפטים אשר צוה ה' אלוקינו:

When your son asks you tomorrow, "What are the testimonies, statutes, and judgments that the Lord our God commanded?"

In this way the last question is explained away altogether.

The *rasha*, in contrast, is not connected to this day or this observance. His mockery and cynicism are pervasive and reach beyond the *Seder*.

4. The other three sons are all listed in singular while the *rasha* is in plural. This may be a message to parents to treat each child as an individual even from the earliest age. A cynical child who mocks tradition may have already exhibited such behavior in early youth. Parents and educators must be attuned to the special attention such a child needs. A story is told of the *Chazon Ish* who was asked by the principal of a school of two hundred and fifty boys about two troublemakers. The principal asked if it would be acceptable to expel the boys as they may adversely influence other students. The *Chazon Ish* responded, "I don't understand. You have two hundred and fifty students and you want to expel the two students who need you the most?"[30] The plural nature of the *rasha*'s verse is an exhortation to parents and educators alike. Not every student fits in the box. The ones that don't need special individual attention or we risk raising a child who asks cynical questions.[31]

5. The *chacham* categorizes what he sees in different ways, but to the *rasha*, observance is simply, "עבודה – laborious work." And, while the Torah itself refers to the Pesach service as עבודה,[32] the contrast still stands, especially in light of all the other contrasts. The *Talmud Yerushalmi* elaborates on the *rasha*'s words in an apparent clarification of his question: "מה הטורח הזה אתם מטריחים עלינו – What is all this burden with which you have burdened us?" The *rasha*'s question is on the עבודה itself. He wonders why we have to bother eating the *korban Pesach* roasted just because that's how they ate it in Egypt. The *rasha* doesn't recognize the

importance of maintaining tradition. We are all trying to connect to our ancestors by actually reliving their actions on this very night, and the *rasha* thinks it's all a boring burden and a waste of time.[33]

All these differences confer upon him the characteristics of a בן נכר.[34] *Onkelos* translates this as an estranged Jew who is not allowed to eat the *korban Pesach*. The reason we don't translate בן נכר as a gentile is because such a designation is already included either in *Shemos* 12:45 or 48, with the words תושב, שכיר, and ערל. The בן נכר is told not to eat the *korban Pesach*. If this referred to a gentile, the verse, which is commanded to Israelites, should have read "כל בן נכר לא יאכל בו – A gentile shall not be fed the *korban Pesach*." Rather, the verse refers to an estranged Jew who may still want to eat the *korban Pesach* even though he was not registered.[35] For this reason, the Haggadah takes a harsh stance on him. He mocks the *avodah* but he wants the meat. Clenching his teeth assures that he won't get any meat of the *korban Pesach*.

We still must define the heresy in his behavior. Our Sages relate that only the violations of idolatry and Shabbos are tantamount to a violation of the entire Torah.[36] The Haggadah seems to add a denial of the proceedings of the Pesach *Seder* to this shortlist of heresies. This is because the mitzvah of *zechiras yetzias Mitzrayim* is the essence of our faith. It is why the opening line of the Decalogue introduces God as the One who took us out of Egypt.[37] The element of the *rasha*'s heresy is that הוציא את עצמו מן הכלל, which literally means he has excluded himself from the community. Our Sages[38] relate how the Roman emperor Titus stabbed the *paroches* of the *Kodesh HaKodashim* and saw blood spurt from it. The Gemara euphemistically describes how he thought he had slain God, so to speak, using the words, וכסבור הרג את עצמו, which *Rashi* explains is a euphemism to refer to God. Based on the omission of God's Name in the *rasha*'s question, we can perhaps euphemistically explain the *rasha*'s heresy of ולפי שהוציא את עצמו מן הכלל; since he left God out of the big picture, he has denied the foundation of our belief.[39]

Regarding our response, the Haggadah's advice of הקהה את שיניו is curious. Perhaps we can connect this answer to an aphorism that appears in *Yirmiyahu* 31:29 and *Yechezkel* 18:2.[40] Cynical contemporaries of these prophets spoke a parable to express their frustration over what they felt was unjust suffering in the years leading up to the fall of Jerusalem.

מה לכם אתם מושלים את המשל הזה על אדמת ישראל לאמר אבות יאכלו בוסר ושני הבנים תקהינה.

What do you mean by quoting this proverb upon the Land of Israel, saying: "Parents eat sour grapes and the teeth of the children rot?"

Over the past two generations many of us have the experience of hearing Holocaust survivors describe their own personal experiences of *yetzias Mitzrayim* from ghettos, death camps, and war zones. The mitzvah of חייב אדם לראות את עצמו כאילו הוא יצא ממצרים comes easy to them. Imagine, if in the midst of these painful stories, an angry voice of cynicism rose at the *Seder* to mock their story of survival, that so many others suffered and did not survive. The story of our redemption begins with similar suffering. Perhaps there is a time to reflect philosophically upon our suffering, but the *Seder* is not the time to do so, and certainly not under the framework of cynicism. For this reason we clench his teeth or we show how his teeth will rot for what he himself ate.[41]

Also, the numerical value of שיניו (366), when subtracted from the numerical value of רשע (570) yields 204, which is the numerical value of צדיק, for every child can be turned around.

The Haggadah's answer to the *rasha* is the Torah's answer to the *she'eino yodei'a lishol*. The *she'eino yodei'a lishol* has not yet demonstrated any

inquisitiveness of the night's proceedings. He can easily be drawn toward the *rasha's* cynicism. For this reason, the Haggadah responds similarly to both of them, only we stress different words for each one. For the *rasha*, the operative word is "לי," to be inclusive. (The operative word for the *she'eino yodei'a lishol* is "זה," as we shall shortly see) The conclusion of this paragraph says that if he maintains his stance of all the contrasts he has with the other sons, such positions would have made it so that he would have remained in Egypt. The Haggadah does not back off of this consideration. It should be noted that in addition to the above contrasts between the *rasha* and the other sons, there is an additional contrast concerning the parental directive. The parents speak directly to the other three sons:

- חכם – ואמרת אליו – You shall say **to him**
- תם – ואמרת אליו –You shall say **to him**
- שאינו יודע לשאול – והגדת לבנך – You shall relate **to your son**

This stands in contrast to the *rasha*. The *Rasha's* answer in the Torah is the Haggadah's answer in Maggid section 16a to explain why the *korban Pesach* was eaten. His response simply begins, ואמרתם. This is the firm stance of ואמרתם alone. Then it is crucial that we begin to speak "to him." We have to start treating him with the care and concern we render the others. Our hope is that once the child feels loved and included, he will return to the path of his family.

The Tanach refers to the children of youth as "כחצים ביד גבור – arrows in the hand of a mighty man."[42] Parents and teachers may take careful aim to assure that the child reaches its target in life. The target is to go from being a קטן, a child, to being a גדול, an adult; from being a taker to being a giver; from being a learner to being a teacher. No matter how precise the aim, once we let go of the arrow (and let go we must – the arrow will *never* reach its target if it remains in our hands), there are many barriers and fickle winds that may prevent the arrow from reaching its target. It is for this very reason that our Sages declared that how our children turn out, depends in addition to other things, on good *mazal*.[43] However, one thing is clear. The closer we hold the arrow to our hearts, the more likely it is that the arrow will reach its desired target. If a child goes "off the *derech*," it is certainly within the realm of the possible to show a firm stance on standards and expectations, yet simultaneously to express unconditional love. The child must never get the picture that we are upset about his behavior because of what others will think or because of what it means to siblings' marriage prospects. Let the child know that our concern is for no one but him. A creative, dynamic, and meaningful *Seder* replete with song and story-telling is a great way to start.

Upon closer analysis we may find that מה זאת is a question that goes beyond its simple translation. The question is asked ten other times in Tanach, and is always followed by the root of the same word: עשה. Here is a full list:

1. "ויאמר ה' אלוקים לאשה **מה זאת עשית**" – The Lord God said to the woman, 'What is this that you have done?'" (*Bereishis* 3:13).

2. "ויקרא פרעה לאברם ויאמר **מה זאת עשית** לי" – Pharaoh called for Avraham and said, 'What is this that you have done to me?'" (*Bereishis* 12:18).

3. "ויאמר אבימלך **מה זאת עשית** לנו" – Avimelech said, 'What is this you have done to us?'" (*Bereishis* 26:10).

4. "ויהי בבקר והנה היא לאה ויאמר אל לבן **מה זאת עשית** לי" – He said to Lavan, 'What is this you have done to me?'" (*Bereishis* 29:25).

5. "ויצא לבם ויחרדו איש אל אחיו לאמר **מה זאת עשה** אלוקים לנו" – Trembling, they turned to one another, saying, 'What is this that God has done to us?'" (*Bereishis* 42:28).

6. "ויאמרו **מה זאת עשינו** כי שלחנו את ישראל מעבדינו" – They said, "What is this we have done, releasing Israel from our service?" (*Shemos* 14:5)

7. "**מה זאת עשית** לנו להוציאנו ממצרים" – What have you done to us, taking us out of Egypt?" (*Shemos* 14:11)

8. "ולא שמעתם בקולי **מה זאת עשיתם**" – You have not obeyed me. What have you done?" (*Shoftim* 2:2)

9. "הלא ידעת כי מושלים בנו פלשתים ומה **זאת עשית** לנו" – You know the Philistines rule over us, what is this you have done to us?" (*Shoftim* 15:11)

10. "וייראו האנשים יראה גדולה ויאמרו אליו **מה זאת עשית**" – The men were greatly terrified and they said to him, 'What is this you have done?'" (*Yonah* 1:10)

In each case, the one asking the question has a claim against the other. For the *tam* it is actually a very thoughtful question and it is asked with humility. The omission of the root of the word עשה makes this the only place in the Tanach where the question מה זאת appears alone. The *tam* is asking why our redemption had so many complications, not unlike Moshe's question to God when he first saw setbacks at the outset of his mission.

וישב משה אל ה' ויאמר ה' למה הרעתה לעם הזה למה שלחתני. ומאז באתי אל פרעה לדבר בשמך הרע לעם הזה והצל לא הצלת את עמך:

Moshe returned to God and said, "Lord, why did You bring harm upon this people? Why did you send me? Ever since I came to Pharaoh to speak in Your Name, he has dealt worse with these people and still You have not delivered Your people."[44]

We answer this thoughtful question with a brief review of these setbacks so that God's power would be universally recognized and so that *we* would commemorate that power in our mitzvos of the redemption of the firstborn and of *tefillin*.[45]

A note of caution – the connection between the *rasha* and the *she'eino yodei'a lishol* was observed earlier. A withdrawn child can easily be drawn in by anyone who pays attention to him and makes him feel important. He may not be able to discern whether he is being drawn in by a moral voice or an immoral one. Now we must be concerned to shelter the *tam* as well. The question מה זאת is a very thoughtful one but it can quickly turn to a very different kind of question which has all the same words in it, namely "מה העבודה הזאת לכם – What is this work to you?" We must answer *every* question and do so thoughtfully, resisting the temptation to answer any question with, "Because I said so."[46]

to warrant an explanation for the difference. The feminine song is a function, says *Tosafos*, of much greater painstaking effort in the redemptive process, one that is needed to a greater extent for a withdrawn child. In addition, את hints at a complete answer from the beginning to the end, leaving out no details. We are to open up to this child from the first letter to the last.[27]

The best mode of education is to educe the teaching material from the child. The most important moment of learning takes place as a child is thinking of asking or answering a question. A good educator can mold any sincere question or answer into a thoughtful vehicle for continuing the discussion at hand. In the laws of *nedarim*, vows, we are sometimes allowed to develop an opening – a "פתח" – for the vow to be annulled. This is done by literally "opening up" a conversation whereby the vow is seen to have been made under erroneous assumptions and is therefore abrogated. We must do something similar for the *she'eino yodei'a lishol*. We must open up to him to get him to open himself[28] and no longer be withdrawn from others.

It would appear from the *Mechilta* that opening up to a student is sound pedagogical advice even if the student is *not* withdrawn. The formula of "פתח" (albeit with the masculine "אתה") appears in the *Mechilta* in connection to the *chacham* as well as the *she'eino yodei'a lishol*.

Although the *she'eino yodei'a lishol* receives the same answer as the *rasha* in the Haggadah, the continuation of his answer in the Torah indicates that he is ready for more than the Pesach observance itself. The *rasha*'s answer in the Torah is limited to the *korban Pesach*.[29] In contrast, the *she'eino yodei'a lishol*'s answer is followed by the observance of *tefillin*, *pidyon haben*, and *talmud Torah*, in addition to *korban Pesach*.

The *rasha* serves as an example for the *she'eino yodei'a lishol*. The Haggadah tells the *rasha* the same answer as the *she'eino yodei'a lishol*, but while we are told "ואמור לו," we don't speak to the *rasha* directly, in second person, but in third person. The *rasha*'s response, if we are speaking to *him*, should have concluded, "אילו היית שם לא היית נגאל – if *you* were there *you* would not have been redeemed."[30]

The Vilna Gaon maintains that the response is by design in third person because it is actually stated to the *she'eino yodei'a lishol*. The teeth being blunted or clenched are indeed those of the *rasha*, so that he remains silent while we turn to the *she'eino yodei'a lishol* and tell him the answer he will receive as well. We tell him to avoid the *rasha*'s pitfalls and we point to the *rasha* and tell the *she'eino yodei'a lishol*: "If he was there in Egypt, he would not have been redeemed, because he removed himself from the *klal*."

The *she'eino yodei'a lishol*, if not given special attention, will likely turn to the direction of the *rasha*,[31] and the same answer they receive brings home this point. While the *rasha*'s answer stresses "לי" so that he feels included, the *she'eino yodei'a lishol*'s answer stresses "זה." He must be shown clear examples to prove every point he is taught. His education must be visual and experiential.[32] The Seder itself is tailored to this type of learning and we see how Maggid Section 8 makes the same point. Some things that are taught are immediately forgotten and some things remain for a long time and continue bearing an influence on knowledge and behavior for years to come.

Consider the following story: A private school was faced with a problem. A number of girls who were beginning to use lipstick would put it on in the school bathrooms and then press their lips on the mirror, leaving hundreds of lip prints. Every night the maintenance man would laboriously remove them from the mirrors and the next day they were all back. The teachers were told to admonish the students to stop this practice but repeated calls went unheeded. Finally the principal decided something had to be done. She called all the girls together around one of the bathrooms and met with the maintenance man there. She explained that the lip prints were causing a major problem for the custodian. To demonstrate how difficult it had been to clean the mirrors, she asked the maintenance man to show the girls how much effort was required. He took out a long-handled squeegee, dipped it in the toilet, and cleaned the mirror with it. From then on, there were no more lip prints on the mirror.

Teachable moments should be lasting memories for all children.

MAGGID SECTION 8 – YACHOL MEI'ROSH CHODESH

1. Why would I suppose the story of Pesach should be told from Rosh Chodesh (presumably Nissan) if the redemption took place on the fifteenth of Nissan?
2. What is the significance of "ביום ההוא – On that day"?
3. What is the significance of "בעבור זה – Because of this"?
4. If ביום ההוא points to a daytime observance, while בעבור זה indicates a nighttime observance, why not simply omit ביום ההוא altogether to avoid any confusion?

יָכוֹל מֵרֹאשׁ חֹדֶשׁ, תַּלְמוּד לוֹמַר בַּיּוֹם הַהוּא. אִי בַּיּוֹם הַהוּא יָכוֹל מִבְּעוֹד יוֹם, תַּלְמוּד לוֹמַר בַּעֲבוּר זֶה. בַּעֲבוּר זֶה לֹא אָמַרְתִּי אֶלָּא בְּשָׁעָה שֶׁיֵּשׁ מַצָּה וּמָרוֹר מוּנָחִים לְפָנֶיךָ:

One might think (that the recounting of the Exodus to one's children) should be done from the first of the month. Therefore, the Torah says, "On that day" (ibid.). But based on the words "on that day," one might think that it should be done while it is still daytime. Therefore, the Torah says, "Because of this" (ibid.), implying that "I am speaking only of the time when matzah and maror are placed before you."

The Wise Son

The observance of Pesach requires more preparation than that of any other holiday. While our Sages bid us to study the laws of all holidays in their time,[46] the laws of Pesach are much more extensive than the laws of all other holidays.[47] For this reason, the Haggadah suggests preparing for the mitzvah of *sippur yetzias Mitzrayim* in advance. Moshe began teaching us the laws of the very first Pesach on Rosh Chodesh Nissan,[48] so the Haggadah suggests the possibility that we should do so as well. The first Pesach observance had four components:

1. Teaching about *korban Pesach* – Rosh Chodesh Nissan
2. Setting aside the *korban Pesach* – The tenth of Nissan
3. Slaughtering the *korban Pesach* – The fourteenth of Nissan
4. Eating the *korban Pesach* – The night of the fifteenth of Nissan

The Pure Son

Our redemption took place in five stages.[47] These stages are:

1. והוצאתי – I will deliver.
2. והצלתי – I will save.
3. וגאלתי – I will redeem.
4. ולקחתי – I will take (as a people).
5. והבאתי – I will bring (to Israel).[48]

Later in Maggid we will refer to fifteen stages of gratitude for our redemption (*Dayeinu*; Maggid Sections 15a–b). Perhaps we would have considered telling the story of that redemption in stages, starting from *Rosh Chodesh*. The Haggadah therefore informs us that the story can only be told as we reenact the events of the night before our redemption with the consumption of (Pesach), matzah, and maror. The story is inextricably tied to the mitzvos of the evening. A number of commentaries have

The Cynical Son

The observance of the *Seder* is a reenactment of the historical accounts of our experiences the night before we left Egypt. That story is told in the Book of *Shemos*, chapter 12. The chapter begins with our first commandment which introduces the account of our redemption as follows:

החדש הזה לכם ראש חדשים ראשון הוא לכם לחדשי השנה:

This month shall be for you the beginning of the months. It is the first of the months of the year for you.

The first half of this verse establishes a lunar calendar so that we can mark the redemption on a certain date and commemorate it on that same date in the future. The second half teaches that Nissan is the first month of the year. A lunar year has eleven fewer days than a solar year and requires adjustments of an additional month every two or three years so that Pesach always falls in the springtime. This is further expressed when the Torah says:

The Withdrawn Son

There are many things an observant Jew needs to learn in order to walk in the path of Torah. A crucial aspect of the night of the *Seder* is to use all the mitzvos of the evening to teach the powerful characteristics of empathy. We try our hardest to empathize with the degradations and deprivations of our ancestors. This is not an intellectual endeavor. If that were so, we would spend the night expounding the text of *Shemos* chapters 1 through 15 in great length and depth. The evening's proceedings are reduced to a two-letter word – זה – and the time for this is none other than the anniversary of the night itself that we left Egypt. This is not a simple task. It may be easier to teach the depths of the storyline of our redemption than to impart empathy. The word זה denotes clarification when confusion or uncertainty exists. Even Moshe experienced this confusion at times and had to be given further clarity, albeit only a few times over a period of forty years. Chazal

The Wise Son – continued

The mitzvah of *sippur yetzias Mitzrayim* is connected to the mitzvah of *eating*, not the mitzvos of *preparation*,[49] since the Torah commands that its observance be ביום ההוא. The word יום attached to a mitzvah generally denotes daytime observance.[50] The words בעבור זה imply that we are pointing at something,[51] which in our case is the (Pesach), matzah, and maror, and these mitzvos are performed at night. This is why *Yachol MeiRosh Chodesh* (Maggid Section 8) concludes that *sippur yetzias Mitzrayim* is inextricably connected to the mitzvos of the evening. These mitzvos are so "enlightening" that the evening itself is like a day.[52] Otherwise the

Torah could have avoided the tension between the two phrases (ביום ההוא denoting day and בעבור זה denoting night) by saying והגדת לבנך בלילה ההוא לאמר בעבור זה.[53] The Torah could have also avoided confusion by omitting ביום ההוא altogether, by saying והגדת לבנך לאמר בעבור זה. For one, without the words ביום ההוא we would have missed the message of this night being as illuminating as the day. In addition, without ביום ההוא, I might have connected בעבור זה to the seven days of eating matzah and no *chametz*, to require *sippur yetzias Mitzrayim* throughout the entire holiday. ביום ההוא therefore limits the mitzvah of *sippur yetzias Mitzrayim* to the *Seder*.

The Cynical Son – continued

היום אתם יוצאים **בחדש האביב:**

*Today you are leaving in the springtime **month**.*[44]

In the very next verse the Torah commands us to observe Pesach:

ועבדת את העבודה הזאת **בחודש הזה:**

*You shall observe in **this month** the following service.*

In addition the Torah commands us:

שמור את **חודש** האביב ועשית פסח:

*Observe the **month** of Aviv and make a Pesach offering.*[45]

Pesach represents our renewal as a people after generations of slavery, so we stress the springtime month of renewal, Nissan, in its observance. This

is why the Torah so often stresses the month of the Pesach observance, and why we might have considered telling the story from Rosh Chodesh.[46]

"ביום ההוא – that day" precludes any possibility of observing *sippur yetzias Mitzrayim* from Rosh Chodesh. However, ההוא is not as precise as "בעבור זה – because of this." Even if the question is asked at an irrelevant time, the one answering the question should be as specific as possible.[47] The mitzvos of this evening take place well into the night. If a child is inclined to fall asleep, perhaps we should react by telling the story מבעוד יום before he falls asleep. To this the Haggadah answers, בעבור זה. If we can be as relevant and specific as possible, the one we are trying to teach is more likely to get it.

The Pure Son – continued

enhanced the scope of בעבור זה by employing numerology, *gematria*, on the word זה to relate to

twelve mitzvos that are performed at the *Seder*.[49]

The Withdrawn Son – continued

teach that Moshe was uncertain about the general ideas of certain mitzvos until God further clarified

them. The common denominator in all these cases is the word זה.[33]

Even Moshe Rabbeinu sometimes had to be told זה. ביום ההוא points to the mitzvos of the evening. We hope that by the time the *Seder* is over, the participants will have a clear view of redemption to proclaim "לשנה הבאה בירושלים – This coming year in Jerusalem!" So we see the importance of זה for the withdrawn child. The same verse that speaks to him also responds to the cynical child, even as we stress לי for him, so that he feels included. However, the זה aspect of the *Seder* is just as important for the cynical child, and the לי aspect is equally important to the withdrawn child. The withdrawn child is very close to falling out, and the cynical child is crying out for clear answers.

Yachol MeiRosh Chodesh has an extra phrase just as the verse it cites does. The passage concludes:

לא אמרתי בעבור זה אלא בשעה שיש מצה ומרור מונחים לפניך:

***I can only say** "it is because of this" at such a time when matzah and maror are placed before you.*[34]

The verse concludes, "והגדת לבנך ביום ההוא **לאמר** בעבור זה עשה ה' לי בצאתי ממצרים – You shall relate to your son on that day, **saying** it is because of this that God acted for me when I left Egypt."

The words לא אמרתי in the *Yachol MeiRosh Chodesh* section of Maggid appear to be extraneous just as the word לאמר is. They both come to stress, therefore, how important it is to connect זה to לאמר. The learning devices we can point to must be explained with words of clarity, compassion, and empathy, so that they are heard.[35] Parents must talk in a way which will make their children listen and parents must listen to their children in a way which will make them want to talk. This is why the verse and the *Yachol MeiRosh Chodesh* section of Maggid stress the root אמר.[36]

One last point. The human brain is more attuned to recognizing visual images than recognizing words. This is why the Written Torah can only be explained according to oral traditions, and our Sages explain that the best way to remember what is not written is through memory devices such as mnemonics and acronyms, and what Chazal refer to as סימניות, which we may term visual devices. The Haggadah is a written text but embedded within that text are many reminders to add visual aids to the learning process. בעבור זה is a clear example of this.[37]

MAGGID SECTION 9 – MI'TCHILAH OVDEI AVODAH ZARAH

1. What is the source of this paragraph and why do we say it?
2. Why does the Haggadah revert to our pre-Patriarchal origins? Shouldn't "אבותינו – our fathers" begin with Avraham?
3. Didn't we already refer to the beginning of the story with *Avadim Hayinu*? This seems to be out of order, as it reverts to a time prior to our slavery in Egypt.
4. There are many extraneous references that require close reading and explanation:
   - Why is it important to mention that our ancestors came from "עבר הנהר – the other side of the river"?
   - What does "מעולם – From very long ago" come to add?
   - Avraham had two brothers, Nachor and Haran. Why only mention Nachor?

- Why refer to "את אביכם את אברהם – **Your father**, Avraham"?
- What is the significance of "ואולך אותו בכל ארץ כנען – I led him through the whole Land of Canaan"?
- If Eisav is mentioned in this passage, why not mention Yishmael? Or, if Yishmael is not mentioned, why mention Eisav?

Note: Question 4 will be answered only to the *tam*.

מִתְּחִלָּה עוֹבְדֵי עֲבוֹדָה זָרָה הָיוּ אֲבוֹתֵינוּ, וְעַכְשָׁיו קֵרְבָנוּ הַמָּקוֹם לַעֲבוֹדָתוֹ, שֶׁנֶּאֱמַר, וַיֹּאמֶר יְהוֹשֻׁעַ אֶל כָּל הָעָם כֹּה אָמַר יְהוָֹה אֱלֹהֵי יִשְׂרָאֵל בְּעֵבֶר הַנָּהָר יָשְׁבוּ אֲבוֹתֵיכֶם מֵעוֹלָם, תֶּרַח אֲבִי אַבְרָהָם וַאֲבִי נָחוֹר, וַיַּעַבְדוּ אֱלֹהִים אֲחֵרִים: וָאֶקַּח אֶת אֲבִיכֶם אֶת אַבְרָהָם מֵעֵבֶר הַנָּהָר, וָאוֹלֵךְ אוֹתוֹ בְּכָל אֶרֶץ כְּנַעַן, וָאַרְבֶּה אֶת זַרְעוֹ, וָאֶתֶּן לוֹ אֶת יִצְחָק: וָאֶתֵּן לְיִצְחָק אֶת יַעֲקֹב וְאֶת עֵשָׂו, וָאֶתֵּן לְעֵשָׂו אֶת הַר שֵׂעִיר לָרֶשֶׁת אוֹתוֹ, וְיַעֲקֹב וּבָנָיו יָרְדוּ מִצְרָיִם:

Originally, our ancestors were idol worshippers, but now the Omnipresent has drawn us near to His service. Thus it says, "Joshua said to all the people: Thus said Hashem, the God of Israel: Your ancestors had always dwelt on the other side of the river – Terach, the father of Avraham and the father of Nachor – and they worshipped other gods. Then I took your father Avraham from the other side of the [Euphrates] River, and I had him travel throughout all of the land of Canaan. I increased his offspring and gave him Yitzchak, and to Yitzchak I gave Yaakov and Esav. To Esav I gave Mount Seir to take possession of, and Yaakov and his sons went down to Egypt" (*Yehoshua* 24:2–4).

The Wise Son

The Mishnah says, "מתחיל בגנות ומסיים בשבח,"[54] that we begin with the shameful part of our history and conclude with praise. It is crucial for us to

The Cynical Son

Historical events must be understood in context. The memory of the experience of migration, rootlessness, slavery, and redemption sets an

The Pure Son

Children have many questions about why we do things, and the best way to answer their questions is to start from the very beginning.

The Withdrawn Son

The Maggid Section of the Haggadah is divided into six parts:[38]

appreciate how far we have come historically, and to do this we revert to a pre-Patriarchal era. In fact, how we fulfill this dictum is a Talmudic dispute between Rav and Shmuel. Shmuel states that we fulfill מתחיל בגנות with the passage of עבדים היינו, while Rav holds that we do so with this section of Maggid. Rav Nachman appears to rule like Shmuel, and we do indeed begin Maggid with *Avadim Hayinu*.[55] Since we say both, we need to understand what stands between Rav and Shmuel.[56] Surely Rav read *Avadim Hayinu* and surely Shmuel recited *Mitchilah Ovedei Avodah Zarah*? Rather, each one wants to stress a different component of the "גנות – disparagement." The purpose of the earlier part of the גנות is to capture the immediate essence of the child's curiosity. The Four Questions must relate directly to *Avadim Hayinu*, and therefore this paragraph immediately follows the *Mah Nishtanah*.[57] Rav prefers to relate back to the totality of the Jewish experience dating back to our earliest origins. That began with the migration of Avraham from Mesopotamia to Canaan and fits in a broader historical theme at this juncture of the Haggadah. In fact, the entire Maggid Section now turns toward the historical experience of the nation in general. The Jew is constantly remembering the lessons of history. Chazal connect the Egyptian exile with Avraham's actions in *Parashas Lech Lecha*.[58] *Ramban* considers it a reaction to Avraham's descent to Egypt during the famine he experienced upon arrival to Canaan.[59] *Abarbanel* goes so far as to connect the major portions of the *Seder* to the sale of Yosef.[60] The Jew constantly seeks to learn messages of history through the lens of morality. We lost Shiloh because of the misconduct of the sons of Eli. We lost the First Temple because of violations of cardinal mitzvos, and we lost the Second Temple because of baseless hatred.[61] In all three cases, a historian might prefer to explain that we suffered these losses to an overwhelming force of an enemy's might. Not so according to the reader of the Haggadah. Our historical vicissitudes fluctuate due to our moral stances. If immorality caused us to be defeated and chained to slave ships to be taken to distant lands, we always felt our fate could be changed by rising to the moral standards God expects of us.[62] The section of *Mitchilah Ovedei Avodah Zarah* demonstrates how far we've come and what we left behind.

indelible mark on our religious outlook. On the heels of a cataclysmic exodus from Egypt, our ancestors experienced a religious and national awakening when they received God's word at Sinai, an enjoinder to constantly remember.[48] The Decalogue opens with a reminder that God redeemed us from Egypt, and commands us to remember and sanctify Shabbos. That sanctity is a weekly reminder of events of the past, from Creation to the redemption we commemorate on Pesach.[49] Our prophets and sages never failed to remind us of our past misdeeds. Our history is not perfect and we don't expect our leaders to be perfect.[50] We do not even consider that our Messianic savior must be perfect,[51] or any Biblical character for that matter.[52] Our collective history as well has a checkered past and the Haggadah, which moves us to be proud of the present, bids us to remember and appreciate how far we've come, and how thankful we must feel toward God. For this reason, we revert to Terach and our slavery, which are shameful and disparaging periods of our past. There is a Talmudic dispute that debates how far we must revert in reference to this shame.[53] It would appear to be more appropriate to refer to *Avadim Hayinu* (the opinion of Shmuel in the dispute) to refer to the event we commemorate at the *Seder*.

The Cynical Son – continued

The disputant of this opinion (Rav) considers it even more worthy to refer further back in our history to an even greater shame – an idolatrous past. The greater the shame, the greater the appreciation of our current state.

The redemption from Egypt is the lynchpin in a long history of a people experiencing broad vicissitudes of life and towering waves of ups and downs.[54] The contrast between עובדי עבודה זרה and קרבנו המקום לעבודתו is what Rav wants to stress. An idolater is excluded from eating the *korban Pesach*.[55] Yet, Rav stresses that we also started this way and God turned our history around.[56]

The Pure Son – continued

This is what Yehoshua does at the end of his life when he exhorts the people to choose the service of God over idolatry, pointing out that idolatry is part of our past.

Along the way we will elaborate upon six specific points.

(1) Why is it important to mention that our ancestors came from "עבר הנהר – the other side of the river"?

The reference to עבר הנהר is a reminder of a change of our destiny. Avraham was already advanced in age without children when God commanded him to move to another place. Avraham's destiny and that of his descendants would be tied to that place from then on. By crossing to the other side of the Euphrates from Ur Kasdim, Avraham would symbolically place himself on the other side of the ancient world[50] in his belief in a moral, monotheistic Deity, and the willingness to obey His commands.

(2) What does "מעולם – from very long ago" come to add?

מעולם generally connotes something everlasting, as in the verse ימלוך ה' לעולם.[51] However, it can also refer to a very long time,[52] and refers to how far back Avraham's Mesopotamian roots spread. But they did not necessarily originate there. When Avraham first came to Canaan, the Torah states "והכנעני אז בארץ – the Canaanites were then in the land," implying that they were not always there. Rashi explains that the Canaanites conquered this land from Shem and forced them out.[53] Even though Avraham's ancestors lived in the North for many years, he and his descendants would not be taking someone else's land, but reclaiming their own.[54] Even if the Jews are cast from their land and destiny for what seems like forever, God's plan for us always awaits and our mission as His people always beckons.

(3) Avraham had two brothers, Nachor and Haran. Why only mention Nachor?

Terach is the only person in the Torah who has a son who bears the same name as his father.[55] Terach's father was named Nachor and his son was named Nachor. In the Torah, most names are based on events or sentiments of the day, and children are generally not named after other relatives. The exception in the case of Nachor may be an attempt to hold on to practices of old.[56] This is often a good thing, but now God wants Avraham to make a clean break with everything from the past. Although Avraham made a clean break from his family, he knew there remained a positive strand of tradition, as is exemplified here. Perhaps for this reason he insisted on returning to his family to find a wife for Yitzchak even though God had told Avraham to leave them.

(4) Why refer to "את אביכם את אברהם – Your father, Avraham"?

Yehoshua's speech begins with a reference to "אבותיכם – your fathers," and includes Terach along with Avraham because he too left Mesopotamia with Avraham, but he never arrived in Canaan. The change in destiny, the break from the past, and the chosenness of Avraham, begins with "ואקח את

אביכם – **I took your father**," and this refers only to Avraham. Chazal explain that Terach repented at the end of his life to follow Avraham's path, but he never quite made it to join his destiny. The word "ואקח – I took," shares the same root with the last of the four expressions of redemption that would characterize the story of the Exodus, of "והוצאתי – I will free you," "והצלתי – I will save you," "וגאלתי – I will redeem you," and finally "ולקחתי – **I will take you**."

The root לקח is the expression the Torah uses for marriage,[57] as if to say that God took Avraham and us into a marriage relationship.

(5) What is the significance of ואולך אותו בכל ארץ כנען?

God told Avraham to traverse the Land of Israel in its length and width.[58] This was to strengthen his descendants' future right to this land. Chazal refer to the land as ירושה היא לכם מאבותיכם,[59] an inheritance they have received from their ancestors. *Ramban*[60] explains that it was important for Avraham to experience traversing the land unimpeded by Canaanite interference as a sign of future success in the conquest of the land by Yehoshua.

There are different opinions as to the age at which Avraham recognized the monotheistic and moralistic nature of God. Chazal give the ages of three or forty-eight.[61] All agree, as these passages in Yehoshua clearly tell us, that Avraham was born into an idolatrous family. He was seventy-five upon his arrival in Israel. The generations between Shem and Terach began to propagate at ages ranging from late twenties to mid-thirties. *Abarbanel* says that the purpose of this additional phrase is to remind us of how significantly God changed Avraham's life. In Mesopotamia, Avraham started with no faith, no children, and no land, and his brothers had already had children by then. Avraham's heart had long stirred him to grasp the existence of a benevolent and moral Divine Creator, and the Creator promised him children and a land. The Israelites, hearing Yehoshua's words, were about

to experience the fulfillment of this promise.

(6) If Eisav is mentioned, why not mention Yishmael, or if Yishmael is not mentioned why mention Eisav?

The fulfillment of the promises to Avraham of becoming a great nation was meant to be through Yitzchak alone,[62] and this promise went further through Yaakov alone.[63] It seems that Yishmael accepted his secondary status to his younger brother; after all, Yitzchak was the son of the matriarch while Yishmael was the son of the bondswoman. In addition, Avraham in his lifetime accorded secondary status to all his sons, compared to Yitzchak.[64] However, Eisav never ceded his position as firstborn willingly. Although he sold his birthright, he never acknowledged the validity of this sale.[65] If Eisav or his descendants would ever lay claim to the Land of Israel in fulfillment of the Abrahamic covenant, let it be known that the inheritors of the land would first be slaves in Egypt before acquiring such an inheritance, as was predicted in the *Bris Bein HaBesarim*, *Bereishis* 15:7–16. Eisav never paid that debt, but we did.

Rashi hints to this in the very first words Moshe was commanded to declare to Pharaoh:

בני בכורי ישראל:

My son, My firstborn is Israel[66]

Rashi renders two interpretations, one *peshat* (simple, straightforward meaning) and one *derash* (deeper meaning). The difficulty in this verse is the word בכורי. It usually refers to a firstborn, but as *Rashi* points out from *Tehillim* 89:28, it can also be an expression of importance.[67] Just as a בכור is the child who makes these two people become parents, so too Avraham's descendants are, as it were, God's בכור insofar as we brought God's fame to the world, a point that the section of *Mitchilah Ovedei Avodah Zarah* intends to make. The *peshat* refers to Israel as God's important nation, perhaps based on the similarity between the root words

The Pure Son — continued

"בכור – firstborn," and "בחור – chosen." Then *Rashi* renders a *derash* in which בכור maintains its general meaning of "firstborn." According to this interpretation, Moshe's opening statement is taken out of historical context in having Moshe declare that the true firstborn of God is ישראל, not as a nation in contrast with Egypt, but as a person in contrast with Eisav. In light of the end of the *Mitchilah Ovedei Avodah Zarah* section, we can understand the reason to be told this at the beginning of the redemption story in *Sefer Shemos*. It is only with the advent of the completion of the exile in Egypt that Eisav can never again lay claim to the Land of Israel.

The Withdrawn Son — continued

1. והגדת לבנך, which are answers to the child
2. ביום ההוא, which connects to history
3. לאמר, which are answers for adults
4. בעבור זה, which is experiential observance
5. עשה ה' לי, which is personal connection
6. בצאתי ממצרים, which is praise and recognition of salvation

In the fulfillment of מתחיל בגנות, Rav and Shmuel don't argue about what to say, but about where to say it. If we must refer to our shameful past, Shmuel prefers the theme at hand, the Egyptian slavery which will speak directly to children in the והגדת לבנך section of the Haggadah. Rav prefers the fulfillment of מתחיל בגנות ומסיים בשבח to be in the longer segment of the Midrashic expositions which speak more to adults, reverting to an earlier time in history.

Egyptian history bears no witness to Moshe or to explicit reference to our exodus because the custom of their record keepers was to expunge all such failures from historical records. This is decidedly not true of our Tanach, nor of the *Seder*. Unpleasant references are not swept under the carpet. They are placed before us so we can learn from the errors of the past, in order to find resolution. Some obvious Biblical examples come to mind. *Sefer Bereishis* is replete with failures of siblings to get along in practically every generation. The Book does not hide these failures and they lead to resolution between Yosef and his brothers as a harbinger for the brotherly peace,[39] between Ephraim and Menasheh,[40] and ultimately, between Moshe and Aharon.[41] For another example, the Book of Rus is written to demonstrate that the lineage of David HaMelech, although from Moabite stock, was accepted in earlier times. The story does not attempt to squelch the opposition to this position. It clearly cites Ploni Almoni's rejection of Rus, even though this was not the prevailing opinion.[42] The *Seder* at first weakens us with גנות. But as sure as a good workout, which first weakens muscle tissue only to subsequently become stronger, so too, the גנות of our past ultimately strengthens us to confront the challenges we face as a people in the present.

MAGGID SECTION 10 – BARUCH SHOMER HAVTACHASO L'YISRAEL

1. What is the promise that is being kept in this section of *Maggid*, and why is God praised for keeping His promise?
2. How can we reconcile the different sources and opinions of the amount of time we spent in Egypt? (God told Avraham that there would be four hundred years of exile

בָּרוּךְ שׁוֹמֵר הַבְטָחָתוֹ לְיִשְׂרָאֵל, בָּרוּךְ הוּא. שֶׁהַקָּדוֹשׁ בָּרוּךְ הוּא חִשַּׁב אֶת הַקֵּץ, לַעֲשׂוֹת כְּמָה שֶׁאָמַר לְאַבְרָהָם אָבִינוּ בִּבְרִית בֵּין הַבְּתָרִים, שֶׁנֶּאֱמַר, וַיֹּאמֶר לְאַבְרָם יָדֹעַ תֵּדַע כִּי גֵר יִהְיֶה זַרְעֲךָ בְּאֶרֶץ לֹא לָהֶם וַעֲבָדוּם וְעִנּוּ אֹתָם אַרְבַּע מֵאוֹת שָׁנָה: וְגַם אֶת הַגּוֹי אֲשֶׁר יַעֲבֹדוּ דָּן אָנֹכִי, וְאַחֲרֵי כֵן יֵצְאוּ בִּרְכֻשׁ גָּדוֹל:

Blessed be the One Who keeps His promise to Israel! Blessed be He! For the Holy One, blessed is He, calculated the end [of our captivity], in order to fulfill what He had said to our forefather Avraham at the Covenant Between the Parts, as it says, "And He said to Avraham: 'Know with certainty that your offspring will be strangers in a land not theirs, and [your offspring] will serve them, and they will oppress [your offspring], for four hundred years. And also the nation whom they will serve, I will judge, and afterwards they will leave with great possessions'" (*Bereishis* 15:13-14).

The Wise Son

1. *Baruch Shomer Havtachaso L'Yisrael*, which is Maggid Section 10, is a response to the last words of *Mitchilah Ovedei Avodah Zarah*, which is Maggid Section 9, "וַיַעֲקֹב וּבָנָיו יָרְדוּ מִצְרָיְמָה." These words are an expression of the Rabbinic dictum,

The Cynical Son

This is our expression of gratitude that the fulfillment of the promise to Avraham in *Bereishis* chapter 15 is through Israel and not any of the other descendants of Avraham, as the end of *Mitchilah Ovedei Avodah Zarah* (Maggid Section 9) indicates.[57]

The Pure Son

1. We thank God for keeping a close watch on the events in Egypt. There were times when we may have felt abandoned, but God was always watching.[68] It is for this reason, that the word שמר can be found many times throughout the Pesach story and its observance.[69]

The Withdrawn Son

1. We praise God for reducing the amount of time we were meant to spend in Egypt.[43]

2. *Abarbanel* says that thirty years were added to the decree of four hundred because of the sinning of the Israelites in Egypt.[44] The *Shelah* adds that the

"כשם שמברכים על הטוב כך מברכים על הרע" – Just as we bless God on the good, we bless God on the bad."[63] This is our acknowledgement that every part of our experience in Egypt was part of a Divine plan.[64]

2. The decree of living in a foreign land began based on the words, "גר יהיה זרעך – your descendants will be strangers," starting from the birth of Yitzchak.[65] From the time of Yitzchak's birth to *yetzias Mitzrayim* was indeed four hundred years.[66] The problem with this resolution is that the verse states that we would be mistreated and enslaved for four hundred years, which did not begin with the birth of Yitzchak! A novel answer to this can be reached by explaining the verse with the approach of סירוס המקרא, which literally means "cutting up the text." It reorders certain clauses or words in the verse.[67] Applied to our verse, we read:

A. "ידע תדע כי גר יהיה זרעך בארץ לא להם" –Know well that your offspring will be strangers in a strange land not theirs."

B. "ועבדום וענו אותם – And they will be enslaved and oppressed."

C. "ארבע מאות שנה" – Four hundred years."

What סירוס המקרא does is that it switches phrases B and C, so that the verse reads in a way that the four hundred years speak to the time of being in a strange land, not to the time of servitude. That time frame is left undetermined as if to say:

ידע תדע כי גר יהיה זרעך בארץ לא להם

ארבע מאות שנה

ועבדום וענו אותם:

This is to say that all the years that Avraham, Yitzchak, and Yaakov lived in Israel, they sojourned as strangers. Avraham did not complain about the difficulty in purchasing land from the Hittites.[68] Yaakov similarly insisted on purchasing land in Shechem,[69] and Yitzchak didn't complain about his difficulties in striking

water for wells in the midst of the Philistines.[70] They accepted these hardships as part of God's plan.[71]

3. Chazal[72] say that the Egyptian exile was a consequence of Avraham's lack of faith in asking "במה אדע כי אירשנה – How do I know that I will inherit it?" The exile atoned for this.[73]

4. The reason the Egyptians were punished for fulfilling the decree of servitude is that they went well beyond "ועבדום וענו אותם – and they will enslave them and afflict them," by embittering the lives of the Israelites and murdering their sons. Many years later, Nevuchadnetzar king of Babylon was called upon to fulfill God's decree against a sinning nation of Israel. Because of this mission he is referred to as God's slave.[74] He too went beyond his decree, and was thus punished as well.[75] The same can be said of the Assyrians[76] and their punishment.[77] The prophet Zechariah reviews these events by saying "וקצף גדול אני קוצף על הגוים השאננים אשר אני קצפתי מעט והמה עזרו להרעה – I am very angry with those nations that are at ease for I was only angry a little, **but they overdid the punishment**."[78]

5. God preceded his command to Moshe to instruct B'nei Yisrael to ask for vessels of gold and silver as follows:

דבר נא באזני העם:

Please speak unto the people.[79]

Chazal comment on the need for God to beseech Moshe with the word נא.[80] They relate that when Moshe heard this command, he was reluctant to fulfill it. We should be satisfied just to leave with our lives, rather than be bogged down with so much wealth. God preempted this reluctance by adding the word נא to the command. This was meant to cajole the Jewish People to fulfill the promise that was made to Avraham that his descendants would leave servitude with wealth. If not, Avraham may retort that God kept his promise of "ועבדום וענו אותם – they will enslave and afflict them," but he did not fulfill His promise of "ואחרי כן יצאו ברכוש גדול" – They will afterward go free with a great possession."

This Talmudic conversation is perplexing. Surely God ought to keep His promise regardless of Avraham's reaction. *HaKesav VeHaKabalah*[81] resolves this by redefining the רכוש גדול. Even though the promise was that the Israelites would *leave* Egypt with a great possession, in actuality, the wealth was in something that was already set aside for them, so they were technically leaving Egypt with it in their possession. This was the Torah. God would be in fulfillment of His promise to Avraham even without material wealth. The reason for God's insistence on the gold and silver was to fulfill what Avraham thought God meant this great possession was.

Shmuel David Luzzatto expresses in a number of places that the Torah omits a number of generations between Yaakov and Moshe. He says that it is inconceivable that the numbers of Levites could have climbed to over twenty thousand given the generations mentioned in *Shemos* 6:18. Rather, he claims that the generations that are mentioned – Leivi then Kehas and then Amram – represent three main families by which the Tribe of Leivi were known. As long as a father was alive, his tribe was known by his name, and remained united under that name for some time after his death until further divided by later descendants. Leivi's family stayed undivided, according to this line of thought, for 137 years after Leivi was born.[58] Then Leivi's family was divided into three groups, Gershon, Kehas, and Merari. The main family of these three, Kehas, stayed united until 133 years after his birth[59] and then divided into four groups – Amram, Yitzhar, Chevron, and Uziel, which lasted 137 years.[60] If we add these three totals and include the 17 years of Yaakov after he arrived in Egypt, the total is 424 years, which according to *Shadal*, was rounded off to four hundred and thirty.[61]

Abarbanel contends that the Egyptian exile came as a result of the sale of Yosef. This can be seen as a punishment to atone for sin or simply a result of the events themselves. Avraham is not assessed of this reason because it hadn't happened yet.

Free will is an essential tenet of Jewish philosophy. Even if everything the Egyptians did was preordained, the fact is that no one individual Egyptian was chosen by God in advance to afflict the Israelites. Since every single Egyptian could have exercised his or her free will and not afflict us, therefore, the ones that did are to be punished even if they are collectively in fulfillment of a Divine plan.[62]

5. We are commanded not to abhor the Egyptian because we were strangers in his land.[63] At the time we entered Egypt we were invited as honored guests, as one of our own saved their economy and their society. Yosef, like so many Jews over the millennia, improved life in the Diaspora for the host nation, only to be abused, tormented, murdered or expelled over time. In the very least, we would leave Egypt with the wages of our labor, to which the *Baruch Shomer Havtachaso L'Yisrael* section alludes, with "ואחרי כן יצאו ברכוש גדול – Afterward they will leave with **a great possession**." Chazal speak of the lawsuit the Egyptians filed against us in the court of Alexander the Great for the money we took from them when we left Egypt.[64] The case was dropped when it was pointed out that their wealth amounted to less than the wages due for so many years of servitude.

2. The four hundred years of subjugation was not meant to be a measure of time, but an intensity of servitude. Avraham's descendants would have to endure four hundred years worth of servitude, and we praise God in *Baruch Shomer Havtachaso L'Yisrael* (Maggid Section 10) for limiting the servitude to 210 years because of its intensity.[70] *Shibbolei HaLeket* finds a hint to this shortening of 190 years in the words, הקדוש ברוך הוא חשב את הקץ, that God considered the numerical value of קץ (190) to be included in the four-hundred-year decree. These 190 years were subsumed in the 60 years of Yitzchak's life before Yaakov was born, and the 130 years of Yaakov before he came to Egypt, and thus decreased the time in Egypt by that number. *Tiferes Yisrael*[71] finds symbolism in this quickening of the redemption in the eating of matzah and maror. The bitterness of our servitude symbolized by the maror hastened our redemption, symbolized by the matzah. The *Vilna Gaon* finds an allusion to this in the cantillation to the Torah's words that are cited by the Haggadah as the reason why we eat maror. וימררו את חייהם has the cantillation קדמא ואזלא, two words which not only have the numerical value of 190,

but allude to this hastening of the redemption, as these words in Aramaic literally mean "to precede and go ahead," as if to say, "Get up and go," earlier than an appointed time.[72]

3. *Ramban*[73] contends that Avraham demonstrated a lack of faith in leaving Egypt during the famine that he experienced upon arriving in Canaan. In addition, he compromised Sarah's safety in his strategy of dealing with the mortal threat he perceived in his travels.

4. *Ramban*[74] points out that if an individual was decreed on Rosh Hashanah to die the following year, the murderer who kills him would surely not be absolved of the crime because he was fulfilling the decree. So too the Egyptians would be punished.

5. The "רכוש גדול – great possession" can also refer to the Land of Israel. B'nei Yisrael actually left Egypt with a deed to the Land. The Talmud[75] says that this was part of the question of the daughters of Tzelafchad, regarding how they would inherit the land set aside for their father, who never made it into Israel. Here too, God would be in full compliance with his promise to Avraham, even without wealth.[76]

thirty years were added because of the sale of Yosef, because Yosef was thirty when he rose to power.

The inconsistency between 400 and 430 is considered by Chazal. *Seder Olam Rabbah*[45] states that the 400-year reckoning begins with Yitzchak's birth, while the 430-year reckoning begins from *Bris Bein HaBesarim* (*Bereishis* capter 15), which was thirty years earlier.[46] This would put Avraham's age at seventy in *Bereishis* chapter 15. The problem with this is that Avraham was seventy-five when he arrived at Canaan, in *Bereishis* 12:4. The answer that the two chapters are not ordered chronologically is complicated by

the fact that chapter 15 begins with the words "אחר הדברים האלה – **After** these events." Although that would seem to place chapter 15 *after* the previous chapters, perhaps we can still maintain *Seder Olam*'s chronology in light of the use of the past perfect in chapter 15. That chapter begins אחר הדברים האלה היה as opposed to the more common ויהי אחר הדברים האלה. The past perfect pushes the narrative of that chapter ahead of previous chapters.[47]

Rashi, after a long attempt to reconcile these numbers, writes,[48] "וזה אחד מן הדברים ששינו לתלמי המלך," this is one of the things that they changed before King Ptolemy. This refers to the episode of Ptolemy who compelled the Sages to translate the Torah into Greek.[49] Throughout their work, the Sages felt that misconceptions in the eyes of the non-Jewish readers regarding nuaces that a literal reader would miss was an impetus for them to alter certain translations accordingly. One of these corrections concerned the reference of our story of the time we spent in Egypt as four hundred and thirty years. Their emendation reads as follows: "The sojourning of the People of Israel who dwelt in Egypt *and in other lands* was four hundred and thirty years." As such, the decree of four hundred years began long before we came to Egypt.[50]

3. The purpose of the beginning of our nationhood as slaves in a strange land was to inculcate within our national consciousness a sensitivity to the plight of the less fortunate. No less than thirty-six times does the Torah remind us of the fair treatment of the stranger.[51]

4. We can add to this question the problem of Pharaoh being punished for something he was forced to do. Pharaoh's heart was hardened by God.[52] *Rashi* and *Ibn Ezra* to this verse explain that Pharaoh was never forced to do anything. After Pharaoh hardened his own heart so many times, his own free will was veritably taken from him. This is linguistically noted from the first five plagues where the text reads וַיְּחַזֵּק לֵב פַּרְעֹה, which means "he hardened his own heart," to the last five plagues where the text reads לֵב פַּרְעֹה וַיְּחַזֵּק, as if to say that his heart was hardened from outside. *Rashi* also points out that even if this seems unfair, such wicked and cruel people do not deserve fair treatment.[53]

5. When Avraham came to Canaan, the Midrash says that God told him, "צֵא וּכְבוֹשׁ אֶת הַדֶּרֶךְ לְפָנַי בָּנֶיךָ – Go forge a path before your descendants."[54] Avraham's life served as a template for future generations.[55] Perhaps he understood this when he accepted Pharaoh's generosity,[56] yet rejected the gifts of the king of Sodom.[57] Avraham forged a path before his descendants by accepting this wealth. This would also serve as a template to assure that the Hebrew slaves would leave servitude with gifts and sustenance.[58] In his Haggadah, the *Baal HaTanya* understands that the Israelites would expect to be paid for their labor upon leaving Egypt, and the command to Moshe to ask for gold, silver, and garments was to add to their reward for obeying a command.[59]

MAGGID SECTION 11 – V'HEE SHE'AMDAH

1. What does וְהִיא refer to, that has stood by us all these years?
2. What is the purpose of the repetitions of this elongated text?
3. Is it really true that in every generation "עוֹמְדִים עָלֵינוּ לְכַלּוֹתֵינוּ – the nations rise up against us to destroy us"?
4. Why do we raise the cup when reciting this Maggid Section?

The matzah is covered, and the cup of wine is raised while reciting the following paragraph:

וְהִיא שֶׁעָמְדָה לַאֲבוֹתֵינוּ וְלָנוּ, שֶׁלֹּא אֶחָד בִּלְבַד עָמַד עָלֵינוּ לְכַלּוֹתֵינוּ, אֶלָּא

And it is this that has stood by our fathers and by us! For it is not just one individual who rose

שֶׁבְּכָל דּוֹר וָדוֹר עוֹמְדִים עָלֵינוּ לְכַלּוֹתֵינוּ, וְהַקָּדוֹשׁ בָּרוּךְ הוּא מַצִּילֵנוּ מִיָּדָם:

against us to annihilate us, but in every single generation people rise up against us to annihilate us, and the Holy One, blessed is He, saves us from their hands!

The Wise Son

1. This chapter is about Jewish survival and והיא refers to the function of that survival. What has stood up for us in every generation is the promise that God made to Avraham in *Bereishis* chapter 15, referred to in the previous paragraph.[82] Although the promise related to the redemption from Egypt (לאבותינו), the passage of *V'Hee She'Amdah* relates also to future generations (לנו) as well. Chazal explain Avraham's reaction to the report of the exile:

והנה אימה חשיכה גדולה נופלת עליו.

A great dark dread descended upon him.[83]

Each word or phrase is expounded to refer to another exile.

1. "אימה – dread" refers to *Galus Bavel*.
2. "חשיכה – dark" refers to *Golus Madai*.

The Pure Son

1. The commands to Avraham when God laid out Avraham's destiny represent the secret of our survival. Avraham was told to cut various animals in half and place them together. These animals represent the nations of the world.[77] Avraham's descendants are represented by the dove[78] and Avraham was told not to divide it. The division of the animals represent the nations, and points to the fact that when one nation is host to another, the guest nation tends to assimilate and lose its cultural distinction. Not so with the Jews. We have found ourselves under the sovereignty of many nations, yet a sizable number of us have always managed to maintain our distinctive status. The reason is in the symbolism of the dove. The dove is the only bird that will only mate with one other bird. The Jewish People as a

The Cynical Son

1. והיא refers to the very end of the *Baruch Shomer Havtachaso L'Yisrael* section. The thing that has stood up for us for so long is the "רכוש גדול – great possession" that God gave us when we left Egypt. This refers to our chosenness in receiving the Torah and the Land of Israel, in addition to a blessing of material wealth. It is this very chosenness that causes the nations to do what this Maggid Section continues to point out. The three definitions of רכוש גדול in *Baruch Shomer Havtachaso L'Yisrael* are the main sources of anti-Semitism to our own day. They are the Torah,[65] material wealth, and the Land of Israel. Every generation has its own challenges and ours today seems to be this last definition. Many anti-Semites today hide behind a veneer of anti-Zionism. We are strengthened by this Maggid

The Withdrawn Son

1. The promise that *Baruch Shomer Havtachaso L'Yisrael* refers to is the promise at the end of *Sefer Vayikra* that no matter how far we stray and how severely we are punished for it, God will never utterly wipe us out. The promise is:

לא מאסתים ולא געלתים לכלותם להפר בריתי אתם:

I will not reject them or spurn them so as to destroy them, annulling My covenant with them.[60]

2. The fact that we have relived the subjugation in Egypt so many times in our own history is precisely what has kept the flame of *zechiras yetzias Mitzrayim* alive. Jews living under the murderous yoke of Romans, Crusaders, Inquisitors, pogroms, and Nazism knew what it was like to eat the bread of affliction. They knew when they said והקב"ה מצילנו מידם that it

3. "גדולה – great" refers to *Golus Yavan*.
4. "נופלת עליו – fell upon him" refers to *Golus Edom*.

God showed Avraham these subsequent exiles and their redemptions as well. This is all part of the promise to which היא refers.[84]

2. *Baruch Shomer Havtachaso L'Yisrael* is itself the secret of our survival. When the enemy oppresses us, we call out to God and this oppression is a motivation to repentance – and it works to our advantage. This is the essence of the cycles of events in the Book of *Shoftim* in which Israel's sinfulness is followed by a nation rising to subjugate us. This is followed by a period of oppression and servitude which drives us again to repentance. "שלא אחד בלבד עמד עלינו לכלותינו – That not just one has risen up against us to destroy us," is precisely the impetus to return to God's graces. Chazal say that Haman's ring (that is, the decree of annihilation, signed with his ring) had a more powerful effect on our repentance than the admonitions of all our prophets and prophetesses.[85]

3. There are two types of enemies of the Jews and both would like to "לכלותינו," put an end to us. One tries to kill us with "kindness" while hiding his nefarious intent. We can't quite determine his intention outright because he is good at keeping it secret. The other enemy does not hide his intentions or at least his ability to destroy the Jew. These two paradigms are represented by two colors in the narratives of Yaakov's early married life. At first he confronts Lavan who calls Yaakov his brother – הכי אחי אתה [86]– and claims good intent, but the truth is, according to the homiletic exposition of the Haggadah, "ארמי אבד אבי – an Aramean (Lavan) sought to destroy my father (Yaakov)." Lavan's name literally means "white" and this color represents his hatred because it

tries to go unnoticed. The second paradigm is that of the color red, epitomizing open hatred. Eisav, who is Edom (*Bereishis* 25:30; 36:1) which means red, does not attempt to hide his venom for Yaakov and comes to meet his brother with four hundred men. If Eisav does not intend to actually kill his brother in the end, at the very least he wants to demonstrate that he can. Both Lavan and Edom have the same intention, "לכלותינו," yet they go about it in different ways. As such, we can say that in every generation, Jews have been challenged with attempts to put an end to us, one way or another.

4. The four cups at the *Seder* correspond to the four redemptions discussed in *Shemos* 6:6–7.[87] Each cup at the *Seder* is drunk over a particular mitzvah.

- The first cup, celebrating the promise of "והוצאתי אתכם מתחת סבלת מצרים – I will free you from the labors of the Egyptians," is drunk over *kiddush hayom*, the sanctification of the holiday.

- The second cup, celebrating the promise of "והצלתי אתכם מעבדתם – I will deliver you from their bondage," is drunk over *sippur yetzias Mitzrayim*, telling the story of the redemption.

- The third cup, celebrating the promise of "וגאלתי אתכם – I will redeem you," is drunk over *birchas hamazon*, grace after the meal.

- The fourth cup, celebrating the promise of "ולקחתי אתכם לי לעם – I will take you to be My people," is drunk over *Hallel*, laudatory praise.

The second mitzvah, which is the recitation of Maggid, corresponds to "והצלתי – I will deliver you." As such, a prayer that concludes with והקב"ה מצילנו מידם, God **delivers us** from their hands, deserves to have the cup accentuated and raised.

Section to stand up to such hatred and lies and speak truth to power.

2. The repetitions of phrases in *Baruch Shomer Havtachaso L'Yisrael* is a function of history repeating itself. The nations that despised us did not change their tune of hatred when we assimilated. The price of some degree of acceptance for the Jew was a full relinquishment of any Jewish identity whatsoever. This was true during the Inquisition and it was true before and after emancipation as well. In modern times, the Jew seems to be able to embrace modernity in many parts of the world without the necessity of breaking off the yoke of Heaven. In some periods, our distinctions were considered and accentuated to our disadvantage,[66] while in others, our attempts to assimilate irked the host nation even more.[67]

3. When Lavan sought to harm Yaakov as Yaakov escaped from his home, God warned Lavan:

השמר לך פן תדבר עם יעקב מטוב עד רע:

Beware of attempting anything with Yaakov good or bad.[68]

Whatever a wicked person has in store for the righteous, even if it is considered a good action, it is nonetheless bad for the righteous. In the instance of Lavan, this refers to his request that Yaakov return with him to Haran, counter to Yaakov's intent as well as God's command.[69] Whatever the intent of our enemies, there is an underlying current of לכלותינו.

4. Throughout history, a number of revolutionary or independence movements were plagued with horrific violence committed by the ones who had just recently been freed against their former tormenters and often against innocent bystanders. Great purges followed the French and Russian revolutions and many others. The intoxication of freedom turned these people into slaves to their unquenchable lust for revenge and recompense. We raise a glass at such a time to demonstrate our control. We are free. We can imbibe the wine of liberty but we are still in control. We will raise a glass but we will not drink. The Torah puts us in control as our independence was guided and directed.

nation have stayed true to God through the exile, like the dove to its mate. It is for this reason that we are often compared to the dove. This is what has stood for us over time.

2. The defeat of Israel at the hands of our enemies is a profanation of God's holy Name. Moshe used this idea effectively in the Wilderness when advocating that God forgive B'nei Yisrael.[79] The Philistines, after capturing the holy Ark, boasted of the power of their god.[80] The Assyrians made similar statements,[81] and *Parashas Ha'azinu* addresses the same point.[82] God allows this profanation in order to avoid an even greater *chillul Hashem*, namely that we continue to thrive while acting immorally. This gives the impression that such behavior is acceptable to God, and is a *chillul Hashem*. The nations who

have tried to destroy us are only strengthened by our lack of mitzvah observance. From Bilaam to Achashveirosh, our enemies know this and try to conquer us in this manner. In the ancient world, when one nation conquered another, it was a sign that the conquering nation's god or gods defeated the vanquished nation's god or gods. To some extent, the Israelites themselves expressed similar sentiments when they wouldn't believe Yirmiyahu that God would allow His own Temple to be destroyed. Yirmiyahu informed them that in light of Israel's violation of God's word, God's Temple had become a den of iniquity.[83] A flourishing, economically successful nation like this is a great *chillul Hashem* because it lends the impression that God is satisfied with such behavior. God's abundant patience with us sometimes allowed such success to continue even as widows and orphans were being oppressed. Such was the case leading to the end of the Northern Kingdom.

In the end, nation after nation may rise to put an end to us,[84] but God always saves a remnant to carry the torch of our nationhood.

3. There is a more recent phenomenon of how we are treated in the Diaspora, which may not have as nefarious intent as the transparent behavior of Lavan and the bloody hatred of Edom, but its end is the same. The Jew did not have much opportunity for intermarriage in most of our history even if we wanted it. Throughout our long and bitter Diaspora since the Roman exile, our numbers have continued to remain stagnant or even to dwindle because of the sword of persecution or forced conversion. Since the emancipation of the Jew, the allure of assimilation and intermarriage have similarly decimated our numbers. In this way we may render עומדים עלינו לכלותינו either according to its plain meaning to destroy us, or as a *derash* "to make us a כלה, a bride," namely, to be willing to marry us.[85] Either way, the ends are the same; the next generation is practically lost to Judaism.

4. The *Seder* constantly reminds us of the redemptive salvation at God's Hands and where we would be if not for that salvation. The Psalmist connects salvation to celebration with drink by declaring:

כוס ישועות אשא ובשם ה' אקרא:

I will raise the cup of salvations and call in the Name of God.[86]

We introduce *Havdalah* every *Motzaei Shabbos* with verses of ישועה, salvation, which lead to the crescendo of these introductory verses and end with the abovementioned verse before we raise our cup reciting the blessing over wine. Wine gladdens the heart[87] and a glad heart wants to sing. The salvation we speak of in this section of Maggid is not dissimilar to the salvation experienced at the Red Sea, when Moshe and Israel spontaneously burst into poetic song, with *Az Yashir*. For this reason we tend to sing – and not just recite – *V'Hee She'Amdah* at the *Seder*, and raising the glass points to the appreciation of God's redemption.[88] It's as though we are stopping to toast and recognize God's salvation, as the verse says, "התיצבו וראו את ישועת ה' – Stand and observe the salvation of God."[89]

was personal. Otherwise we do our best to imaginatively recreate such subjugation in order to inculcate a sense of gratitude at the *Seder*.

3. There are many causes over the years that have threatened our existence. In every generation we must be aware of those causes. Jewish continuity requires a vigorous and strong educational system to draw the children into an active Jewish lifestyle. Even when we are able to overcome all the other obstacles facing us over time throughout the ages, it is all for naught if the next generation is not similarly engaged. This section of Maggid ends "והקב"ה מצילנו מידם – God saves us from **their hands**," which can also mean that our salvation will come

from the hands of the enemy itself. This was the case with Moshe, who was raised as an Egyptian. It was true in the Purim story where our salvation came from the Persian king himself, the very source of the decree to destroy us in the first place. The flip side of this is that for the next generation to feel the need to continue in the paths of our ancestors, *we* need to be engaged to assure that the tantalizing assimilation forces don't drive them away. The end of this section of Maggid acknowledges that we do so with God's help.

4. A wine glass reminds us of our distinctiveness as a people. Jewish practice forbids us to drink wine with gentiles. Originally, this was because

wine was usually used with idolatrous libations, but subsequently, the prohibition was broadened to socializing and fraternizing, as a precaution against intermarriage.[61] Our Sages say that even Haman used this law to convince Achashveirosh to exterminate us.[62] The purpose of the prohibition is not to consider ourselves superior to the population around us. It is rather to maintain our distinctions of Torah and mitzvah observance that could not possibly flourish in an atmosphere of rampant intermarriage. Moreover, our prophets bid us to improve our Diaspora environment and pray for the success of our host nation even as we maintain our distinction.[63]

The raised glass reminds us of these distinctions and how crucial they are to our survival.

MAGGID SECTION 12 – TZEI U'LEMAD

1. What is the nature of *Tzei U'Lemad*, and why is it here?
2. Why does this Maggid Section begin with the words צא ולמד?
3. Why does the Haggadah concentrate on Lavan and not on our other adversaries such as Eisav, Amalek, or Pharaoh?
4. In what way does Lavan attempt "לעקור את הכל – to uproot everything"?[7]

The cup is put down, and the matzah is uncovered.

צֵא וּלְמַד מַה בִּקֵּשׁ לָבָן הָאֲרַמִּי לַעֲשׂוֹת לְיַעֲקֹב אָבִינוּ, שֶׁפַּרְעֹה לֹא גָזַר אֶלָּא עַל הַזְּכָרִים, וְלָבָן בִּקֵּשׁ לַעֲקוֹר אֶת הַכֹּל.

Go out and learn what Lavan the Aramean wanted to do to our father Yaakov. For Pharaoh decreed only against the male children, but Lavan sought to obliterate everyone,

The Wise Son

1. This short section of Maggid introduces the main section of Maggid,[88] connecting it to *Tzei U'Lemad* (Maggid Section 11). God has saved us from so many enemies in the past, but the first one who threatened the Jewish Nation in totality

The Cynical Son

Our first experience of exile as a people actually started in *Sefer Bereishis*, well before we descended to Egypt. All but one of Yaakov's children were born in exile, and the promise of Avraham's descendants being strangers in a strange land

The Pure Son

1. This Maggid Section and the one that follows continue an essential theme of the Haggadah of מתחיל בגנות ומסיים בשבח. The entire *Seder* is replete with reminders of this theme, such as eating matzah and maror which remind us of the גנות of servitude, and dipping and reclining

The Withdrawn Son

1. The archenemy of the *Seder* is Lavan, who appears quite friendly and generous at first glance. But his true colors come through even though his name bespeaks a lack of color. White appears to be colorless, but in reality, it is a combination of *all* colors on the spectrum.

was Lavan.[89] It connects to *Mikra Bikkurim* (Maggid Section 13) by explaining how we came to be in Egypt.

2. The terminology צא ולמד, which means "go out and learn," appears often in Chazal.[90] Its use in the Haggadah, though, correlates specifically to Yaakov, Lavan, and *yetzias Mitzrayim*. At this point of the Haggadah we are beginning to realize the correlation between our Torah stories of exile and our numerous historical exiles up to the present time. The word צא fits Yaakov's departure from Lavan when God told him, "קום צא מן הארץ הזאת – Arise and **go out** from this land."[91] One would normally expect the more common "לך – go." Perhaps the Haggadah wants to stress the connection between Yaakov's departure from Lavan with יציאת מצרים.[92] In both stories the escapees left under a pretense the host misunderstood. In the case of Lavan, Yaakov left without notice and in the case of Egypt, Pharaoh thought the Israelites would return after three days.[93] In both stories Lavan and Pharaoh chase after the escapees on the third day of their escape, and in both, the escapees are overcome on the seventh day, and only God's intervention saves the day. Because of these connections, Lavan is referenced here. In order to fully understand

Lavan's intentions, we must "צא ולמד," leave his story and compare him to Pharaoh.

3. Lavan and Pharaoh share a common hatred of us. Their hatred was fabricated by stressing an imagined fear. Lavan claims that Yaakov represents an economic threat to his sons,[94] while Pharaoh fabricates a threat from a people who would take over their land.[95] Nothing was further from the truth in both cases. Yaakov was the one who brought prosperity to Lavan,[96] and when the Israelites *did* have a chance to take over the land during the plague of Darkness, they did not at all do so.[97] This would be a canard leveled at us by many others throughout history,[98] and because of Lavan's comparison to Pharaoh, he is mentioned here. The difference between the two is the relative intended level of destruction. צא ולמד teaches us to leave Lavan's story and connect him to Pharaoh to see that Lavan's intent was more devastating.

4. The Haggadah's contrast of Lavan with Pharaoh indicates that Lavan's intent went beyond Pharaoh's. *Maharal* points out that while Pharaoh killed only the males, Lavan confronted Yaakov with the intent to do harm to Yaakov's sons as well as Yaakov's daughters.[99] Had he not been thwarted by God, the Haggadah tells us, he would have destroyed the entire nation of Israel as it then existed.

came with no explicit time frame of when it would begin. It may appear that the exile God predicted to Avraham started when Yaakov arrived in Aram. Lavan's treatment of Yaakov[70] could be considered the fulfillment of "ועבדום וענו אותם – that they will enslave and oppress them,"[71] and Yaakov actually did leave "ברכוש גדול – with great possession."[72]

2. צא ולמד means to inform the reader that in order to fully appreciate the threat that Lavan represented we must depart from the simple storyline that appears in the narratives of *Sefer Bereishis*.[73] The obvious direct cause of our time in Egypt was the jealousy that Yaakov's sons

had for Yosef, their younger brother. Indirectly, Lavan was the cause of the jealousy by switching Leah and Rachel. If not for this deception, Yosef would have been the firstborn and there would have been no cause for jealousy.[74]

3. Another way of explaining this phrase is that *Arami Oved Avi* does not refer to Lavan at all. In its plain meaning, it refers either to Avraham[75] or Yaakov[76] and its meaning is, "my father was a lost Aramean." However, the Haggadah refers to the tradition that Lavan is paradigmatic of the oppressors of our people in the Diaspora.[77]

The Cynical Son – continued

4. The greatest threat to our existence from Lavan was not Lavan's nefarious plans for Yaakov and his family. God protected us from that threat.[78] A far greater threat to us was our exposure to Lavan in the first place. For example, Yaakov begins and ends *Parashas Vayeitzei* by dreaming about lofty angels. In between, he dreams about the very mundane sheep and goats and he works out a plan to level the playing field to Lavan's deceptions. Yaakov's exposure to Lavan puts him at great risk. The risk is that Yaakov may become like Lavan,[79] but God saved him and instructed him to leave before Lavan's influence could affect Yaakov to too great an extent.[80]

The Pure Son – continued

which bespeak the comforts of freedom. Earlier references to this theme take the שבח to service of God and receiving the Torah. This section of the Haggadah goes one step further to include entry into the Promised Land.

2. *V'Hee She'Amdah* details how often God has saved us from the clutches of those who would destroy us. The more one studies, the more one realizes that debt we owe God for our very survival. On the face of it, Lavan did nothing to us, but if we go out and delve into the text we will see that if not for God's intervention,[90] Lavan would have caused us great harm.[91]

3. Lavan and Pharaoh represent the oppressors of our people who hate us without cause. Yosef's contribution to Egyptian society is soon forgotten. Yaakov's contribution to Lavan is similarly forgotten. The Jew would contribute phenomenally to societies across the globe throughout history, and these paradigms of hatred would follow them wherever they would go.[92]

4. Once again, צא ולמד – by delving deeper into *Bereishis* narratives, we may answer this question as well. Before offering a sacrifice to God at Beis El, Yaakov commanded his household to remove idolatrous images from their midst.[93] While some indicate that these idols came from the recently acquired spoils of Shechem,[94] it is possible that these were remnants of gods of Lavan that were taken when they left. They may have had similar intentions as Rachel had in taking her father's *teraphim*,[95] but in the end it would have deleterious effect upon Yaakov's children and he thus commanded their removal. Had we remained in Aram much longer we may have grown משועבד, dependent, upon Aramean society, so God told us to leave that place. By leaving, we could, from a different vantage point, learn and become aware of what living with Lavan did to us. This is yet another meaning behind צא ולמד.

The Withdrawn Son – continued

Lavan's heart and mouth are never consistent. We will soon see that Pharaoh treated us the same way, "אנוס על פי הדבור – by Divine decree." The conditions of our entry into the land were quickly changed, the same way Lavan changed the conditions of Yaakov's employment. With these similarities, we can understand how the reckoning of the four-hundred-year exile ran through the lives of the Patriarchs.[64]

2. We must delve in great depth to determine the totality of Lavan's deception and destructive intent. It is the intent of the Haggadah to train the children to understand the lesson of the *Haftarah* of the *Sidra* of Lavan's treachery – *Vayeitzei*.[65] In that prophecy Hoshea refers to Lavan's double-dealing and corruption, and that Yaakov survived with the help of God. Hoshea's point is that the contemporary threat Israel experienced from

Aram will have the same end, namely salvation from God. This is precisely the message of the *Tzei U'Lemad* section of Maggid. In this vein, perhaps we can vocalize not צֵא וְלְמַד but צֵא וְלַמֵּד; teach this very point to the children at the *Seder so that they may apply the experiences of our past exiles to our current situation.*

3. We must always be concerned with the enemy who hides his true intentions behind a veil of deception and chicanery. Lavan's intentions are harder to read because he doesn't broadcast them the way Eisav does. This reverts to why this section begins צֵא וְלְמַד; we need to be vigilant in anticipating and reading these intentions. As an example, some enemies of Israel openly declare their intent to destroy us while others negotiate publicly with us as they privately plan our destruction all the same. The second paradigm resembles Lavan and is, by some measure, a more dangerous type of enemy.[66]

4. Yaakov clearly saw the threat to the future of his family as he was leaving Lavan. At some point, he felt he was better off confronting the threat of Eisav rather than continually experiencing the threat of Lavan. Yaakov's mother Rivkah assured him that when Eisav's anger would subside, she would send for him,[67] and so far, no such instruction had come. As far as Yaakov was concerned, that threat of Eisav's anger was still upon him and he therefore prepared accordingly.[68] There is another time in *Sefer Bereishis* where Yaakov consciously prefers another confrontation to a return to Lavan. When the famine caused Yaakov to seek other food sources, he chose Egypt over the much closer Aram[69] because he wanted to avoid any other confrontation with Eisav or having to return to Lavan – and even the unfamiliar terrain of Egypt was preferable to this. The verses in *Devarim* that the Haggadah is about to expound directly connect Lavan's actions with our descent to Egypt. These imply that it was a direct result of Lavan's oppression that we descended to Egypt during the famine. The *Tzei U'Lemad* section explains why Yaakov would do so.

MAGGID SECTION 13 – MIKRA BIKKURIM

The Haggadah cites a series of verses from *Sefer Devarim* (26:5–7) which are then expounded to describe the daily suffering of the Egyptian exile and slavery. The verses were recited by those who brought their first fruits to God's Sanctuary. The exposition stems from the *Midrash Halachah* to *Devarim*, known as the *Sifri*, with some slight changes.[8]

There are numerous Biblical sources that review the Egyptian experience.[9] Why does the Haggadah specifically choose these verses?

שֶׁנֶּאֱמַר, אֲרַמִּי אֹבֵד אָבִי וַיֵּרֶד מִצְרַיְמָה וַיָּגָר שָׁם בִּמְתֵי מְעָט, וַיְהִי שָׁם לְגוֹי גָּדוֹל עָצוּם וָרָב:

As it says, "An Aramean [sought to] destroy my forefather. And he went down to Egypt and sojourned there with a small number of people, and there he became a great, powerful, and numerous nation" (*Devarim* 26:5).

The Wise Son

We purposely expound these verses because of their relationship to the mitzvah of *bikkurim*, first fruits. The culmination of our redemption was entry into the Holy Land promised to our Patriarchs, where we could follow the Torah and all of God's commandments.[100] The full culmination of the process would be to have a continuation of the Divine Presence we experienced at the mountain,[101] which would be the construction of God's Sanctuary in the Land of Israel. It took 440 years from our entry into the Land until we were finally able to build the Temple in Jerusalem,[102] but in the interim the holy place stood at Gilgal, Shiloh, Nov, and Givon.[103] These verses embody the connection between our redemption and its culmination, namely the entry to the land of Israel and the mitzvos we perform there.[104]

The Pure Son

Moshe's opening words to Pharaoh were:

בני בכורי ישראל.

*My son, **My firstborn**, is Israel.[96]*

The first laws taught after we left Egypt were the laws of *kedushas bechor*, the sanctity of the firstborn. This mitzvah reflects our desire to reserve our best and first for God or for holiness. *Bikkurim* is one of several such examples[97] and demonstrates that we have successfully made the transition from slaves to become a responsible, free nation.

The Cynical Son

For so many years we had been toiling in Egypt for the sake of others. Our backbreaking work fed the Egyptians, built their towers and edifices, cleared their swamps and tilled their soil. The bringing of *bikkurim* represents our use of our resources for our purposes. *Shir HaShirim Rabbah*, which expounds the verses of *Shir HaShirim* as a relationship between God and His people, refers to our experience in Egypt metaphorically in chapter 1 verse 6.

בני אמי נחרו בי.

The sons of my mother abused and enslaved me.

Egypt is from Cham and we are from Shem – sons of the same mother.

שמוני נטרה את הכרמים.

They forced me to guard their vineyards and tend to their needs.

The Withdrawn Son

Shortly after leaving Egypt, we were charged with an elaborate project. For so long, we had been producing food we could never eat, producing services we could never use, and building structures we could never enter. Now that we left Egypt, God put us in charge of constructing a Sanctuary that would harness our considerable latent talents. That Sanctuary took thirty-nine major categories of labor which could be divided in four categories; using agriculture to prepare food, using agriculture to make clothing, using skins and leathers to prepare tents and garments, and using natural materials to prepare buildings for residence. In essence, all of man's necessary abilities for basic life needs would be wrapped up in the project of building God's Sanctuary. The reference to these verses connects us to this Sanctuary better than any other and for this reason the Haggadah continues with these expositions.

כרמי שלי לא נטרתי.

I was not able to tend to my own vineyard.

But now with our freedom we *would* be able to

tend to our land and proudly declare that freedom in the *bikkurim* ceremony. For this reason, these verses are expounded here.[81]

IN THE UPCOMING sections, we are presenting one explanation of each exposition for all the sons together.

MAGGID SECTION 13a – VA'YEIRED MITZRAIMAH

1. Why and how was Yaakov's descent to Egypt characterized as אנוס על פי הדיבור, and in what way do we derive this from the words וירד מצרימה?
2. How was Yaakov's descent to Egypt אנוס על פי הדבור?
3. In what way do the words וירד מצרימה teach that they descended in a manner characterized as אנוס על פי הדבור?

וַיֵּרֶד מִצְרַיְמָה, אָנוּס עַל פִּי הַדִּבּוּר:

And he went down to Egypt – compelled by Divine decree.

All Four Sons

13a. אנוס refers to an act that is done either against one's will or beyond one's control. The words על פי הדיבור are used by Chazal to refer to a Divine decree.[1]

Surely by the time Yaakov descended to Egypt, he would have willingly left Canaan to escape the famine and to see his son, Yosef, who would continue to provide food for the family. In reality, Yaakov may have balked at leaving for Egypt just as his father, Yitzchak, was told not to go to Egypt during a famine.[2] Instead, Yitzchak settled in Be'er Sheva,[3] where Yaakov stopped off on his way to Egypt[4] to offer sacrifices. The verse specifically refers to Yaakov offering a sacrifice to the God of Yitzchak, his father – further connecting these two events. It was in Be'er Sheva where God told Yaakov to descend to Egypt and not to fear

such a move.[5] Yaakov had cause to fear that the beginning of the exile would entail servitude and that perhaps they would all be enslaved upon arrival in Egypt.[6] God allayed these fears, and Yaakov cautiously descended to a new land.

Take note that in contrast to other paragraphs in this section of Maggid, this exposition does not say כמו שנאמר or מלמד. The fact is that אנוס על פי הדיבור is *not* derived from וירד מצרימה. In fact, the *Sifri*, which is the source of this, does not contain this exposition at all. The continuation of the verse implies that Yaakov knew what he was doing and intended to return.

That being said, many commentaries derive the אונס from the verb וירד as opposed to ויבא, ויצא, or וילך.[7] Yaakov's journey to Egypt seems to be one of free will and an exercise of his own choice due to circumstance. The words אָנוּס עַל פִּי הַדִּבּוּר, however, indicate that it was all part of a Divine plan. This can possibly fit with *Ramban*'s explanation that the Egyptian exile came as recompense for Avraham's journey to Egypt in time of famine.[8] Had Avraham remained in Israel during that famine it is likely that Yaakov would have done the same, given the fact that by the time he left he knew his source of food would continue unabated. Yaakov could have remained in Canaan, while being supported by Yosef.

MAGGID SECTION 13B – VA'YAGAR SHAM

How does וַיָּגָר שָׁם indicate that Yaakov intended to stay in Egypt temporarily?

וַיָּגָר שָׁם, מְלַמֵּד שֶׁלֹּא יָרַד יַעֲקֹב אָבִינוּ לְהִשְׁתַּקֵּעַ בְּמִצְרַיִם אֶלָּא לָגוּר שָׁם, שֶׁנֶּאֱמַר, וַיֹּאמְרוּ אֶל פַּרְעֹה לָגוּר בָּאָרֶץ בָּאנוּ, כִּי אֵין מִרְעֶה לַצֹּאן אֲשֶׁר לַעֲבָדֶיךָ, כִּי כָבֵד הָרָעָב בְּאֶרֶץ כְּנָעַן, וְעַתָּה יֵשְׁבוּ נָא עֲבָדֶיךָ בְּאֶרֶץ גֹּשֶׁן:

And sojourned there – this teaches that our father Yaakov did not go down to settle in Egypt permanently, but to (temporarily) sojourn there. Thus it says, "[Yaakov's sons] said to Pharaoh, 'We have come to sojourn in the land, for there is no pasture for your servants' sheep, because the famine is severe in the land of Canaan. So now, let your servants please dwell in the land of Goshen'" (*Bereishis* 47:4).

All Four Sons

13b. The choice of the words וַיָּגָר שָׁם as opposed to וַיֵּשֶׁב שָׁם may teach this.[9] In the proof text cited from *Bereishis*, Yaakov and his sons make it clear that they are in Egypt solely because of the famine, implying that with the end of the famine, they intend to return to Canaan. It was only with the change of circumstance that they ended up staying in Egypt. We can also see the primacy given to וַיָּגָר שָׁם in the verse by its placement right after וַיֵּרֶד מִצְרַיְמָה. Since בִּמְתֵי מְעָט describes their numbers upon arrival, the verse should have read "וַיֵּרֶד מִצְרַיְמָה בִּמְתֵי מְעָט וַיָּגָר שָׁם – They descended to Egypt few in numbers and they resided there," and not "וַיֵּרֶד מִצְרַיְמָה וַיָּגָר שָׁם בִּמְתֵי מְעָט."

By moving וַיָּגָר שָׁם up in the verse, we are told that the purpose of the descent was only for a temporary stay.[10]

בְּמְתֵי מְעָט, כְּמָה שֶׁנֶּאֱמַר, בְּשִׁבְעִים נֶפֶשׁ יָרְדוּ אֲבֹתֶיךָ מִצְרָיְמָה, וְעַתָּה שָׂמְךָ יהוה אֱלֹהֶיךָ כְּכוֹכְבֵי הַשָּׁמַיִם לָרֹב:

With a small number of people - as it says, "With seventy souls your forefathers went down to Egypt, and now Hashem your God has made you as numerous as the stars of heaven" (*Devarim* 10:22).

All Four Sons

13c. The number seventy in this context is relative. Any verse cited in *Bereishis* describing the seventy souls descending to Egypt would appear to be a *large* family. In contrast, the *Devarim* citation contrasts the number seventy with the stars of the heavens. This reference of our numbers appears in a section of *Devarim* (10:12–22) that is intent on teaching God's great might and His charge for a moral nation that would redeem and protect the weak and the stranger the same way He protected us. This section concludes with the "rags to riches" reference of going from seventy souls to numbers as great as the stars of the sky.[11]

וַיְהִי שָׁם לְגוֹי, מְלַמֵּד שֶׁהָיוּ יִשְׂרָאֵל מְצֻיָּנִים שָׁם:

And there he became a nation - this teaches that the Israelites were distinctive there.

All Four Sons

13d. Chazal tell us that the Israelites remained distinct by their clothes, their language, their names, as well as their residence. The word מצוינים is used to refer to something outstanding, as we may recall from an excellent grade where a teacher wrote מצוין across the test.[12] The *Mechilta* adds that they remained distinct by their morality.[13]

The Torah's use of גוי as opposed to עם further denotes this distinction of a nation rather than a people. This also points to their distinction.[14]

In the first reference in *Shemos* where it would appear that the Jews lost their distinction, their problems began to sprout. The verse states that

וַתִּמָּלֵא הָאָרֶץ אֹתָם,[15] the Land of Egypt became filled with the Israelites presumably even beyond Goshen. The Midrash homiletically reveals that they were even found in the theater and circuses, which at that time (interpolated from such Roman gatherings) were places of idolatry, licentiousness, and murder. Once again, our problems come off the heels of our immorality.

MAGGID SECTION 13e – GADOL V'ATZUM

Why are these two words of גדול ועצום given to exposition together?

גָּדוֹל עָצוּם, כְּמָה שֶׁנֶּאֱמַר, וּבְנֵי יִשְׂרָאֵל פָּרוּ וַיִּשְׁרְצוּ וַיִּרְבּוּ וַיַּעַצְמוּ בִּמְאֹד מְאֹד וַתִּמָּלֵא הָאָרֶץ אֹתָם:

Great, powerful – as it says, "And the Children of Israel were fruitful and proliferated and became very, very powerful, and the land became filled with them" (*Shemos* 1:7).

All Four Sons

13e. The passage וַיְהִי שָׁם לְגוֹי גָּדוֹל עָצוּם וָרָב, which translates as "there he became a great and very populous nation," uses three words at the end of the verse to describe גוי.[16] The Haggadah however, wishes to expound upon ורב on its own. As such, גדול and עצום are paired to underscore the prolific birthrates of the Israelites in Egypt. גדול refers to the sheer numbers, while עצום refers to the strength of the children even though they were born to slaves.[17] The proof text from *Shemos* that elaborates on these words actually contains the same root, which is ויעצמו. It is also possible that גדול refers to the importance of the nation in the eyes of the Egyptians. The same understanding of the word גדול can be found in a description of Moshe.[18]

MAGGID SECTION 13f – VA'RAV

1. Why is this proof text used to describe how numerous we were?
2. What is the background of these verses?
3. What is the overall message of these verses?

וָרָב, כְּמָה שֶׁנֶּאֱמַר, רְבָבָה כְּצֶמַח הַשָּׂדֶה נְתַתִּיךְ, וַתִּרְבִּי וַתִּגְדְּלִי וַתָּבֹאִי בַּעֲדִי עֲדָיִים,

And numerous – as it says, "I made you as numerous as the plants of the field; you increased and grew

שָׁדַיִם נָכֹנוּ וּשְׂעָרֵךְ צִמֵּחַ וְאַתְּ עֵרֹם וְעֶרְיָה׃
וָאֶעֱבֹר עָלַיִךְ וָאֶרְאֵךְ מִתְבּוֹסֶסֶת בְּדָמָיִךְ,
וָאֹמַר לָךְ בְּדָמַיִךְ חֲיִי, וָאֹמַר לָךְ בְּדָמַיִךְ חֲיִי׃

and you came to have great charm, beautiful of figure and your hair sprouting, but you were naked and bare" (*Yechezkel* 16:7). "I passed by you and saw you wallowing in your blood, and I said to you, 'By your blood you shall live!' I said to you, 'By your blood you shall live!'" (*Yechezkel* 16:6).

All Four Sons

13f. The word ורב is not an adjective (numerous), rather, it is a verb (increasing). As such the Haggadah uses a proof text רבבה כצמח השדה where this very root is used similarly. ורב is not simply another word for how numerous we became. The verse compares our growth to the vegetation of the fields, and this metaphor bears several messages. Just as a seed, before it sprouts, must first decompose in the ground, so too does the nation of Israel rise to the first sprouting of redemption after despair and destruction. This has been true throughout our history, and it is also why our prophets refer to our redemption and redeemer in terms of this type of rise.

Yeshayahu refers to Mashiach as a root and a branch.[19]

Yirmiyahu refers to Mashiach as a צמח צדק, a righteous growth.[20]

Yechezkel refers to two redemptive figures – Mashiach ben David and Mashiach ben Yosef – as trees.[21]

Zechariah names Mashiach "צמח" outright.[22] A צמח grows slowly but surely and describes the slow process in which Mashiach's arrival will take place.

The more one cuts and prunes vegetation, the better it grows. So too, the more Pharaoh afflicted the Jews, the more they procreated, as the verse states: "וכאשר יענו אותו כן ירבה וכן יפרץ – The more they were oppressed the more they increased and spread out."

The proof text for ורב, beginning רבבה כצמח השדה, increasing like the plants of the field, appears in *Yechezkel* 16:3–14, and describes our origins as a nation. The prophet metaphorically describes an abandoned newborn baby neither cleaned nor swaddled, but rolling in filth and blood. The baby found pity in no one's eyes and was left for dead. The baby is the Israelite nation whose birth and origins were quite inglorious. We were left for dead as a nation, bloodied and sullied by years of degradation, depravation, blood, and sweat. God Himself, however, took pity and cleaned, anointed, and clothed the baby. Yechezkel continues to describe the Israelite historical experience to his own days, but the Haggadah does not the quote narrative to that extent. As we grew and matured we should have insulated ourselves in the protective clothing of God's commandments, but we remained ערום ועריה, naked and bare. The Haggadah wishes to stress the verse ואמר לך בדמיך חיי ואמר לך בדמיך חיי, that twice assures us that we shall live in spite of, or perhaps even because of, the blood spilled.[23]

The overall message therefore is consistent with our tradition that Mashiach is born on Tishah B'Av. From the ashes of our worst destructions rise our salvations. The verse that twice mentions living through blood, is expanded by Chazal to refer to the blood of circumcision and the blood of a *korban*.[24] These commitments and others have ensured that we will continue to increase.

MAGGID SECTION 13ɢ – VA'YAREI'U

What is the significance of this proof text from ויריעו אותנו?

וַיָּרֵעוּ אֹתָנוּ הַמִּצְרִים וַיְעַנּוּנוּ, וַיִּתְּנוּ עָלֵינוּ עֲבֹדָה קָשָׁה:

וַיָּרֵעוּ אֹתָנוּ הַמִּצְרִים, כְּמָה שֶׁנֶּאֱמַר, הָבָה נִתְחַכְּמָה לוֹ פֶּן יִרְבֶּה וְהָיָה כִּי תִקְרֶאנָה מִלְחָמָה וְנוֹסַף גַּם הוּא עַל שֹׂנְאֵינוּ וְנִלְחַם בָּנוּ וְעָלָה מִן הָאָרֶץ:

The Egyptians did evil to us and afflicted us, and forced hard labor upon us (*Devarim* 26:6).

The Egyptians did evil to us – as it says, "Come, let us deal wisely with them, lest they multiply, and when there is a war they will join our enemies and fight us, and leave the land" (*Shemos* 1:10).

All Four Sons

13g. In order to answer this question, we must differentiate between the phrases וירעו לנו, which the haggadah does not say, and וירעו אותנו, which it does.[25]

וירעו לנו would mean "they perpetrated evil acts against us." While this is certainly what they did, וירעו אותנו adds a sinister dimension to what the Egyptians did. וירעו אותנו means "they made us out to be evil." In stages, they slowly made us out to be a pariah people until their own populace and even others agreed that we deserved what we were getting. This is similar to the incremental subhumanization that the Nazis (ימ״ש) perpetrated against the Jews throughout the 1930s. *Ramban* shows that in Egypt this took five stages. In the ancient world, if you were not native to your residence, you had to pay a special foreigner tax to live there. Understandably, Yosef's family was exempt from this tax as they were invited guests of Pharaoh in gratitude of all that Yosef had done to save Egypt. After some time though, when the Israelite contribution to saving Egypt was forgotten, the nefarious plan against them started to take shape, as our proof text indicates.

Pharaoh knows he can't visit his ultimate goal immediately. He must test the waters of his population and surroundings by usurping rights and privileges of the Israelites in increments, much as the Nazis did in the 1930s. At first he placed the foreigner tax upon the Israelites so that they no longer enjoyed the favored status of members of Yosef's nation. The king saw to it that no one remembered Yosef anyway.[26] The tax likely took the form of manual labor and was common in the ancient world. Our Sages point out that the Jews did not complain about this because the Egyptians convinced them in a friendly manner that paying this tax was part of their civic duty for the privilege of living in Egypt. Many Jews felt beholden to Egypt and felt more Egyptian than Hebrew. They were the ones who filled the theaters and circuses. In any event, this is perhaps alluded to in the word וירעו, which, related to רֵעַ, friend, can also mean "they befriended us." After some time, this labor took on the form of much more laborious tasks and is the subject of exposition later in our verse. The verses in *Shemos* reveal however, that from the very outset Pharaoh intended all the stages of his subjugation. Had the extent of his decree been limited to paying the special tax, this could have perhaps fulfilled our servitude requirement from the *Bris Bein HaBesarim*. Perhaps even the next stage of subjugation was needed to fully fulfill "ועבדום וענו אותם – They will **enslave and oppress** them." The point is that the verse "וישימו עליו שרי מסים למען ענותם בסבלותם – They set taskmasters over them to opress them with forced labor," indicates that it was Pharaoh's intention all along to afflict

us and as we will see, to annihilate us.

Finally, the proof text of וירעו אותנו refers to a plan of action, not the action itself. *Malbim* shows from the use of "רוח רעיון" in *Koheles* 2:22 that the root of וירעו can be connected to a thought process. As such, the Haggadah describes Pharaoh's plan for the Jews as a thought process, a meeting of minds to discuss what to do about his "Israelite problem," similar to such meetings throughout the 1930s in Europe.[27] Pharaoh, like the Germans, saw no objections to their actions from their advanced society and plowed ahead toward his nefarious goals.

MAGGID SECTION 13ʜ – VA'YE'ANUNU

See above Maggid Section 13g. This refers to the first stage of subjugation. *Ramban* refers to five such stages as follows:

1. שרי מסים – Tax masters.
2. ויעבדו מצרים את בני ישראל בפרך – Hard labor.
3. וימררו את חייהם – Embittered lives.
4. מילדות העבריות – The midwives killing the boys secretly.
5. ויאמר לכל עמו כל הבן הילוד היאורה תשליכהו – Open genocide.

Note that there are five stages of redemption in *Shemos* 6:6–8. Perhaps these correspond to these five levels of subjugation. It seems that another word was needed to undo each of these bitter levels of subjugation.[10]

וַיְעַנּוּנוּ, כְּמָה שֶׁנֶּאֱמַר, וַיָּשִׂימוּ עָלָיו שָׂרֵי מִסִּים לְמַעַן עַנֹּתוֹ בְּסִבְלֹתָם, וַיִּבֶן עָרֵי מִסְכְּנוֹת לְפַרְעֹה אֶת פִּתֹם וְאֶת רַעַמְסֵס:

And afflicted us – as it says, "And they placed taskmasters over them in order to afflict them with their burdens, and they built storage cities for Pharaoh – Pithom and Raamses" (*Shemos* 1:11).

MAGGID SECTION 13i – VA'YITNU ALEINU

This is the second stage of subjugation above. פרך describes useless, backbreaking work that is meant to oppress and dehumanize. It turns people into beasts of burden unable to enjoy the toil of their labors. The Haggadah lists ויתנו עלינו עבודה קשה and ויענונו as separate entities to be expounded upon because of Pharaoh's plan of incremental subjugation. Its ultimate purpose was to instill in the Egyptian populace an intense hatred for the Israelites, as the verse reads "ויקצו מפני בני ישראל – The Egyptians were disgusted by the Israelites."[11] After the populace had been trained for some time to despise us it would have been much easier for Pharaoh to say "לכל עמו – to his entire nation,"[12] to fill the Nile with blood of Israelite boys. Pharaoh couldn't do this without a complicit nation. The one moral and courageous Egyptian, Pharaoh's daughter, who stood up to Pharaoh's nefarious decree, saved and nurtured Moshe, and is remembered by us in a good light. We see that this hatred was also part of God's plan.[13]

וַיִּתְּנוּ עָלֵינוּ עֲבֹדָה קָשָׁה, כְּמָה שֶׁנֶּאֱמַר, וַיַּעֲבִדוּ מִצְרַיִם אֶת בְּנֵי יִשְׂרָאֵל בְּפָרֶךְ:

And forced hard labor upon us – as it is says, "And the Egyptians forced the Children of Israel to do crushing labor" (*Shemos* 1:13).

MAGGID SECTION 13j – VA'NITZAK EL HASHEM

What was the nature of the supplication to God?

וַנִּצְעַק אֶל יהוה אֱלֹהֵי אֲבֹתֵינוּ וַיִּשְׁמַע יהוה אֶת קֹלֵנוּ וַיַּרְא אֶת עָנְיֵנוּ וְאֶת עֲמָלֵנוּ וְאֶת לַחֲצֵנוּ:

And we cried out to Hashem, the God of our fathers, and Hashem heard our voice and saw our affliction, our travail, and our oppression (*Devarim* 26:7).

וַנִּצְעַק אֶל יהוה אֱלֹהֵי אֲבֹתֵינוּ, כְּמָה שֶׁנֶּאֱמַר, וַיְהִי בַיָּמִים הָרַבִּים הָהֵם וַיָּמָת מֶלֶךְ מִצְרַיִם וַיֵּאָנְחוּ בְנֵי יִשְׂרָאֵל מִן הָעֲבֹדָה וַיִּזְעָקוּ, וַתַּעַל שַׁוְעָתָם אֶל הָאֱלֹהִים מִן הָעֲבֹדָה:

And we cried out to Hashem, the God of our fathers – as it says, "It happened during those long days that the king of Egypt died, and the Children of Israel groaned because of the labor, and they cried out. And their plea from their labor ascended to God" (*Shemos* 2:23).

13j. It would appear from the proof text in *Shemos* that the Israelites were not crying out in repentance. The verse makes no reference to how their prayers were directed, only that they cried out from, or because of, their slavery.[28] This is in contrast to our verse, which directs the cries to God and makes reference to our Patriarchs. This may be a reminder that even if we had no merit at all, God would still redeem us simply because we turned to Him.

The Israelites were not accustomed to prayer. According to Chazal they were unable to pray on a regular basis.[29] The death of Pharaoh, however, gave them cause to cry out. To the Egyptian it seemed that they were mourning the loss. In reality though, they were either crying out from their affliction, or reaching out to God's mercies, and the reaction of God follows.[30]

MAGGID SECTION 13ᴋ – VA'YISHMA HASHEM

1. Was God oblivious to the pain and cries of B'nei Yisrael before this?
2. Why does the verse refer to God's covenant with Avraham, Yitzchak, and Yaakov if the covenant was made solely with Avraham (in *Bereishis* 15)?

וַיִּשְׁמַע יהוה אֶת קֹלֵנוּ, כְּמָה שֶׁנֶּאֱמַר, וַיִּשְׁמַע אֱלֹהִים אֶת נַאֲקָתָם, וַיִּזְכֹּר אֱלֹהִים אֶת בְּרִיתוֹ אֶת אַבְרָהָם אֶת יִצְחָק וְאֶת יַעֲקֹב:

And Hashem heard our voice – as it says, "And God heard their groaning, and God remembered His covenant with Avraham, with Yitzchak, and with Yaakov" (ibid. 2:24).

13k. When Yaakov descended to Egypt, God told him (*Bereishis* 46:3–4): "Fear not to go down to Egypt, for I will make you there into a great nation. I Myself will go down with you to Egypt and I Myself will bring you back." Even when it seemed otherwise, God was always with us. Chazal give several symbolisms to explain why God appeared to Moshe in a burning thornbush that could not be consumed. Among them are:

1. We cannot be destroyed, as symbolized by the fact that the bush burned but did not burn up. Our enemies will try to destroy us but they will not succeed.

2. God especially concerns Himself with the downtrodden, as is symbolized by His appearance in a lowly thornbush.

3. It was easy to enter Egypt, but leaving will involve difficulty, as is symbolized by thorns turned inward where the hand can easily be thrust in, while pulling out is painful.

4. God is in pain with us, symbolized by Him being in the midst of the fire and the thornbush.

From all these explanations and more,[31] *Rashi* chose the last one to indicate that throughout our entire time in Egypt, God, so to speak, felt our pain,[32] only it was not yet proper to act on it until the appointed time. This was determined in the covenant that God forged with Avraham, in *Bereishis* chapter 15. That covenant was renewed with Yitzchak[33] and with Yaakov,[34] so our proof text makes reference to them as well.

MAGGID SECTION 13ʟ – VA'YAR ES ANYEINU

How is a description of intimacy hinted at in the word עִנּוּי?

וַיַּרְא אֶת עָנְיֵנוּ, זוֹ פְּרִישׁוּת דֶּרֶךְ אֶרֶץ, כְּמָה שֶׁנֶּאֱמַר, וַיַּרְא אֱלֹהִים אֶת בְּנֵי יִשְׂרָאֵל וַיֵּדַע אֱלֹהִים:

And saw our affliction – this refers to the disruption of family life, as it says, "God saw the children of Israel, and God knew" (ibid. 2:25).

All Four Sons

13ʟ. The Haggadah already expounded on the word ויענונו above and therefore this word of similar root must mean something else.[35] This was an affliction that only God could see. Usually the verb וירא in the Torah is followed by the thing that is seen. In the proof text cited from *Shemos*, all God sees is B'nei Yisrael. God saw something that was antithetical to his covenant with Avraham. God promised Avraham's descendants would be great in number. But with a cessation of intimacy, this promise would never be realized.[36]

The Israelites did not want to bring more children into the world of destruction and suffering.[37]

The word עניו itself hints at such abstinence, as Chazal expound from *Bereishis* 31:50, as well as *Vayikra* 16:31.[38] In addition, the words וידע אלקים may also hint at the definition of עניו as a reference to a cessation of intimacy, as the Tanach refers to intimate relations with the expression, וידע. For reasons of modesty the Torah euphemistically refers to intimate relations with these words.[39]

MAGGID SECTION 13ᴍ – V'ES AMALEINU

How does עמלינו connect to בנים? And what is the point of adding וכל הבת תחיון?

וְאֶת עֲמָלֵנוּ, אֵלּוּ הַבָּנִים, כְּמָה שֶׁנֶּאֱמַר, כָּל הַבֵּן הַיִּלּוֹד הַיְאֹרָה תַּשְׁלִיכֻהוּ וְכָל הַבַּת תְּחַיּוּן:

And our travail – this refers to the children, as it says, "Every boy that is born you shall throw into the river, but spare all the daughters" (ibid. 1:22).

13m. Yeshayahu blesses us with the words, "לֹא יָגְעוּ לָרִיק וְלֹא יֵלְדוּ לַבֶּהָלָה – We shall not toil to no purpose nor bear offspring in vain." [40] There is no greater investment of time and energy than in bearing and raising children. To contemplate that after all the trouble of bearing and rearing children that it would all be for naught is here described as עָמָל, striving. We see the specific connection in the verse, "כִּי אָדָם לְעָמָל יוּלָּד – Man is born to toil."[41]

Pharaoh's intention in letting the girls live was not an altruistic gesture. According to *Ramban*, our experiences in Egypt mirrored Avraham's journey there. Like Avraham, we came to Egypt to survive a famine. Like Avraham, we faced danger there and the danger came specifically to Sarah.

Pharaoh's intent for the Israelite girls was for them to quickly assimilate into Egyptian culture the way Pharaoh had wanted to take Sarah. In both cases, God interceded and smote Pharaoh and the Egyptians with plagues and afflictions until Avraham and B'nei Yisrael left there with great wealth and possessions.[42] Perhaps this is why Avraham accepted Pharaoh's wealth but refused the wealth of Sodom. He may have also wanted that no one should say, "Pharaoh made me rich" the same way he didn't want anyone saying, "the King of Sodom made me rich." However, he knew that in Egypt he was setting up the future for his descendants, and accepted the wealth of Pharaoh as a harbinger of his descendants leaving with Egyptian wealth as well.

MAGGID SECTION 13N – V'ES LACHATZEINU

Why does the Haggadah introduce "דְּחַק – pressure"? The Haggadah should have moved directly to the *Shemos* verse which mentions לַחַץ itself, which we immediately mention; "וְגַם רָאִיתִי אֶת הַלַּחַץ אֲשֶׁר מִצְרַיִם לֹחֲצִים אֹתָם – I have seen how the Egyptians oppress them."[14]

וְאֶת לַחֲצֵנוּ, זוֹ הַדְּחַק, כְּמָה שֶׁנֶּאֱמַר, וְגַם רָאִיתִי אֶת הַלַּחַץ אֲשֶׁר מִצְרַיִם לֹחֲצִים אֹתָם:

And our oppression – this refers to the pressure, as it is said, "And I have also seen the pressure with which the Egyptians oppress them" (ibid. 3:9).

13n. The word לַחַץ can refer to pressure due to deprivation of basic necessities, as in "לֶחֶם צַר וּמַיִם לַחַץ – meager bread and scant water."[43] It can refer to physical confinement in a tight space, as in "וַתִּלְחַץ אֶל הַקִּיר – she squeezed (his foot) against the wall."[44] It can also refer to general oppression as in "וַיִּלְחָצוּם אוֹיְבֵיהֶם – their enemies oppressed them."[45]

By defining the לַחַץ as דְּחַק, it seems that these are all similar, in that someone feels "constricted," whether by the deprivation of basic necessities, the lack of space, or the very real dangers posed

by the enemy. The Haggadah's definition is thus related to all three definitions of the word. It would appear that the Haggadah means to stress the second and possibly third meaning. The Egyptians placed unrealistic expectations of what each Israelite could do and punished anyone who didn't meet their expectation. We in fact see דְּחַק and לַחַץ used in the same verse: "כִּי יִנָּחֵם ה' מִזַּאֲקָתָם מִפְּנֵי לֹחֲצֵיהֶם וְדֹחֲקֵיהֶם – The Lord would be moved to pity by their moaning because of those who **oppressed** and **crushed** them."[46]

MAGGID SECTION 13o – VA'YOTZIENU HASHEM

The emphasis of this description is that God acted alone in the original Pesach story on the night of the fifteenth of Nissan.

1. If so, why does the Torah speak of a מַשְׁחִית, a destroyer, killing the Egyptian firstborns (*Shemos* 12:23)?
2. How can we tell from ויוציאנו ה' ממצרים that He acted alone?
3. If the purpose of passing over the Israelite homes was to save their firstborn sons, why was it necessary for *all* homes, even ones where there were no firstborns, to have blood placed on the doorposts?

וַיּוֹצִאֵנוּ יהוה מִמִּצְרַיִם בְּיָד חֲזָקָה וּבִזְרֹעַ נְטוּיָה וּבְמֹרָא גָּדֹל וּבְאֹתוֹת וּבְמֹפְתִים:

And Hashem took us out of Egypt with a strong hand and an outstretched arm, and with great awe, and with signs, and with wonders (*Devarim* 26:8).

וַיּוֹצִאֵנוּ יהוה מִמִּצְרַיִם, לֹא עַל יְדֵי מַלְאָךְ וְלֹא עַל יְדֵי שָׂרָף וְלֹא עַל יְדֵי שָׁלִיחַ, אֶלָּא הַקָּדוֹשׁ בָּרוּךְ הוּא בִּכְבוֹדוֹ וּבְעַצְמוֹ, שֶׁנֶּאֱמַר, וְעָבַרְתִּי בְאֶרֶץ מִצְרַיִם בַּלַּיְלָה הַזֶּה, וְהִכֵּיתִי כָל בְּכוֹר בְּאֶרֶץ מִצְרַיִם מֵאָדָם וְעַד בְּהֵמָה וּבְכָל אֱלֹהֵי מִצְרַיִם אֶעֱשֶׂה שְׁפָטִים אֲנִי יהוה:

וְעָבַרְתִּי בְאֶרֶץ מִצְרַיִם בַּלַּיְלָה הַזֶּה, אֲנִי וְלֹא מַלְאָךְ: וְהִכֵּיתִי כָל בְּכוֹר בְּאֶרֶץ מִצְרַיִם, אֲנִי וְלֹא שָׂרָף: וּבְכָל אֱלֹהֵי מִצְרַיִם אֶעֱשֶׂה שְׁפָטִים, אֲנִי וְלֹא הַשָּׁלִיחַ:

אֲנִי יהוה, אֲנִי הוּא וְלֹא אַחֵר:

And Hashem took us out of Egypt – not through an angel, not through a seraph and not through an agent, but the Holy One, blessed is He, in His glory, by Himself. Thus it says, "I will pass through the land of Egypt on that night, and I will strike every firstborn in the land of Egypt from man to beast, and against all the gods of Egypt I will mete out judgments, I am Hashem" (*Shemos* 12:12). I will pass through the land of Egypt on that night – I and not an angel; and I will strike every firstborn in the land of Egypt – I and not a seraph; and against all the gods of Egypt I will mete out judgments – I and not an agent; I am Hashem – it is I, and no one else.

13o. Since the previous verse mentions God a number of times, this verse could have simply continued ויוציאנו ממצרים. The repetition of God's Name – ויוציאנו ה' ממצרים – teaches that God Himself enacted all the miracles and wonders of the events of the night of Pesach. The destroyer mentioned in *Shemos* 12:23 seems to refer to the plague itself from God.[47] It could also refer to religiously zealous Egyptians who were prevented from entering our homes to wreak vengeance on us for slaughtering their gods for our *korban Pesach*.[48] It could also refer to angels acting out God's bidding precisely.[49] It could also be that the משחית, destroyer, that God didn't allow into houses with blood on the doorpost was the general destroyer who takes people when their time comes.[50] In a nation of six hundred thousand men between the ages of twenty and sixty there are bound to be a few hundred whose time was up that night. No one died that night if there was blood on their doorpost. This

interpretation of משחית bears no connection to God's sole performance of the last Plague.[51]

There was a great cry in Egypt that night to the extent the verse says "אין בית אשר אין שם מת – There was no house where there was not someone dead."[52] But surely there could be numerous situations in which a household had no firstborn males. Why must *every* household suffer a loss? Although the Tenth Plague seems to wreak vengeance for the infanticide in the beginning of the Egyptian subjugation, which only involved boys, there are some opinions that firstborn girls were also affected by this Plague.[53] In the event that there was no firstborn at all in the household, the oldest person would be affected. This being the case, it is clear that every house needed protection.[54] Perhaps we can suggest that firstborn males were killed by God alone, as Maggid Section 13o states. Firstborn girls or other oldest members of households were killed by the destroyer.

MAGGID SECTION 13p – B'YAD CHAZAKAH

Why is the Fifth Plague, *Dever*, singled out to represent יד חזקה? Surely יד חזקה should represent *all* the plagues!

בְּיָד חֲזָקָה, זוּ הַדֶּבֶר, כְּמָה שֶׁנֶּאֱמַר, הִנֵּה יַד יהוה הוֹיָה בְּמִקְנְךָ אֲשֶׁר בַּשָּׂדֶה בַּסּוּסִים בַּחֲמֹרִים בַּגְּמַלִּים בַּבָּקָר וּבַצֹּאן, דֶּבֶר כָּבֵד מְאֹד:

With a strong hand – this refers to the pestilence, as it says, "Behold, the hand of Hashem will be upon your livestock in the field, upon the horses, the donkeys, the camels, the cattle, and the sheep, [with] a very severe pestilence" (ibid. 9:3).

13p. The דבר referred to here does not necessarily refer to the Fifth Plague, but to a pestilence that accompanied every plague.[55] Alternatively, the

mere reference to יד in the verse describing the fifth plague connects to יד חזקה.

MAGGID SECTION 13ǫ – U'VIZRO'A NETUYAH

How does "זרוע נטויה – an outstretched arm" refer to חרב, the sword, considering that the redemption from Egypt doesn't reference a sword at all? The proof text refers to Yerushalayim!

וּבִזְרֹעַ נְטוּיָה, זוּ הַחֶרֶב, כְּמָה שֶׁנֶּאֱמַר, וְחַרְבּוֹ שְׁלוּפָה בְּיָדוֹ נְטוּיָה עַל יְרוּשָׁלָיִם:

And with an outstretched arm – this refers to the sword, as it says, "His sword was drawn in his hand, stretched out over Jerusalem" (*I Divrei Hayamim* 21:16).

All Four Sons

13q. The sword here is a reference to the sword that killed the firstborn in the Tenth Plague. As such, the first half of this common term "וביד חזקה ובזרוע נטויה – With a strong hand and an outstretched arm" refers to the Fifth Plague, and the second half refers to the Tenth Plague. We see that the redemption should have come after the Fifth Plague, of *Dever*, but that the remaining plagues were added to show God's power and so that His Name would be proclaimed throughout the land; "בעבור הראותך את כחי ולמען ספר שמי בכל הארץ – In order to show you My power, and in order that My fame may resound throughout the world."[56] There are also other connections between the Plague of *Dever* and חרב, the sword. When Moshe originally confronted Pharaoh, Moshe warned that if Pharaoh refused Moshe's demands to sacrifice unto God, He would punish them with pestilence and the sword: "ונזבחה לה' אלקינו פן יפגעו בדבר או בחרב."[57] Pharaoh did indeed refuse, and *Dever* and the sword did indeed follow.[58]

There is a difference in Pharaoh's reaction to the first five plagues and the last five plagues. There is a subtle difference to describe Pharaoh's defiance.[59] The Torah's words to describe Pharaoh's defiance in the first five plagues is "ויחזק לב פרעה – Pharaoh's heart was hardened." In the second five it is "ויחזק לב פרעה – A subject (God, sometimes unmentioned) hardened Pharaoh's heart." In the first five plagues leading up to *Dever*, Pharaoh hardened his own heart. In the last five, it was as though God hardened it because by then Pharaoh became so ingrained in his defiance, it was as if his free will was revoked.

The connection of the words "חרב – sword" and "נטויה – outstretched" in the proof text is enough to draw the allusion to the sword of the Tenth Plague.

We have seen and we will again see a theme of redemption of the *Seder* connecting to entry into the Land of Israel and the building of the Temple. The verse cited here is immediately followed by King David purchasing the land where the Temple would be built.[60]

MAGGID SECTION 13ʀ – U'VEMORA GADOL

How do the words וּבְמֹרָא גָּדֹל refer to the revelation of Divine Presence?

וּבְמֹרָא גָּדֹל, זוֹ גִּילּוּי שְׁכִינָה, כְּמָה שֶׁנֶּאֱמַר, אוֹ הֲנִסָּה אֱלֹהִים לָבוֹא לָקַחַת לוֹ גוֹי מִקֶּרֶב גּוֹי בְּמַסֹּת בְּאֹתֹת וּבְמוֹפְתִים וּבְמִלְחָמָה וּבְיָד חֲזָקָה וּבִזְרוֹעַ נְטוּיָה וּבְמוֹרָאִים גְּדֹלִים כְּכֹל אֲשֶׁר עָשָׂה לָכֶם יְהוָה אֱלֹהֵיכֶם בְּמִצְרַיִם לְעֵינֶיךָ:

And with great awe – this refers to the revelation of the Divine Presence, as it says, "Or has any god ever attempted to go and take for himself a nation from the midst of another nation, with trials, signs, and wonders, with wars and with a strong hand and an outstretched arm and with great terrors, like all that Hashem your God did for you in Egypt before your eyes?" (*Devarim* 4:34).

All Four Sons

13r. The purpose of *yetzias Mitzrayim* was not simply to take the Israelites out of Egypt. As we saw above in *Avadim Hayinu* (Maggid Section 3), the Egyptian way of life had made its imprint on us to the point that God had to reveal Himself in a way that would take Egypt out of us. The only way one nation could be successfully extracted out of another would be through מוֹרָא גָּדוֹל. *Targum Onkelos* translates מוֹרָא גָּדוֹל as וּבְחֶזְוָנָא רַבָּא, as if to connect the word מוֹרָא to מַרְאֶה, "something to be seen." God appeared for all to see, in an awesome fashion. Only in this way could Israel successfully depart from the depravity of Egypt.

MAGGID SECTION 13s – U'VE'OSOS

1. Why does the Haggadah connect אוֹתוֹת to the vehicle that brought the plagues and not to the plagues themselves?
2. To which אוֹתוֹת does the *derash* refer?

וּבְאֹתוֹת, זֶה הַמַּטֶּה, כְּמָה שֶׁנֶּאֱמַר, וְאֶת הַמַּטֶּה הַזֶּה תִּקַּח בְּיָדֶךָ אֲשֶׁר תַּעֲשֶׂה בּוֹ אֶת הָאֹתֹת:

And with signs – this refers to the staff, as it says, "Take this staff in your hand, with which you shall perform the signs" (*Shemos* 4:17).

13s. The Haggadah prefers not to relate the אותות to the plagues themselves because previous references in the Midrashic exposition already made such allusions.[61]

The citation of *Shemos* 4:7 has a specific purpose. At the Burning Bush God told Moshe that the people would at first accept Moshe's mission, but that part of the plan is for Pharaoh to stubbornly refuse Moshe. At that point, Moshe considers the possibility that the people won't believe him. He feared that in the wake of Pharaoh's refusal, his people would reject him, because if God really had sent him, then Pharaoh wouldn't be able to interfere with God's plan. *Ramban* says that Moshe was justified in his complaint, and God's response was to have Moshe show certain miracles to impress the people that Pharaoh's refusal is *part* of God's plan and that he had not appeared before Pharaoh on his own.[62] In a broader sense, it refers to the signs that would follow in *Sefer Shemos*, many of which were initiated with Moshe's staff.

MAGGID SECTION 13T – U'VEMOFSIM

1. Why does the word מופתים refer specifically to the *Makah* of *Dam*?
2. What is the difference between an אות and a מופת?

וּבְמֹפְתִים, זֶה הַדָּם, כְּמָה שֶׁנֶּאֱמַר, וְנָתַתִּי מוֹפְתִים בַּשָּׁמַיִם וּבָאָרֶץ:

And with wonders – this refers to the blood, as it says, "And I shall place wonders in heaven and on earth" (*Yoel* 3:3).

It is customary to dip a finger in the second cup of wine a total of sixteen times throughout the *Seder*. (The wine is to be dabbed on a napkin and not drunk.)

The following three words are said while each participant dips their finger:

דָּם וָאֵשׁ וְתִימְרוֹת עָשָׁן:

Blood and fire and pillars of smoke (*Shemos* 4:17).

13t. God showed Moshe three miracles at the Burning Bush:

1. A stick turning to a snake and then back to a stick.
2. His hand turning leprous and then reverting to healthy flesh.
3. Water turning to blood.

Since of these three, only one was replicated in Egypt, then the plural מופתים – miracles – must refer to *Dam*. Also, the prophet Yoel uses the three words,[63] (1) "דם – blood," (2) "אש – fire," (3) "ותמרות עשן – and pillars of smoke." Once again, only blood is replicated from the Ten Plagues, hence the plural מופתים, if referring to a Plague, must be the *Makah* of *Dam*.

Although it has been shown that the Plagues were expounded earlier in *Devarim* 26:8, we shall see why the *Makah* of *Dam* is treated separately. The Plagues began as a continuum of what at first appeared as natural consequences of preceding events. The blood caused the frogs to leave the water and the frogs spread lice which bred wild animals, which brought pestilence, etc. In this scheme, only the first plague could be called a מופת, while the others are אותות.

A מופת is generally considered more wondrous than an אות. The translations of these words bear this message, as אות means a sign, while מופת means a wonder.[64] To be sure, both are meant to bear a message, albeit on different levels. For this reason, the first two miracles God showed Moshe are called אותות because they are less convincing than the third. If Pharaoh wouldn't be convinced by the first two signs, he would be influenced by a מופת, which our exposition connects to the Plague of Blood. The citation from the prophet Yoel is instructive. The verses from *Yoel* have the same purpose as the verse from *Shemos*, namely to inspire a skeptical audience to believe in and trust the mission of God. Like so many parts of the *Seder*, those few words attempt to relate our past redemption in Egypt with the future redemption in the case of all mankind.

It is worthwhile to cite the entire chapter where the citation from *Yoel* appears:

וְהָיָה אַחֲרֵי כֵן אֶשְׁפּוֹךְ אֶת רוּחִי עַל כָּל בָּשָׂר וְנִבְּאוּ בְּנֵיכֶם וּבְנוֹתֵיכֶם זִקְנֵיכֶם חֲלֹמוֹת יַחֲלֹמוּן בַּחוּרֵיכֶם חֶזְיֹנוֹת יִרְאוּ. וְגַם עַל הָעֲבָדִים וְעַל

הַשְּׁפָחוֹת בַּיָּמִים הָהֵמָּה אֶשְׁפּוֹךְ אֶת רוּחִי. וְנָתַתִּי מוֹפְתִים בַּשָּׁמַיִם וּבָאָרֶץ דָּם וָאֵשׁ וְתִימֲרוֹת עָשָׁן. הַשֶּׁמֶשׁ יֵהָפֵךְ לְחֹשֶׁךְ וְהַיָּרֵחַ לְדָם לִפְנֵי בּוֹא יוֹם ה' הַגָּדוֹל וְהַנּוֹרָא. וְהָיָה כֹּל אֲשֶׁר יִקְרָא בְּשֵׁם ה' יִמָּלֵט כִּי בְּהַר צִיּוֹן וּבִירוּשָׁלַ͏ִם תִּהְיֶה פְלֵיטָה כַּאֲשֶׁר אָמַר ה' וּבַשְּׂרִידִים אֲשֶׁר ה' קֹרֵא. כִּי הִנֵּה בַּיָּמִים הָהֵמָּה וּבָעֵת הַהִיא אֲשֶׁר אָשִׁיב אֶת שְׁבוּת יְהוּדָה וִירוּשָׁלָ͏ִם:

And it shall come to pass afterward that I will pour out My spirit upon all flesh, and your sons and daughters shall prophesy; your elders shall dream dreams, your young men shall see visions. And even upon the slaves and the maidservants in those days will I pour out My spirit. And I will perform signs in the heavens and on the earth: blood, fire, and pillars of smoke. The sun shall turn to darkness, and the moon to blood, prior to the coming of the great and awesome day of the Lord. And it shall come to pass that whoever shall call in the name of the Lord shall be delivered, for on Mount Zion and in Jerusalem there shall be a deliverance, as the Lord said, and among the survivors whom the Lord invites. For behold, in those days and in that time when I return the captivity of Judah and Jerusalem. (Yoel 3:1–4:1)

This is an expression of our hope that our original redemption from Egypt will serve as an inspiration to aspire to the future redemption.

MAGGID SECTION 14A – DAVAR ACHER

Each question has one answer for all four sons.

1. Why does the section of the Ten Plagues begin with דבר אחר?
2. How do these phrases allude to the Ten Plagues?
3. What is the purpose of the closing statement, אלו עשר מכות אשר הביא הקדוש ברוך הוא וכו'?
4. The end of this passage, על המצרים במצרים, appears superfluous. What is its purpose?

דָּבָר אַחֵר, בְּיָד חֲזָקָה שְׁתַּיִם, וּבִזְרֹעַ נְטוּיָה שְׁתַּיִם, וּבְמֹרָא גָדֹל שְׁתַּיִם, וּבְאֹתוֹת שְׁתַּיִם, וּבְמֹפְתִים שְׁתַּיִם:

Another explanation of the verse is: "With a strong hand" indicates two plagues; "with an outstretched arm" indicates two plagues; "with great terrors" indicates two plagues; "with signs" indicates two plagues; and "with wonders" indicates two plagues.

All Four Sons

1. The exposition of the last five phrases – ביד חזקה, ובזרוע נטויה, ובמורא גדול, ובאותות and במופתים – have all been referenced to specific plagues or modes of bringing them as is evident in Maggid Sections 13 o–t. These expositions are problematic for a number of reasons.

- *Dever*, the Fifth Plague, is expounded in the beginning of the verse (ביד חזקה), while *Dam*, the First Plague is expounded at the end of the verse (ובמופתים).

- The proof text for *Dam* (Yoel 3:3) is not connected to *yetzias Mitzrayim*, but to the Future Redemption.

- It would seem preferable to expound these words to refer to all Ten Plagues rather than to limit them to *Dever* and *Dam*.

Therefore, the Haggadah gives another interpretation to these phrases, דבר אחר. This interpretation indeed alludes to all Ten Plagues.

2. The second interpretation expounds the Ten Plagues from five phrases, because, in order to derive the five items of the first interpretation, namely (1) דבר – ביד החזקה, (2) חרב – ובזרוע נטויה, (3) גלוי שכינה – ובמורא גדול, (4) מטה – ובאותות, (5) דם – ובמופתים, the verse could have read "ביד נטויה ובמורא ובאות ובמופת – with an outstretched arm, and with awesomeness and with an instructive sign and punishing miracle."

All five expositions could have been derived from these words themselves. The extra word in the first three phrases and the plural form of the fourth and fifth derivation turn the five derivations to ten, hence the hint to Ten Plagues.[65] This derivation also neatly divides the Ten Plagues into five groups of two.[66]

- (1) Blood and (2) Frogs – Derived from the water.
- (3) Lice and (4) Wild animals – Derived from the earth.
- (5) Pestilence and (6) Boils – Derived from airborne infection.
- (7) Hail and (8) Locusts – Derived from high in the sky.
- (9) Darkness and (10) Death of the Firstborn – Supernatural acts from the Heavens.

3. The Ten Plagues came in a progression that could allow Pharaoh to consider that each one came on the heels of the previous one. The blood could be explained as clay falling from upstream avalanches that muddied the waters, killing all the fish and driving all the frogs out of the water. The frogs brought the lice which in turn brought wild animals which brought airborne diseases. By this time, Pharaoh's heart was so stiffened, that nothing could move him. The *Eser Makkos* section of Maggid stresses that all Ten Plagues stemmed from a preordained plan from God and was no coincidence.

4. The purpose of the Plagues was to teach the Egyptians and the Israelites the awesome power of God and that such a power will extract one nation from another to fulfill a promise to that nation. For this to be effective, citizens from other nations dwelling in Egypt, and Egyptians dwelling among other nations, did not need to be afflicted by these plagues. Therefore, the Haggadah stresses that God visited Ten Plagues on the *Egyptians* in *Egypt*.[67]

MAGGID SECTION 14B – EILU ESER MAKKOS

1. What is the point of the progression of the Ten Plagues?
2. What is the origin of the custom to dip a finger in wine for each Plague?
3. What is the purpose of Rabbi Yehudah's mnemonics?
4. The עשר מכות are usually translated as the "Ten Plagues." Why does the Haggadah use the term מכות, which literally connotes "beatings"?

אֵלוּ עֶשֶׂר מַכּוֹת שֶׁהֵבִיא הַקָּדוֹשׁ בָּרוּךְ הוּא עַל הַמִּצְרִים בְּמִצְרַיִם, וְאֵלוּ הֵן:

These are the ten plagues, which the Holy One, blessed is He, brought upon the Egyptians:

Some wine is spilled out with the mention of each of the ten plagues, as well as the Rabbi Yehuda's three-word acronym.

דָּם, צְפַרְדֵּעַ, כִּנִּים, עָרוֹב, דֶּבֶר, שְׁחִין, בָּרָד, אַרְבֶּה, חוֹשֶׁךְ, מַכַּת בְּכוֹרוֹת:

Blood, Frogs, Lice, Mixed Beasts, Pestilence, Boils, Hail, Locusts, Darkness, the Plague of the Firstborn.

רַבִּי יְהוּדָה הָיָה נוֹתֵן בָּהֶם סִמָּנִים, דְּצַ"ךְ, עַדַ"שׁ, בְּאַחַ"ב:

Rabbi Yehuda used to combine their initials into an acronym: D'TzaCh, ADaSh, Be'AChaV.

The Wise Son

1. One of the purposes of the plagues was to teach Pharaoh the utter futility of his initial response to Moshe and Aharon's request for

The Cynical Son

1. One of the outcomes of the plagues is Hashem's declaration, "ובכל אלהי מצרים אעשה שפטים – I will mete out punishments to all the gods of Egypt."[82]

The Pure Son

1. The plagues were meant to teach both Egyptians and Israelites of God's purpose and plan. Until the Egyptian redemption, God appeared as the

The Withdrawn Son

1. *Abarbanel* explains the Ten Plagues as the fulfillment of *Bereishis* 15:14, "I will execute judgment on the nation they will serve." He does

time off to celebrate before God in the desert. Pharaoh's response was:

מי ה' אשר אשמע בקולו לשלח את ישראל לא ידעתי את ה' וגם את ישראל לא אשלח:

Who is the Lord that I should heed Him and send Israel out? I do not know the Lord nor will I send out Israel.[105]

Ritva notes that in this statement, Pharaoh denied three basic tenets of our faith:

1. The belief in the existence of a Prime Cause
2. The belief that God is aware of man's deeds, and rewards or punishes man according to those deeds
3. The belief that God communicates His thoughts and intentions through His prophets and messengers

The first three plagues demonstrate God as a Primordial Cause who changes the primordial stuff of creation – water[106] – which in turn led to the second and third plagues. It is in this context that God tells Moshe to tell Pharaoh "בזאת תדע כי אני ה' – With this you shall know that I am the Lord."[107]

The second set of three plagues is meant to teach Pharaoh that a heavenly Judge rules over the land and weighs the deeds of man in reward and punishment. This is why the plague of *Arov*, for the first time, makes specific reference to the difference between the Israelites and the Egyptians,[108] as does the next plague, *Dever*.[109] Once again, this set of three plagues begins with a lesson for Pharaoh.

למען תדע כי אני ה' בקרב הארץ:

So that you should know that I, the Lord, am in the midst of the land.[110]

This realization would go one step beyond the last one. This time, Pharaoh is informed that God exerts his judgments not only from the Heavens, but to the earth as well, in the midst of man's activities and directives.

The third set of plagues demonstrate God's communication of His Will through His prophets and messengers. This set begins with an offer to the people to prevent the havoc that will be wrought upon them by bringing their livestock indoors.[111] The workings of a prophet is to extend the opportunity of salvation to God-fearing people, and that opportunity is offered here. Pharaoh does come to learn in this plague that the messengers of God are efficacious in their entreaties, as Pharaoh lowers himself to beg Moshe to pray on his behalf.[112] While it is true that Pharaoh had already asked this in the first set of plagues,[113] here Pharaoh significantly humbles himself before Moshe.[114] Pharaoh finally recognizes the prophetic standing of Moshe and Aharon.[115]

2. The sixteen dippings at this point of the *Seder* represent numerous sentiments, ranging from sorrow over loss of life, to recognition of God's involvement in *our* lives. The number sixteen is an important number as it follows the transitional number of fifteen that shows up so often at the *Seder*.[116] The number sixteen asks, "Where do we go from here?" "How has the *Seder* transformed me this night?" To be able to simultaneously render gratitude for our salvation while diminishing our joy of the loss of those from whose deadly grip we were saved, shows a profound degree of emotional control.[117] It is a celebration of life, which connects to *all* the dippings at the *Seder*. These sixteen, and two more dippings that are mentioned in the *Mah Nishtanah*, namely karpas in salt water and maror in *charoses*, total eighteen which is the numerical value (*gematria*) of the Hebrew word for "alive" – חי. Rabbi Elazar of Worms, also known as the *Rokeach*, points to the Hebrew word for plague, דבר, which appears sixteen times in the rebukements of the prophet Yirmiyahu. The sixteen dippings are meant to counter these sixteen plagues. *Rokeach* says we also counter these sixteen allusions of דבר with sixteen *aliyos* to the Torah each week,[118] as well as sixteen regular weekly offerings in the Beis Hamikdash; fourteen regular daily *tamid* offerings and the two extra Shabbos *mussaf* offerings.[119] The message is that our regular mitzvah observance can offset any plague.

3. The Talmud tells a story of the descendants of Eisav who petitioned Alexander the Great for a share in the Land of Israel, since they were also descended from Avraham. The rebuttal of the Jews was, that the promise God made to Avraham that his descendants would inherit the land of Canaan, would necessarily follow a period of slavery and subjugation. Eisav's descendants never paid that debt. In fact, in his youth, Eisav sold whatever claim he had on Yaakov. In that story, Yaakov solidified the sale of Eisav's birthright portion with a serving of lentils. The mnemonic of Rabbi Yehudah makes reference to this sale and bids us to rejoice in the purchase of the brother's birthright with lentils.

דצ"ך – Rejoice

עד"ש – Lentils

באח"ב – Of Your Brother

This was a battle against the gods of Egypt. In battle, mortal kings cut off their enemy's water supply, and then blow trumpets to instill fear. *Rashi* extends this explanation of the first two plagues. When the waters of the Nile turned to blood, the Egyptians were forced to scramble for water,[83] and the croaking of the frogs was so loud, Moshe had to scream[84] to be heard over them.[85]

Also, the Nile was a god worshipped by the Egyptians and surely its turning to blood was a demoralizing factor in the storyline. The Egyptians also worshipped a fertility goddess named Heqet who was represented in the form of a human body with the head of a frog and was worshipped by Egyptians just at the moment of birth.[86] A frog also represents the highest number in Egyptian hieroglyphics, one million. The frog in the second plague likely reminded the Egyptians of the vast numbers of Hebrews they had diminished through the workings of the midwives and Pharaoh's infanticide. The next five plagues all stress how animals were affected by the plagues. Animals were worshipped in Egypt and these plagues likely caused additional torment.[87] The Egyptians also worshipped the sun god, Ra, and it seems that Pharaoh makes a specific reference to this god. When Moshe demanded time off to serve God in the desert, Pharaoh warned that if so many people ventured under the hot sun, "ראו כי רעה נגד פניכם," which may be understood as meaning "See that that Ra is facing against you."[88] *Rashi* explains that רעה mentioned in this verse refers to a star the Egyptians worshipped; this may be understood as referring to the sun. For this reason, the next plague after Pharaoh said this was Locusts, which is described by the Torah as covering the earth in darkness.[89] The blinding thickness of the locusts was followed by a significant blow to the sun-worshipping Egyptians – three days of total darkness. The tenth plague is especially directed toward judgments against the gods of Egypt.[90] The Egyptians worshipped the ram, an adult male sheep, especially at that time of year – early spring – when Aries, the ram, was the constellation above. By slaughtering a sheep, the Israelites would be demonstrating their utter contempt of the Egyptians whom they had feared for so long. They would add bravado to their contempt by preparing the sacrifice in a way that would be most noticeable, by roasting it whole on a spit for all Egyptians to see and smell, after which they dabbed the blood of the Egyptian god on their doorposts and lintels. After all of this, the Israelites were ready to put the fear of the One and true God ahead of their former fears, especially now that the gods of Egypt had been revealed as useless.[91]

Egyptian sources seem to make reference to much of this and what follows are interesting parallels. This source is from a papyrus unearthed in 1822 near the pyramids at Saara. The Museum of Leiden in the Netherlands purchased the papyrus in 1828 and it was translated into English by Egyptologist Sir Alan Gardiner in 1909 and published as "The Admonition of an Egyptian Sage." The text is a lengthy complaint, and a litany of woes of a priest named Ipuwer, against the king.[92]

We have broken up the text of the papyrus according to the order of the *Makkos*.

Makkas Dam

Papyrus 7:4: *Behold Egypt is poured out like water. He who poured water on the ground, he has captured the strong man in misery.*[93]

Papyrus 2:6: *Blood is everywhere.*

Papyrus 2:10: *Forsooth, the river is blood.*

Makkas Dever

Papyrus 2:6: *Plague is throughout the land.*

Makkas Barad

Papyrus 2:10: *Forsooth, gates, columns, and walls are consumed with fire.*[94]

Makkas Arbeh

Papyrus 6:2–4: *Forsooth, no fruits or herbs are found. Grain has perished on every side.*[95]

Makkas Choshech

Papyrus 9:8–10: *Mirth has perished and is no longer. There is groaning throughout the land mingled with lamentations. The land is in darkness.*

Makkas Bechoros

Papyrus 2:13: *Forsooth, men are few. He who places his brother in the ground is everywhere.*

Papyrus 4:3: *Children of princes are dashed against walls. The offspring of nobility are laid out on the high ground.*

In the aftermath of these plagues, the Israelites left Egypt with great wealth,[96] they were joined by a mixed multitude of followers,[97] and were protected by a pillar of fire.[98]

Consider the following sources in this same source.

The Wealth of Egypt

Papyrus 2:4: *Forsooth, poor men have become the owners of good things. He who could not make his own sandals is now the possessor of riches.*

Papyrus 3:3: *Gold, blue stone, silver...are fastened to the necks of female slaves.*

Papyrus 8:2: *Behold, the poor of the land have become rich and the possessor of property has become one who has nothing.*

The Mixed Multitude

Papyrus 3:14: *Those who were Egyptians have become foreigners.*

Pillar of Fire

Papyrus 7:1: *Behold, the fire mounted up on high. Its burning goes forth before the enemies of the land.*

These sources capture the terror and misery experienced by the Egyptians during the plagues.

2. Our observance of Pesach, unlike any other Torah holiday,[99] involves the death and suffering of others. In order not to gloat over the downfall of our enemies, we invoke the sentiment of the Biblical verse, "בנפל אויבך אל תשמח – Do not rejoice at the fall of your enemy."[100] We shed these symbolic tears for the enemy with these dippings.[101]

3. Rabbi Yehudah made mnemonics to facilitate remembering lists. He does so regarding the *Lechem HaPanim* in the *Mishkan*.[102] It's important to know the order of the plagues because they come in groups of three for a series of reasons (see the previous section).

Rabbi Yehudah's mnemonics point to this direction of the order of the plagues. The third of each group affected the bodies of the Egyptians the most, and Pharaoh was never warned about these. This is the framework of the verse, "הן כל אלה יפעל אל פעמים שלש עם גבר – God does all these things two or three times with man."[103] [104]

The Pure Son – continued

One who makes promises and predictions for His people.[98] The plagues represent the beginning of the fulfillment of these promises.[99] Insofar as the plagues were meant to instill faith in those who witnessed them, *Maharal* connects the Ten Plagues to the Ten Utterances through which the world was created,[100] which follow here:

The First Utterance: "בראשית ברא אלוקים – In the beginning, God created." (*Bereishis* 1:1)

The Second Utterance: "יהי אור – Let there be light." (verse 3)

The Third Utterance: "יהי רקיע – Let there be a firmament." (verse 6)

The Fourth Utterance: "יקוו המים וכו' – Let the waters gather...and let the dry land appear." (verse 9)

The Fifth Utterance: "תדשא הארץ דשא – Let the earth sprout vegetation." (verse 11)

The Sixth Utterance: "יהי מאורות – Let there be luminaries." (verse 14)

The Seventh Utterance: "ישרצו המים – Let the waters teem with crawling creatures." (verse 20)

The Eighth Utterance: "תוצא הארץ נפש חיה – Let the earth bring forth living creatures." (verse 24)

The Ninth Utterance: "נעשה אדם בצלמינו – Let Us make man in Our image." (verse 26)

The Tenth Utterance: "הנה נתתי לכם את כל עשב זרע זרע וכו' לכם יהיה לאכלה – I have given to you all herbage yielding seed...it shall be yours for food." (verse 29)

Maharal connects the Ten Plagues to the Ten Utterances of Creation, but not in order. He points out that in the three chapters of *Tehillim* which refer to the plagues,[101] they are also not in order.

Makkas Dam **connects to the Tenth Utterance** – The plague of Blood deprived man and beast of their sustenance and corresponds to what encapsulates creation.

Makkas Tzefardeya **connects to the Seventh Utterance** – The frogs escaped from the water in droves as the creatures swarmed from water.

Makkas Kinnim **connects to the Fourth Utterance** – The ground was beaten to put forth lice, corresponding to the waters being gathered so that the dry land would appear.

Makkas Arov **connects to the Eighth Utterance** – The wild beasts correspond to the Earth bringing forth living creatures.

Makkas Dever **connects to the Sixth Utterance** – The pestilence was spread through airborne contact of what we breathe. *Maharal* connects this to all heavenly objects, which also affect the air we breathe.

Makkas Shechin **connects to the Ninth Utterance** – The boils, more than any other plague, caused an immediate diminution of the bodily form, corresponding to the creation of Man.

Makkas Barad **connects to the Third Utterance** – The hail stems from the firmament where the upper and lower waters were separated.

Makkas Arbeh **connects to the Fifth Utterance** – The locusts destroyed all vegetation.

Makkas Choshech **connects to the Second Utterance** – The darkness corresponds to the light of Creation.

Makkas Bechoros **connects to the Fifth Utterance** – The firstborn represents the building block of family,[102] just as "בראשית ברא אלוקים – In the beginning, God created" established the fact of Creation.

The Ten Plagues thus point to a Prime Cause and a Director, as much as the Creation of the universe itself.

2. This observance is part of an explanation extended for saying only half-*Hallel* on the last six days of Pesach. Our joy is curtailed as a result of these losses. The Talmud connects the half-*Hallel* of Pesach to the fact that while the sacrifices of Sukkos are always changing, those of Pesach remain consistent throughout the holiday.[103] Our Sages maintain that the seventy bulls of Sukkos are brought for the nations of the world,[104] and this ever-changing sacrificial order maintains a level of joy that warrants full *Hallel*. But on Pesach, we can't maintain such a level because of the loss of life that is a part of the story. The cups of wine at the *Seder* are a type of libation that is diminished on Pesach because of the loss of life.

3. The Torah says the plague of *Arbeh* was the worst of its kind up to that point and it will never again be like this.[105] Yet the prophet Yoel says that a plague of locusts in *his* day was the worst ever![106] A number of solutions to this have been suggested.

Rashi: The plague in *Shemos* was only the species of locusts called *arbeh*. The plague in *Yoel* was of many species of locusts, for, Yoel mentions species of *gazam*, *yelek*, and *chesil*, as well. While the total devastation in *Yoel* was greater, technically speaking, the plague of *Arbeh* itself was greater in Egypt.

Ibn Ezra: The plague in *Shemos* refers to Egypt. The plague in *Yoel* was in Israel.

Abarbanel: There is no contradiction at all. Yoel's four types of "locusts" aren't locusts at all. They represent four nations that will wreak havoc upon the Israelites, as no nation had done before.

Radak: *Radak* points to a problem according to *Rashi*, based on three chapters of *Tehillim* 78, 105, and 106, which contain references to the Ten Plagues. These chapters mention not only species of *arbeh*-locusts, but other types of locusts as well! This poses a powerful question of *Rashi's* explanation that the Egyptian plague was limited to species of *arbeh*-locusts alone. *Radak* answers that the account in *Sefer Tehillim* of the plagues is written in a poetic fashion and it relates the events in a poetic form that takes liberties with some descriptions and also changes the order of the plagues. Rabbi Yehudah's list informs us that his list of the plagues is the accurate one.[107]

The Withdrawn Son – continued

so by explaining each plague with a dimension of מדה כנגד מדה, measure-for-measure punishment.

Makkas Dam – The river was turned to blood because of the blood of newborn Hebrew males that was spilled when they were thrown in the river.

Makkas Tzefardeya – The frogs croaked at such a pitch that even Moshe had to scream above them in order to hear himself (*Shemos* 8:8). This recalls the bitter screams of the mothers as their sons were snatched from them and cast in the Nile.

Makkas Kinnim – The lice was beaten from the

ground in retaliation for the backbreaking toil of the Israelites who cultivated the fields for food they would not eat.

Makkas Arov – Wild beasts ran to and fro, indiscriminately wreaking havoc on anyone in their path, as recompense for all the people of Egypt who abused the Jews with all sorts of indiscriminate work.

Makkas Dever – Egyptian livestock was killed by pestilence as retribution for the neglect of the Israelites in caring for their own livestock due to grinding preoccupation with their slave labor.

Makkas Shechin – The boils that covered the entire bodies of the Egyptians prevented marital intimacy as punishment for depriving the Israelites of such.[70]

Makkas Barad – The hail came as recompense for the insults, indignities, and stones that the Egyptians rained down on the Israelites.

Makkas Barad – The locusts devoured all Egyptian produce as recompense for all the food the Israelites produced for the Egyptians while eating none for themselves.

Makkas Choshech – The darkness descended upon the Egyptians as a consequence of the despair and darkness of the slavery that was cast upon the Israelites.

Makkas Bechoros – The firstborn of the Egyptians were killed because they subjugated, enslaved, and killed the children of the Firstborn of God.[71]

2. We are at the stage of the *Seder* when we are taking full recognition of the miracles of our redemption. Pharaoh's own magicians first realized this when they could not match the plague of Lice despite having matched Moshe's miracles of blood and frogs (albeit on a much smaller scale).[72] After this realization they said, "אצבע אלוקים היא – It is the finger of God."[73] The numerical value of the Hebrew word היא is sixteen, and hints to the sixteen dips of the forefinger[74] in the wine.[75]

3. The Arizal notes that the numerical value of the ten letters in Rabbi Yehudah's mnemonic – דצ"ך עד"ש באח"ב – add up to 501. This is a hint to what Pharaoh initially said to Moshe:

מי ה' **אשר** אשמע בקולו?

Who is God that I should heed his voice?[76]

By the time he would experience the plagues, adding up to 501 – the numerical value of אשר, he *would* come to listen to Moshe. This number also connects to the next section, in which three *Tanna'im* discuss how many plagues the Egyptians experienced at the Sea in addition to what they experienced in Egypt. Rabbi Yosi says fifty, Rabbi Eliezer says two hundred, and Rabbi Akiva says two hundred and fifty totaling five hundred, one less than 501 of these letters.[77]

MAGGID SECTION 14C – RABBI YOSI HAGELILI

Each question has one answer for all four sons.

1. What is the purpose of the three lists of plagues that the Egyptians experienced? What is the point of referring to so many plagues? Are these numbers contradicted by *Avos* 5:5 which states that there were ten plagues in Egypt and ten plagues at the Sea?

2. What exactly is Rabbi Yosi HaGelili's point? We don't need any exposition to derive ten plagues in Egypt. The Torah says so. Furthermore, he ignores the original question and speaks only of what transpired at the Sea!

3. Why should the expression of אצבע of Pharaoh's magicians be used to determine the extent of the plagues? Moshe himself uses the word יד in the Plague of *Dever* and the Haggadah describes ביד חזקה as *Dever* for this very reason (See above, *Tzei U'Lemad*, Maggid Section 12). In fact, the word יד appears numerous times to describe the plagues, certainly more often than אצבע.

4. What is the essential difference between Rabbi Eliezer and Rabbi Akiva over whether to multiply the plagues by four or five?

רַבִּי יוֹסֵי הַגְּלִילִי אוֹמֵר, מִנַּיִן אַתָּה אוֹמֵר שֶׁלָּקוּ הַמִּצְרִים בְּמִצְרַיִם עֶשֶׂר מַכּוֹת וְעַל הַיָּם לָקוּ חֲמִשִּׁים מַכּוֹת. בְּמִצְרַיִם מָה הוּא אוֹמֵר, וַיֹּאמְרוּ הַחַרְטֻמִּם אֶל פַּרְעֹה אֶצְבַּע אֱלֹהִים הוּא. וְעַל הַיָּם מָה הוּא אוֹמֵר, וַיַּרְא יִשְׂרָאֵל אֶת הַיָּד הַגְּדֹלָה אֲשֶׁר עָשָׂה יְהוָה בְּמִצְרַיִם וַיִּירְאוּ הָעָם אֶת יְהוָה וַיַּאֲמִינוּ בַּיהוָה וּבְמֹשֶׁה עַבְדּוֹ: כַּמָּה לָקוּ בְּאֶצְבַּע עֶשֶׂר מַכּוֹת. אֱמֹר מֵעַתָּה, בְּמִצְרַיִם לָקוּ עֶשֶׂר מַכּוֹת וְעַל הַיָּם לָקוּ חֲמִשִּׁים מַכּוֹת:

Rabbi Yosi Haglili said: How can it be shown that the Egyptians suffered ten plagues in Egypt and then suffered fifty plagues at the sea? What does it say about [the plagues of] Egypt? "The magicians said to Pharaoh: This is the finger of God" (Shemos 8:15). But when it comes to [the plagues of] the sea it says, "Israel saw the great hand that Hashem wielded against Egypt, and the people feared Hashem, and they believed in Hashem and in His servant Moshe" (ibid. 14:31). Now, how many plagues did they suffer by God's "finger"? Ten plagues! Hence, you may infer that in Egypt they suffered ten plagues, while at the sea they suffered fifty plagues!

רַבִּי אֱלִיעֶזֶר אוֹמֵר, מִנַּיִן שֶׁכָּל מַכָּה וּמַכָּה שֶׁהֵבִיא הַקָּדוֹשׁ בָּרוּךְ הוּא עַל הַמִּצְרִים בְּמִצְרַיִם הָיְתָה שֶׁל אַרְבַּע מַכּוֹת, שֶׁנֶּאֱמַר, יְשַׁלַּח בָּם חֲרוֹן אַפּוֹ עֶבְרָה וָזַעַם וְצָרָה מִשְׁלַחַת מַלְאֲכֵי רָעִים: עֶבְרָה, אַחַת. וָזַעַם, שְׁתַּיִם. וְצָרָה, שָׁלֹשׁ. מִשְׁלַחַת מַלְאֲכֵי רָעִים, אַרְבַּע. אֱמֹר מֵעַתָּה, בְּמִצְרַיִם לָקוּ אַרְבָּעִים מַכּוֹת וְעַל הַיָּם לָקוּ מָאתַיִם מַכּוֹת:

Rabbi Eliezer said: How can it be shown that each plague that the Holy One, blessed is He, inflicted upon the Egyptians in Egypt actually consisted of four plagues? Because it says, "He sent against them the heat of His anger, wrath and fury and calamity, a delegation of agents of evil" (Tehillim 78:49): wrath – one, fury – two, calamity – three, a delegation of agents of evil – four. Hence, you may infer that in Egypt they suffered forty plagues, while at the sea they suffered two hundred plagues.

רַבִּי עֲקִיבָא אוֹמֵר, מִנַּיִן שֶׁכָּל מַכָּה וּמַכָּה שֶׁהֵבִיא הַקָּדוֹשׁ בָּרוּךְ הוּא עַל הַמִּצְרִים בְּמִצְרַיִם הָיְתָה שֶׁל חָמֵשׁ מַכּוֹת, שֶׁנֶּאֱמַר, יְשַׁלַּח בָּם חֲרוֹן אַפּוֹ עֶבְרָה וָזַעַם וְצָרָה מִשְׁלַחַת מַלְאֲכֵי רָעִים: חֲרוֹן אַפּוֹ, אַחַת. עֶבְרָה, שְׁתַּיִם. וָזַעַם, שָׁלֹשׁ. וְצָרָה, אַרְבַּע. מִשְׁלַחַת מַלְאֲכֵי רָעִים, חָמֵשׁ. אֱמֹר מֵעַתָּה, בְּמִצְרַיִם לָקוּ חֲמִשִּׁים מַכּוֹת וְעַל הַיָּם לָקוּ חֲמִשִּׁים וּמָאתַיִם מַכּוֹת:

Rabbi Akiva said: How can it be shown that each plague that the Holy One, blessed is He, inflicted upon the Egyptians in Egypt actually consisted of five plagues? Because it says, "He sent against them the heat of His anger, wrath and fury and calamity, a delegation of agents of evil": the heat of His anger - one, wrath - two, fury - three, calamity - four, a delegation of agents of evil - five. Hence, you may infer that in Egypt they suffered fifty plagues, while at the sea they suffered two hundred and fifty plagues.

All Four Sons

1. When we left Egypt, God told us that if we heed His word, then "כָּל הַמַּחֲלָה אֲשֶׁר שַׂמְתִּי בְמִצְרַיִם לֹא אָשִׂים עָלֶיךָ – Any of the diseases that I placed in Egypt, I will not bring upon you."[68] If so, it stands to reason that the more plagues that were visited upon Egypt, the fewer will be visited upon us. Therefore, these Sages use a combination of expositions to increase the number of Egyptian plagues.[69]

The Mishnah in the tenth chapter of *Maseches Pesachim*, which extends an overview of the Haggadah, makes no reference to this section. It is not mentioned in *Rambam*'s Haggadah either. It stands to reason that on a night when we remember the *korban Pesach* and the Exodus from Egypt, we find no need to jump ahead to what happened a week later at the *Yam Suf*. That being said, there may be a good reason to include the miracles of *Yam Suf* at the *Seder*. Until then we were still in the mode of runaway slaves.[70] Our faith was not fully formulated until then either, as the Haggadah points out by citing our faith

in God and Moshe at the *Yam Suf* "וַיַּאֲמִינוּ בַּה' וּבְמֹשֶׁה עַבְדּוֹ – And they believed in God and Moshe His servant."[71] The Mishnah (*Avos* 5:5) refers to ten *miracles* in Egypt and ten *miracles* at the Sea. These paragraphs refer to *plagues* upon the Egyptians at the sea. The Mishnah refers to miracles wrought for *us* at the Sea, and these are two separate things.

2. Rabbi Yosi is not asking how we know there were ten plagues in Egypt. The Haggadah had just made reference to that. Rather he is saying the following: Now that we know there were ten plagues in Egypt, how do we know there were fifty at the Sea? Proof that this is so is that he doesn't answer the original question at all and skips over to the plagues at the Sea. In addition to enhancing the Egyptian plight, which diminishes ours, these Sages connect the events of the seventh day of our redemption, to the redemption itself. It is for this reason that some commentators and *poskim* have discussed whether or not we can fulfill the daily mitzvah of *zechiras yetzias Mitzrayim* by reciting *Az Yashir*.[72]

3. The phrase "אצבע אלוקים היא – It is the finger of God" was an admission from Pharaoh's magicians that the plagues must be the workings of a powerful God on a mission. Until then they had been able to replicate the blood and the frogs, albeit on a smaller scale. The Plague of Lice was one of which the Egyptians were forced to concede the true nature of the Plagues. For this reason, it serves as a paradigm for the total number of plagues. While there are indeed numerous references to the Hand of God enacting the Plagues, Rabbi Yosi prefers the words of the Egyptians themselves. Such would be a true and full admission of God's power and plan.[73]

4. Rabbi Akiva multiplied the fifty plagues at the Sea by five, based on *Tehillim* 78:49, which says, "ישלח בם – He will send into your midst…"

1. "חרון אפו – His fierce anger."
2. "עברה – fury."
3. "וזעם – and wrath."

4. "וצרה – and trouble."
5. "משלחת מלאכי רעים – a band of emissaries of evil."

Rabbi Akiva simply cites every statement as an additional point to add to the total. Rabbi Eliezer chose to omit the reference of "חרון אפו – His fierce anger" for a few reasons. First, it is written in a different form, as a general description of God's wrath, as it appears in the possessive. The words that follow are in a different form. If "חרון אפו – His fierce anger" was to be counted in the list, then "עברה – fury" should have been preceded by a letter ו. It seems that the last four words or phrases are specific references to describe the general statement that precedes them. Rabbi Akiva's desire to add more and more plagues to the list, for the reason cited above, was enough to make him disregard these points. The key here is not the exposition of *Tehillim* words but to free Israel from future מחלות.

MAGGID SECTION 15A – *KAMAH MAALOS TOVOS/DAYEINU*

Each question has one answer for all four sons.

1. What is the point of the introduction of *Kamah Maalos Tovos* in this section of the Haggadah?
2. Why is the word מעלות, which means stages or steps, used to describe all that God did for us?
3. What does דיינו mean? If it means "it would have sufficed," would it have really sufficed for us to be taken to Mount Sinai if we had not been given the Torah?
4. What is the point of the progression of the passages of Dayeinu? How can we say that it would have sufficed if we had not been taken to Israel? Didn't God promise this to us?
5. Why does דיינו conclude with the building of the Temple? How is that related to the Haggadah?

כַּמָּה מַעֲלוֹת טוֹבוֹת לַמָּקוֹם עָלֵינוּ:

How grateful we must be to the Omnipresent for all the levels of kindness He has done for us!

אִלּוּ הוֹצִיאָנוּ מִמִּצְרַיִם וְלֹא עָשָׂה בָהֶם שְׁפָטִים, דַּיֵּנוּ.

If He had brought us out of Egypt, but not meted out judgments against them – it would have been sufficient for us!

אִלּוּ עָשָׂה בָהֶם שְׁפָטִים וְלֹא עָשָׂה בֵאלֹהֵיהֶם, דַּיֵּנוּ.

If He had meted out judgments against them, but not against their gods – it would have been sufficient for us!

אִלּוּ עָשָׂה בֵאלֹהֵיהֶם וְלֹא הָרַג אֶת בְּכוֹרֵיהֶם, דַּיֵּנוּ.

If He had done so against their gods, but not slain their firstborn – it would have been sufficient for us!

אִלּוּ הָרַג אֶת בְּכוֹרֵיהֶם וְלֹא נָתַן לָנוּ אֶת מָמוֹנָם, דַּיֵּנוּ.

If He had slain their firstborn, but not given us their money – it would have been sufficient for us!

אִלּוּ נָתַן לָנוּ אֶת מָמוֹנָם וְלֹא קָרַע לָנוּ אֶת הַיָּם, דַּיֵּנוּ.

If He had given us their money, but not split the sea for us – it would have been sufficient for us!

אִלּוּ קָרַע לָנוּ אֶת הַיָּם וְלֹא הֶעֱבִירָנוּ בְּתוֹכוֹ בֶּחָרָבָה, דַּיֵּנוּ.

If He had split the sea for us, but had not led us through it on dry land – it would have been sufficient for us!

אִלּוּ הֶעֱבִירָנוּ בְתוֹכוֹ בֶּחָרָבָה וְלֹא שִׁקַּע צָרֵינוּ בְּתוֹכוֹ, דַּיֵּנוּ.

If He had led us through on dry land, but not submerged our enemies in it – it would have been sufficient for us!

אִלּוּ שִׁקַּע צָרֵינוּ בְּתוֹכוֹ וְלֹא סִפֵּק צָרְכֵּנוּ בַּמִּדְבָּר אַרְבָּעִים שָׁנָה, דַּיֵּנוּ.

If He had submerged our enemies in it, but not supplied our needs in the desert for forty years – it would have been sufficient for us!

אִלּוּ סִפֵּק צָרְכֵּנוּ בַּמִּדְבָּר אַרְבָּעִים שָׁנָה וְלֹא הֶאֱכִילָנוּ אֶת הַמָּן, דַּיֵּנוּ.

If He had supplied our needs in the desert for forty years, but not fed us manna – it would have been sufficient for us!

אִלּוּ הֶאֱכִילָנוּ אֶת הַמָּן וְלֹא נָתַן לָנוּ אֶת הַשַּׁבָּת, דַּיֵּנוּ.

אִלּוּ נָתַן לָנוּ אֶת הַשַּׁבָּת וְלֹא קֵרְבָנוּ לִפְנֵי הַר סִינַי, דַּיֵּנוּ.

אִלּוּ קֵרְבָנוּ לִפְנֵי הַר סִינַי וְלֹא נָתַן לָנוּ אֶת הַתּוֹרָה, דַּיֵּנוּ.

אִלּוּ נָתַן לָנוּ אֶת הַתּוֹרָה וְלֹא הִכְנִיסָנוּ לְאֶרֶץ יִשְׂרָאֵל, דַּיֵּנוּ.

אִלּוּ הִכְנִיסָנוּ לְאֶרֶץ יִשְׂרָאֵל וְלֹא בָנָה לָנוּ אֶת בֵּית הַבְּחִירָה, דַּיֵּנוּ.

If He had fed us manna, but not given us the Sabbath - it would have been sufficient for us!

If He had given us the Sabbath, but not brought us before Mount Sinai - it would have been sufficient for us!

If He had brought us before Mount Sinai, but not given us the Torah - it would have been sufficient for us!

If He had given us the Torah, but not taken us into the Land of Israel - it would have been sufficient for us!

If He had taken us into the land of Israel, but not built the Temple for us - it would have been sufficient for us!

All Four Sons

1. This section of the Haggadah is a bridge. According to some commentaries, it connects to the section just before it by referring to the numerous miracles God performed for us in Egypt and at the Sea. Three Sages had just made this point (in the discussion of the *Makkos*, in Maggid Section 14b) and *Dayeinu* continues on this theme.[74] Others consider this to be a bridge to the next section of the Haggadah, which stresses the gratitude we owe God. Our salvation came in stages just as the subjugation came in stages.[75]

The Talmud teaches that we are to thank God[76] when we experience one of the following four ordeals:

1. Leaving captivity.
2. Crossing a body of water.
3. Crossing a desert.
4. Experiencing a threat to life.

Our departure from Egypt and its aftermath comprised all four of these.[77] As such the *korban Pesach* can be considered a type of *korban todah*. Both are considered *shelamim* and therefore would normally be eaten for two days. Yet the *korban todah* has the time limit of more strict sacrifices, insofar as it can only be eaten for one day.[78] The *Netziv*[79] explains that the purpose of limiting the time of eating the *korban todah* is to increase the amount of eaters who are invited to partake of the sacrifice, for the only way to fully consume it by an earlier time is by inviting more people to share in its meats and breads. Thus, the one who demonstrates his gratitude to God will have a large audience with whom to share his experiences.

This is what we are all doing at the *Seder*[80] as we add expressions of gratitude during the Maggid Section of the Haggadah. In many homes, this is an opportunity for Holocaust survivors to relate their miraculous tales of survival. It is because of this element of gratitude that we tend to sing *Dayeinu*. Many Biblical verses draw the connection between gratitude and song, such as

טוב להודות לה' ולזמר לשמך עליון:

It is good to praise the Lord to sing hymns to Your Name on most high.[81]

This is an obligation. It is *incumbent* upon us to react this way. This is why the Haggadah says:

כמה מעלות טובות המקום **עלינו.**

How many stages of benevolence did the Omnipresent grant ***us.***[82]

2. מעלות means "levels," or stages, and we touched upon this in answer 1 above. The fact that *Dayeinu* refers to fifteen מעלות seems to correlate to the fifteen Psalms that begin with the words "שיר המעלות – Song of Ascents" (*Tehillim* chapters 120–134). There were also fifteen steps leading to the Temple Courtyard at the Gates of Nikanor.[83] The number fifteen has great significance for the *Seder* night. To begin with, the festival occurs on the fifteenth of the month. Rav Shimshon Raphael Hirsch[84] correlates the relationship between God and His people regarding each holiday and the size of the moon, or the calendar date on which the holiday falls. On Pesach night, the moon is full, demonstrating God's full influence over us on that holiday. This is also true of Sukkos, which also takes place under a full moon. The protection God extended in the desert was complete and required no effort on our part. This stands in contrast to Shavuos which commemorates the giving of the Torah, at which time the moon is half full. This is because the Torah is a partnership between the Giver and the recipient as Teacher and student. All these elements are mentioned in *Dayeinu*.

The significance of the number fifteen can be seen at the start of every Haggadah as we begin the proceedings of the evening, referring to fifteen parts of the *Seder* that we cover in an orderly fashion (hence the name of the event – *Seder*).

Chazal[85] point to a microcosm of our history in a way that resembles the cycle of the moon's appearance on earth through the month. Our history begins with Avraham and resembles the new moon. The moon waxes for fifteen days, and similarly, in the fifteenth generation from Avraham the Temple is built, and this corresponds to the fifteenth מעלה of *Dayeinu*.[86] Shlomo's son, Rechavam, was already born when the Temple was built,[87] so if we count from his son Aviyah, the destruction of the Temple is, again, after fifteen generations.[88] This represents the waning of the moon from its fullness on the fifteenth until the next new moon. Our early history resembles the stages of the moon's growth and is hinted in the words, "החדש הזה לכם – This month is for you." The Midrash understands this to mean that we are like the moon, constantly waxing and waning. The number fifteen represents our peak, and the full moon at the *Seder* reminds us of this.[89]

Of course, the key element of the observance of the evening, the *korban Pesach*, requires the Temple, and that is our fifteenth stage of *Dayeinu*. Fifteen is thus a transitional number. It is meant to change us and prepare us for a new stage in life, as if we are climbing all fifteen steps leading up to the Temple Courtyard, singing another "Song of Ascents" at each stage. The fifteenth level of *Dayeinu* has us contemplating a return to Temple observance and the purity from sin that such an era will usher. (See the end of question 3, next paragraph.)

According to *Malbim*, *Maalos* are expressions of praise, as in לעלה ולקלס or ויתהדר **ויתעלה** ויתהלל from our *Kaddish* liturgy. Each of these fifteen מעלות is reason enough unto itself to praise God.[90]

3. The key to understanding the term of "*Dayeinu*" is its translation; "It would have sufficed *for us.*" The point was made immediately with הוציאנו אילו,

if God had taken **us** from Egypt. This was a point made earlier at *Avadim Hayinu* and is the essence of the rest of Maggid. We begin by remembering these seminal historical events. We are actually reliving these events, one by one. Each definitive stage of our liberation from Egypt is a complete event for us unto itself, as we experience each one in the present. Altogether they comprise a complete narrative, leading slaves to peoplehood and nationhood, united by their observance of the law, in their land. We must see these passages in this light because it would be absurd to contemplate how it would have sufficed without some of the fifteen stages of *Dayeinu*. Surely owning the wealth of Egypt would be meaningless if the Egyptians had slaughtered us at the *Yam Suf*. Surely it would be absurd to line up the entire nation at Mount Sinai and not receive the Torah! At every stage of *Dayeinu* we felt the utter fullness of that moment until we were ready to advance to another stage.

This can relate to the stages of life. At a boy's bris, his parents are enjoying the fullness of the moment, without necessarily thinking of his bar mitzvah or his *aufruf*. When a young couple marries they are not necessarily contemplating how to celebrate their twenty-fifth wedding anniversary or preparing for retirement. They are simply enjoying the experience of the moment, and we savor every stage of our liberation as a major event unto itself.

Malbim answers this basic difficulty of *Dayeinu* by explaining that each stage unto itself would require a demonstration of gratitude on our part. *Dayeinu* does *not* mean that it would have sufficed for us to receive the first miracle of each line but not the second. In some cases that would be absurd (as above). Rather, we would be required to thank God separately at every stage of these events. Yet, God added miracle upon miracle and מעלה upon מעלה until we reach the crescendo of all fifteen מעלות.

4. The points of progression of *Dayeinu* will be made by lining up each מעלה.

Dayeinu Stages 1 and 2
אילו הוציאנו ממצרים ולא עשה בהם שפטים

The main remembrance of the evening is, of course, our redemption from Egypt, but only with our firsthand experience of the judgments of God through the Plagues could we be sure that *we* were the chosen of God. Of course, we do not say *Dayeinu* for not having experienced אילו הוציאנו ממצרים. There is no story at all without that.

Dayeinu Stage 3
אילו עשה בהם שפטים ולא עשה באלהיהם

In the ancient world a nation felt that its success was a function of the strength and power of its god. Only with the judgments upon the gods of Egypt did we feel the full manifestation of God's chosenness. This explains the main observance of the *korban Pesach* the night before we left Egypt. (See Maggid Section 14b – Cynic).

Dayeinu Stage 4
אילו עשה באלהיהם ולא הרג את בכוריהם

The preoccupation of the Egyptians with the death and burial of their firstborn meant that they were distracted from the fact that we left Egypt, "בעצם היום הזה," right under their noses, and we had nothing to fear.[91]

Dayeinu Stage 5
אילו הרג את בכוריהם ולא נתן לנו את ממונם

This was in fulfillment of the promise God made to Avraham, of "ואחרי כן יצאו ברכוש גדול" – They will leave with a great possession."[92] This is why Avraham had no compunction accepting gifts from Pharaoh[93] although he refused to have anyone consider that the king of Sodom made him rich.[94] Avraham didn't mind being enriched by the king of Egypt because this would be a harbinger of the time when his descendants would leave Egypt with great wealth.[95] These last three items – the gods, firstborn, and wealth – are the things people cherish the most; their religion, their family, and their possessions.[96] All these were forfeit from the Egyptians.

Dayeinu Stage 6

אילו נתן לנו את ממונם **ולא קרע לנו את הים**

This line proves our point above regarding what *Dayeinu* means. If God had not split the Sea, we would all have been killed. How would that have sufficed? Some commentaries explain that God could have saved us in a more natural way.[97] While there have been attempts to show how a long and steady wind could split a sea like the *Yam Suf* for several hours, of course the miracle is that it happened just when we needed it to. The common terminology to describe this event is קריעת ים סוף, the **tearing** of the *Yam Suf*, based on this reference.

Dayeinu Stage 7

אילו קרע לנו את הים **ולא העבירנו בתוכו בחרבה**

While we refer to the splitting of the Yam Suf as קריעת ים סוף, the Torah uses a different root, "בקע," as in "ויבקעו המים."[98] After this, the Israelites walked on dry land, יבשה.[99] This terminology bespeaks a total separation between the water and the dry land and is the source for the Midrashim that speak of the great comfort the Israelites experienced when crossing the Sea.[100] *Kamah Maalos Tovos/Dayeinu* uses the expression בחרבה, which is found in *Tehillim* in the poetic reference "ויגער בים ויחרב – He rebuked the Yam Suf and it dried up."[101] Our feet did not become mired in the muck of the sea bed. The wind totally dried out the ground upon which we trod.[102]

Dayeinu Stage 8

אילו העבירנו בתוכו בחרבה **ולא שקע צרינו בתוכו**

Until our oppressors drowned and until we saw them utterly defeated, our salvation was not complete. This is why the term "ויושע – God saved," does not appear until after our enemies were engulfed by the waters of Yam Suf.[103] Until then we still felt like runaway slaves.[104] This too, was a component of our redemption that deserves gratitude unto itself.

Dayeinu Stage 9

אילו שקע צרינו בתוכו ולא ספק צרכינו במדבר ארבעים שנה

We would never have survived so long in the desert without sustenance. In this liturgy this sustenance comes in the form of ספק. This word captures the essence of *Dayeinu*. Our needs were supported until we had מספיק, enough. This includes food, clothing, shoes, and shelter.[105]

Dayeinu Stage 10

אילו ספק צרכינו במדבר ארבעים שנה ולא האכילנו את המן

The *mahn* is treated separately here because of the way it came to us – directly from God. He could have had us fed in some other form, and for this direct connection we are especially grateful. (This may be why we don't mention the Well from which we drank that followed us in the desert, for that did not come directly from God, as the *mahn* did). Chazal connect whatever Avraham did for the angels in *Bereishis* chapter 18 with God's care for us in the desert.[106] Avraham himself offered them bread,[107] so bread came to us directly from God.[108] Avraham, however, had water brought by someone else,[109] so our water did not come directly from God, but from a Well. Additionally, God could have had us cultivate our own food in the desert.

Dayeinu Stage 11

אילו האכילנו את המן **ולא נתן לנו את השבת**

Shabbos was commanded in the context of the collection of the *mahn*,[110] before Matan Torah, so it is singled out here. Of course, Shabbos is mentioned in *Bereishis*,[111] and according to our Sages was offered to us as a day of rest even as we were enslaved.[112]

Dayeinu Stage 12

אילו נתן לנו את השבת ולא קרבנו לפני הר סני

The experience at Sinai was first and foremost

an experience of קירבה, drawing close to God. The purpose of Shabbos observance is to feel released from mundane and material constraints and activities, in order to harness our spiritual capabilities to commit ourselves to full Torah observance. Thus, we thank Hashem for the lower level of *kirvah*, even if He would have not allowed us the more elevated level. Simply encamping at Mount Sinai, as our Sages say, "כאיש אחד בלב אחד – as one man with one heart,"[113] enhanced that spirit.

Dayeinu Stage 13

אילו קרבנו לפני הר סיני ולא נתן לנו את התורה

At the very outset of Moshe's mission, God told him that after the redemption, "תעבדון את האלוקים על ההר הזה – You shall serve God on this mountain."[114] The purpose of this connection was to transition from doing the bidding of Pharaoh to doing the bidding of God. The extra letter ן at the end of תעבדון even hints to the fact that such a service would take place fifty days after the redemption, as the extra letter has the numerical value 50.

Dayeinu Stage 14

אילו נתן לנו את התורה ולא הכניסנו לארץ ישראל

It surely would not have sufficed for us to become a nation without the Torah as much as it would not have sufficed for us to become a nation without a land. Entry into the land that God promised Avraham, Yitzchak, and Yaakov was part of God's message to Moshe at the Burning Bush.[115] Two earlier "gifts" from God appear as אילו נתן לנו את השבת, If God had **given us** the Shabbos, and אילו נתן לנו את התורה, If God had **given us** the Shabbos. The Shabbos and the Torah are our gifts in perpetuity. However, the Land of Israel is not. We must deserve it, and if we don't, it can be lost (God forbid). For this reason, the latter half of this line doesn't say ולא נתן לנו את ארץ ישראל, And He had not *given us* the Land of Israel. While all other ancient nations soon lost their identity when they lost their homeland, the Israelites survived many long bitter exiles

because of their adherence to the Torah.

Dayeinu Stage 15

אילו הכניסנו לארץ ישראל ולא בנה לנו את בית הבחירה

This expression is difficult. Surely *we* built the Sanctuaries that stood in the desert, in Gilgal, Shiloh, Nov, and Givon, as well as the holy Temple in Jerusalem. The answer is a technicality. God didn't build the Temple just as He didn't "take" us out of Egypt. That would be הוצאה ממצרים, **taking out** of Egypt. We refer to our redemption as יציאת מצרים because the phrase refers to what *we* did. We filed out of Egypt and entered the Land of Israel under God's guidance and supervision.[116] So too did we build the Temple in the same way. That being said, *Rashi* states that the Third Temple will be built by God himself![117] Alternatively, the line only speaks of the Temple in Jerusalem which was a grand improvement over the temporary Sanctuaries that stood before it. The Temple in Jerusalem was built under direct instruction from God, from *Devarim* 12:11, to *Shmuel II* 24:18–25, to *Divrei HaYamim I* 28:19.

5. The Haggadah takes us on a journey to a distant past that begins even before Avraham was chosen by God to change the face of the Ancient Near East. The vicissitudes of our history saw migrations, trials, exiles, slaveries, redemptions, conquests, successful monarchies, and crumbled kingdoms. The *Seder* is very much about the past but also fundamentally about Jewish continuity, hence the concentration on children and experiential education. Today that experience revolves around matzah, maror, *charoses*, reclining, salt water, karpas, a shank bone, wine, pillows, traditional foods, horseradish, and additional traditions every family brings to the *Seder*. We name the holiday Pesach. The most indispensable element of all this is the one we no longer have – the *korban Pesach* – because there is no Altar upon which to offer it. Surely then, it is appropriate to conclude the song of our gratitude with the hope of performing the service of the

evening in its fullness in a rebuilt Temple. We began the proceedings of the evening with the hope of being free and in Israel.[118] We begin the concluding parts of the *Seder* by repeating those aspirations by asserting "לשנה הבאה בירושלים – This coming year in Jerusalem."

MAGGID SECTION 15B – AL ACHAS KAMAH – REVIEW OF DAYEINU

Why does this paragraph repeat the fifteen praises of *Dayeinu*?

עַל אַחַת כַּמָּה וְכַמָּה טוֹבָה כְפוּלָה וּמְכֻפֶּלֶת לַמָּקוֹם עָלֵינוּ, שֶׁהוֹצִיאָנוּ מִמִּצְרַיִם, וְעָשָׂה בָהֶם שְׁפָטִים, וְעָשָׂה בֵאלֹהֵיהֶם, וְהָרַג אֶת בְּכוֹרֵיהֶם, וְנָתַן לָנוּ אֶת מָמוֹנָם, וְקָרַע לָנוּ אֶת הַיָּם, וְהֶעֱבִירָנוּ בְתוֹכוֹ בֶּחָרָבָה, וְשִׁקַּע צָרֵינוּ בְּתוֹכוֹ, וְסִפֵּק צָרְכֵּנוּ בַּמִּדְבָּר אַרְבָּעִים שָׁנָה, וְהֶאֱכִילָנוּ אֶת הַמָּן, וְנָתַן לָנוּ אֶת הַשַּׁבָּת, וְקֵרְבָנוּ לִפְנֵי הַר סִינַי, וְנָתַן לָנוּ אֶת הַתּוֹרָה, וְהִכְנִיסָנוּ לְאֶרֶץ יִשְׂרָאֵל, וּבָנָה לָנוּ אֶת בֵּית הַבְּחִירָה לְכַפֵּר עַל כָּל עֲוֹנוֹתֵינוּ:

How much more so, then, must we be grateful to the Omnipresent for the manifold, repeated beneficence that He has bestowed upon us. For He brought us out of Egypt, meted out judgments against them, did so also against their gods, slew their firstborn, gave us their money, split the sea for us, led us through it on dry land, submerged our enemies in it, supplied our needs in the desert for forty years, fed us manna, gave us the Sabbath, brought us before Mount Sinai, gave us the Torah, took us into the Land of Israel, and built the Temple for us, to atone for all our sins.

All Four Sons

There is precedence for this type of repetitive configuration between Maggid Section 15a and 15b. *Tehillim* chapters 135 and 136 are two chapters that immediately follow the fifteen chapters of שיר המעלות. We have already established the relationship between these fifteen chapters and the *Seder*, as well as the Beis Hamikdash.[119]

Tehillim 135 and 136 largely focus on the redemption from Egypt and its aftermath. We are reminded of this event time and again in our observances and commemorations. In contrast to *yetzias Mitzrayim*, which is referenced dozens of times by the prophets, *Matan Torah* is hardly mentioned at all outside of the Chumash itself.[120]

This is because *Matan Torah* is a unique experience that is not to be replicated. We have the same Torah that was revealed at Sinai and it will not ever change.[121] In contrast, the redemption from Egypt serves as a paradigm for all future redemptions and may even be eclipsed by future redemptions.[122]

The *Shelah HaKadosh* suggests that we repeat these benefits to indicate God's redemption on our behalf in this world as well as the next world.[123] This is an esoteric idea that states that every physical and material act or acquisition in this world has a counterpart in the spiritual realm of the next world. Maggid Section 15b reminds us as such to assure that we turn our physical redemption to a spiritual direction. We see that *Dayeinu* itself concludes with a spiritual direction, mentioning *Matan Torah*, the Land of Israel, and the Holy Temple. The *Shelah* maintains that even these essential Jewish principles need reminders that the physical observances of Torah and mitzvos done only in Israel and even in the Holy Temple, must be directed to a moral and spiritual consideration. We are, after all, imperfect, and this paragraph therefore concludes with a reference to atonement of sins.

By repeating the fifteen מעלות of *Dayeinu* in Maggid Section 15b, we double the number fifteen to thirty, and our Sages teach that kingship is acquired through thirty מעלות.[124] King David was thirty years old when he assumed the throne and this is the numerical value of his tribe, יהודה.[125] This element of kingship connects once again to the building of the Temple, the main objective of our next king.

MAGGID SECTION 16 – RABBAN GAMLIEL HAYAH OMER

Each question has one answer for all four sons.

1. Why does the Haggadah read Rabban Gamliel *used* to say, when the discussion of the number of *Makkos* (in Maggid Section 14b) reads Rabbi Eliezer, Rabbi Yosi HaGelili, and Rabbi Akiva *say*? Why doesn't this section of Maggid similarly begin, רבן גמליאל אומר?
2. Why do we not simply say "חייבים אנחנו לאמר שלשה דברים אלו – We are obligated to say these three things"?
3. What is so special about the mitzvos of Pesach, matzah, and maror, that requires us to be cognizant of their reasons? We don't find this requirement regarding other commandments.
4. What is the obligation that is not fulfilled if we don't say these three paragraphs?

רַבָּן גַּמְלִיאֵל הָיָה אוֹמֵר, כָּל שֶׁלֹּא אָמַר שְׁלֹשָׁה דְבָרִים אֵלּוּ בַּפֶּסַח לֹא יָצָא יְדֵי חוֹבָתוֹ, וְאֵלּוּ הֵן: פֶּסַח, מַצָּה, וּמָרוֹר:

Rabban Gamliel used to say: Whoever does not talk about [the symbolism of] the following three things on Pesach has not fulfilled his obligation – the Pesach offering, matzah, and maror.

1. Until now, the operative word for telling the story stems from the verse, "והגדת לבנך – You shall **relate** to your son, and hence our text is called the הגדה. Here a different root is used; "כל שלא אמר שלשה דברים אלו – Whoever doesn't **say** these three things." אמר is a term for a soft-spoken expression.[126] We are at the very end of Maggid and Rabban Gamliel tells us that after all this, the main part of Maggid is the recitation of these three paragraphs. The source of *Rabban Gamliel Hayah Omer* is a Mishnah in *Pesachim*.[127] Everything else in Maggid is a give and take of a leader of the Seder relating Maggid's passages to the Seder's participants. This section must be recited and understood by all. We must recite these passages even if no child asks a question. This is why our passage begins, רבן גמליאל היה אומר. He would always be sure to say this, even if not prompted at all.[128]

2. Had Rabban Gamliel simply said "חייבים אנחנו לאמר שלשה דברים אלו – We are obligated to say these three things," one might have drawn the conclusion that our obligations are fulfilled when we answer everyone's questions. This paragraph goes one step further. Even if every question is answered, and even if no questions are asked, we must recite these three passages.

3. *Tosafos*[129] explains the special nature of these three mitzvos, deriving from the Torah itself. "ואמרתם זבח פסח הוא לה' – You shall say it is a Passover sacrifice to God," is a command to explain the *korban Pesach* in words. This relates back to the soft expression of אמירה that we saw above in the words of Rabban Gamliel. Matzah and Maror, which are juxtaposed to Pesach,[130] are thus included in this directive. *Maharsha* objects

to this source. He points to the general rule that a mitzvah involving an action itself, such as eating, is sufficiently fulfilled in the action itself, and need not be accompanied by a realization of the reason for the mitzvah.[131] *Maharsha* considers this rule regarding *korban Pesach*, and by extension, matzah and maror, to be a special rule concerning the first commandments we received as a nation. These three mitzvos essentially created us as a people and therefore require special attention. A function of this is the fact that the Passover offering is the only non-sin offering that is disqualified if not brought with the proper intent.[132]

Malbim considers the source of this requirement to be the same verse that teaches the recitation of the Haggadah itself, of והגדת לבנך ביום ההוא לאמר בעבור; When we say "בעבור זה עשה ה' לי בצאתי ממצרים זה – Because of **this**," God took us out of Egypt, we refer to Pesach, matzah, and maror. This can only make sense if we explain these three and is the crescendo of what we said earlier; *Yachol MeiRosh Chodesh* (Maggid Section 8). The Haggadah rejects the proposal of telling the story of Pesach from *Rosh Chodesh* or even by day because the story must be connected to the mitzvos of the evening, namely Pesach, matzah, and maror.

4. The obligation that is not fulfilled if we don't recite these three paragraphs is not the three mitzvos they describe, but it is the essential mitzvah of *sippur yetzias Mitzrayim*. Therefore, this is the most important part of Maggid, so that if we said everything else in Maggid but not these paragraphs, we would not fulfill the mitzvah. Conversely, if we only said these paragraphs we *would* fulfill Maggid.

MAGGID SECTION 16A - PESACH

1. What does the word "Pesach" literally mean? The root of the word פסח is used as a verb in four different contexts in the Torah. The first is of course in our context and is used

When saying the words, "The Pesach offering, which our ancestors ate," one should glance at the shank bone on the Seder plate. However, the shank bone should not be raised.

פֶּסַח שֶׁהָיוּ אֲבוֹתֵינוּ אוֹכְלִים בִּזְמַן שֶׁבֵּית הַמִּקְדָּשׁ הָיָה קַיָּם, עַל שׁוּם מָה. עַל שׁוּם שֶׁפָּסַח הַקָּדוֹשׁ בָּרוּךְ הוּא עַל בָּתֵּי אֲבוֹתֵינוּ בְּמִצְרַיִם. שֶׁנֶּאֱמַר, וַאֲמַרְתֶּם זֶבַח פֶּסַח הוּא לַיהוָה אֲשֶׁר פָּסַח עַל בָּתֵּי בְנֵי יִשְׂרָאֵל בְּמִצְרַיִם בְּנָגְפּוֹ אֶת מִצְרַיִם וְאֶת בָּתֵּינוּ הִצִּיל וַיִּקֹּד הָעָם וַיִּשְׁתַּחֲווּ:

The Pesach offering, which our ancestors ate when the Temple was still standing – what does it represent? It represents the fact that the Holy One, blessed is He, passed over our ancestors' houses in Egypt, as it says, "You shall say: It is a Pesach offering to Hashem, offered because He passed over the houses of the Children of Israel in Egypt when He smote the Egyptians, and He saved our houses. And the people bowed and prostrated themselves" (*Shemos* 12:27).

The Wise Son

1. The night before we left Egypt is described as a time of חִפָּזוֹן, a time of great haste[120] and nervous excitement. One of the Biblical sources of פסח as a verb is also a function of haste:

וַתִּשָּׂאֵהוּ אֹמַנְתּוֹ וַתָּנֹס וַיְהִי בְחָפְזָהּ לָנוּס וַיִּפֹּל וַיִּפָּסֵחַ:

His nurse picked him up and fled, but as she was fleeing in haste, he fell and was lamed.[121]

The Cynical Son

1. In the days of Eliyahu HaNavi, the Israelites divided their devotion between the true God and the idolatrous worship of *Baal*. Eliyahu devised a test to determine which side indeed held the truth. In so doing he asked "עַד מָתַי אַתֶּם פֹּסְחִים עַל שְׁתֵּי הַסְּעִפִּים – How long will you keep hopping between two opinions."[105]

The Pure Son

1. *Targum Onkelos* renders the word פסח as וְיֵחוֹס, which means that God "pitied" us. The night before we left Egypt was a night of wrath and required an extra effort of pity for the Israelites to not be caught up in it. Our Sages tell us that "כֵּיוָן שֶׁנִּתְּנָה רְשׁוּת לַמַּשְׁחִית אֵינוֹ מַבְחִין בֵּין צַדִּיקִים לָרְשָׁעִים – once the destroyer has been given permission,

The Withdrawn Son

1. The prophet Yeshayahu speaks of God's salvation of His people in the future.

כְּצִפֳּרִים עָפוֹת כֵּן יָגֵן ה' צְבָאוֹת עַל יְרוּשָׁלִַם גָּנוֹן וְהִצִּיל **פָּסֹחַ** וְהִמְלִיט:

*Like the birds that fly, so will the Lord shield Jerusalem, shielding, saving, **protecting**, and rescuing.*[78]

ויפסח literally means, "He became crippled." In our context this can mean that God "stopped" at our houses to assure that the destroyer does not enter. This explains the etymological connection between the words for our holiday and the cripple.

2. The focus of this answer is not the redemption from Egypt per se, but the fact that God chose between the houses to spare and the houses not to spare. Rav Aharon Soloveitchik profoundly broadens the scope of how God saved us from Egyptian bondage in a chapter of his book, *Logic of the Heart, Logic of the Mind*.[122] The chapter is called, "Pesach: Developing Our Sense of Freedom."[123] The thesis of this chapter is that we were saved in more ways than one in the saga of our redemption from Egypt. That we were physically liberated is obvious, but we were in need also of an equally crucial freedom to spare us of the ills associated with other liberation movements in history. Many such cases have been followed by periods of chaos and bloodshed. Even loyal supporters of the French Revolution were often caught in the mass killings of Robespierre. Similar atrocities followed the Russian Bolshevik Revolution of 1917. These destructive forces, argues Rav Soloveitchik, stem from several forces and manifest themselves in four ways:

1. A reigning sense of confusion often follows a shift in power. This phenomenon recently appeared in segments of the former Soviet Union as communism crumbled, leading to reprehensible ethnic violence. The same can be said across sections of the disappointing outcome of the "Arab Spring."

2. Upon liberation, victims of persecution tend to throw off all shackles of moral law.

3. An oppressed people seeks revenge and cruelly lashes out at all and, too often, blameless and innocent bystanders are caught up in the violence against oppressors.

4. Perhaps the most destructive factor isn't the actual physical backlash, but the loss of values in the struggle, leading to a culture consumed in years of turmoil and searching for renewed identity.

The passage explaining Pesach demonstrates why the destructive elements associated with liberation movements throughout history found no expression in the Exodus from Egypt.

On the tenth of Nissan the Israelites were commanded to set aside the lamb which was to be sacrificed and eaten on the eve of their departure four days later. The Israelites were instructed to form groups of households in preparation for the anticipated event. Being busy with these preparations was meant to prevent rampant disorder and to quell chaos. Their sense of expectation was suffused with the performance of a number of mitzvos in order to prevent moral decay. Our freedom is directed to the observance of mitzvos. We were also instructed not to leave our houses in order to quell the urge or opportunity for revenge.[124] Order and decorum were guaranteed, and by slaughtering the god of the Egyptians, the male sheep, which rules on high as Aries at the time of year of our redemption, we were sure to disavow ourselves of the culture of the vanquished regime. No one would look back longingly on the Egyptians as Lot's wife looked back from Sodom. This was the time to utterly split with the Egyptians. The entire preparation of the *korban Pesach* underlies this point. We roasted the Pesach so the Egyptians could smell what we were doing to their gods. We roasted it whole so they could see what we were doing to their gods. And to fully show our break with the past, we dabbed its blood conspicuously on our doorposts for all to see. In this way we fulfilled "משכו וקחו לכם צאן – Go pick out lambs,"[125] which our Sages expound: "משכו מעבודת כוכבים והדבקו במצוה – turn aside from idolatry and cling to the mitzvah."[126]

The destroyer that God did not allow into our homes was the very destructive forces that so badly tainted other liberation movements, and this passage explains that best.

The Cynical Son – continued

The Aramaic word used by *Targum Yonasan* in translation of פסחים is פליגין, which denotes division, ambivalence, and lack of determination. Our Sages tell of a large majority of Israelites who preferred to remain in Egypt, even after all they had seen. While they do say that most of them were lost in the plague of Darkness, this connotation of פסח implies that even at this time, God divided His actions. Although the general action in Egypt was one of destruction, God divided and separated this action from Israelite homes. there was some ambivalence on God's part about who deserved to leave and who didn't.

2. This is the actual answer given to the *rasha*'s question in the Torah of מה העבודה הזאת לכם.[106] The Haggadah itself concentrates on his use of the excluding word, לכם. Some commentaries concentrate on a reference to what he sees as עבודה, or hard work, instead of meaningful and uplifting ritual.[107] However, Rav Aharon Lichtenstein[108] focuses on his word "הזאת – *this* work." The question, says Rav Aharon, does not mean to annul Divine Service, but to question its particular form. His question doesn't mean to cast off God's service altogether. His question is less extreme and therefore, perhaps more dangerous. The other three sons would never acquiesce to a full abandonment of Divine Service. What is *this* service to you is a challenge to adapt to reality as he sees it. This passage of Haggadah is an excellent response to such a claim. The parents' answer relates to the commandment of "*Pesach Doros,*" the observance of future generations. Since we currently are not offering or eating the *korban Pesach*, we refer back to the Temple times and we don't point to anything during this recitation (not even the *z'roa* on the *Seder* plate which commemorates the *korban Pesach*). The original Pesach in Egypt was quite different than that of subsequent years. They prepared the *korban* well in advance. They dipped hyssop in blood to smear on their doorposts. They sat with loins girded, shoes on their feet, and staffs in hand ready to leave in a hurry. All these obligations are absent from the Pesach of later generations.

This explanation of the Pesach effectively tells children that there is room for change when necessary in accordance with a changing reality. The commandment of the Pesach sacrifice for the generations symbolizes the change. However, we must also bear in mind the final words of the verse.

ויקד העם וישתחוו:

The people bowed low.[109]

Change is essential and the great Torah sages throughout history have applied halachah to the particular conditions of each and every generation. This must be done, however, with complete dedication to halachah and its obligations, rather than out of a desire to submit to fashionable philosophies.

There is a tendency, says Rav Aharon Lichtenstein, for parents when questioned by their children to dismiss the questions and to remain frozen and inflexible. And sometimes there is an opposite tendency to submit altogether to the spirit of the times and to children's youthful impatience, leading to a shift in the fundamental precepts of our religion for the sake of making life easier. This answer explaining the Pesach attempts to indicate a middle path to observe in every question.

he does not discern between the righteous and the wicked."[108] If not for this special pity, the Israelites might have fallen into its grip as well. For this reason they were warned: "אל תצאו איש מפתח ביתו עד בוקר – No man shall leave his house before morning."[109] *Ramban* likens this exhortation to the prohibition of those leaving Sodom from looking back as the city was being destroyed. God will only pass over in pity those who do not gloat over the destruction of others or long for what they are leaving behind.

2. The essential point of this answer is the contrast between "בנגפו את מצרים – When he smote the Egyptians" and "את בתינו הציל – And he saved our houses."[110] Pharaoh had originally rejected Moshe's mission by declaring that he knew not of any God of Israel.[111] The way the ancient pagan

viewed the relationship between a people and its deity is that a god's strength and power is a function of the success of his or her worshippers. Pharaoh would naturally reject the demands of any deity whose worshippers were lowly slaves. The plagues and the observance of *korban Pesach* were meant to teach Pharaoh that there is a single God controlling the destiny of the world, and that that God favors Israel despite their enslavement. Pharaoh cannot fathom how the God of slaves could possibly be powerful enough to challenge Egypt. An ancestor of these slaves, Yosef, convinced another Pharaoh of the ability of the weak to overpower the will of the strong as only Yosef could explain Pharaoh's inconceivable dreams of the weak devouring the strong. This was a message the second Pharaoh would learn very well with our redemption.

This usage directly connects passing over with protection. This is indeed the rendition of *Targum Yonasan ben Uziel* to the Torah, which translates ופסח as ויגן. God protected us then, and we continue to benefit from this protection, as we call the night of Pesach ליל שמורים.[79]

2. The Haggadah includes an addendum to the explanation of Pesach that is not needed to answer the essential question the passage raises. "ויקד העם וישתחו – The people bowed low"

is included because it is the end of the verse itself. *Rashi* cites that the Israelites bowed and prostrated themselves על בשורת הבנים, because of the news that they would have children who could be engaged with the stories they had experienced. The Haggadah is about continuity, about passing tradition from one generation to the next. Any child who shows up at the *Seder*, even if he at first is withdrawn to the point of not asking questions, still gives his parents *nachas* and a reason to be thankful.

MAGGID SECTION 16B – MATZAH

1. How does Rabban Gamliel consider his answer to מצה זו שאנו אוכלים על שום מה as the reason for eating matzah, when the command to do so preceded the Exodus by two weeks?

2. Why does the Pesach passage refer to God as הקדוש ברוך הוא, and the Matzah passage refers to Him as מלך מלכי המלכים הקדוש ברוך הוא?

מַצָה זוּ שֶׁאָנוּ אוֹכְלִים עַל שׁוּם מָה. עַל שׁוּם שֶׁלֹּא הִסְפִּיק בְּצֵקָם שֶׁל אֲבוֹתֵינוּ לְהַחֲמִיץ, עַד שֶׁנִּגְלָה עֲלֵיהֶם מֶלֶךְ מַלְכֵי הַמְּלָכִים הַקָּדוֹשׁ בָּרוּךְ הוּא וּגְאָלָם, שֶׁנֶּאֱמַר, וַיֹּאפוּ אֶת הַבָּצֵק אֲשֶׁר הוֹצִיאוּ מִמִּצְרַיִם עֻגֹת מַצּוֹת כִּי לֹא חָמֵץ, כִּי גֹרְשׁוּ מִמִּצְרַיִם וְלֹא יָכְלוּ לְהִתְמַהְמֵהַּ וְגַם צֵדָה לֹא עָשׂוּ לָהֶם:

This matzah that we eat – what does it represent? It represents the fact that the dough of our ancestors did not have a chance to become leavened before the King of the kings of kings, the Holy One, blessed is He, appeared to them and redeemed them, as it says, "And they baked the dough that they had brought out of Egypt into unleavened cakes, for it had not become leavened; for they were driven out of Egypt and were unable to delay, nor had they prepared any food for themselves" (Shemos 12:39).

The Wise Son

1. *Abarbanel* points to two separate observances of matzah to capture two separate reasons for eating matzah in the Torah, once together with the *korban Pesach* and maror,[127] and once to be eaten alone. The first observance of matzah is a reminder of bitter enslavement while the second is to recall deliverance. *Abarbanel* explains this dichotomy as follows: The matzah the Jews were commanded to eat at the very first *Seder*,[128] which took place even before they left Egypt, was to symbolize the affliction of slavery. Surely they

The Cynical Son

1. The idea that we would leave in haste is essential to the Pesach narrative. We would not stay in this place one moment more than necessary. The haste is symbolized by the bread product we eat and the chametz we don't eat during this festival. *Ibn Ezra* points out that matzah was actually the bread product we ate during the years of slavery. This is because, given a limited supply of flour and other ingredients, it would make the most sense for slaves to bake a product that does not need other ingredients

The Pure Son

1. The haste of the liberation speaks to the praise of Israel. It stresses our full and total dependence upon God's providence and care. For this reason, the Torah refers to the holiday as חג המצות. The term פסח as used in the Torah usually refers to the *korban*, or the period of time from the fourteenth of Nissan until the morning of the fifteenth when the *korban Pesach* is prepared, offered, and eaten. This name refers to what God did and is a name that stresses His praises. Rav Leivi Yitzchak of Berditchov explains this as a function of a verse

The Withdrawn Son

1. It's all about the rush. We didn't have to be in a rush. We had two weeks to prepare for the redemption. Nonetheless, the rush was crucial to our redemptive process and matzah is the food of rushing. This rush is similar to that of Lot leaving Sodom.[80] There could be no room for longing for anything left behind. As it is, some Israelites did agitate for the good times in Egypt,[81] and Moshe's reaction to this trespass appears to be his most drastic in the entire Torah.[82] That being said, matzah is the food for people in a rush

The Wise Son – continued

could have been instructed in advance to prepare bread with time to rise. They had two weeks to prepare for this. But this would not have symbolized slavery. The matzah of subsequent years, says *Abarbanel*, would symbolize the haste of our liberation, and is therefore prepared in the same way.

2. Pesach represents our rejection of the gods of Egypt while matzah represents our acknowledgement of God. We could only acknowledge God after rejection of our past, and eating the *korban Pesach* together with matzah reminds us of the Holy One, Blessed be He. But the matzah takes us one step further – to a recognition of the King Who is King of Kings.

The Cynical Son – continued

besides the basic minimum of flour and water. Such a product would remain in the digestive system longer and thus satisfy for a longer period of time. This fits with the earlier liturgy of הא לחמא עניא די אכלו אבהתנא בארעא דמצרים. We didn't just eat matzah the night before and in the aftermath of our redemption. We ate it **in** Egypt as well. There is another point to eating matzah in comemoration of our redemption from Egypt. That country is considered the first to introduce yeast for bread. Chametz products are therefore associated with ancient Egypt, and what better way to turn our backs on our experience in Egypt than to refrain from what yeast produces, and to

eat a bread product baked without it.

2. The source of the reference to God as מלך מלכי המלכים is the Book of *Daniel* 2:37. Daniel refers to Nevuchadnetzar as a king who is "king of kings." Our passage has the first reference to מלך as the King of the one who would be called king of kings.[110] The eating of the *korban Pesach* is a natural rejection of the gods of Egypt as explained above. Therefore, הקדוש ברוך הוא suffices as a reference to God. The eating of the matzah is a reminder of what we ate in Egypt or the haste in which we left, so the reference to God needs to be more emphatic.

The Pure Son – continued

in the *Megillah* we read on Pesach, *Shir HaShirim*. The verse is "אני לדודי ודודי לי – I am for my beloved and my beloved for me." The lovestruck man and woman in the *Megillah* symbolizes the love of God and His people. He demonstrates His love for us by referring to the holiday as חג המצות, as above, and we demonstrate our love for God by referring to the holiday as חג הפסח. We stress what God did and the Torah stresses what *we* did.

2. The preparation, slaughtering, and eating of the *korban Pesach* involved considerable sacrifice on the parts of the Israelites. At the time of the fourth plague, of *Arov*, Pharaoh suggested that the Israelites serve their God, but, instead of a three-day journey in the desert, to perform the service not far from Egypt. To this Moshe rejoined:

הן נזבח את תועבת מצרים לעיניהם ולא יסקלונו:

Were we to sacrifice what is detestable to the Egyptians before their eyes, would they not stone us?[112]

Evidently this fear dissipated over time to the point where the Israelites offered the *korban Pesach* right under the noses of the Egyptians. This audacity was a necessary component of our redemption and involved a great commitment. It may be that the eating of matzah involved an even greater commitment, as the passage ends "וגם צדה לא עשו להם – They made no provisions for themselves."[113] According to *Rashi* this is what Yirmiyahu had in mind when he introduces his first prophecy for the nation; remembering better days between God and His people.

זכרתי לך חסד נעוריך אהבת כלולתיך לכתך אחרי במדבר בארץ לא זרועה:

I remember the devotion of your youth, your love as a bride. How you followed Me in the wilderness in a land not sown.[114]

Our personal sacrifice in offering the *korban Pesach* drew us closer to הקדוש ברוך הוא, but our willingness to follow Him blindly into the desert demonstrated our subordination to מלך מלכי המלכים as well.

in two other places as well. Avraham feeds his guests in a relaxed and laid-back manner so he serves them עוגות, cakes. Lot, on the other hand, is pressed for time and must move quickly so he serves *matzos*.[83] Also, the necromancer serves *matzos* to the very rushed King Shaul after she was asked to to revive Shmuel for him.[84]

Although our first redemption came about in haste to symbolize our utter rejection of everything Egyptian, our future redemption, says the prophet Yeshayahu, will not have this consideration. By that time, we will have the resources to already be removed from the likes of the impurity of Egypt. His prophecy reads "כי לא בחפזון תצאו ובמנוסה לא תלכון – You will not depart in haste, nor will you leave in flight."[85]

2. The festival of Pesach, in the Torah's use of the term, lasts less than one day. It starts at midday of the fourteenth of Nissan and concludes the next morning. When we finished eating the *korban Pesach*, we were ready to leave Egypt. The Festival of Matzos continues for seven days because the acknowledgement of God as the undisputed Master of our destiny came only after seven days. Until the seventh day, we felt like runaway slaves.[86] On Rosh Hashanah we say a prayer at a body of water to symbolize the continuity of the kingdom and kingship of God.[87] This service is called *Tashlich* and, in concert with this reason for *Tashlich*, the true and absolute crowning of God as our King came also at a body of water; at *Krias Yam Suf*, seven days after we left Egypt. These seven days connect to our eating *matzos* and hence חג המצות, and therefore, the paragraph explaining *matzos* refers to God as מלך מלכי המלכים. It took one day to acknowledge הקדוש ברוך הוא – the day of the eating of *korban Pesach*. But it took seven days, the days of eating matzah, to acknowledge מלך מלכי המלכים.

MAGGID SECTION 16C – MAROR

1. What is the full extent of the reason for eating maror?
2. At this point of the *Seder* why are we stressing the bitterness of slavery? Haven't we already fulfilled our obligation of מתחיל בגנות?

The maror is raised and shown to the participants.

מָרוֹר זֶה שֶׁאָנוּ אוֹכְלִים עַל שׁוּם מָה. עַל שׁוּם שֶׁמֵּרְרוּ הַמִּצְרִים אֶת חַיֵּי אֲבוֹתֵינוּ

This maror that we eat – what does it represent? It represents the fact that the Egyptians embittered the lives of our ancestors

בְּמִצְרַיִם, שֶׁנֶּאֱמַר, וַיְמָרְרוּ אֶת חַיֵּיהֶם בַּעֲבֹדָה קָשָׁה בְּחֹמֶר וּבִלְבֵנִים וּבְכָל עֲבֹדָה בַּשָּׂדֶה, אֵת כָּל עֲבֹדָתָם אֲשֶׁר עָבְדוּ בָהֶם בְּפָרֶךְ:

in Egypt, as it says, "And they embittered their lives with hard labor, with mortar and bricks, and with all sorts of work in the field; all their work with which they enslaved them with backbreaking labor" (*Shemos* 1:14).

The Wise Son

1. The verse cited here doesn't explain why we eat maror, but we can deduce on our own that the command to eat bitter herbs is to remember the bitterness of our slavery. The Mishnah[129] indicates that the bitter food we eat must be of the ground and preferably a leafy vegetable. The *Rokeach* derives from a verse in *Mishlei* that the best choice for maror is romaine lettuce.[130] The *Rokeach* also rules that if leafy vegetables are not available, we may use horseradish. Many Ashkenazic *poskim* allowed horseradish because leaves were often not available. Bitter leaves are always preferable, though, because they not only remind us of the bitterness of the slavery, but also of the foods we ate at the time.[131]

The Cynical Son

1. *Ibn Ezra* and *Abarbanel* point to the eating habits of those who live in dry climates. They tend to eat bitter and spicy foods that cause the tastebuds to salivate and help with digestion. According to this, maror, like matzah, not only reminded us of an aspect of our slavery and redemption, but was the actual food we ate in Egypt. It may have also served as a condiment inside a sandwich.[111]

2. The embitterment in Egypt actually has a positive side to it. It assured that we would never get too comfortable there as to lose our distinction as a people. At first this almost happened. We were originally designated to reside in Goshen to remain distinct from the temptations of Egypt. We

The Pure Son

1. Since the *korban Pesach* served as a means to wean us away from idolatrous practice, the matzah and maror serve an additional purpose beyond all the memories these foods would evoke. The Torah tells us to refrain from adding yeast and honey to our sacrifices.[115] *Rambam*[116] suggests that this was an idolatrous practice to mask the foods to which these items were added in taste and in appearance. Our first *korban* would negate these ideas. We are only to add salt to all our sacrifices. Salt neither hides nor masks taste, but it enhances it. The matzah and maror we add to the *korban Pesach*, in addition to all its other purposes, would negate the two forbidden ingredients above. The matzah would negate the

The Withdrawn Son

1. Imagine a long day of arduous backbreaking work in the fields or mud pits, under the burning heat of the scorching sun. Imagine that after such a long day all we would have to eat was food akin to matzah and maror. If we are fortunate enough today not to suffer such slavery and to have better food to eat, we should be sensitive to those who are less fortunate than we are. The Talmud[88] reminds us that our experience as strangers in a strange land has led to the fair treatment of the stranger to be the most commonly repeated mitzvah of the entire Torah. More often than idolatry, Shabbos, *kashrus*, or any other mitzvah, the Torah wants us to learn the lesson of our subjugation and spare others

The Wise Son – continued

2. Eating matzah and the *korban Pesach* more readily connects to salvation and thanksgiving than does our eating maror. Yet we can find some degree of consolation in eating maror as well. The time of our subjugation was preordained at four hundred years,[132] yet our Sages explain that the time we spent in Egypt was considerably less.[133] Our Sages explain that due to the extra bitterness imposed upon us beyond the ועבדום וענו אותם, servitude and affliction said to Avraham, our subjugation in Egypt was compressed to a shorter amount of time.[134] The Vilna Gaon, in his Haggadah commentary, suggests a hint to this effect by pointing to the cantillation of the words in the Torah "וימררו את חייהם – They embittered their lives." The name of the cantillation on these words is קדמא ואזלא, which literally means "to precede and go ahead." Four hundred years of servitude were compressed into the 210 years they spent in Egypt. This is further hinted through the numerical value of קדמא ואזלא which is 190, the amount subtracted from the original reckoning. In this way the maror serves as a reminder of salvation as well.

The Cynical Son – continued

quickly grew to the point that the Torah describes as: "ותמלא הארץ אותם – The land was filled with them," which our Sages explain means that we were found everywhere, including in the theaters, circuses, and places of idolatry, immorality, and bloodshed. We wanted to be more Egyptian than the Egyptians. This is where Pharaoh had enough of the encroaching Israelites. Forgetting all that the Yosef had done for them, Pharaoh enacted laws to subjugate the Israelites and this in effect guaranteed that we wouldn't ever be accepted into Egyptian society. This idea is hinted in our passage with the inclusion of one extra word. The Haggadah says:

על שום שמררו המצרים את חיי אבותינו במצרים:

*Because the Egyptians embittered our ancestors' lives **in Egypt**.*

Why does the Haggadah feel the need to stress that these events happened במצרים? Where else did all this happen but in Egypt? Egypt was a large land that had a main city.[112] The Israelites were meant to stay in Goshen, away from this main city, and their attempt to live in the main city of Egypt was rebuffed by Pharaoh. In the end, this reference to why we eat maror is actually what preserved us as a people, and is thus a source of consolation.

The Pure Son – continued

yeast and the maror would negate the honey. Thus the matzah and maror together with the *korban Pesach* shared a common purpose.

2. In *Likutei Maharan*,[117] Rav Nachman of Breslov finds a positive message behind the bitterness of the maror. Rav Nachman describes the sweet serenity we experience when we know our life has meaning and purpose. This meaning brings us tranquility and harmony when we realize we are fulfilling God's will. But we can only recognize the sweet serenity after first experiencing the bitterness, and the absence of peace and serenity. Darkness helps us appreciate light, impurity helps us appreciate purity, and death helps us appreciate life. So too, the bitterness of maror prepares us with the necessary frame of mind to appreciate the redemption we commemorate at the *Seder*.

from the same experience. This is why we began to tell the story of Egypt by inviting others to our *Seder*.[89]

2. Our Sages[90] prefer lettuce, called חסה in Hebrew, to fulfill the mitzvah of eating maror. The word חסה stems from the root for "חס – pity."[91] *Abarbanel* describes how all three of these foods represent contrasting ideas. The *korban Pesach* reminds us of God's judgments against the Egyptians and His mercy in passing over our homes and sparing us. The matzah represents the bread of affliction that is naturally the food for slaves, and simultaneously it is the food of our redemption which came so quickly we had no time for the dough to rise for bread. The maror shows both the bitterness of slavery and the mercy God showed us on the day of our salvation.

MAGGID SECTION 17 – BE'CHOL DOR VADOR

Questions 3 and 4 are answered to all four sons.

1. Is there a practical way to regard ourselves as though *we* left Egypt, beyond what we've been doing at the *Seder*?
2. Why does the *Be'chol Dor VaDor* passage change expressions from the root יצא to גאל?
3. What does the second verse, "ואותנו הוציא משם – He brought us out from there," add to the first verse, "עשה ה' לי – God did for me"? Don't *both* teach that we must feel that we actually left slavery in Egypt?
4. The end of *Be'chol Dor VaDor* seems to imply that the necessity to consider ourselves as if we left Egypt applies only to those who live in Israel.[16] How does this pertain to those who were born and live in exile?

בְּכָל דּוֹר וָדוֹר חַיָּב אָדָם לִרְאוֹת אֶת עַצְמוֹ כְּאִלּוּ הוּא יָצָא מִמִּצְרַיִם. שֶׁנֶּאֱמַר, וְהִגַּדְתָּ לְבִנְךָ בַּיּוֹם הַהוּא לֵאמֹר בַּעֲבוּר זֶה עָשָׂה יְהוָֹה לִי בְּצֵאתִי מִמִּצְרָיִם. לֹא אֶת אֲבוֹתֵינוּ בִּלְבָד גָּאַל הַקָּדוֹשׁ בָּרוּךְ הוּא, אֶלָּא אַף אוֹתָנוּ גָּאַל עִמָּהֶם. שֶׁנֶּאֱמַר, וְאוֹתָנוּ הוֹצִיא מִשָּׁם, לְמַעַן הָבִיא אוֹתָנוּ לָתֶת לָנוּ אֶת הָאָרֶץ אֲשֶׁר נִשְׁבַּע לַאֲבוֹתֵינוּ:

In each and every generation, a person is obligated to regard himself as if he himself had left Egypt, as it says, "You shall tell your son on that day: 'Because of this Hashem did for me when I left Egypt'" (*Shemos* 13:8). It was not only our ancestors that the Holy One, blessed is He, redeemed from Egypt; rather, He redeemed us with them as well, as it is says, "He brought us out from there, in order to bring us [here] to give us the land that He swore to our forefathers" (*Devarim* 6:21-3).

The Wise Son

1. *Tehillim* 106 recreates our experiences in the Egyptian bondage and redemption. Toward the end of the chapter, we say, "וירא **בצר להם** בשמעו את רנתם – He saw **their distress** when He heard their outcry."[135] These words "בצר להם" serve as a template for future examples of salvation at God's Hand. The very next chapter of *Tehillim* is the source for the Talmudic dictum, ארבעה צריכים להודות, four groups of people are required to declare their gratitude to Hashem.[136] This refers to a *korban todah*, a thanksgiving offering, and is manifest today in the blessing called *Birchas HaGomel*. This blessing is said nowadays by the four groups in *Tehillim* 107. Each group cries out to God in their distress, and the same words are used for each group, as in the previous chapter, "בצר להם." The four groups are:

1. those who cross a desert;
2. those who leave incarceration;
3. those who were sick or had undergone a general threat to life;
4. those who cross an ocean or sea.[137]

The Pure Son

There is a daily mitzvah to remember the Egyptian redemption, based on the verse

למען תזכור את יום צאתך מארץ מצרים כל ימי חייך:

So that you may remember the day of your departure from the Land of Egypt as long as you live.

See above in Maggid Section 5 (*Amar Rabbi Elazar ben Azaryah*) regarding why *Rambam* did not count this mitzvah in his list of 613 mitzvos of the Torah. Basically, the daily mitzvah to remember the Egyptian redemption is already a mitzvah. It is the mitzvah of faith, and faith in Judaism goes beyond belief in God's existence or that God created the universe and left it to its own devices. The mitzvah that commands faith, according to *Rambam*, refers to God as the One who took us out of Egypt.[118] God not only created us, He redeemed us. He continues to care for us and is concerned with our welfare and morality.

The Cynical Son

1. There is a very common activity to which we can commit ourselves that is an excellent fulfillment of our paragraph's obligation. The Talmud[113] makes references to the fact that the most commonly repeated mitzvah of the Torah is the fair treatment of the strangers in Egypt. Therefore, every time we empathize with someone less fortunate, we are in essence imagining ourselves as having left Egypt. This is why we began the *Seder* with invitations to the hungry and those in need.

2. This passage is an important reminder that God is not only a מוציא who physically took us out of Egypt; He is also a גואל who redeems us as well. *Ibn Ezra*[114] describes the difference between these two terms. He cites Rav Yehudah HaLeivi who likens God's role in Creation to a מוציא; One who brings out all matter to be formed into the Universe. He then refers to God's role in *yetzias Mitzrayim* as that of a גואל, a Redeemer who continues to be concerned with the Universe He

The Withdrawn Son

1. Many of our mitzvos require us to remember. On a daily basis we are to remember the redemption from Egypt and this is performed by simply making reference to it. We also have a daily mitzvah to remember Shabbos. On the first six days of the week, we do this by reciting the daily *Shir Shel Yom* at the end of the morning service, as the Levites did in the Temple.[92] The numbers of the days of the week themselves remind us how close we are to Shabbos.[93] On Shabbos itself we fulfill this mitzvah by making *Kiddush* and sanctifying the day. We remember our dear departed several days a year by saying *Yizkor*.[94] Once a year we publicly gather to remember the treacherous hatred of Amalek and to commit to its eradication and we publicly declare "זכור את אשר עשה לך עמלק – Remember what Amalek did to you."

Our calendar and our rituals are punctuated with

The Wise Son – continued

Upon leaving Egypt, we did all four of these, so the Egyptian salvation is paradigmatic of all future salvations. Every time we *bentch gomel* or acknowledge God's role in assisting us in our daily existential struggles, we are in essence regarding ourselves as if we left Egypt ourselves.[138]

2. The root גאל usually has the connotation of redemption. However, it can also mean "to acquire," as in the mitzvah of גאולת שדה, the redemption of a field[139] or in the story of the marriage of Ruth, when Boaz said "אם יגאלך טוב יגאל – If he will act as a redeemer, good! Let him redeem."[140] The word גאל in the *Bechol Dor VaDor* section stresses not only our redemption, but our acquisition as a People by God, to be His Chosen People.[141]

The Cynical Son – continued

brought out. Explaining why God would appear to the Israelites in the Decalogue as the Redeemer rather than the Creator, *Ibn Ezra* himself says that it was preferable for the Israelites to be introduced to God in a manner of an event that they had just experienced, namely, *yetzias Mitzrayim*. Creation was too esoteric an idea for them to grasp. Rav Yehudah HaLeivi explains the difference between the two. The מוציא acts for the moment of the deliverance. The גאל continues to deliver as an ongoing historical growth process.[115] This may be why we bless God on bread as המוציא לחם מן הארץ – **Who brings forth** bread from the earth. Surely wheat is taken from the earth, not bread. Rather, God wants the process of deliverance and redemption to be a partnership. God will initiate the process by being a מוציא and then we must be partners to bring about the גאולה. Our passage makes this point by moving from one root to the other.[116]

The Pure Son – continued

Anyone who sees God in the daily vicissitudes of life, who considers that the daily struggles of our existence are eased by God's presence and direction, fulfills the dictates of this section of the Haggadah. There is a simple way to fulfill this mitzvah on a daily basis: when reciting the seventh blessing in the daily *Amidah*, which is here translated: "Behold our affliction, take up our grievance, and redeem us speedily for Your Name's sake for You are a powerful redeemer. Blessed are you, God, the Redeemer of Israel."

2. We change from יצא to גאל to teach that the process of גאולה is a continual endeavor. As the *Dayeinu* passage clearly demonstrates, our גאולה is an ongoing experience that proceeds in stages.[119] The first mitzvah the Torah mentions after we left Egypt was meant to make redeemers of us. Just as God spared and redeemed our firstborn in Egypt, so too does He command redemption of our firstborn males in the immediate aftermath of our deliverance.[120] This makes us partners in the redemptive process. Indeed, the *tam*'s question at the Seder, "מה זאת,"[121] is actually a question on *pidyon haben*, the redemption of the firstborn male. The answer to why we do *pidyon haben* is the same as the explanation of the proceedings at the Seder; "'כי בחזק יד הוציאנו ה ממצרים מבית עבדים – For it was with a mighty Hand that God brought us out from Egypt, the house of bondage." [122] This explains why *Bechol Dor VaDor* switches from יצא to גאל.

remembrance, and Pesach night is very much part of that. We perform rituals and tell stories to keep our redemption fresh in our minds. The night of Pesach is called ליל שמורים, a night of being watched.[95] In Akkadian, an ancient Semitic language, the root שמר means to carefully hold on to a feeling, almost to the point of bearing a grudge.[96] The rituals of the evening and the stories we tell assure that we will imagine that we left Egypt ourselves. This is not only true of remembering the redemption from Egypt; it is a necessary component of all of our remembrances. We will better remember the tragedy of Rabbi Akiva's students if we observe the rituals of the mourning period of *Sefiras Ha'Omer*.[97] In the same vein, we will better remember the tragedy of the Holocaust if we set that remembrance to

ritual on *Yom HaShoah* or Kristallnacht events. This can include candle lighting, recitation of special readings, or special קל מלא רחמים prayers at *Yizkor*, handing out pictures of Shoah victims for everyone to remember at *Yizkor*, indicating that we are all mourners for the Shoah. The *Seder* has taught us that setting remembrances to rituals is the surest way to know that our memories will remain fresh.

2. In a literal sense, "ואותנו הוציא משם – He took us from there," does not refer to the way that the term הוצאה is generally used. God did not literally *take* us out of Egypt. We walked out on our own, in the wake of His numerous miracles. We were partners, so to say, in our past redemption, as we must be in future redemptions.

All Four Sons

3. This passage actually attempts to capture all four of the parents' answers or statements to their children. The Torah's answer to the *chacham* includes the second verse ואותנו הוציא משם,[133] and is very close to the *tam*'s answer. The response to both the *rasha* and the *she'eino yodei'a lishol* is the first verse. The *Bechol Dor VaDor* section of the Haggadah is in essence saying that we will best attain the continuity of generation to generation (בכל דור ודור) if we take stock of our children's unique qualities when we engage them. That being said, the first verse refers to children whose parents actually left Egypt. Future generations of children whose parents were never in Egypt are the subjects of the second verse.

4. The Haggadah seems to be written for those in exile. The beginning of the proceedings note that we are stranded "here" and enslaved and we hope to hold next year's *Seder* in freedom and in Israel. Toward the end we pray that next year we will be in Jerusalem. We see that entry into the Land of Israel is as much a part of our *zechiras yetzias Mitzrayim*,[134] as it was part of God's original message to Moshe

at the Burning Bush.[135] The *Rabban Gamliel Hayah Omer* section of Maggid refers to three things we say at the *Seder*, which serves as a way for our generation to connect to what our ancestors did in Egypt and as they left Egypt.

Korban Pesach, matzah, and maror can be connected to the three leaders who enacted our redemption and assured our safety and protection in its aftermath. They are Moshe, Aharon and Miriam.[136] The prophet Michah refers to all three as active players in our redemption.

כי העלתיך מארץ מצרים ומבית עבדים פדיתיך ואשלח לפניך את משה אהרון ומרים:

For I brought you up from the land of Egypt, I redeemed you from the house of bondage, and I sent before you Moshe, Aharon, and Miriam.[137]

Our Sages explain that B'nei Yisrael were protected by the Clouds of Glory and the Pillar of Fire in the merit of Aharon, that the *mahn* fell in the merit of Moshe, and that the Well followed them in the desert in the merit of Miriam.[138]

It seems that the Israelites became so dependent

on this support and protection that they couldn't imagine deserving these merits or their own. When the ten *meraglim* returned from their scouting mission with a negative report, they set the decree in motion for the generation to spend the next thirty-eight years in the desert. In the aftermath of that debacle, three commandments were instructed to us:

1. *Nesachim* – Libations that accompany animal offerings.[139]
2. *Challah* – Sanctification of part of the dough of baked goods.[140]
3. *Tzitzis* – Worn at the corners of our garments.[141]

Each of these commandments was meant to teach B'nei Yisrael that they could merit these protections and gifts on their own. The *nesachim* would merit the rain they would need, the *challah* would assure they would merit abundant grain,[142] and the *tzitzis* would be a source of physical protection.

Since the Haggadah juxtaposes *korban Pesach*, matzah, and maror to *Bechol Dor VaDor*, which concludes with the ultimate purpose of entry into the Land, we can now extend these three to our three leaders. *Korban Pesach* involved God's protection of our homes from the destroyer the night before we left Egypt.[143] This connects to the protective Clouds of Glory. The matzah connects to Moshe, as he is the one in whose merit the *mahn* fell. And the maror (מרור) connects to Miriam (מרים) by her very name. A Midrashic source indicates that the bitterness of our slavery began with the birth of Miriam; "ולפיכך נקראת מרים על שום שמררו המצרים את חייהם – She was thus named Miriam, because the Egyptians embittered their lives."[144] This is the very verse that was cited in Maggid Section 16c for the reason for eating maror.[145] The passage of *Bechol Dor VaDor* (Maggid Section 17) therefore teaches that by saying these three paragraphs of *Rabban Gamliel Hayah Omer* (Maggid Sections 16a–c), we will merit a return to our Land.

MAGGID SECTION 18: LEFICHACH

1. What is the nature of this section of Maggid?
2. Why are there so many different expressions of praise? Isn't it considered counterproductive to praise God so effusively?[17]
3. What does "כל הנסים האלה – all these miracles," refer to? What follows is merely an elaboration on the original theme of redemption, but doesn't seem to reference any particular miracle.
4. Why does *Lefichach* repeat so many examples of what God did for us?

The matzah is covered, and the cup of wine is raised while reciting the following paragraph. (Some have the custom to continue to raise the cup until it is drunk, after the blessing *Gaal Yisrael*.)

לְפִיכָךְ אֲנַחְנוּ חַיָּבִים לְהוֹדוֹת לְהַלֵּל לְשַׁבֵּחַ לְפָאֵר לְרוֹמֵם לְהַדֵּר לְבָרֵךְ לְעַלֵּה וּלְקַלֵּס לְמִי שֶׁעָשָׂה לַאֲבוֹתֵינוּ וְלָנוּ אֶת כָּל

Therefore, we are obligated to thank, to praise, to laud, to glorify, to exalt, to honor, to bless, to elevate, and to extol the One Who performed all these miracles for our

הַנִּסִּים הָאֵלֶּה. הוֹצִיאָנוּ מֵעַבְדוּת לְחֵרוּת, מִיָּגוֹן לְשִׂמְחָה, מֵאֵבֶל לְיוֹם טוֹב, וּמֵאֲפֵלָה לְאוֹר גָּדוֹל, וּמִשִּׁעְבּוּד לִגְאֻלָּה, וְנֹאמַר לְפָנָיו שִׁירָה חֲדָשָׁה הַלְלוּיָהּ:

ancestors – and for us. He took us out from slavery to freedom, from sadness to joy, from mourning to festivity, from darkness to great light, and from subjugation to redemption. Now let us recite before Him a new song – Halleluyah!

The Wise Son

1. We are up to the part of the Haggadah that conveys the message that we all left Egypt, and we are all indebted. Maggid began with such a theme (see *Avadim Hayinu*: Maggid Section 3), and now we give this theme practical application in profuse praise. We learned above of the Rabbinic dictum "ארבעה צריכים להודות – four types of people are obliged to thank God" (see *Bechol Dor VaDor*: Maggid Section 17, The Wise Son – Question 1). Our passage says in contemplation of all that God had done for us, that we are להודות חייבים, obligated to show gratitude.

2. Our text of the Haggadah has nine expressions of praise. *Abarbanel's* text omitted two of these

The Cynical Son

1. The *Lefichach* section of Maggid introduces what many feel is the introduction to a blessing upon the evening's proceedings. We had a similar reference above in *Baruch HaMakom* – (see Maggid Section 6, The Cynical Son – question 1).

2. *Lefichach* lists nine expressions of praise leading into the word הללויה, which begins with our saying the first part of *Hallel*.[117] Chazal point to ten synonyms of praise in *Sefer Tehillim* and the greatest of all is הללויה.[118] It would seem that our passage purposely lists nine expressions to lead into the tenth, to parallel the point of Chazal above. That being said, Chazal also warn us to be careful not to overdo our profuse praise of God. After all how can a human, with finite knowledge

The Pure Son

1. The *Lefichach* section of Maggid arouses within us the crescendo of our recognition of the purpose of the entire evening, which is to go to the next step, which is the very obligation we speak of in this passage. Now we are ready to receive God's word, which is why, when that Word is revealed, it is done with an introduction of *yetzias Mitzrayim*:

אנכי ה' אלוקיך אשר הוצאתיך מארץ מצרים מבית עבדים:

I am the Lord your God who brought you forth from the land of Egypt from the house of bondage.

2. *Abarbanel*, who lists seven expressions of praise in his Haggadah, connects these words to seven benefits we derived from our redemption.

The Withdrawn Son

1. The *Lefichach* section of Maggid is our blessing of witnessing the place of our ancestor's miracles. This parallels the addition of *Al HaNissim* to the *Amidah* and *Birchas HaMazon* on Chanukah and Purim. Since we are reliving what our ancestors did the night before they left Egypt, it is as if we actually see the place of the miracle itself.[98]

2. The *Lefichach* section of Maggid refers to four ways in which we were elevated with our redemption from שעבוד to גאולה. We went from:

1. Slavery to freedom
2. Anguish to joy
3. Mourning to festivity
4. Darkness to great light

expressions, the praises of "להלל – to glorify," and "לקלס – to celebrate,"[142] and he explains that the seven expressions mentioned correspond to seven tenets of faith derived from the Egyptian redemption and its aftermath:

1. The existence of a Prime Mover[143]
2. God's Unity and uniqueness[144]
3. God's Omniscience[145]
4. The tenets of reward and punishment[146]
5. God's Omnipotence[147]
6. The world is a creation of a Divine design[148]
7. The reality of prophecy[149]

3. The purpose of the *Lefichach* section of Maggid is to connect everything we have read in the Haggadah up to this point. The miracles referred to here are those listed earlier in Maggid, especially in Maggid Sections 15a–b. This underscores the message that the themes and emotions mentioned in *Lefichach* relate to all of Maggid.

4. The *Vilna Gaon* classifies five separate transitions that we underwent in light of the five phrases of *Lefichach*. The full process of our turning from slaves to free people in a productive Torah society would require all these transitions. He further explains these phrases to serve us in our transitions throughout history.

1. מעבדות לחרות – **From slavery to freedom:** This is the Exodus from Egypt. We refer to Pesach as "זמן חרותינו – the time of our freedom." The word חרות does not appear throughout the entire Tanach. It is the word used *by Targum Onkelos* for the words דרור,[150] and חפשי,[151] in the Torah, and by *Targum Yonasan* for דרור in *Nevi'im*.[152] The closest we get to this word in the Torah is that the

words of the *Aseres HaDibros* were "חרות על הלוחות – **engraved** onto the Tablets."[153] Our Sages expound the similar sounding "חָרוּת – engraved," and "חֵרוּת – free," to teach that only one who is involved in Torah study is truly free.[154]

2. מיגון לשמחה – **From anguish to joy:** Splitting of the Yam Suf. We recreate this event every day at the end of *Pesukei D'Zimra*. The *Mishnah Berurah* calls for us to recite the *Shiras HaYam* in the following way:

ויאמר שירת הים **בשמחה** וידמה בדעתו כאילו באותו היום עבר הים.

We should say Shiras HaYam **joyously** *and consider it as if we crossed the Sea on that very day.*[155]

3. מאבל ליום טוב – **From mourning to festivity:** This mourning refers to our remorse after the Golden Calf. The Torah relates: ויתאבלו ולא שתו איש עדיו עליו — They mourned, and no man put on his ornaments.[156]

In the wake of the forgiveness for the Golden Calf, we returned to God's good graces and this was the source of establishing a *Yom Tov*.[157]

4. מאפלה לאור גדול – **From darkness to great light:** From the desert, a place of darkness, death, and barrenness to the land of spiritual light, Israel.

5. משעבוד לגאולה – **From subjugation to redemption:** This refers to the numerous subjugations of *Sefer Shoftim* and *Sefer Shmuel* before the Davidic dynasty brought us to our ultimate redemption and autonomy.[158] We pray this evening to replicate these elements of redemption.

The Cynical Son – continued

and ability, adequately encapsulate the full praise due to God who is infinite and beyond our comprehension.[119]

3. The *Lefichach* section of Maggid does not list any specific miracles, to teach us that our belief in Hashem, in Moshe's mission, or in that of any prophet, is not conditional to any performance of miracles. This is not to say that miracles did not take place, only that our faith transcends such belief.[120]

4. *Abarbanel* relates these five stages of God's compassion to His people to correspond to five specific levels of subjugation the Israelites experienced in Egypt.[121]

1. מעבדות לחרות – **from slavery to freedom.** We were subordinate to the will of the Egyptians.

2. מיגון לשמחה – **from anguish to joy.** We were in a perpetual state of depression and degradation.

3. מאבל ליום טוב – **from mourning to festivity.** We were enslaved to the point of having no personal time. Our time was not our own.[122]

4. מאפלה לאור גדול – **from darkness to great light.** The slavery snuffed out our spirit and our faith in a better day.

5. משעבוד לגאולה – **from subjugation to redemption.** The slavery put our destiny to the whim of the taskmaster and the force of the lash.

We would be able to appreciate our freedom and redemption by establishing a calendar whereby we could celebrate holidays with rejoicing, where we could ignite our spirits and prepare for a better day.

The Pure Son – continued

They are:

1. Freedom
2. Recompense from our enemies
3. The *rechush gadol*, great wealth, with which we left Egypt[123]
4. Respect
5. Complete belief
6. The Torah
7. The Promised Land

3. The general reference to miracles in our passage underscores the principle that while the miracles in Egypt were meant to teach Pharaoh of God's might and justice, the main purpose was to be an everlasting source of our original connection to God as a people, which is the main purpose of the *Seder* itself.[124]

4. *Abarbanel* also connects these five phrases to

five separate major subjugations in our history. He adjusts their order to fit the historical order of these subjugations. They are:

1. מעבדות לחרות: **Egyptian** slavery turned to **freedom** with the Exodus.

2. משעבוד לגאולה: **Babylonian** servitude turned to **redemption** when we returned to Israel to rebuild the Temple.

3. מיגון לשמחה: The agony of the **Persian** decrees turned to **joy**, as we were saved and granted permission to rebuild Jerusalem.

4. מאבל ליום טוב: The mournful subjugation at the hand of the **Greeks** turned us to revolt and our victorious rebellion led to a *Yom Tov* during the Chanukah period.

5. מאפלה לאור גדול: The darkness of the **Edomite** exile is one that we look to emerge from with **great light**, namely, the Messianic era.

Rashbatz is cited by *Torah Sheleimah*, with a version that has eight expressions of praise.[99] Since the Haggadah referred to double the goodness from God (see Maggid Section 15b; על אחת כמה וכמה טובה כפולה ומכופלת המקום עלינו), it is proper for us to express eight words of praise for the four elevations above.

3. Actually, the phrases that follow the reference to miracles *do* hint to the miracles of *Sefer Shemos*. See the answers to the next question.

4. These five phrases are introductory expressions for what we are about to say: *Hallel*.

1. **מעבדות לחרות**: This corresponds to "בצאת ישראל ממצרים – When Israel went forth from Egypt."[100]

2. **מיגון לשמחה**: The desperation of our slavery where Egyptians worshipped graven images, was turned to the joy of blessings of God's favor. This corresponds to the description of idols and the blessings of 'ה זכרנו יברך.[101]

3. **מאבל ליום טוב**: This offsets "צרה ויגון אמצא ובשם ה' אקרא – I found trouble and sorrow and I called the Name of God."[102]

4. **מאפלה לאור גדול**: The "great light" is a function of God's *chessed* that He performs on our behalf. Just as Pharaoh came to recognize God, so too all the nations of the world will come to know God and praise Him. Throughout world history, whenever Jews thrive, the world prospers. Conversely, the suffering of Jews is a harbinger of global deprivation. When the world will realize its beneficence is a function of God's *chessed* to us, *Tehillim* 117, which discusses the nations of the world recognizing and praising God's *chessed* to us will be realized.

5. **משעבוד לגאולה**: Our salvation is stressed again and again in the last chapter of *Hallel*. If God supports me, how can I be afraid of any enemy? The relevant verses are:

עזי וזמרת י-ה ויהי לי לישועה:

The Lord is my strength and might, He has become my salvation.[103]

קול רינה וישועה באהלי צדיקים:

The tents of the righteous resound with joyous shouts of salvation.[104]

אודך כי עניתני ותהי לי לישועה:

I praise You for You have answered me and have become my salvation.[105]

אנא ה' הושיעה נא:

O Lord save us.[106]

MAGGID SECTION 19 – HALLEL: TEHILLIM 113 – 114

1. What is the message of these two chapters of *Tehillim*, 113 and 114?
2. Why do we recite part of *Hallel* before the meal and the rest after the meal? If the beginning of *Hallel* is part of Maggid, why is it mentioned at the very end of the *Seder*'s list, before *Nirtzah*, and why is there no blessing on this *Hallel*?

הַלְלוּיָהּ, הַלְלוּ עַבְדֵי יהוה, הַלְלוּ אֶת שֵׁם יהוה: יְהִי שֵׁם יהוה מְבֹרָךְ, מֵעַתָּה וְעַד

Halleluyah! Praise, you servants of Hashem, praise the name of Hashem! May Hashem's name be blessed from now to eternity. From

עוֹלָם: מִמִּזְרַח שֶׁמֶשׁ עַד מְבוֹאוֹ, מְהֻלָּל שֵׁם יְהוָה: רָם עַל כָּל גּוֹיִם יְהוָה, עַל הַשָּׁמַיִם כְּבוֹדוֹ: מִי כַּיהוָה אֱלֹהֵינוּ, הַמַּגְבִּיהִי לָשָׁבֶת: הַמַּשְׁפִּילִי לִרְאוֹת, בַּשָּׁמַיִם וּבָאָרֶץ: מְקִימִי מֵעָפָר דָּל, מֵאַשְׁפֹּת יָרִים אֶבְיוֹן: לְהוֹשִׁיבִי עִם נְדִיבִים, עִם נְדִיבֵי עַמּוֹ: מוֹשִׁיבִי עֲקֶרֶת הַבַּיִת, אֵם הַבָּנִים שְׂמֵחָה, הַלְלוּיָהּ:

the place of the rising of the sun to the place of its setting Hashem's name is praised. Hashem is raised above all nations, His glory is over the heavens. Who is like Hashem our God, Who dwells on high, and lowers Himself to look upon heaven and earth! He raises up the poor from the dust, He lifts the needy from the trash heaps – to seat them with nobles, with the nobles of His people. He causes the barren woman to be established with a family, a joyful mother of children. Halleluyah! (*Tehillim* 113)

בְּצֵאת יִשְׂרָאֵל מִמִּצְרָיִם, בֵּית יַעֲקֹב מֵעַם לֹעֵז: הָיְתָה יְהוּדָה לְקָדְשׁוֹ יִשְׂרָאֵל מַמְשְׁלוֹתָיו: הַיָּם רָאָה וַיָּנֹס, הַיַּרְדֵּן יִסֹּב לְאָחוֹר: הֶהָרִים רָקְדוּ כְאֵילִים, גְּבָעוֹת כִּבְנֵי צֹאן: מַה לְּךָ הַיָּם כִּי תָנוּס, הַיַּרְדֵּן תִּסֹּב לְאָחוֹר: הֶהָרִים תִּרְקְדוּ כְאֵילִים, גְּבָעוֹת כִּבְנֵי צֹאן: מִלְּפְנֵי אָדוֹן חוּלִי אָרֶץ מִלְּפְנֵי אֱלוֹהַּ יַעֲקֹב: הַהֹפְכִי הַצּוּר אֲגַם מָיִם, חַלָּמִישׁ לְמַעְיְנוֹ מָיִם:

When Israel went out of Egypt, the House of Yaakov from a people of a foreign language, Yehuda became His sanctifier, Israel His dominions. The sea saw and fled, the Jordan turned back. The mountains skipped like rams, the hills like young sheep. What is with you, O sea, that you flee, O Jordan, that you turn back? You mountains, why do you skip like rams; you hills, like young sheep? Tremble, O earth, from before Hashem, from before the God of Yaakov, Who transforms a rock into a pool of water, a hard stone into a spring of water! (*Tehillim* 114)

The Wise Son

1. Verse 113: 'הללו את שם ה – **Let us praise God.** We can never know the true essence of God. Our feeble minds cannot comprehend the fullness of God's Being. Even our greatest prophet, Moshe, was told "לא יראני האדם וחי – Man cannot see Me and live."[159] Rather, we can only hope to comprehend the Eminence of God through His Name. This is why Moshe, at the Burning Bush, asked God for His Name. This reflects the revelation with which we comprehend Him. For instance, God's Name as אלקים represents Him within a framework of justice,[160] or, put in other words, nature.[161] Moshe himself expressed his doubts at the beginning of his mission, and God reminded him that in the unfolding of the Exodus from Egypt, God's Name will be known and evident to all.[162]

Verse 114: The word denoting the splitting of the Sea is וינס. Elsewhere in *Tehillim* we find the terminology, "לגוזר ים סוף לגזרים – The Sea was divided into divisions."[163] The Torah's word for the split

The Cynical Son

1. Verse 113: 'הללו עבדי ה – **Let the servants of God praise Him.** The incorporation of Maggid, to this point, has hopefully transformed us to be עבדי ה', servants of God, with all that such a status entails. We did not leave the slavery of Egypt to become enslaved by our passions, but to become עבדי ה'. The mantra of the Soviet Jewry movement in America was "Let My People Go," a loose translation of שלח את עמי, which means "Send My People Out."[123] We were free to serve God here and we agitated to assure that our brethren could enjoy those freedoms as well. The correct mantra though would have included the end of that demand, which usually concluded "ויעבדוני – so that they may serve Me." Moshe demanded our freedom so that we could serve God. This is the purpose of the Exodus and is demonstrated by the beginning of *Hallel*.

Verse 114: This is a poetic form of the Sea simply acting in concert with all the other supernatural events of the Exodus. It figuratively saw what

The Pure Son

1. Verse 113: מעתה ועד עולם – **From this time and forever.** Until the Exodus, God had not manifested the full demonstration of His Omnipotence for the masses. This was a necessary prelude to *Matan Torah*, whereby the Chosen People would accept the preamble or command of "אנכי ה' אלקיך אשר הוצאתיך מארץ מצרים מבית עבדים – I am the Lord your God who has taken you out of the Land of Egypt from the house of bondage."[125] "מעתה – from this time," above, refers to the Exodus. From then on, *Hallel* is appropriate to say in perpetuity. With the Torah in our possession, we would be "free" in perpetuity. For this reason, our liturgy refers to *yetzias Mitzrayim* as "חרות עולם – eternal freedom."[126] If we say *Hallel*, we are free.[127] Even when enslaved to another nation, an עבד ה' feels assured that the slavery is temporary, as in Egypt. The beginning of Hallel stresses this feeling.

Verse 114: The Sea saw the word "וינס" in order

The Withdrawn Son

1. Verse 113: המגביהי לשבת המשפילי לראות בשמים ובארץ – He is enthroned on high yet deigns to look upon heaven and earth.

The Talmud states: "כל מקום שאתה מוצא גבורתו של הקב"ה אתה מוצא ענוותנותו – Wherever you see the greatness of God, you see the humility of God."[107]

The essential point of our redemption is that God defeated the mightiest army and the most powerful king in the world for the sake of a weak and enslaved nation. The Egyptian exile was set in motion by an earlier Egyptian king who was mystified by fat cows and fat ears of grain being devoured by thin cows and thin ears of grain. Only the Hebrew could explain its meaning, and it comes through clearly with the above words. The Torah is replete with mitzvos that care for the poor, the unfortunate, the stranger, the widowed, the orphaned, and the infirmed. It reserves its greatest calumny and scorn for the nation of Amalek for attacking us at a time of

The Wise Son – continued

is a rare word,[164] ויבקעו המים, and it is only used as a verb in four contexts.[165] The first describes how the heavens opened for the Flood in the days of Noach: נבקעו כל מעינות תהום רבה.[166] Another occurrence describes how the earth opened to swallow Korach and his camp; ותבקע האדמה.[167] In light of these two verses and our source, it seems the word is reserved for miraculous openings. But it is the fourth, quite natural, reference that leads to a beautiful and meaningful exposition of the impetus for the Sea to split. Chazal describe the Sea's reaction to God ordering it to split.[168] The Sea, like all of nature, prefers its natural state and wants to stay in its natural form. When the Sea asked why it should run counter to its nature by splitting, God let it see the fourth root of בקע, reminding it of a man who profoundly went counter to his nature in the performance of God's will in the test of *Akeidas Yitzchak*; "ויבקע עצי עולה – Avraham split the "wood of the offering," i.e., of his son,[169] whom he would bring up to God. When the Sea saw that Avraham ran counter to his nature, it did so as well.[170]

2. Chazal derive from a Biblical source to recite *Hallel* on *Yom Tov*.[171] Yeshayahu refers to a joyous time, when "השיר יהיה לכם כליל התקדש חג – For you there shall be singing as on a night when a festival is hallowed."[172] Chazal connect this verse to the Pesach *Seder* and this very recitation.[173] The *Hallel* that is recited in some synagogues on the night of the *Sedarim* is a fulfillment of the requirement of the *Yom Tov* night which Yeshayahu mentions, or possibly a demonstration of *zecher l'Mikdash*, since *Hallel* was recited when the *korban Pesach* was brought in the Temple.[174] The *Hallel* at the *Seder*, however, is a fulfillment of *sippur yetzias Mitzrayim*.[175] Since there is no blessing on Maggid, there is no blessing on this *Hallel*.[176] And, to demonstrate that this *Hallel* is set apart, we interrupt it with the mitzvos of the evening, just as *sippur Yetzias Mitzrayim* is tied into the mitzvos of the evening.[177]

The Cynical Son – continued

had transpired and continued to perform its duty in the same vein.

2. Each cup at the *Seder* is connected to a mitzvah. The first is for *kiddush*, the second for *sippur yetzias Mitzrayim*, the third, for *Birchas HaMazon* and the fourth for *Hallel*. *Hallel* begins just as we complete the mitzvah of the second cup, so we break up the *Hallel* and refer to *Hallel* when we finish it, since a mitzvah is called after its completion.[124] Since many have the custom to recite the *Hallel* in the synagogue, there is no blessing in the Haggadah even for those who don't recite *Hallel* with *Maariv*.[125]

The Pure Son – continued

to split. This word appears only twice by the time of *Krias Yam Suf*, and the first time describes Yosef's reaction to Potifar's wife. Yosef was under exorbitant pressure to submit to the demands of Potifar's wife. He knew he would suffer at her hands if he refused her. He had every reason to give in and one reason to refuse: it was morally wrong. Our Sages even explain that he was inclined to submit,[128] but in the end he resisted, which the Torah describes using the expression "וינס ויצא החוצה – He fled and went outside."[129] The Sea would not split until shown how Yosef went against his inclination. At that point the Sea also went against its inclination and split.[130]

2. The Talmud explains that we recite *Hallel* at the *Seder* because it mentions five crucial points.[131]

1. **The Exodus from Egypt**: "בצאת ישראל ממצרים – When the Israelites went forth from Egypt" (*Tehillim* 114:1).
2. **The splitting of the Red Sea**: "הים ראה וינס – The Sea saw and fled" (*Tehillim* 114:3).

3. *Matan Torah*: "ההרים רקדו כאלים – The mountains danced like rams" (*Tehillim* 114:4).

4. **The resurrection of the dead**: אתהלך לפני ה' בארצות החיים – I will walk before God in the land of the living" (*Tehillim* 116:9).

5. **The birth pangs prior to the Messianic Age**: לא לנו ה' לא לנו – Not to us, Lord. Not to us" (*Tehillim* 115:1).

Maggid ends with a blessing of redemption and it is clear from this Gemara that the first three of these – the Exodus, *Krias Yam Suf*, and *Matan Torah* – are captured by the first two chapters of *Hallel*. The other chapters capture themes that are germane to other parts of the *Seder* that are performed after the meal. Hence *Hallel* is broken up into two parts.

weakness and frailty, and striking at our weakest people in the back lines. Imagine then, the rewards in store for those who imitate God above and help the weakest among us.

Verse 114: The second time וינס appears in the Torah is when Moshe, for the first time, is shown a sign that runs counter to nature. The staff in his hand turned to a snake and he reacted with astonished fright; "וינס מפניו – He recoiled from it." The Sea saw from the very outset all of Moshe's heroic acts on behalf of his people and then decided to help Moshe complete the deliverance of his people by splitting and returning just in time.

2. On the night of the slaying of the firstborn, we were told not to leave our homes.[108] The night that Lot was saved (which our Sages say was the fifteenth of Nissan)[109] he was told not to look upon Sodom as it was being destroyed.[110] These commands were meant to assure that we would not gloat over the defeat of the enemy. The Talmud discusses the reason for changing from full-*Hallel* to half-*Hallel* starting with *Chol HaMoed Pesach*, while *Hallel* remains full for the entirety of Sukkos.[111] Since Sukkos has a change in its sacrifices each day,[112] the holiday is renewed with each new day. Pesach, however, has the same offering each day and therefore since the holiday does not renew itself this way, *Hallel* is diminished starting *Chol HaMoed*.

This explanation stands in contrast to an explanation in *Midrash Harninu* cited by the Codes,[113] that we diminish our joy on Pesach because its observance involved the death of the firstborn, and of those who drowned at Yam Suf.

Perhaps, rather than offering a new reason for half-*Hallel* on Pesach, these sources are suggesting a reason for the Gemara's explanation of the difference between Pesach and Sukkos. Chazal say that the bulls we brought on Sukkos, descending daily from thirteen on the first day of *Yom Tov* to seven on the final day of *Yom Tov*, which number seventy in total, were brought for the sake of the seventy nations of the world.[114] The prophet Zechariah understands Sukkos as a universal holiday and bids us to invite the nations of the world to join us in the sukkah, which symbolizes peace.[115] For this reason we pray nightly, "ופרוש עלינו סוכת שלומך – Spread upon us the **sukkah** of Your peace."[116] This may also be the reason why, according to the *Aggadah*, when the nations of the world ask God for a mitzvah, they were granted the mitzvah of sukkah.[117] This stands in sharp contrast to *korban Pesach* where the Torah warns us "כל בן נכר לא יאכל בו – No foreigner may eat it,"[118] and "כל ערל לא יאכל בו – No uncircumcised person may eat it."[119] This holiday does not have the universal aspect of Sukkos and for this reason the seventy bulls brought on that holiday are not replicated on Pesach. Perhaps for this reason we divide the *Hallel* of the *Seder*, and just say enough of *Hallel* to complete the essence of the command of Maggid, בעבור זה עשה ה' לי בצאתי ממצרים, Because of this that

God did for me **when I went forth from Egypt**. We recite just enough of *Hallel* until we reach the chapter which begins "בצאת ישראל ממצרים – When Israel went forth from Egypt."

MAGGID SECTION 20 – BIRCHAS HEGEULAH

1. What is the nature of this blessing?

2. Why do some *Haggados* change the order of the references to פסחים and זבחים on *Motzaei Shabbos*?

3. In the *Lefichach* section of Maggid we praise God: "שעשה לאבותינו ולנו את כל הנסים האלו – that He wrought all these miracles for our fathers and for us." This makes sense. We project the redemption of our ancestors upon ourselves. In *Birchas HeGeulah* (Maggid Section 20) we say: "אשר גאלנו וגאל את אבותינו – He redeemed us and redeemed our fathers." Why is the order switched?

4. Why does *Lefichach* (Maggid Section 18) refer to the song as שירה חדשה, in the feminine form of the word, while *Birchas HeGeulah* (Maggid Section 20) refers to שיר חדש, in the masculine?

The cup of wine is held in the hand as the following paragraph is recited:

בָּרוּךְ אַתָּה יהוה אֱלֹהֵינוּ מֶלֶךְ הָעוֹלָם, אֲשֶׁר גְּאָלָנוּ וְגָאַל אֶת אֲבוֹתֵינוּ מִמִּצְרַיִם, וְהִגִּיעָנוּ הַלַּיְלָה הַזֶּה לֶאֱכָל בּוֹ מַצָּה וּמָרוֹר. כֵּן יהוה אֱלֹהֵינוּ וֵאלֹהֵי אֲבוֹתֵינוּ יַגִּיעֵנוּ לְמוֹעֲדִים וְלִרְגָלִים אֲחֵרִים הַבָּאִים לִקְרָאתֵנוּ לְשָׁלוֹם, שְׂמֵחִים בְּבִנְיַן עִירֶךָ, וְשָׂשִׂים בַּעֲבוֹדָתֶךָ, וְנֹאכַל שָׁם מִן הַזְּבָחִים וּמִן הַפְּסָחִים (במוצש"ק מִן הַפְּסָחִים וּמִן הַזְּבָחִים) אֲשֶׁר יַגִּיעַ דָּמָם עַל קִיר מִזְבַּחֲךָ לְרָצוֹן וְנוֹדֶה לְךָ שִׁיר חָדָשׁ עַל גְּאֻלָּתֵנוּ וְעַל פְּדוּת נַפְשֵׁנוּ: בָּרוּךְ אַתָּה יהוה גָּאַל יִשְׂרָאֵל:

Blessed are You, Hashem, our God, King of the universe, Who has redeemed us and redeemed our ancestors from Egypt, and allowed us to reach this night, to eat matzah and maror on it. So too, Hashem, our God and the God of our fathers, allow us to reach in peace other holidays and festivals in the future, happy in the rebuilding of Your city, and joyful in Your Temple service. And there we will partake of sacrifices and Pesach offerings (on Saturday night reverse the order: of Pesach offerings and sacrifices), whose blood will be poured on the wall of Your altar for Your acceptance, and we will give thanks to You with a new song over our redemption and the salvation of our souls. Blessed are You, Hashem, Who redeemed Israel.

בָּרוּךְ אַתָּה יהוה אֱלֹהֵינוּ מֶלֶךְ הָעוֹלָם, בּוֹרֵא פְּרִי הַגָּפֶן:

Blessed are You, Hashem, our God, King of the universe, Who creates the fruit of the vine.

The wine is now drunk while reclining on the left side.

The Wise Son

1. The Mishnah[178] requires Maggid to חותם בגאולה, to conclude with a blessing of redemption, and records a dispute as to the extent of the blessing:

Rabbi Tarfon says that the blessing's formula is "אשר גאלנו וגאל את אבותינו ממצרים – He redeemed us and redeemed our ancestors in Egypt."

Rabbi Akiva says that the blessing's formula is "כן ה' אלוקינו ואלקי אבותינו יגיענו למועדים ולרגלים אחרים וכו' – So shall the Lord our God and God of our fathers enable us to attain other festivals and pilgrimages."

Also, Rabbi Akiva requires the blessing to end "ברוך אתה ה' גאל ישראל – Blessed are you, God, the Redeemer of Israel," and Rabbi Tarfon does not have this requirement.

Rav Ze'ev Mishel is quoted in *Haggadas*

The Cynical Son

1. *Maharal* explains that this blessing is meant to impress upon us the obligation of חייב אדם לראות את עצמו כאילו הוא יצא ממצרים, that each person must consider himself as if he left Egypt. The Mishnah in *Berachos*[126] speaks of four types of people who are צריכים להודות, they *need* to express gratitude to God.[127] At this point, we go beyond this to say we are חייב to do so. They are *obligated*. Recently a parent came to me to complain of her child who was not behaving properly to her. She asked, "Don't I *deserve* her respect?" I responded, "Regardless of what you deserve, she's *obligated* to respect you." The purpose of the *Birchas HeGeulah* section of Maggid is to remind us of our obligations.

2. *Haggadah Sheleimah* suggests that this change is based on a scribal error. The opinion that we

The Pure Son

1. *Shibbolei HaLeket* considers this blessing to be in the place of a *birchas hamitzvah* of *sippur yetzias Mitzrayim*. Usually blessings on mitzvos are said עובר לעשייתן, before doing the mitzvah, and there was a hint to this earlier in Maggid Section 6, *Baruch HaMakom*.[132] The reason for saying it now is to teach the inextricable connection referenced numerous times already, between *sippur yetziyas Mitzrayim* and the mitzvos of Matzah and Maror, which are about to be fulfilled.

2. The change is based on a mistaken understanding of what this blessing entails. If it is a prayer for subsequent years for our aspirations of Pesach, then there may be a reason to switch the order, as suggested above. In such a case, זבחים refers to the specific offering of the *chagigah* of the fourteenth of Nissan. However, if it is a general prayer for a

The Withdrawn Son

1. On Chanukah and Purim we recite the blessing "שעשה נסים לאבותינו בימים ההם בזמן הזה – Who performed miracles for our ancestors in those days at this time." *Rashi* says that the *berachah* of אשר גאלנו stands in the place of the *berachah* of שעשה נסים לאבותינו. Our survival has been miraculous and we stress this through this blessing. Our redemption from Egypt serves as a paradigm for our future aspirations as we find in the verse:

כימי צאתך מארץ מצרים אראנו נפלאות:

As in the days when you left the land of Egypt, I will show you miracles.[120]

2. Rav Yaakov Emden[121] explains that there is no question to ask here. When Pesach falls on a Sunday, there is no *chagigah* offered on Shabbos at all, so there is no need to switch the order.

Mei'Otzreinu HaYashan,[179] explaining this dispute as a function of two approaches to Roman subjugation. Rabbi Tarfon held the opinion that we should keep a low profile and obey Roman decrees. He felt that rebellion was futile and could only lead to severe disappointment and failure. Therefore, for him, it was enough to end Maggid with a short blessing calling attention to the past, and not drawing any additional attention to our aspirations for the present or future. Rabbi Akiva, on the other hand, held fast to the revolt at hand, in support of Bar Kochba.[180] He felt that Maggid reaches its crescendo with reference not only to the past, but to the future as well. For this reason, he adds a prayer for our return to the sacrificial order[181] and greatly enlarges the scope of the blessing with a concluding line, "ברוך אתה ה׳ גאל ישראל – Blessed are you, God, the Redeemer of Israel."

2. זבחים here refers to the *korban chagigah*[182] eaten before the *korban Pesach*, so that the *korban Pesach* can be eaten on an almost-full stomach,[183] על השובע, while satiated. *Yerushalmi Pesachim*[184] explains that this is to prevent the breaking of the bones which would violate the Torah's commandment.[185] *Mordechai*[186] explains that the *chagigah* is brought first because it can be offered all day in the Temple, as opposed to the *korban Pesach* which can only be brought in the afternoon. However, when Pesach falls on a Sunday, the זבחים are not offered on the eve of

Pesach because, while the *korban Pesach* does override Shabbos,[187] the *chagigah* does not.[188] Therefore, the order is switched for *Motzaei Shabbos*. In that case, the *korban Pesach* is offered first, and the *chagigah* is offered the next day.[189]

3. The order is switched because *Lefichach* (Maggid Section 18) and *Birchas HeGeulah* (Maggid Section 20) have two different purposes. *Lefichach* concentrates on the miracles of the past, and in that case, the miracles of the Egyptian redemption outweigh all others, so we refer first to what was done for our ancestors. *Birchas HeGeulah*, however, projects upon the future, and therefore concentrates first upon us. The prophet Yirmiyahu predicts that the miracles of the ingathering of the exiles will be even greater than the miracles of the Exodus from Egypt.[190]

4. These songs are sung at the advent of our future redemption. Based on the prophecies of Yechezkel[191] and Zechariah,[192] our Sages predicted that our redemption would be preceded by a period known as חבלי משיח, the birth pangs of Mashiach. Just as a birth comes with great pain, so too have our past redemptions been preceded by great historical trials and tribulations. This is denoted, according to Chazal,[193] by the feminine שירה חדשה. However, our future redemption, which is the focus of *Birchas HeGeulah*, will have no such pain again and is therefore referred as a masculine שיר חדש.[194]

The Cynical Son – continued

always say מן הפסחים ומן הזבחים is from the version of the Mishnah in the *Talmud Yerushalmi*. This notation was listed as במש״ב and was meant to signify במשנה שבירושלמי and was mistakenly interpreted as במוצאי שבת.

3. The *Aruch HaShulchan* says that we should always represent ourselves first, as in our prayers when we say, "אלוקינו ואלוקי אבותינו – Our God and the God of our fathers." The question therefore isn't why

we place ourselves first in *Birchas HeGeulah* but why we place our ancestors first in *Lefichach*. This is a special consideration for the *Seder* because the essence of the evening is to recall what was done for us at a specific time. Of course we continue to detail the impact of that redemption for all subsequent generations, as we especially did in *V'Hee She'Amdah* (Maggid Section 11).

4. *Lefichach* refers to the miracles of Egypt,

The Cynical Son – continued

which culminated with the *Shiras HaYam*, which is referred to as the feminine expression השירה הזאת.[128] In contrast, *Birchas HeGeulah* uses the plain word for song, which is the masculine term שיר, and it is defined as a שיר חדש.

The Pure Son – continued

return to our sacrificial order, then there is no need to switch the order at all.

3. The reference to miracles brings up the past, so we stress the past first in *Lefichach* (Maggid Section 18). *Birchas HeGeulah* (Maggid Section 20) is about redemption, and if we don't feel our place in the continuum of God's plan, we won't recognize the past redemption either.

4. The reference to the masculine hints to a שיר חדש, to a pain-free redemptive age. This is hinted in the liturgy of the *Birchas HaMazon*. We say הרחמן הוא ישבור עולנו מעל צוארינו והוא יוליכנו קוממיות לארצינו – May the Merciful One break the yoke from our shoulders and bring us upright into our Land." This is clearly a paraphrase of the Biblical verse "ואשבור מטות עולכם ואולך אתכם קוממיות – I will break the bars of your yoke and make you walk upright."[133] The Torah speaks of breaking the bars of the yoke, while the *Birchas HaMazon* speaks of breaking the entire yoke. The Torah version refers to the broken bar of the yoke, with the yoke left intact. This is symbolic of releasing us from the Egyptian burden, even as the yoke of other nations might subsequently be upon us. However, the *Birchas HaMazon* liturgy looks to a time when the yoke is broken altogether as we are released from שעבוד מלכיות, the burdens of the exile, altogether and forever.

The Withdrawn Son – continued

3. We understand why our ancestors are mentioned first in *Lefichach*, for the miracles that were wrought for them were openly recognizable, while the daily miracles wrought for us are not. However, when we refer to our redemption, *we* must be mentioned first for a simple reason. Our Sages say that every generation is weaker in spirituality than the previous one. This is known as *yeridas hadoros*, and is a function of a greater and greater distance in time from revelation and prophecy. As such, every subsequent generation is in a greater need for redemption and must therefore be mentioned first.

4. The feminine phrase שירה חדשה in *Lefichach* refers to our reaction to the redemption from Egypt, in which the Israelites remained passive as they were redeemed by the miraculous outstretched hand of God. *Birchas HeGeulah* references the masculine שיר חדש, to indicate a more active role that we would have to play in subsequent redemptions to our own day. The denotation of femininity to a more passive role is consistent with Chazal's depiction of gender roles in the time of *Yetzias Mitzrayim*. The righteous women cajole the men to hope for a better day when the men are ready to surrender to the hopelessness of the bitter exile. Miriam convinces her father to renew his hope for salvation, and all we see are women in the efforts of saving the day for our nation in the beginning of *Sefer Shemos*. Yirmiyahu predicts that women will emerge from this passivity in the Messianic age in the following prophecy: "כי ברא ה' חדשה בארץ נקבה תסובב גבר – God has created a new thing on Earth. A woman shall court a man."[122] *Rashi* understands the woman and the man to be symbolic of the relationship between God and His people. Throughout Biblical history, God sent prophets to us to exhort us to improve our ways. The new thing is that in the future, He

will not send prophets to pursue us, but we will have to search to find Him.[123] In this allegory, the woman is Israel and the man is God.[124] According to *Malbim*,[125] the female represents the Land of Israel, and the male represents the People of Israel.[126] Our Sages explain that since man lost his rib,[127] he is the one who must engage in the search for it.[128] This is why the man pursues the woman for marriage. So too, a people pursues a land for inhabitance.[129] However, Yirmiyahu is predicting that in the future, the Land will pursue us. This prophecy was realized by the Persians inviting us to return to Israel after the Babylonian exile. The land, as it were, invited us to return. *Malbim*, living in the latter half of the nineteenth century, predicted that we would return to Israel in the future under similar circumstances, invited to do so by the nations of the world. We were not worthy for the full realization of this prophecy, but the advent of our successful return to our Holy Land is no less miraculous, as we are closer than we have been in nearly two thousand years to finally realizing the dream of a renewed Temple and an ability to eat the *korban Pesach* once again.

I conclude with the simplest explanation of Yirmiyahu's prophecy, that שיר חדש and שירה חדשה join together in serving Hashem as we march toward the Messianic age. "נקבה תסובב גבר – The female shall encircle the man" means that women will emerge to have a crucial role in our future redemption, and they will do so openly and significantly. They will do so in the classroom, in media, in print, and in the community. The withdrawn child will be opened up because את פתח לו. In second person feminine, the woman will open up to him and thus open him up and bring out his full potential, as we move through these exciting times to our redemption.

רחצה

Since it is forbidden to interrupt unnecessarily between the washing of the hands and the eating of the Korech sandwich, the leader should relate to the participants the various rules of matzah consumption before washing his hands. He should remind everyone that they must eat a *k'zayis* of matzah within a time span of *k'dei achilas pras* (two minutes according to the most stringent opinion; four or even nine minutes according to more lenient opinions) and that the matzah and Korech must be eaten while reclining to the left side. The hands are washed in preparation for the meal and the following blessing is recited:

בָּרוּךְ אַתָּה יהוה אֱלֹהֵינוּ מֶלֶךְ הָעוֹלָם, אֲשֶׁר קִדְּשָׁנוּ בְּמִצְוֹתָיו וְצִוָּנוּ עַל נְטִילַת יָדָיִם:

Blessed are You, Hashem, our God, King of the universe, Who has sanctified us through His commandments and commanded us concerning the washing of the hands.

מוֹצִיא

The three matzos are held, and the following blessing is recited:

בָּרוּךְ אַתָּה יהוה אֱלֹהֵינוּ מֶלֶךְ הָעוֹלָם, הַמּוֹצִיא לֶחֶם מִן הָאָרֶץ:

Blessed are You, Hashem, our God, King of the universe, Who brings forth bread from the earth.

מַצָּה

The bottom matzah is released. The following blessing is recited while holding the top two matzos:

בָּרוּךְ אַתָּה יהוה אֱלֹהֵינוּ מֶלֶךְ הָעוֹלָם, אֲשֶׁר קִדְּשָׁנוּ בְּמִצְוֹתָיו וְצִוָּנוּ עַל אֲכִילַת מַצָּה:

Blessed are You, Hashem, our God, King of the universe, Who has sanctified us through His commandments and commanded us concerning the eating of matzah.

A *k'zayis* of matzah is eaten while reclining on the left side.

מָרוֹר

A *k'zayis* of maror is dipped in charoses. The charoses should then be shaken off the maror (so as not to sweeten its bitter taste), and the following blessing is recited:

בָּרוּךְ אַתָּה יהוה אֱלֹהֵינוּ מֶלֶךְ הָעוֹלָם, אֲשֶׁר קִדְּשָׁנוּ בְּמִצְוֹתָיו וְצִוָּנוּ עַל אֲכִילַת מָרוֹר:

Blessed are You, Hashem, our God, King of the universe, Who has sanctified us through His commandments and commanded us concerning the eating of maror.

The *k'zayis* of maror is eaten (without reclining).

כּוֹרֵךְ

A *k'zayis* of the bottom matzah is taken together with a *k'zayis* of maror (some people dip the maror in charoses), and the following is recited:

זֵכֶר לְמִקְדָּשׁ כְּהִלֵּל.
כֵּן עָשָׂה הִלֵּל, בִּזְמַן שֶׁבֵּית הַמִּקְדָּשׁ הָיָה קַיָּם, הָיָה כּוֹרֵךְ מַצָּה וּמָרוֹר וְאוֹכֵל בְּיַחַד, לְקַיֵּם מַה שֶּׁנֶּאֱמַר, עַל מַצּוֹת וּמְרֹרִים יֹאכְלֻהוּ:

In remembrance of the Temple, like Hillel. This is what Hillel did, when the Temple was still standing. He would combine matzah and maror and eat them together, in fulfillment of what it says: "They shall eat it together with matzos and maror" (*Bamidbar* 9:11).

The matzah-and-maror combination is eaten while reclining on the left side.

שלחן עורך

It is customary to eat eggs at the beginning of the meal. Care should be taken to leave enough time in order to be able to eat the Afikoman before halachic midnight. One should also be sure to leave some appetite for the Afikoman.

צפון

At the end of the meal, a *k'zayis* (according to some, two *k'zeisim*) of the matzah that was hidden away earlier is eaten as the Afikoman. The Afikoman should be eaten while reclining on the left side. One may not eat anything after the Afikoman, nor may he drink anything (besides the third and fourth cups of wine) other than water.

בָּרֵךְ

The third cup of wine, over which the Grace is recited, is poured. It is customary for the master of the house to lead the Grace at the Seder.

שִׁיר הַמַּעֲלוֹת, בְּשׁוּב יְהֹוָה אֶת שִׁיבַת צִיּוֹן הָיִינוּ כְּחֹלְמִים: אָז יִמָּלֵא שְׂחוֹק פִּינוּ וּלְשׁוֹנֵנוּ רִנָּה, אָז יֹאמְרוּ בַגּוֹיִם הִגְדִּיל יְהֹוָה לַעֲשׂוֹת עִם אֵלֶּה: הִגְדִּיל יְהֹוָה לַעֲשׂוֹת עִמָּנוּ הָיִינוּ שְׂמֵחִים: שׁוּבָה יְהֹוָה אֶת שְׁבִיתֵנוּ כַּאֲפִיקִים בַּנֶּגֶב: הַזֹּרְעִים בְּדִמְעָה בְּרִנָּה יִקְצֹרוּ: הָלוֹךְ יֵלֵךְ וּבָכֹה נֹשֵׂא מֶשֶׁךְ הַזָּרַע בֹּא יָבֹא בְרִנָּה נֹשֵׂא אֲלֻמֹּתָיו:

A song of ascents. When Hashem will return the exiles of Zion, we will be like dreamers. Then our mouth will be filled with laughter, and our tongue with shouts of joy. Then will they say among the nations, "Hashem has done great things for these people." Hashem has done great things for us. Then we will be joyful. Hashem, return our exiles, like streams in parched land. Those who sow in tears will reap with shouts of joy. He keeps going along weeping, carrying the load of seed; but he will surely come back with shouts of joy, carrying his sheaves (*Tehillim* 126).

The following invitation to say Grace is added when there are three adult males present. When ten adult males are present, the words in parentheses are also added.

המזמן: רַבּוֹתַי נְבָרֵךְ:

Leader: Gentlemen, let us say Grace!

המסובים: יְהִי שֵׁם יהוה מְבֹרָךְ מֵעַתָּה וְעַד עוֹלָם:

Others: May the Name of Hashem be blessed from now to eternity.

המזמן: יְהִי שֵׁם יהוה מְבֹרָךְ מֵעַתָּה וְעַד עוֹלָם: בִּרְשׁוּת מָרָנָן וְרַבָּנָן וְרַבּוֹתַי, נְבָרֵךְ (אֱלֹהֵינוּ) שֶׁאָכַלְנוּ מִשֶּׁלּוֹ:

Leader: May the Name of Hashem be blessed from now to eternity. With the permission of my masters, teachers and gentlemen, let us bless Him (our God), of Whose [bounty] we have eaten.

המסובים: בָּרוּךְ (אֱלֹהֵינוּ) שֶׁאָכַלְנוּ מִשֶּׁלּוֹ וּבְטוּבוֹ חָיִינוּ:

Others: Blessed be He (our God) of Whose bounty we have eaten, and by Whose grace we live.

המזמן: בָּרוּךְ (אֱלֹהֵינוּ) שֶׁאָכַלְנוּ מִשֶּׁלּוֹ וּבְטוּבוֹ חָיִינוּ:

Leader: Blessed be He (our God) of Whose bounty we have eaten, and by Whose grace we live.

בָּרוּךְ אַתָּה יהוה אֱלֹהֵינוּ מֶלֶךְ הָעוֹלָם, הַזָּן אֶת הָעוֹלָם כֻּלּוֹ בְּטוּבוֹ בְּחֵן בְּחֶסֶד וּבְרַחֲמִים, הוּא נוֹתֵן לֶחֶם לְכָל בָּשָׂר כִּי לְעוֹלָם חַסְדּוֹ, וּבְטוּבוֹ הַגָּדוֹל תָּמִיד לֹא חָסַר לָנוּ וְאַל יֶחְסַר לָנוּ מָזוֹן לְעוֹלָם וָעֶד, בַּעֲבוּר שְׁמוֹ הַגָּדוֹל, כִּי הוּא אֵל זָן וּמְפַרְנֵס לַכֹּל וּמֵטִיב לַכֹּל, וּמֵכִין מָזוֹן לְכָל בְּרִיּוֹתָיו אֲשֶׁר בָּרָא. בָּרוּךְ אַתָּה יהוה, הַזָּן אֶת הַכֹּל:

Blessed are You, Hashem, our God, King of the universe, Who feeds the whole world in His benevolence, with graciousness, with kindness and with compassion. He "gives food to all flesh, for His kindness is forever" (*Tehillim* 136:25). And in His great benevolence, we have never lacked food, nor will we ever lack food, for the sake of His great Name, for He is God, Who feeds and sustains all, is benevolent to all, and prepares food for all His creatures that He created. Blessed are You, Hashem, Who provides food for all.

נוֹדֶה לְךָ יהוה אֱלֹהֵינוּ עַל שֶׁהִנְחַלְתָּ לַאֲבוֹתֵינוּ, אֶרֶץ חֶמְדָּה טוֹבָה וּרְחָבָה, וְעַל שֶׁהוֹצֵאתָנוּ יהוה אֱלֹהֵינוּ מֵאֶרֶץ מִצְרַיִם, וּפְדִיתָנוּ מִבֵּית עֲבָדִים, וְעַל בְּרִיתְךָ שֶׁחָתַמְתָּ בִּבְשָׂרֵנוּ, וְעַל תּוֹרָתְךָ שֶׁלִּמַּדְתָּנוּ, וְעַל חֻקֶּיךָ שֶׁהוֹדַעְתָּנוּ, וְעַל חַיִּים חֵן וָחֶסֶד שֶׁחוֹנַנְתָּנוּ, וְעַל אֲכִילַת מָזוֹן שָׁאַתָּה זָן וּמְפַרְנֵס אוֹתָנוּ תָּמִיד, בְּכָל יוֹם וּבְכָל עֵת וּבְכָל שָׁעָה:

We thank You, Hashem, our God, for having bestowed upon our ancestors a precious, good and spacious land; for having brought us out, Hashem our God, from the land of Egypt and redeeming us from the house of bondage; for Your covenant, which You have sealed in our flesh, and for Your Torah, which You have taught us; for Your statutes, which You have made known to us; for life, grace and kindness which You have graciously granted us; and for our eating of the food that You provide and sustain us with constantly, every day, at all times, and at every hour.

וְעַל הַכֹּל יהוה אֱלֹהֵינוּ אֲנַחְנוּ מוֹדִים לָךְ, וּמְבָרְכִים אוֹתָךְ, יִתְבָּרַךְ שִׁמְךָ בְּפִי כָּל חַי תָּמִיד לְעוֹלָם וָעֶד. כַּכָּתוּב, וְאָכַלְתָּ וְשָׂבָעְתָּ, וּבֵרַכְתָּ אֶת יהוה אֱלֹהֶיךָ עַל הָאָרֶץ הַטֹּבָה אֲשֶׁר נָתַן לָךְ. בָּרוּךְ אַתָּה יהוה עַל הָאָרֶץ וְעַל הַמָּזוֹן:

For everything, Hashem our God, we are thankful to You and bless You. May Your Name always be blessed in the mouth of every living being, forever. Thus it is written: "And you will eat and become sated, and you shall bless Hashem your God for the fine land that He has given you" (*Devarim* 8:10). Blessed are You, Hashem, for the land and for the food.

רַחֵם נָא יהוה אֱלֹהֵינוּ, עַל יִשְׂרָאֵל עַמֶּךָ, וְעַל יְרוּשָׁלַיִם עִירֶךָ, וְעַל צִיּוֹן מִשְׁכַּן כְּבוֹדֶךָ, וְעַל מַלְכוּת בֵּית דָּוִד מְשִׁיחֶךָ, וְעַל הַבַּיִת הַגָּדוֹל וְהַקָּדוֹשׁ שֶׁנִּקְרָא שִׁמְךָ עָלָיו. אֱלֹהֵינוּ אָבִינוּ, רְעֵנוּ זוּנֵנוּ פַּרְנְסֵנוּ וְכַלְכְּלֵנוּ וְהַרְוִיחֵנוּ, וְהַרְוַח לָנוּ יהוה אֱלֹהֵינוּ מְהֵרָה מִכָּל צָרוֹתֵינוּ. וְנָא אַל תַּצְרִיכֵנוּ יהוה אֱלֹהֵינוּ לֹא לִידֵי מַתְּנַת בָּשָׂר וָדָם, וְלֹא לִידֵי הַלְוָאָתָם, כִּי אִם לְיָדְךָ הַמְּלֵאָה הַפְּתוּחָה הַקְּדוֹשָׁה וְהָרְחָבָה, שֶׁלֹּא נֵבוֹשׁ וְלֹא נִכָּלֵם לְעוֹלָם וָעֶד:

Have mercy, Hashem our God, upon Israel Your people, upon Jerusalem Your city, upon Zion the abode of Your glory, upon the kingship of the House of David Your anointed one, and upon the great and holy Temple with which Your name is associated. Our God, our Father! Provide for us, nourish us, sustain us, support us and relieve us; and speedily grant us relief, Hashem our God, from all our troubles. And do not make us dependent, Hashem our God, upon gifts of mortal men nor upon their loans - but only upon Your full, open, holy and bountiful hand, that we may never be ashamed or embarrassed.

On Shabbos, the following paragraph is added:

רְצֵה וְהַחֲלִיצֵנוּ יהוה אֱלֹהֵינוּ בְּמִצְוֹתֶיךָ, וּבְמִצְוַת יוֹם הַשְּׁבִיעִי הַשַּׁבָּת הַגָּדוֹל וְהַקָּדוֹשׁ הַזֶּה, כִּי יוֹם זֶה גָּדוֹל וְקָדוֹשׁ הוּא לְפָנֶיךָ, לִשְׁבָּת בּוֹ וְלָנוּחַ

May it please You, Hashem our God, to grant us strength through Your commandments, and through the commandment of the seventh day – this great and holy Sabbath. For this day is a great and holy one before You, to refrain from work and to rest on it with love, in accordance with the commandment of Your will. And may it be Your will, Hashem, our God, to grant us tranquility, that there should be no misfortune, sorrow or anguish on our day of our rest. And allow us to behold, Hashem our God, the solace of Zion Your city and the rebuilding of Jerusalem Your holy city, for You are the Master of salvations and the Master of consolations.

בּוֹ בְּאַהֲבָה כְּמִצְוַת רְצוֹנֶךָ, וּבִרְצוֹנְךָ הָנִיחַ לָנוּ יהוה אֱלֹהֵינוּ שֶׁלֹּא תְהֵא צָרָה וְיָגוֹן וַאֲנָחָה בְּיוֹם מְנוּחָתֵנוּ, וְהַרְאֵנוּ יהוה אֱלֹהֵינוּ בְּנֶחָמַת צִיּוֹן עִירֶךָ וּבְבִנְיַן יְרוּשָׁלַיִם עִיר קָדְשֶׁךָ, כִּי אַתָּה הוּא בַּעַל הַיְשׁוּעוֹת וּבַעַל הַנֶּחָמוֹת:

Our God and God of our fathers! May they ascend, come and reach, be seen and accepted, heard, recalled and remembered before You – the remembrance and recollection of us, the remembrance of our fathers, the remembrance of the Messiah, the descendant of David Your servant, the remembrance of Jerusalem Your holy city, and the remembrance of all Your people the House of Israel, for deliverance, welfare, grace, kindness, mercy, life and peace, on this day of the Festival of Matzos. Remember us on it, Hashem, our God, for good; recall us on it for a blessing; and spare us on it for life. And with a word of salvation and compassion, pity us and be gracious to us, and have mercy upon us and save us; for our eyes are [lifted] towards You, for You are a gracious and merciful God (and King).

אֱלֹהֵינוּ וֵאלֹהֵי אֲבוֹתֵינוּ, יַעֲלֶה וְיָבֹא וְיַגִּיעַ וְיֵרָאֶה וְיֵרָצֶה וְיִשָּׁמַע וְיִפָּקֵד וְיִזָּכֵר זִכְרוֹנֵנוּ וּפִקְדוֹנֵנוּ, וְזִכְרוֹן אֲבוֹתֵינוּ, וְזִכְרוֹן מָשִׁיחַ בֶּן דָּוִד עַבְדֶּךָ, וְזִכְרוֹן יְרוּשָׁלַיִם עִיר קָדְשֶׁךָ, וְזִכְרוֹן כָּל עַמְּךָ בֵּית יִשְׂרָאֵל לְפָנֶיךָ, לִפְלֵיטָה לְטוֹבָה לְחֵן וּלְחֶסֶד וּלְרַחֲמִים לְחַיִּים וּלְשָׁלוֹם בְּיוֹם חַג הַמַּצּוֹת הַזֶּה, זָכְרֵנוּ יהוה אֱלֹהֵינוּ בּוֹ לְטוֹבָה, וּפָקְדֵנוּ בוֹ לִבְרָכָה, וְהוֹשִׁיעֵנוּ בוֹ לְחַיִּים, וּבִדְבַר יְשׁוּעָה וְרַחֲמִים חוּס וְחָנֵּנוּ וְרַחֵם עָלֵינוּ וְהוֹשִׁיעֵנוּ, כִּי אֵלֶיךָ עֵינֵינוּ, כִּי אֵל מֶלֶךְ חַנּוּן וְרַחוּם אָתָּה:

וּבְנֵה יְרוּשָׁלַיִם עִיר הַקֹּדֶשׁ בִּמְהֵרָה בְּיָמֵינוּ. בָּרוּךְ אַתָּה יהוה בּוֹנֵה בְרַחֲמָיו יְרוּשָׁלָיִם, אָמֵן:

Rebuild Jerusalem the holy city speedily in our days. Blessed are You, Hashem, Who rebuilds Jerusalem in His mercy. Amen.

בָּרוּךְ אַתָּה יהוה אֱלֹהֵינוּ מֶלֶךְ הָעוֹלָם, הָאֵל אָבִינוּ מַלְכֵּנוּ אַדִּירֵנוּ בּוֹרְאֵנוּ גּוֹאֲלֵנוּ יוֹצְרֵנוּ קְדוֹשֵׁנוּ קְדוֹשׁ יַעֲקֹב, רוֹעֵנוּ רוֹעֵה יִשְׂרָאֵל, הַמֶּלֶךְ הַטּוֹב וְהַמֵּטִיב לַכֹּל, שֶׁבְּכָל יוֹם וָיוֹם הוּא הֵטִיב הוּא מֵטִיב הוּא יֵיטִיב לָנוּ, הוּא גְמָלָנוּ הוּא גוֹמְלֵנוּ הוּא יִגְמְלֵנוּ לָעַד, לְחֵן וּלְחֶסֶד וּלְרַחֲמִים וּלְרֶוַח הַצָּלָה וְהַצְלָחָה, בְּרָכָה וִישׁוּעָה נֶחָמָה פַּרְנָסָה וְכַלְכָּלָה, וְרַחֲמִים וְחַיִּים וְשָׁלוֹם וְכָל טוֹב, וּמִכָּל טוּב לְעוֹלָם אַל יְחַסְּרֵנוּ:

Blessed are You, Hashem, our God, King of the universe, the God, our Father, our Mighty One, our Creator, our Redeemer, our Maker, our Holy One, the Holy One of Yaakov, our Shepherd, the Shepherd of Israel, the King Who is benevolent and bestows benevolence upon all, Who each and every day has done good for us, does good for us, and will do good for us; He has bestowed upon us, bestows upon us, and will forever bestow upon us grace, kindness and mercy, relief, salvation, success, blessing, deliverance, consolation, sustenance and nourishment, mercy, life, peace and all goodness; and may He never allow us any lack of bounty.

הָרַחֲמָן, הוּא יִמְלֹךְ עָלֵינוּ לְעוֹלָם וָעֶד:

May the Merciful One reign over us forever and ever.

הָרַחֲמָן, הוּא יִתְבָּרַךְ בַּשָּׁמַיִם וּבָאָרֶץ:

May the Merciful One be blessed in heaven and on earth.

הָרַחֲמָן, הוּא יִשְׁתַּבַּח לְדוֹר דּוֹרִים, וְיִתְפָּאַר בָּנוּ לָעַד וּלְנֵצַח נְצָחִים, וְיִתְהַדַּר בָּנוּ לָעַד וּלְעוֹלְמֵי עוֹלָמִים:

May the Merciful One be praised for all generations, and may He be glorified among us forever and ever, and may He be honored among us for all eternity.

הָרַחֲמָן, הוּא יְפַרְנְסֵנוּ בְּכָבוֹד:

May the Merciful One grant us honorable sustenance.

הָרַחֲמָן, הוּא יִשְׁבּוֹר עוֹל גָּלוּתֵנוּ מֵעַל צַוָּארֵנוּ וְהוּא יוֹלִיכֵנוּ קוֹמְמִיּוּת לְאַרְצֵנוּ:

May the Merciful One break off our yoke from our necks and lead us upright to our land.

הָרַחֲמָן, הוּא יִשְׁלַח לָנוּ בְּרָכָה מְרֻבָּה בַּבַּיִת הַזֶּה, וְעַל שֻׁלְחָן זֶה שֶׁאָכַלְנוּ עָלָיו:

May the Merciful One send us abundant blessing into this house, and upon this table at which we have eaten.

הָרַחֲמָן, הוּא יִשְׁלַח לָנוּ אֶת אֵלִיָּהוּ הַנָּבִיא זָכוּר לַטּוֹב וִיבַשֶּׂר לָנוּ בְּשׂוֹרוֹת טוֹבוֹת יְשׁוּעוֹת וְנֶחָמוֹת:

May the Merciful One send us Elijah the Prophet - may he be remembered for a blessing - to proclaim good tidings of salvation and consolation to us.

הָרַחֲמָן, הוּא יְבָרֵךְ אֶת [אָבִי מוֹרִי] בַּעַל הַבַּיִת הַזֶּה וְאֶת [אִמִּי מוֹרָתִי] בַּעֲלַת הַבַּיִת הַזֶּה, אוֹתָם וְאֶת בֵּיתָם וְאֶת זַרְעָם וְאֶת כָּל אֲשֶׁר לָהֶם, אוֹתָנוּ וְאֶת כָּל אֲשֶׁר לָנוּ, כְּמוֹ שֶׁנִּתְבָּרְכוּ אֲבוֹתֵינוּ אַבְרָהָם יִצְחָק וְיַעֲקֹב בַּכֹּל מִכֹּל כֹּל, כֵּן יְבָרֵךְ אוֹתָנוּ כֻּלָּנוּ יַחַד, בִּבְרָכָה שְׁלֵמָה, וְנֹאמַר אָמֵן:

May the Merciful One bless [my father, my teacher] the master of this house and [my mother, my teacher] the lady of this house – them, their household, their offspring, and all that is theirs, as well as us and all that is ours. Just as our forefathers Avraham, Yitzchak and Yaakov, were blessed with everything, from everything, and everything, so may He bless all of us together, with a complete blessing. And let us say Amen.

בַּמָּרוֹם יְלַמְּדוּ עֲלֵיהֶם וְעָלֵינוּ זְכוּת שֶׁתְּהֵא לְמִשְׁמֶרֶת שָׁלוֹם, וְנִשָּׂא בְרָכָה מֵאֵת יהוה וּצְדָקָה מֵאֱלֹהֵי יִשְׁעֵנוּ, וְנִמְצָא חֵן וְשֵׂכֶל טוֹב בְּעֵינֵי אֱלֹהִים וְאָדָם:

On High, may there be invoked merit for them and for us, which will serve them as a safeguard for peace. And may we receive blessing from Hashem and kindness from the God of our salvation, and may we find grace and good repute in the eyes of God and man.

הָרַחֲמָן, הוּא יַנְחִילֵנוּ יוֹם שֶׁכֻּלוֹ שַׁבָּת וּמְנוּחָה לְחַיֵּי הָעוֹלָמִים:

May the Merciful One allow us to inherit that day that will be a complete Sabbath and rest, for eternal life.

הָרַחֲמָן הוּא יַנְחִילֵנוּ יוֹם שֶׁכֻּלוֹ טוֹב. יוֹם שֶׁכֻּלוֹ אָרוּךְ, יוֹם שֶׁצַּדִּיקִים יוֹשְׁבִים וְעַטְרוֹתֵיהֶם בְּרָאשֵׁיהֶם וְנֶהֱנִים מִזִּיו הַשְּׁכִינָה, וִיהִי חֶלְקֵנוּ עִמָּהֶם:

May the Merciful One allow us to inherit that day that will be total goodness, that day when the righteous sit with their crowns of glory on their heads, benefiting from the splendor of the Divine Presence; and may our portion be among them.

הָרַחֲמָן, הוּא יְזַכֵּנוּ לִימוֹת הַמָּשִׁיחַ וּלְחַיֵּי הָעוֹלָם הַבָּא:

May the Merciful One grant us the privilege of experiencing the Messianic era and the life of the Next World. He is a tower of His king's salvation, and does kindness for His anointed one, for David and his descendants forever.

מִגְדּוֹל יְשׁוּעוֹת מַלְכּוֹ וְעֹשֶׂה חֶסֶד לִמְשִׁיחוֹ לְדָוִד וּלְזַרְעוֹ עַד עוֹלָם: עֹשֶׂה שָׁלוֹם בִּמְרוֹמָיו הוּא יַעֲשֶׂה שָׁלוֹם עָלֵינוּ וְעַל כָּל יִשְׂרָאֵל, וְאִמְרוּ אָמֵן:

He Who makes peace in His heights – may He make peace over us and over all Israel. And say, Amen.

יְראוּ אֶת יהוה קְדֹשָׁיו, כִּי אֵין מַחְסוֹר לִירֵאָיו: כְּפִירִים רָשׁוּ וְרָעֵבוּ, וְדֹרְשֵׁי יהוה לֹא יַחְסְרוּ כָל טוֹב: הוֹדוּ לַיהוה כִּי טוֹב, כִּי לְעוֹלָם חַסְדּוֹ: פּוֹתֵחַ אֶת יָדֶךָ, וּמַשְׂבִּיעַ לְכָל חַי רָצוֹן: בָּרוּךְ הַגֶּבֶר אֲשֶׁר יִבְטַח בַּיהוה, וְהָיָה יְהוָה מִבְטַחוֹ: נַעַר הָיִיתִי גַּם זָקַנְתִּי, וְלֹא

Fear Hashem, you, His holy ones, for those who fear Him want for nothing. Young lions may be deprived and go hungry, but those who seek out Hashem shall not lack any goodness. Give thanks to Hashem, for He is good, for His kindness is forever. You open Your hand and satisfy the desire of every living thing. Blessed be the man who trusts in Hashem and makes Hashem his security. I was once a boy, and have also grown old, and I have never seen a righteous man forsaken or his offspring begging

רָאִיתִי צַדִּיק נֶעֱזָב וְזַרְעוֹ מְבַקֶּשׁ לָחֶם: יהוה עֹז לְעַמּוֹ יִתֵּן, יהוה יְבָרֵךְ אֶת עַמּוֹ בַשָּׁלוֹם:

for bread. Hashem will give strength to His people; Hashem will bless His people with peace.

בָּרוּךְ אַתָּה יהוה אֱלֹהֵינוּ מֶלֶךְ הָעוֹלָם, בּוֹרֵא פְּרִי הַגָּפֶן:

Blessed are You, Hashem, our God, King of the universe, who creates the fruit of the vine.

The third cup of wine is now drunk while reclining on the left side.

The Cup of Eliyahu is now filled. There are those who pour the fourth cup of wine at this point as well. (Others pour it after the recitation of these verses.) The door of the house is opened as the following verses are recited. (Some have the custom to rise while reciting these passages.)

שְׁפֹךְ חֲמָתְךָ אֶל הַגּוֹיִם אֲשֶׁר לֹא יְדָעוּךָ וְעַל מַמְלָכוֹת אֲשֶׁר בְּשִׁמְךָ לֹא קָרָאוּ: כִּי אָכַל אֶת יַעֲקֹב וְאֶת נָוֵהוּ הֵשַׁמּוּ: שְׁפָךְ עֲלֵיהֶם זַעְמֶךָ וַחֲרוֹן אַפְּךָ יַשִּׂיגֵם: תִּרְדֹּף בְּאַף וְתַשְׁמִידֵם מִתַּחַת שְׁמֵי יהוה:

Pour out Your wrath upon the nations that do not acknowledge You and upon the kingdoms that do not call upon Your Name. For they have devoured Yaakov and laid waste his abode (*Tehillim* 79:6-7). Pour out Your fury upon them, and let the heat of Your anger overtake them

(ibid. 69:25). Pursue [them] with anger, and destroy them from beneath the heavens of Hashem (*Eichah* 3:66).

The door is closed.

הלל

The fourth cup of wine is poured. The remaining part of Hallel is now recited.

לֹא לָנוּ יהוה לֹא לָנוּ, כִּי לְשִׁמְךָ תֵּן כָּבוֹד עַל חַסְדְּךָ עַל אֲמִתֶּךָ: לָמָּה יֹאמְרוּ הַגּוֹיִם, אַיֵּה נָא אֱלֹהֵיהֶם: וֵאלֹהֵינוּ בַשָּׁמָיִם, כֹּל אֲשֶׁר חָפֵץ עָשָׂה: עֲצַבֵּיהֶם כֶּסֶף וְזָהָב, מַעֲשֵׂה יְדֵי אָדָם: פֶּה לָהֶם וְלֹא יְדַבֵּרוּ, עֵינַיִם לָהֶם וְלֹא

Not for us, Hashem, not for us, but for Your Name give glory, for the sake of Your kindness and Your truth. Why should the nations say, "Where, now, is their God?" But our God is in heaven; He does whatever He desires. Their idols are silver and gold, the

יִרְאוּ: אָזְנַיִם לָהֶם וְלֹא יִשְׁמָעוּ, אַף לָהֶם וְלֹא יְרִיחוּן: יְדֵיהֶם וְלֹא יְמִישׁוּן רַגְלֵיהֶם וְלֹא יְהַלֵּכוּ, לֹא יֶהְגּוּ בִּגְרוֹנָם: כְּמוֹהֶם יִהְיוּ עֹשֵׂיהֶם, כֹּל אֲשֶׁר בֹּטֵחַ בָּהֶם: יִשְׂרָאֵל בְּטַח בַּיהוה, עֶזְרָם וּמָגִנָּם הוּא: בֵּית אַהֲרֹן בִּטְחוּ בַּיהוה, עֶזְרָם וּמָגִנָּם הוּא: יִרְאֵי יהוה בִּטְחוּ בַיהוה, עֶזְרָם וּמָגִנָּם הוּא:

product of human hands. They have a mouth but cannot speak; they have eyes but cannot see; they have ears but cannot hear; they have a nose but cannot smell; they have hands but cannot feel; they have feet but cannot walk; they can utter no sound with their throat. May those who make them be like them – all those who trust in them! Israel, trust in Hashem; He is their help and their shield. House of Aaron, trust in Hashem; He is their help and their shield. You who fear Hashem, trust in Hashem; He is their help and their shield. (*Tehillim* 115).

יהוה זְכָרָנוּ יְבָרֵךְ, יְבָרֵךְ אֶת בֵּית יִשְׂרָאֵל, יְבָרֵךְ אֶת בֵּית אַהֲרֹן: יְבָרֵךְ יִרְאֵי יהוה, הַקְּטַנִּים עִם הַגְּדֹלִים: יֹסֵף יְהוָה עֲלֵיכֶם, עֲלֵיכֶם וְעַל בְּנֵיכֶם: בְּרוּכִים אַתֶּם לַיהוה, עֹשֵׂה שָׁמַיִם וָאָרֶץ: הַשָּׁמַיִם שָׁמַיִם לַיהוה, וְהָאָרֶץ נָתַן לִבְנֵי אָדָם: לֹא הַמֵּתִים יְהַלְלוּ יָהּ, וְלֹא כָּל יֹרְדֵי דוּמָה: וַאֲנַחְנוּ נְבָרֵךְ יָהּ, מֵעַתָּה וְעַד עוֹלָם, הַלְלוּיָהּ:

Hashem, Who has always remembered us, will bless – He will bless the House of Israel, He will bless the House of Aaron, He will bless those who fear Hashem, the smaller ones along with the greater ones. Hashem will increase you – you and your children. Blessed are you for Hashem, the Maker of heaven and earth. The heavens are the heavens of Hashem, but the earth He gave to mankind. The dead do not praise God, nor do those who go down to the grave. But we will bless God, from now to eternity. Halleluyah!

אָהַבְתִּי כִּי יִשְׁמַע יהוה, אֶת קוֹלִי תַּחֲנוּנָי: כִּי הִטָּה אָזְנוֹ לִי, וּבְיָמַי אֶקְרָא: אֲפָפוּנִי חֶבְלֵי מָוֶת, וּמְצָרֵי שְׁאוֹל מְצָאוּנִי, צָרָה וְיָגוֹן אֶמְצָא: וּבְשֵׁם יהוה אֶקְרָא,

I loved that Hashem hears my voice, my prayers. For He inclined His ear to me, so all my days I will call [Him]. The pains of death encompassed me, and the anguish of dying came upon me, I encounter

אָנָּה יהוה מַלְּטָה נַפְשִׁי: חַנּוּן יהוה וְצַדִּיק, וֵאלֹהֵינוּ מְרַחֵם: שֹׁמֵר פְּתָאיִם יהוה, דַּלֹּתִי וְלִי יְהוֹשִׁיעַ: שׁוּבִי נַפְשִׁי לִמְנוּחָיְכִי, כִּי יהוה גָּמַל עָלָיְכִי: כִּי חִלַּצְתָּ נַפְשִׁי מִמָּוֶת, אֶת עֵינִי מִן דִּמְעָה אֶת רַגְלִי מִדֶּחִי: אֶתְהַלֵּךְ לִפְנֵי יהוה, בְּאַרְצוֹת הַחַיִּים: הֶאֱמַנְתִּי כִּי אֲדַבֵּר, אֲנִי עָנִיתִי מְאֹד: אֲנִי אָמַרְתִּי בְחָפְזִי, כָּל הָאָדָם כֹּזֵב:

misfortune and sorrow – and I call out in the name of Hashem, "Please, Hashem, rescue my life!" Hashem is gracious and righteous, and our God shows compassion. Hashem watches over simple people; when I sink low He will save me. Return, my soul, to your rest, for Hashem has dealt kindly with you. For You have released my soul from death, my eyes from tears, my foot from stumbling. I will walk before Hashem in the lands of the living. I had faith when I said, "I am greatly distressed"; I said in my haste, "All men are deceitful" (*Tehillim* 116).

מָה אָשִׁיב לַיהוה, כָּל תַּגְמוּלוֹהִי עָלָי: כּוֹס יְשׁוּעוֹת אֶשָּׂא, וּבְשֵׁם יהוה אֶקְרָא: נְדָרַי לַיהוה אֲשַׁלֵּם, נֶגְדָה נָא לְכָל עַמּוֹ: יָקָר בְּעֵינֵי יהוה, הַמָּוְתָה לַחֲסִידָיו: אָנָּה יהוה כִּי אֲנִי עַבְדֶּךָ, אֲנִי עַבְדְּךָ בֶּן אֲמָתֶךָ, פִּתַּחְתָּ לְמוֹסֵרָי: לְךָ אֶזְבַּח זֶבַח תּוֹדָה וּבְשֵׁם יהוה אֶקְרָא: נְדָרַי לַיהוה אֲשַׁלֵּם, נֶגְדָה נָא לְכָל עַמּוֹ: בְּחַצְרוֹת בֵּית יהוה, בְּתוֹכֵכִי יְרוּשָׁלָיִם, הַלְלוּיָהּ:

With what can I repay Hashem for all His kindness to me? I will raise a cup of salvation and call the name of Hashem. I will fulfill my vows to Hashem now, in the presence of all His people. The death of His pious ones is difficult in the eyes of Hashem. I thank you, Hashem, for I am Your servant; I am Your servant, the son of Your maidservant, and You have broken open my bonds. I will sacrifice a thanksgiving-offering to You, and I will call the name of Hashem. I will fulfill my vows to Hashem now, in the presence of all His people, in the courtyards of the Temple of Hashem, in the midst of Jerusalem. Halleluyah!

הַלְלוּ אֶת יהוה כָּל גּוֹיִם, שַׁבְּחוּהוּ כָּל הָאֻמִּים: כִּי גָבַר עָלֵינוּ חַסְדּוֹ, וֶאֱמֶת יהוה לְעוֹלָם, הַלְלוּיָהּ:

Praise Hashem, all nations! Laud Him, all peoples! For His kindness has overwhelmed us, and the truth of Hashem is forever. Halleluyah (*Tehillim* 117)!

If there are three adult males present at the Seder, the following four verses are recited responsively:

הוֹדוּ לַיהוה כִּי טוֹב כִּי לְעוֹלָם חַסְדּוֹ:

יֹאמַר נָא יִשְׂרָאֵל כִּי לְעוֹלָם חַסְדּוֹ:

יֹאמְרוּ נָא בֵית אַהֲרֹן כִּי לְעוֹלָם חַסְדּוֹ:

יֹאמְרוּ נָא יִרְאֵי יהוה כִּי לְעוֹלָם חַסְדּוֹ:

Give thanks to Hashem, for He is good, for His kindness is forever.

Let Israel say: For His kindness is forever.

Let the House of Aaron say: For His kindness is forever.

Let those who fear Hashem say: For His kindness is forever (*Tehillim* 118).

מִן הַמֵּצַר קָרָאתִי יָּהּ, עָנָנִי בַמֶּרְחָב יָהּ: יהוה לִי לֹא אִירָא, מַה יַּעֲשֶׂה לִי אָדָם: יהוה לִי בְּעֹזְרָי, וַאֲנִי אֶרְאֶה בְשֹׂנְאָי: טוֹב לַחֲסוֹת בַּיהוה, מִבְּטֹחַ בָּאָדָם: טוֹב לַחֲסוֹת בַּיהוה, מִבְּטֹחַ בִּנְדִיבִים: כָּל גּוֹיִם סְבָבוּנִי, בְּשֵׁם יהוה כִּי אֲמִילַם: סַבּוּנִי גַם סְבָבוּנִי, בְּשֵׁם יהוה כִּי אֲמִילַם: סַבּוּנִי כִדְבוֹרִים דֹּעֲכוּ כְּאֵשׁ קוֹצִים, בְּשֵׁם יהוה כִּי אֲמִילַם: דָּחֹה דְחִיתַנִי לִנְפֹּל, וַיהוה עֲזָרָנִי: עָזִּי וְזִמְרָת יָהּ, וַיְהִי לִי לִישׁוּעָה: קוֹל רִנָּה וִישׁוּעָה בְּאָהֳלֵי צַדִּיקִים, יְמִין יהוה עֹשָׂה חָיִל: יְמִין יהוה רוֹמֵמָה, יְמִין יהוה עֹשָׂה חָיִל: לֹא אָמוּת כִּי אֶחְיֶה, וַאֲסַפֵּר מַעֲשֵׂי יָהּ:

Out of the narrow straits I called to God; God answered me by [granting me] spaciousness. Hashem is with me, I shall not fear; what can man do to me? Hashem is with me among those who help me, and I will see my enemies' [downfall]. It is better to seek shelter with Hashem than to trust in man; it is better to seek shelter in Hashem than to trust in nobles. If all the nations surround me, I will cut them down in the name of Hashem. If they surround me and they encompass me, I will cut them down in the name of Hashem. If they surround me like bees, they are extinguished like a fire of thorns; I will cut them down in the Name

יִסֹּר יִסְּרַנִּי יָּה, וְלַמָּוֶת לֹא נְתָנָנִי: פִּתְחוּ לִי שַׁעֲרֵי צֶדֶק, אָבֹא בָם אוֹדֶה יָּה: זֶה הַשַּׁעַר לַיהוה, צַדִּיקִים יָבֹאוּ בוֹ: אוֹדְךָ כִּי עֲנִיתָנִי, וַתְּהִי לִי לִישׁוּעָה: אוֹדְךָ כִּי עֲנִיתָנִי, וַתְּהִי לִי לִישׁוּעָה: אֶבֶן מָאֲסוּ הַבּוֹנִים, הָיְתָה לְרֹאשׁ פִּנָּה: אֶבֶן מָאֲסוּ הַבּוֹנִים, הָיְתָה לְרֹאשׁ פִּנָּה: מֵאֵת יהוה הָיְתָה זֹּאת, הִיא נִפְלָאת בְּעֵינֵינוּ: מֵאֵת יהוה הָיְתָה זֹּאת, הִיא נִפְלָאת בְּעֵינֵינוּ: זֶה הַיּוֹם עָשָׂה יהוה, נָגִילָה וְנִשְׂמְחָה בוֹ: זֶה הַיּוֹם עָשָׂה יהוה, נָגִילָה וְנִשְׂמְחָה בוֹ:

of Hashem. You may push me repeatedly to make me fall, but Hashem helps me. God is my strength and my song, and He has always been my salvation. The sound of shouts of joy and salvation is in the tents of the righteous: "The right hand of Hashem acts valiantly. The right hand of Hashem is exalted; the right hand of Hashem acts valiantly!" I shall not die, but I shall live, and I shall relate the deeds of God. God may chastise me, but He has not given me over to death. Open for me the gates of righteousness; I will enter them and give thanks to God. This is the gate of Hashem; the righteous will enter it. I give thanks to You for You have answered me, and You have been my salvation. I give thanks to You for You have answered me, and You have been my salvation. The stone rejected by the builders has become the main cornerstone. The stone rejected by the builders has become the main cornerstone. This took place because of Hashem; it is wondrous in our eyes. This took place because of Hashem; it is wondrous in our eyes. This is the day that Hashem has made, let us be glad and rejoice on it. This is the day that Hashem has made, let us be glad and rejoice on it.

If there are three adult males present at the Seder, the following four phrases are recited responsively:

אָנָּא יהוה הוֹשִׁיעָה נָּא:
אָנָּא יהוה הוֹשִׁיעָה נָּא:

Please, Hashem, save us now! Please, Hashem, save us now!

אָנָּא יהוה הַצְלִיחָה נָּא:
אָנָּא יהוה הַצְלִיחָה נָּא:

Please, Hashem, grant us success now! Please, Hashem, grant us success now!

בָּרוּךְ הַבָּא בְּשֵׁם יהוה, בֵּרַכְנוּכֶם מִבֵּית יהוה: בָּרוּךְ הַבָּא בְּשֵׁם יהוה, בֵּרַכְנוּכֶם

Blessed is he who comes in the name of Hashem; we bless you from the House of Hashem. Blessed is he

מִבֵּית יְהוָה: אֵל יְהוָה וַיָּאֶר לָנוּ, אִסְרוּ חַג בַּעֲבֹתִים עַד קַרְנוֹת הַמִּזְבֵּחַ: אֵל יְהוָה וַיָּאֶר לָנוּ, אִסְרוּ חַג בַּעֲבֹתִים עַד קַרְנוֹת הַמִּזְבֵּחַ: אֵלִי אַתָּה וְאוֹדֶךָּ, אֱלֹהַי אֲרוֹמְמֶךָּ: אֵלִי אַתָּה וְאוֹדֶךָּ, אֱלֹהַי אֲרוֹמְמֶךָּ: הוֹדוּ לַיהוָה כִּי טוֹב, כִּי לְעוֹלָם חַסְדּוֹ: הוֹדוּ לַיהוָה כִּי טוֹב, כִּי לְעוֹלָם חַסְדּוֹ:

who comes in the name of Hashem; we bless you from the House of Hashem. Hashem is God, and He made light shine for us; bind the festival-offering up to the corners of the altar. Hashem is God, and He made light shine for us; bind the festival-offering up to the corners of the altar. You are my God and I will give thanks to You; my God, I will exalt You. You are my God and I will give thanks to You; my God, I will exalt You. Give thanks to Hashem, for He is good, for His kindness is forever. Give thanks to Hashem, for He is good, for His kindness is forever.

יְהַלְלוּךָ יְהוָה אֱלֹהֵינוּ כָּל מַעֲשֶׂיךָ, וַחֲסִידֶיךָ צַדִּיקִים עוֹשֵׂי רְצוֹנֶךָ, וְכָל עַמְּךָ בֵּית יִשְׂרָאֵל, בְּרִנָּה יוֹדוּ וִיבָרְכוּ וִישַׁבְּחוּ וִיפָאֲרוּ וִירוֹמְמוּ וְיַעֲרִיצוּ וְיַקְדִּישׁוּ וְיַמְלִיכוּ אֶת שִׁמְךָ מַלְכֵּנוּ, כִּי לְךָ טוֹב לְהוֹדוֹת וּלְשִׁמְךָ נָאֶה לְזַמֵּר, כִּי מֵעוֹלָם וְעַד עוֹלָם אַתָּה אֵל:

All Your works shall praise You, Hashem, our God, along with Your pious ones, the righteous who do Your will. And all Your people, the House of Israel, with shouts of joy, will give thanks, bless, laud, glorify, exalt, acclaim, sanctify, and proclaim the sovereignty of Your Name, our King. For it is good to give thanks to You, and it is befitting to sing to Your Name, for You are God for all eternity.

הוֹדוּ לַיהוָה כִּי טוֹב
כִּי לְעוֹלָם חַסְדּוֹ:

Give thanks to Hashem, for He is good, for His kindness is forever.

הוֹדוּ לֵאלֹהֵי הָאֱלֹהִים
כִּי לְעוֹלָם חַסְדּוֹ:

Give thanks to the God of gods, for His kindness is forever.

הוֹדוּ לַאֲדֹנֵי הָאֲדֹנִים
כִּי לְעוֹלָם חַסְדּוֹ:

Give thanks to the Lord of lords, for His kindness is forever.

לְעֹשֵׂה נִפְלָאוֹת גְּדֹלוֹת לְבַדּוֹ

כִּי לְעוֹלָם חַסְדּוֹ:

To the One Who alone does great wonders, for His kindness is forever.

לְעֹשֵׂה הַשָּׁמַיִם בִּתְבוּנָה

כִּי לְעוֹלָם חַסְדּוֹ:

To the One Who made the heavens with understanding, for His kindness is forever.

לְרֹקַע הָאָרֶץ עַל הַמָּיִם

כִּי לְעוֹלָם חַסְדּוֹ:

To the One Who stretched out the earth over the waters, for His kindness is forever.

לְעֹשֵׂה אוֹרִים גְּדֹלִים

כִּי לְעוֹלָם חַסְדּוֹ:

To the One Who made the great lights, for His kindness is forever.

אֶת הַשֶּׁמֶשׁ לְמֶמְשֶׁלֶת בַּיּוֹם

כִּי לְעוֹלָם חַסְדּוֹ:

The sun to rule by day, for His kindness is forever.

אֶת הַיָּרֵחַ וְכוֹכָבִים לְמֶמְשְׁלוֹת בַּלַּיְלָה

כִּי לְעוֹלָם חַסְדּוֹ:

The moon and stars to rule by night, for His kindness is forever.

לְמַכֵּה מִצְרַיִם בִּבְכוֹרֵיהֶם

כִּי לְעוֹלָם חַסְדּוֹ:

To the One Who struck Egypt in their firstborn, for His kindness is forever.

וַיּוֹצֵא יִשְׂרָאֵל מִתּוֹכָם

כִּי לְעוֹלָם חַסְדּוֹ:

And took Israel out of their midst, for His kindness is forever.

בְּיָד חֲזָקָה וּבִזְרוֹעַ נְטוּיָה

כִּי לְעוֹלָם חַסְדּוֹ:

With a strong hand and with an outstretched arm, for His kindness is forever.

לְגֹזֵר יַם סוּף לִגְזָרִים

כִּי לְעוֹלָם חַסְדּוֹ:

To the One Who carved the Red Sea into sections, for His kindness is forever.

וְהֶעֱבִיר יִשְׂרָאֵל בְּתוֹכוֹ

כִּי לְעוֹלָם חַסְדּוֹ:

And had Israel pass through it, for His kindness is forever.

וְנִעֵר פַּרְעֹה וְחֵילוֹ בְיַם סוּף

כִּי לְעוֹלָם חַסְדּוֹ:

And stirred up Pharaoh and his army in the Red Sea, for His kindness is forever.

לְמוֹלִיךְ עַמּוֹ בַּמִּדְבָּר	To the One Who led His people through the desert, for His kindness is forever.	
כִּי לְעוֹלָם חַסְדּוֹ:		
לְמַכֵּה מְלָכִים גְּדֹלִים	To the One Who struck great kings, for His kindness is forever.	
כִּי לְעוֹלָם חַסְדּוֹ:		
וַיַּהֲרֹג מְלָכִים אַדִּירִים	And killed mighty kings, for His kindness is forever.	
כִּי לְעוֹלָם חַסְדּוֹ:		
לְסִיחוֹן מֶלֶךְ הָאֱמֹרִי	Sichon, king of the Amorites, for His kindness is forever.	
כִּי לְעוֹלָם חַסְדּוֹ:		
וּלְעוֹג מֶלֶךְ הַבָּשָׁן	And Og, king of Bashan, for His kindness is forever.	
כִּי לְעוֹלָם חַסְדּוֹ:		
וְנָתַן אַרְצָם לְנַחֲלָה	And gave their land as an inheritance, for His kindness is forever.	
כִּי לְעוֹלָם חַסְדּוֹ:		
נַחֲלָה לְיִשְׂרָאֵל עַבְדּוֹ	An inheritance to His servant Israel, for His kindness is forever.	
כִּי לְעוֹלָם חַסְדּוֹ:		
שֶׁבְּשִׁפְלֵנוּ זָכַר לָנוּ	[To the One] Who remembered us when we were lowly, for His kindness is forever.	
כִּי לְעוֹלָם חַסְדּוֹ:		
וַיִּפְרְקֵנוּ מִצָּרֵינוּ	And delivered us from our enemies, for His kindness is forever.	
כִּי לְעוֹלָם חַסְדּוֹ:		
נֹתֵן לֶחֶם לְכָל בָּשָׂר	He gives food to all flesh, for His kindness is forever.	
כִּי לְעוֹלָם חַסְדּוֹ:		
הוֹדוּ לְאֵל הַשָּׁמָיִם	Give thanks to the God of heaven, for His kindness is forever (*Tehillim* 136 – the "Great Hallel").	
כִּי לְעוֹלָם חַסְדּוֹ:		

נִשְׁמַת כָּל חַי תְּבָרֵךְ אֶת שִׁמְךָ יהוה אֱלֹהֵינוּ, וְרוּחַ כָּל בָּשָׂר תְּפָאֵר וּתְרוֹמֵם זִכְרְךָ מַלְכֵּנוּ תָּמִיד, מִן הָעוֹלָם וְעַד הָעוֹלָם אַתָּה אֵל, וּמִבַּלְעָדֶיךָ אֵין לָנוּ מֶלֶךְ גּוֹאֵל וּמוֹשִׁיעַ, פּוֹדֶה וּמַצִּיל וּמְפַרְנֵס וּמְרַחֵם בְּכָל עֵת צָרָה וְצוּקָה, אֵין לָנוּ מֶלֶךְ אֶלָּא אָתָּה. אֱלֹהֵי הָרִאשׁוֹנִים וְהָאַחֲרוֹנִים, אֱלוֹהַּ כָּל בְּרִיּוֹת, אֲדוֹן כָּל תּוֹלָדוֹת, הַמְהֻלָּל בְּרֹב הַתִּשְׁבָּחוֹת, הַמְנַהֵג עוֹלָמוֹ בְּחֶסֶד וּבְרִיּוֹתָיו בְּרַחֲמִים. וַיהוה לֹא יָנוּם וְלֹא יִישָׁן, הַמְעוֹרֵר יְשֵׁנִים, וְהַמֵּקִיץ נִרְדָּמִים, וְהַמֵּשִׂיחַ אִלְּמִים, וְהַמַּתִּיר אֲסוּרִים, וְהַסּוֹמֵךְ נוֹפְלִים, וְהַזּוֹקֵף כְּפוּפִים. לְךָ לְבַדְּךָ אֲנַחְנוּ מוֹדִים. אִלּוּ פִינוּ מָלֵא שִׁירָה כַּיָּם, וּלְשׁוֹנֵנוּ רִנָּה כַּהֲמוֹן גַּלָּיו, וְשִׂפְתוֹתֵינוּ שֶׁבַח כְּמֶרְחֲבֵי רָקִיעַ, וְעֵינֵינוּ מְאִירוֹת כַּשֶּׁמֶשׁ וְכַיָּרֵחַ, וְיָדֵינוּ פְרוּשׂוֹת כְּנִשְׁרֵי שָׁמָיִם, וְרַגְלֵינוּ קַלּוֹת כָּאַיָּלוֹת, אֵין אֲנַחְנוּ מַסְפִּיקִים לְהוֹדוֹת לְךָ יהוה אֱלֹהֵינוּ וֵאלֹהֵי אֲבוֹתֵינוּ, וּלְבָרֵךְ אֶת שִׁמְךָ עַל אַחַת מֵאֶלֶף אֶלֶף אַלְפֵי אֲלָפִים וְרִבֵּי רְבָבוֹת פְּעָמִים, הַטּוֹבוֹת שֶׁעָשִׂיתָ עִם

The soul of every living being shall bless Your Name, Hashem, our God; and the spirit of all flesh shall always glorify and exalt Your remembrance, our King. For all eternity You are God, and other than You we have no king who redeems and saves us. You deliver, rescue, sustain, and show mercy in all times of trouble and distress; we have no king but You – the God of the first and of the last, God of all creatures, Lord of all generations, Who is lauded with a multitude of praises, Who guides His world with kindness and His creatures with compassion. Hashem neither slumbers nor sleeps; He awakens sleepers and rouses those who slumber; He makes the mute speak, releases the bound, supports those who are falling and straightens those who are bent over. To You alone do we give thanks. Even if our mouths were as full with song as the sea, and our tongues [as full] with shouts of joy as the multitudes of its waves, and our lips [as full] with praise as the expanse of the sky, and our eyes as gleaming as the sun and the moon, and our hands as spread out as the eagles of heaven, and our feet as swift as hinds – we would still be insufficient to thank You, Hashem, our God and God of our fathers, and to bless Your name for even one of the millions and billions of benevolent acts that You have done for our fathers and for us. You redeemed us from Egypt, Hashem, our God, and You delivered us from the house of

אֲבוֹתֵינוּ וְעִמָּנוּ. מִמִּצְרַיִם גְּאַלְתָּנוּ יהוה אֱלֹהֵינוּ וּמִבֵּית עֲבָדִים פְּדִיתָנוּ, בְּרָעָב זַנְתָּנוּ וּבְשָׂבָע כִּלְכַּלְתָּנוּ, מֵחֶרֶב הִצַּלְתָּנוּ וּמִדֶּבֶר מִלַּטְתָּנוּ, וּמֵחֳלָיִם רָעִים וְנֶאֱמָנִים דִּלִּיתָנוּ. עַד הֵנָּה עֲזָרוּנוּ רַחֲמֶיךָ וְלֹא עֲזָבוּנוּ חֲסָדֶיךָ, וְאַל תִּטְּשֵׁנוּ יהוה אֱלֹהֵינוּ לָנֶצַח. עַל כֵּן אֵבָרִים שֶׁפִּלַּגְתָּ בָּנוּ, וְרוּחַ וּנְשָׁמָה שֶׁנָּפַחְתָּ בְּאַפֵּינוּ, וְלָשׁוֹן אֲשֶׁר שַׂמְתָּ בְּפֵינוּ, הֵן הֵם יוֹדוּ וִיבָרְכוּ וִישַׁבְּחוּ וִיפָאֲרוּ וִירוֹמְמוּ וְיַעֲרִיצוּ וְיַקְדִּישׁוּ וְיַמְלִיכוּ אֶת שִׁמְךָ מַלְכֵּנוּ. כִּי כָל פֶּה לְךָ יוֹדֶה, וְכָל לָשׁוֹן לְךָ תִשָּׁבַע, וְכָל בֶּרֶךְ לְךָ תִכְרַע, וְכָל קוֹמָה לְפָנֶיךָ תִשְׁתַּחֲוֶה, וְכָל לְבָבוֹת יִירָאוּךָ, וְכָל קֶרֶב וּכְלָיוֹת יְזַמְּרוּ לִשְׁמֶךָ, כַּדָּבָר שֶׁכָּתוּב, כָּל עַצְמוֹתַי תֹּאמַרְנָה יהוה מִי כָמוֹךָ. מַצִּיל עָנִי מֵחָזָק מִמֶּנּוּ, וְעָנִי וְאֶבְיוֹן מִגֹּזְלוֹ. מִי יִדְמֶה לָּךְ וּמִי יִשְׁוֶה לָּךְ וּמִי יַעֲרָךְ לָךְ, הָאֵל הַגָּדוֹל הַגִּבּוֹר וְהַנּוֹרָא אֵל עֶלְיוֹן, קוֹנֵה שָׁמַיִם וָאָרֶץ. נְהַלֶּלְךָ וּנְשַׁבֵּחֲךָ וּנְפָאֶרְךָ וּנְבָרֵךְ אֶת שֵׁם קָדְשֶׁךָ, כָּאָמוּר, לְדָוִד, בָּרְכִי נַפְשִׁי אֶת יהוה, וְכָל קְרָבַי אֶת שֵׁם קָדְשׁוֹ.

bondage. You have fed us during famine and nourished us in times of plenty; You have saved us from the sword and rescued us from pestilence, and extricated us from dire and serious diseases. Up to now Your compassion has always helped us, and Your kindnesses have not left us; so too, do not abandon us, Hashem our God, forever more! Therefore, the limbs that You have supplied us with, and the spirit and soul that You have breathed into our nostrils, and the tongue that You have placed in our mouth – they shall all thank, bless, praise, glorify, exalt, acclaim, sanctify and proclaim the sovereignty of Your name, our King. For every mouth shall give thanks to You, every tongue shall swear allegiance to You, every knee shall kneel to You, every spine shall bow down before You, every heart shall fear You, and every organ and mind shall sing praises to Your Name, as it is written, "All my bones say: Hashem, who is like You? You save the poor man from those stronger than he, and the poor and needy man from one who tries to rob him" (*Tehillim* 35:10). Who can be likened to You, who is equal to You, who can be compared to You, the great, mighty, awesome God, supreme God, Possessor of heaven and earth! We shall praise You, laud You and glorify You, and we will bless Your holy name, as it says, "By David. Bless Hashem, O my soul, and all that is within me [bless] His holy name" (*Tehillim* 103:1).

הָאֵל בְּתַעֲצֻמוֹת עֻזֶּךָ, הַגָּדוֹל בִּכְבוֹד שְׁמֶךָ, הַגִּבּוֹר לָנֶצַח וְהַנּוֹרָא בְּנוֹרְאוֹתֶיךָ, הַמֶּלֶךְ הַיּוֹשֵׁב עַל כִּסֵּא רָם וְנִשָּׂא.

You are the God – in the might of Your strength;

Great in the glory of Your Name;

Mighty forever; and awesome in Your awesome deeds;

The King Who sits upon an exalted and lofty throne.

שׁוֹכֵן עַד מָרוֹם וְקָדוֹשׁ שְׁמוֹ, וְכָתוּב, רַנְּנוּ צַדִּיקִים בַּיהוה, לַיְשָׁרִים נָאוָה תְהִלָּה. בְּפִי יְשָׁרִים תִּתְהַלָּל, וּבְדִבְרֵי צַדִּיקִים תִּתְבָּרַךְ, וּבִלְשׁוֹן חֲסִידִים תִּתְרוֹמָם, וּבְקֶרֶב קְדוֹשִׁים תִּתְקַדָּשׁ.

He abides forever, exalted and holy is His Name. And it is written, "Shout out with joy to Hashem, you righteous ones; it is befitting for the upright to offer praise" (*Tehillim* 33:1). By the mouth of the upright You shall be praised; by the words of the righteous You shall be blessed; by the tongue of the pious You shall be exalted; and among the holy ones You shall be sanctified.

וּבְמַקְהֲלוֹת רִבְבוֹת עַמְּךָ בֵּית יִשְׂרָאֵל, בְּרִנָּה יִתְפָּאַר שִׁמְךָ מַלְכֵּנוּ בְּכָל דּוֹר וָדוֹר, שֶׁכֵּן חוֹבַת כָּל הַיְצוּרִים לְפָנֶיךָ יהוה אֱלֹהֵינוּ וֵאלֹהֵי אֲבוֹתֵינוּ, לְהוֹדוֹת לְהַלֵּל לְשַׁבֵּחַ לְפָאֵר לְרוֹמֵם לְהַדֵּר לְבָרֵךְ לְעַלֵּה וּלְקַלֵּס, עַל כָּל דִּבְרֵי שִׁירוֹת וְתִשְׁבְּחוֹת דָּוִד בֶּן יִשַׁי עַבְדְּךָ מְשִׁיחֶךָ:

And in the assemblies of the myriads of Your people, the House of Israel, Your name shall be glorified with joyful shouts, our King, in every generation. For this is the duty of all creatures before You, Hashem, our God and God of our fathers – to thank, to praise, to laud, to glorify, to exalt, to honor, to bless, to elevate and to extol [You], even beyond all the words of song and praise of David son of Jesse, Your anointed servant.

יִשְׁתַּבַּח שִׁמְךָ לָעַד מַלְכֵּנוּ, הָאֵל הַמֶּלֶךְ הַגָּדוֹל וְהַקָּדוֹשׁ בַּשָּׁמַיִם וּבָאָרֶץ, כִּי לְךָ נָאֶה יהוה אֱלֹהֵינוּ וֵאלֹהֵי אֲבוֹתֵינוּ, שִׁיר וּשְׁבָחָה הַלֵּל וְזִמְרָה עֹז וּמֶמְשָׁלָה נֶצַח גְּדֻלָּה וּגְבוּרָה תְּהִלָּה וְתִפְאֶרֶת קְדֻשָּׁה וּמַלְכוּת בְּרָכוֹת וְהוֹדָאוֹת מֵעַתָּה וְעַד עוֹלָם, בָּרוּךְ אַתָּה יהוה אֵל מֶלֶךְ גָּדוֹל בַּתִּשְׁבָּחוֹת אֵל הַהוֹדָאוֹת, אֲדוֹן הַנִּפְלָאוֹת, הַבּוֹחֵר בְּשִׁירֵי זִמְרָה, מֶלֶךְ אֵל חֵי הָעוֹלָמִים:

May Your Name be praised forever, our King, the God and King Who is great and holy in heaven and on earth. For to You, Hashem, our God and God of our fathers, are befitting song and praise, laud and hymn, strength and dominion, eternity, greatness and might, glorification and splendor, holiness and sovereignty, blessings and thanksgiving – for all eternity. Blessed are You, Hashem, God, King, great in praises, God of thanksgiving, Lord of wonders, Who favors melodious songs of praise, the King, the Life of the universe.

בָּרוּךְ אַתָּה יהוה אֱלֹהֵינוּ מֶלֶךְ הָעוֹלָם, בּוֹרֵא פְּרִי הַגָּפֶן:

Blessed are You, Hashem, our God, King of the universe, Who creates the fruit of the vine.

The fourth cup of wine is now drunk while reclining on the left side. After drinking the fourth cup, the following blessing is recited. (On Shabbos, the words in parentheses are added.)

בָּרוּךְ אַתָּה יהוה אֱלֹהֵינוּ מֶלֶךְ הָעוֹלָם, עַל הַגֶּפֶן וְעַל פְּרִי הַגָּפֶן וְעַל תְּנוּבַת הַשָּׂדֶה וְעַל אֶרֶץ חֶמְדָּה טוֹבָה וּרְחָבָה, שֶׁרָצִיתָ וְהִנְחַלְתָּ לַאֲבוֹתֵינוּ, לֶאֱכֹל מִפִּרְיָהּ וְלִשְׂבֹּעַ מִטּוּבָהּ. רַחֶם (נָא) יהוה אֱלֹהֵינוּ עַל יִשְׂרָאֵל עַמֶּךָ, וְעַל יְרוּשָׁלַיִם עִירֶךָ, וְעַל צִיּוֹן מִשְׁכַּן כְּבוֹדֶךָ וְעַל מִזְבְּחֶךָ וְעַל הֵיכָלֶךָ. וּבְנֵה יְרוּשָׁלַיִם עִיר הַקֹּדֶשׁ בִּמְהֵרָה בְיָמֵינוּ, וְהַעֲלֵנוּ לְתוֹכָהּ וְשַׂמְּחֵנוּ בְּבִנְיָנָהּ וְנֹאכַל מִפִּרְיָהּ וְנִשְׂבַּע

Blessed are You, Hashem our God, King of the universe, for the vine and the fruit of the vine, for the produce of the field, and for the precious, good and spacious land that You saw fit to grant as a possession to our fathers, to eat of its fruit and be sated by its goodness. Have mercy, Hashem our God, on Israel Your people, on Jerusalem Your city, on Zion the abode of Your glory, on Your altar and on Your Temple. Rebuild Jerusalem, the holy city, speedily in

מְטוּבָה, וּנְבָרֶכְךָ עָלֶיהָ בִּקְדֻשָּׁה וּבְטָהֳרָה, (וּרְצֵה וְהַחֲלִיצֵנוּ בְּיוֹם הַשַּׁבָּת הַזֶּה) וְשַׂמְּחֵנוּ בְּיוֹם חַג הַמַּצּוֹת הַזֶּה כִּי אַתָּה יהוה טוֹב וּמֵטִיב לַכֹּל, וְנוֹדֶה לְּךָ עַל הָאָרֶץ וְעַל פְּרִי הַגָּפֶן: בָּרוּךְ אַתָּה יהוה, עַל הָאָרֶץ וְעַל פְּרִי הַגָּפֶן:

our days, and bring us up into it and let us rejoice in its rebuilding; let us partake of its fruits and be sated by its goodness, and bless You upon it in holiness and purity. (May it please You to grant us strength on this Sabbath day,) and remember us for good on this day of the Festival of Matzos. For You, Hashem, are benevolent and bestow benevolence upon all, and we give thanks to You for the land and for the fruit of the vine. Blessed are You, Hashem, for the land and for the fruit of the vine.

נרצה

חֲסַל סִדּוּר פֶּסַח כְּהִלְכָתוֹ, כְּכָל מִשְׁפָּטוֹ וְחֻקָּתוֹ, כַּאֲשֶׁר זָכִינוּ לְסַדֵּר אוֹתוֹ, כֵּן נִזְכֶּה לַעֲשׂוֹתוֹ, זָךְ שׁוֹכֵן מְעוֹנָה, קוֹמֵם קְהַל עֲדַת מִי מָנָה, בְּקָרוֹב נַהֵל נִטְעֵי כַנָּה, פְּדוּיִם לְצִיּוֹן בְּרִנָּה.

This is the completion of the Pesach ceremony according to its rules, in accordance with all its laws and statutes. Just as we merited to present it, so may we merit to perform it. Pure One, Who dwells on high, raise up the congregation of whom it was said, "Who can count them?" (Bamidbar 23:10). Soon lead the plants of your vineyard (Israel), redeemed, to Zion, with shouts of joy.

לְשָׁנָה הַבָּאָה בִּירוּשָׁלָיִם!
NEXT YEAR IN JERUSALEM!

The following poem is recited on the first night:

	וּבְכֵן וַיְהִי בַּחֲצִי הַלַּיְלָה:
בַּלַּיְלָה.	אָז רוֹב נִסִּים הִפְלֵאתָ
הַלַּיְלָה.	בְּרֹאשׁ אַשְׁמוֹרֶת זֶה
לַיְלָה	גֵּר צֶדֶק נִצַּחְתּוֹ כְּנֶחֱלַק לוֹ
	וַיְהִי בַּחֲצִי הַלַּיְלָה:

"It happened at midnight" (*Shemos* 12:29).

Always, You have performed wondrous miracles on this night.

At the beginning of the watches on this night,

You granted victory to the righteous convert (Avraham) when the night was divided in two (*Bereishis* 14:15).

It happened at midnight.

הַלַּיְלָה.	דַּנְתָּ מֶלֶךְ גְּרָר בַּחֲלוֹם
לַיְלָה.	הִפְחַדְתָּ אֲרַמִּי בְּאֶמֶשׁ
לַיְלָה	וַיָּשַׂר יִשְׂרָאֵל לְמַלְאָךְ וַיּוּכַל לוֹ
	וַיְהִי בַּחֲצִי הַלַּיְלָה:

You judged the king of Gerar (Avimelech) in a dream at night (ibid. 20:3).

You frightened the Aramean (Lavan) in the dark of the night (ibid. 31:24).

Israel struggled with an angel and overcame him at night (ibid. 32:25).

It happened at midnight.

הַלַּיְלָה.	זֶרַע בְּכוֹרֵי פַתְרוֹס מָחַצְתָּ בַּחֲצִי
בַּלַּיְלָה.	חֵילָם לֹא מָצְאוּ בְּקוּמָם
לַיְלָה.	טִיסַת נְגִיד חֲרֹשֶׁת סִלִּיתָ בְּכוֹכְבֵי
	וַיְהִי בַּחֲצִי הַלַּיְלָה:

You crushed the firstborn offspring of Pathros (Egypt) at midnight.

They did not find their vigor (firstborn sons) when they awoke in the middle of the night.

You trampled the swift army of the Prince of Harosheth (Sisera) by the stars of the night (*Shoftim* 5:20).

It happened at midnight.

בַּלַּיְלָה.	יָעַץ מְחָרֵף לְנוֹפֵף אִוּוּי הוֹבַשְׁתָּ פְגָרָיו
לַיְלָה.	כָּרַע בֵּל וּמַצָּבוֹ בְּאִישׁוֹן
לַיְלָה.	לְאִישׁ חֲמוּדוֹת נִגְלָה רָז חֲזוֹת
	וַיְהִי בַּחֲצִי הַלַּיְלָה:

The blasphemer (Sancheriv) planned to wave his hand against the cherished Temple; You dried out his corpses overnight (*II Melachim* 19:35).

Bel (Babylonia) and its watchmen collapsed in the dark of night;

To the beloved man (Daniel) was revealed the secret of the vision at night (*Daniel* 5).

It happened at midnight.

בַּלַּיְלָה.	מִשְׁתַּכֵּר בִּכְלֵי קֹדֶשׁ נֶהֱרַג בּוֹ
לַיְלָה.	נוֹשַׁע מִבּוֹר אֲרָיוֹת פּוֹתֵר בְּעִתּוּתֵי
בַּלַּיְלָה.	שִׂנְאָה נָטַר אֲגָגִי וְכָתַב סְפָרִים
	וַיְהִי בַּחֲצִי הַלַּיְלָה:

The one who became drunk drinking from the sacred vessels (Belshazzar) was killed that very night (ibid.).

The one saved from the lion's den (Daniel) interpreted the frightening sight at night (ibid.).

The Agagite (Haman) retained his hatred and wrote writs at night (*Esther* 5:14-6:4).

It happened at midnight.

עוֹרַרְתָּ נִצְחֲךָ עָלָיו בְּנֶדֶד שְׁנַת לַיְלָה.
פּוּרָה תִדְרוֹךְ לְשׁוֹמֵר מַה מִלַּיְלָה.
צָרַח כַּשּׁוֹמֵר וְשָׂח אָתָא בֹקֶר וְגַם לַיְלָה.
וַיְהִי בַּחֲצִי הַלַּיְלָה:

You launched Your triumph against him (Haman) when (Achashverosh's) sleep was disturbed at night (ibid.).

You will trample the vintage of the one (Edom) of whom it was said, "Watchman, what of the night?" (*Yeshayahu* 21:11).

God shouted back like a watchman and said, "Morning is coming, but also night" (ibid. 21:12).

It happened at midnight.

קָרֵב יוֹם אֲשֶׁר הוּא לֹא יוֹם וְלֹא לַיְלָה.
רָם הוֹדַע כִּי לְךָ הַיּוֹם אַף לְךָ הַלַּיְלָה.
שׁוֹמְרִים הַפְקֵד לְעִירְךָ כָּל הַיּוֹם וְכָל הַלַּיְלָה.
תָּאִיר כְּאוֹר יוֹם חֶשְׁכַת הַלַּיְלָה.
וַיְהִי בַּחֲצִי הַלַּיְלָה:

Bring near the day (of the Messiah) which is "neither day nor night" (*Zechariah* 14:7).

Exalted One, make it known that "Yours is the day and Yours is the night" (*Tehillim* 74:16).

Post guardians over Your city all day and all night (*Yeshayahu* 61:6).

Light up the dark of night as brightly as the light of day.

It happened at midnight.

The following poem is recited on the second night. (In Israel, where only one Seder is held, both poems are recited on the first night.)

וּבְכֵן וַאֲמַרְתֶּם זֶבַח פֶּסַח:
אֹמֶץ גְּבוּרוֹתֶיךָ הִפְלֵאתָ בַּפֶּסַח.
בְּרֹאשׁ כָּל מוֹעֲדוֹת נִשֵּׂאתָ פֶּסַח.
גִּלִּיתָ לְאֶזְרָחִי חֲצוֹת לֵיל פֶּסַח.
וַאֲמַרְתֶּם זֶבַח פֶּסַח:

And you shall say, "It is a sacrifice of Pesach" (*Shemos* 12:27).

You demonstrated the power of Your might on Pesach.

You elevated as the first of the holidays, Pesach (*Vayikra* 23:4-5).

You revealed to the Easterner (Avraham) the events of the midnight of Pesach.

And you shall say, "It is a sacrifice of Pesach."

דְּלָתָיו דָּפַקְתָּ כְּחֹם הַיּוֹם בַּפֶּסַח.
הִסְעִיד נוֹצְצִים עֻגוֹת מַצּוֹת בַּפֶּסַח.
וְאֶל הַבָּקָר רָץ זֵכֶר לְשׁוֹר עֵרֶךְ פֶּסַח.
וַאֲמַרְתֶּם זֶבַח פֶּסַח:

You knocked on his (Avraham's) door in the heat of the day on Pesach (*Bereishis* 18:1);

He fed angels unleavened cakes on Pesach (ibid. 18:6);

He ran to take from the cattle (ibid. 18:7), symbolizing the ox brought in conjunction with the sacrifice of Pesach.

And you shall say, "It is a sacrifice of Pesach."

זוֹעֲמוּ סְדוֹמִים וְלֹהֲטוּ בָּאֵשׁ בַּפֶּסַח.
חֻלַּץ לוֹט מֵהֶם וּמַצּוֹת אָפָה בְּקֵץ פֶּסַח.
טֵאטֵאתָ אַדְמַת מוֹף וְנוֹף בְּעָבְרְךָ בַּפֶּסַח.
וַאֲמַרְתֶּם זֶבַח פֶּסַח:

The Sodomites were damned and burnt in fire on Pesach.

Lot was rescued from among them; he baked unleavened bread (ibid. 19:3) at the end of the eve of Pesach.

You wiped out the land of Moph and Noph (Egypt) when You passed through on Pesach.

And you shall say, "It is a sacrifice of Pesach."

יָהּ רֹאשׁ כָּל אוֹן מָחַצְתָּ בְּלֵיל שִׁמּוּר פֶּסַח.

כַּבִּיר עַל בֵּן בְּכוֹר פָּסַחְתָּ בְּדַם פֶּסַח.

לְבִלְתִּי תֵּת מַשְׁחִית לָבֹא בִּפְתָחַי בַּפֶּסַח.

וַאֲמַרְתֶּם זֶבַח פֶּסַח:

God, You crushed the first one of all their child-bearing, on the "night of watching" (*Shemos* 12:42) of Pesach.

Mighty One, You passed over [Your own] firstborn son because of the blood of the Pesach,

Not allowing the Destroyer to enter my doors on Pesach.

And you shall say, "It is a sacrifice of Pesach."

מְסֻגֶּרֶת סֻגְּרָה בְּעִתּוֹתֵי פֶּסַח.

נִשְׁמְדָה מִדְיָן בִּצְלִיל שְׂעוֹרֵי עוֹמֶר פֶּסַח.

שֹׂרְפוּ מִשְׁמַנֵּי פּוּל וְלוּד בִּיקַד יְקוֹד פֶּסַח.

וַאֲמַרְתֶּם זֶבַח פֶּסַח:

The sealed city (Jericho) was handed over during the time of Pesach.

Midian was destroyed through a loaf representing the barley of the Omer-sacrifice of Pesach (*Shoftim* 7:13).

The burly warriors of Pul and Lud (Assyria) were burnt in a conflagration on Pesach (*Yeshayahu* 10:16).

And you shall say, "It is a sacrifice of Pesach."

עוֹד הַיּוֹם בְּנֹב לַעֲמוֹד עַד גָּעָה עוֹנַת פֶּסַח.

פַּס יָד כָּתְבָה לְקַעֲקֵעַ צוּל בַּפֶּסַח.

צָפֹה הַצָּפִית עָרוֹךְ הַשֻּׁלְחָן בַּפֶּסַח.

וַאֲמַרְתֶּם זֶבַח פֶּסַח:

He (Sancheriv) wanted "to reach Nob that very day" (ibid. 10:32) - until it became the season of Pesach.

The palm of a hand wrote an inscription about the crushing of the well-watered country (Babylonia) on Pesach;

"The chandelier was lit and table was set" (ibid. 21:5, describing the downfall of Babylonia) on Pesach.

And you shall say, "It is a sacrifice of Pesach,"

קָהָל כִּנְּסָה הֲדַסָּה צוֹם לְשַׁלֵּשׁ בַּפֶּסַח.

רֹאשׁ מִבֵּית רָשָׁע מָחַצְתָּ בְּעֵץ חֲמִשִּׁים בַּפֶּסַח.

שְׁתֵּי אֵלֶּה רֶגַע תָּבִיא לְעוּצִית בַּפֶּסַח.

תָּעֹז יָדְךָ וְתָרוּם יְמִינְךָ כְּלֵיל הִתְקַדֵּשׁ חַג פֶּסַח.

וַאֲמַרְתֶּם זֶבַח פֶּסַח:

Hadassah assembled the congregation to hold a three-day fast on Pesach (*Esther* 4:16).

You vanquished the chief (Haman) from the wicked family (Amalek) on a fifty-cubit wooden pole on Pesach.

May You bring "these two things" (*Yeshayahu* 47:9) in an instant upon the Utzites (Babylonians) on Pesach!

Let Your hand be strong and Your right hand raised, as on the night of the sanctification of the holiday of Pesach!

And you shall say, "It is a sacrifice of Pesach."

כִּי לוֹ נָאֶה, כִּי לוֹ יָאֶה.

אַדִּיר בִּמְלוּכָה, בָּחוּר כַּהֲלָכָה, גְּדוּדָיו יֹאמְרוּ לוֹ.
לְךָ וּלְךָ, לְךָ כִּי לְךָ, לְךָ אַף לְךָ, לְךָ יְיָ הַמַּמְלָכָה,
כִּי לוֹ נָאֶה, כִּי לוֹ יָאֶה.

To Him it is befitting! To Him it is becoming!

Mighty in dominion, Superior indeed, His legions (angels) say to Him:

To You, to You! To You, indeed to You! To You, only to You! "To you, Hashem, belongs the dominion" (*I Divrei Hayamim* 29:11)!

To Him it is befitting! To Him it is becoming!

דָּגוּל בִּמְלוּכָה, הָדוּר כַּהֲלָכָה, וָתִיקָיו יֹאמְרוּ לוֹ. לְךָ וּלְךָ, לְךָ כִּי לְךָ, לְךָ אַף לְךָ, לְךָ יְיָ הַמַּמְלָכָה, כִּי לוֹ נָאֶה, כִּי לוֹ יָאֶה.

Outstanding in dominion, Glorious indeed, His devoted ones (Israel) say to Him:

To You, to You! To You, indeed to You! To You, only to You! To you, Hashem, belongs the dominion!

To Him it is befitting! To Him it is becoming!

זַכַּאי בִּמְלוּכָה, חָסִין כַּהֲלָכָה, טַפְסְרָיו יֹאמְרוּ לוֹ. לְךָ וּלְךָ, לְךָ כִּי לְךָ, לְךָ אַף לְךָ, לְךָ יְיָ הַמַּמְלָכָה, כִּי לוֹ נָאֶה, כִּי לוֹ יָאֶה.

Pure in dominion, Powerful indeed, His captains (angels) say to Him:

To You, to You! To You, indeed to You! To You, only to You! To you, Hashem, belongs the dominion!

To Him it is befitting! To Him it is becoming!

יָחִיד בִּמְלוּכָה, כַּבִּיר כַּהֲלָכָה, לִמּוּדָיו יֹאמְרוּ לוֹ. לְךָ וּלְךָ, לְךָ כִּי לְךָ, לְךָ אַף לְךָ, לְךָ יְיָ הַמַּמְלָכָה, כִּי לוֹ נָאֶה, כִּי לוֹ יָאֶה.

Unique in dominion, Potent indeed, His learned ones (Israel) say to Him:

To You, to You! To You, indeed to You! To You, only to You! To you, Hashem, belongs the dominion!

To Him it is befitting! To Him it is becoming!

מוֹשֵׁל בִּמְלוּכָה, נוֹרָא כַּהֲלָכָה, סְבִיבָיו יֹאמְרוּ לוֹ. לְךָ וּלְךָ, לְךָ כִּי לְךָ, לְךָ אַף לְךָ, לְךָ יְיָ הַמַּמְלָכָה, כִּי לוֹ נָאֶה, כִּי לוֹ יָאֶה.

Exalted in dominion, Awesome indeed, Those surrounding Him (angels) say to Him:

To You, to You! To You, indeed to You! To You, only to You! To you, Hashem, belongs the dominion!

To Him it is befitting! To Him it is becoming!

עָנָיו בִּמְלוּכָה, פּוֹדֶה כַּהֲלָכָה, צַדִּיקָיו יֹאמְרוּ לוֹ. לְךָ וּלְךָ, לְךָ כִּי לְךָ, לְךָ אַף לְךָ, לְךָ יְיָ הַמַּמְלָכָה, כִּי לוֹ נָאֶה, כִּי לוֹ יָאֶה.

Deigning in dominion, Redeeming indeed, His righteous ones (Israel) say to Him:

To You, to You! To You, indeed to You! To You, only to You! To you, Hashem, belongs the dominion!

To Him it is befitting! To Him it is becoming!

קָדוֹשׁ בִּמְלוּכָה, רַחוּם כַּהֲלָכָה, שִׁנְאַנָּיו יֹאמְרוּ לוֹ. לְךָ וּלְךָ, לְךָ כִּי לְךָ, לְךָ אַף לְךָ, לְךָ יְיָ הַמַּמְלָכָה, כִּי לוֹ נָאֶה, כִּי לוֹ יָאֶה.

Holy in dominion, Compassionate indeed, His *shinanim* (angels) say to Him:

To You, to You! To You, indeed to You! To You, only to You! To you, Hashem, belongs the dominion!

To Him it is befitting! To Him it is becoming!

תַּקִּיף בִּמְלוּכָה, תּוֹמֵךְ כַּהֲלָכָה, תְּמִימָיו יֹאמְרוּ לוֹ. לְךָ וּלְךָ, לְךָ כִּי לְךָ, לְךָ אַף לְךָ, לְךָ יְיָ הַמַּמְלָכָה, כִּי לוֹ נָאֶה, כִּי לוֹ יָאֶה.

Strong in dominion, Supporter indeed, His faithful ones (Israel) say to Him:

To You, to You! To You, indeed to You! To You, only to You! To you, Hashem, belongs the dominion!

To Him it is befitting! To Him it is becoming!

אַדִּיר הוּא יִבְנֶה בֵּיתוֹ בְּקָרוֹב, בִּמְהֵרָה בִּמְהֵרָה בְּיָמֵינוּ בְּקָרוֹב, אֵל בְּנֵה אֵל בְּנֵה, בְּנֵה בֵיתְךָ בְּקָרוֹב.

He is mighty! May He build His Temple soon! Speedily, speedily, in our days, soon! God, build, God build, build Your Temple soon!

בָּחוּר הוּא, גָּדוֹל הוּא, דָּגוּל הוּא, יִבְנֶה בֵּיתוֹ בְּקָרוֹב. בִּמְהֵרָה בִּמְהֵרָה בְּיָמֵינוּ בְּקָרוֹב, אֵל בְּנֵה אֵל בְּנֵה, בְּנֵה בֵיתְךָ בְּקָרוֹב.

He is superior! He is great! He is outstanding! May He build His Temple soon! Speedily, speedily, in our days, soon! God, build, God build, build Your Temple soon!

הָדוּר הוּא, וָתִיק הוּא, זַכַּאי הוּא, חָסִיד הוּא, יִבְנֶה בֵּיתוֹ בְּקָרוֹב, בִּמְהֵרָה בִּמְהֵרָה בְּיָמֵינוּ בְּקָרוֹב, אֵל בְּנֵה אֵל בְּנֵה, בְּנֵה בֵיתְךָ בְּקָרוֹב.

He is glorious! He is virtuous! He is blameless! He is kind! May He build His Temple soon! Speedily, speedily, in our days, soon! God, build, God build, build Your Temple soon!

טָהוֹר הוּא, יָחִיד הוּא, כַּבִּיר הוּא, לָמוּד הוּא, מֶלֶךְ הוּא, נוֹרָא הוּא, סַגִּיב הוּא, עִזּוּז הוּא, פּוֹדֶה הוּא, צַדִּיק הוּא, יִבְנֶה בֵּיתוֹ בְּקָרוֹב, בִּמְהֵרָה בִּמְהֵרָה בְּיָמֵינוּ בְּקָרוֹב, אֵל בְּנֵה אֵל בְּנֵה, בְּנֵה בֵיתְךָ בְּקָרוֹב.

He is pure! He is unique! He is powerful! He is all-knowing! He is King! He is awesome! He is exalted! He is all powerful! He is the Redeemer! He is righteous! May He build His Temple soon! Speedily, speedily, in our days, soon! God, build, God build, build Your Temple soon!

קָדוֹשׁ הוּא, רַחוּם הוּא, שַׁדַּי הוּא, תַּקִּיף הוּא, יִבְנֶה בֵּיתוֹ בְּקָרוֹב, בִּמְהֵרָה בִּמְהֵרָה בְּיָמֵינוּ בְּקָרוֹב, אֵל בְּנֵה אֵל בְּנֵה, בְּנֵה בֵיתְךָ בְּקָרוֹב.

He is holy! He is compassionate! He is the Almighty! He is strong! May He build His Temple soon! Speedily, speedily, in our days, soon! God, build, God build, build Your Temple soon!

אֶחָד מִי יוֹדֵעַ, אֶחָד אֲנִי יוֹדֵעַ, אֶחָד אֱלֹהֵינוּ שֶׁבַּשָּׁמַיִם וּבָאָרֶץ.

Who knows one? I know one!
One is our God, in heaven and on earth.

שְׁנַיִם מִי יוֹדֵעַ, שְׁנַיִם אֲנִי יוֹדֵעַ. שְׁנֵי לוּחוֹת הַבְּרִית, אֶחָד אֱלֹהֵינוּ שֶׁבַּשָּׁמַיִם וּבָאָרֶץ.

Who knows two? I know two!
Two are the tablets of the Covenant; One is our God, in heaven and on earth.

שְׁלֹשָׁה מִי יוֹדֵעַ, שְׁלֹשָׁה אֲנִי יוֹדֵעַ, שְׁלֹשָׁה אָבוֹת, שְׁנֵי לוּחוֹת הַבְּרִית, אֶחָד אֱלֹהֵינוּ שֶׁבַּשָּׁמַיִם וּבָאָרֶץ.

Who knows three? I know three!
Three are the patriarchs; two are the tablets of the Covenant; One is our God, in heaven and on earth.

אַרְבַּע מִי יוֹדֵעַ, אַרְבַּע אֲנִי יוֹדֵעַ, אַרְבַּע אִמָּהוֹת, שְׁלֹשָׁה אָבוֹת, שְׁנֵי לוּחוֹת הַבְּרִית, אֶחָד אֱלֹהֵינוּ שֶׁבַּשָּׁמַיִם וּבָאָרֶץ.

Who knows four? I know four!
Four are the matriarchs; three are the patriarchs; two are the tablets of the Covenant; One is our God, in heaven and on earth.

חֲמִשָּׁה מִי יוֹדֵעַ, חֲמִשָּׁה אֲנִי יוֹדֵעַ, חֲמִשָּׁה חוּמְשֵׁי תוֹרָה, אַרְבַּע אִמָּהוֹת, שְׁלֹשָׁה אָבוֹת, שְׁנֵי לוּחוֹת הַבְּרִית, אֶחָד אֱלֹהֵינוּ שֶׁבַּשָּׁמַיִם וּבָאָרֶץ.

Who knows five? I know five!
Five are the books of the Torah; four are the matriarchs; three are the patriarchs; two are the tablets of the Covenant; One is our God, in heaven and on earth.

שְׁשָׁה מִי יוֹדֵעַ, שִׁשָּׁה אֲנִי יוֹדֵעַ, שִׁשָּׁה סִדְרֵי מִשְׁנָה, חֲמִשָּׁה חוּמְשֵׁי תוֹרָה, אַרְבַּע אִמָּהוֹת, שְׁלֹשָׁה אָבוֹת, שְׁנֵי לוּחוֹת הַבְּרִית, אֶחָד אֱלֹהֵינוּ שֶׁבַּשָּׁמַיִם וּבָאָרֶץ.

שִׁבְעָה מִי יוֹדֵעַ, שִׁבְעָה אֲנִי יוֹדֵעַ, שִׁבְעָה יְמֵי שַׁבְּתָא, שִׁשָּׁה סִדְרֵי מִשְׁנָה, חֲמִשָּׁה חוּמְשֵׁי תוֹרָה, אַרְבַּע אִמָּהוֹת, שְׁלֹשָׁה אָבוֹת, שְׁנֵי לוּחוֹת הַבְּרִית, אֶחָד אֱלֹהֵינוּ שֶׁבַּשָּׁמַיִם וּבָאָרֶץ.

שְׁמוֹנָה מִי יוֹדֵעַ, שְׁמוֹנָה אֲנִי יוֹדֵעַ, שְׁמוֹנָה יְמֵי מִילָה, שִׁבְעָה יְמֵי שַׁבְּתָא, שִׁשָּׁה סִדְרֵי מִשְׁנָה, חֲמִשָּׁה חוּמְשֵׁי תוֹרָה, אַרְבַּע אִמָּהוֹת, שְׁלֹשָׁה אָבוֹת, שְׁנֵי לוּחוֹת הַבְּרִית, אֶחָד אֱלֹהֵינוּ שֶׁבַּשָּׁמַיִם וּבָאָרֶץ.

תִּשְׁעָה מִי יוֹדֵעַ, תִּשְׁעָה אֲנִי יוֹדֵעַ, תִּשְׁעָה יַרְחֵי לֵידָה, שְׁמוֹנָה יְמֵי מִילָה, שִׁבְעָה יְמֵי שַׁבְּתָא, שִׁשָּׁה סִדְרֵי מִשְׁנָה, חֲמִשָּׁה חוּמְשֵׁי תוֹרָה, אַרְבַּע אִמָּהוֹת, שְׁלֹשָׁה אָבוֹת, שְׁנֵי לוּחוֹת הַבְּרִית, אֶחָד אֱלֹהֵינוּ שֶׁבַּשָּׁמַיִם וּבָאָרֶץ.

עֲשָׂרָה מִי יוֹדֵעַ, עֲשָׂרָה אֲנִי יוֹדֵעַ, עֲשָׂרָה דִבְּרַיָּא, תִּשְׁעָה יַרְחֵי לֵידָה, שְׁמוֹנָה יְמֵי מִילָה, שִׁבְעָה יְמֵי שַׁבְּתָא, שִׁשָּׁה סִדְרֵי מִשְׁנָה, חֲמִשָּׁה חוּמְשֵׁי תוֹרָה, אַרְבַּע אִמָּהוֹת, שְׁלֹשָׁה אָבוֹת, שְׁנֵי לוּחוֹת הַבְּרִית, אֶחָד אֱלֹהֵינוּ שֶׁבַּשָּׁמַיִם וּבָאָרֶץ.

אַחַד עָשָׂר מִי יוֹדֵעַ, אַחַד עָשָׂר אֲנִי יוֹדֵעַ, אַחַד עָשָׂר כּוֹכְבַיָּא, עֲשָׂרָה דִבְּרַיָּא, תִּשְׁעָה יַרְחֵי לֵידָה, שְׁמוֹנָה יְמֵי מִילָה, שִׁבְעָה יְמֵי שַׁבְּתָא, שִׁשָּׁה סִדְרֵי מִשְׁנָה, חֲמִשָּׁה חוּמְשֵׁי תוֹרָה, אַרְבַּע אִמָּהוֹת, שְׁלֹשָׁה אָבוֹת, שְׁנֵי לוּחוֹת הַבְּרִית, אֶחָד אֱלֹהֵינוּ שֶׁבַּשָּׁמַיִם וּבָאָרֶץ.

Who knows six? I know six!

Six are the volumes of the Mishnah; five are the books of the Torah; four are the matriarchs; three are the patriarchs; two are the tablets of the Covenant; One is our God, in heaven and on earth.

Who knows seven? I know seven!

Seven are the days of the week; six are the volumes of the Mishnah; five are the books of the Torah; four are the matriarchs; three are the patriarchs; two are the tablets of the Covenant; One is our God, in heaven and on earth.

Who knows eight? I know eight!

Eight are the days until circumcision; seven are the days of the week; six are the volumes of the Mishnah; five are the books of the Torah; four are the matriarchs; three are the patriarchs; two are the tablets of the Covenant; One is our God, in heaven and on earth.

Who knows nine? I know nine!

Nine are the months of pregnancy; eight are the days until circumcision; seven are the days of the week; six are the volumes of the Mishnah; five are the books of the Torah; four are the matriarchs; three are the patriarchs; two are the tablets of the Covenant; One is our God, in heaven and on earth.

Who knows ten? I know ten!

Ten are the Commandments; nine are the months of pregnancy; eight are the days until circumcision; seven are the days of the week; six are the volumes of the Mishnah; five are the books of the Torah; four are the matriarchs; three are the patriarchs; two are the tablets of the Covenant; One is our God, in heaven and on earth.

Who knows eleven? I know eleven!

Eleven are the stars (of Joseph's dream); ten are the Commandments; nine are the months of pregnancy; eight are the days until circumcision; seven are the days of the week; six are the volumes of the Mishnah; five are the books of the Torah; four are the matriarchs; three are the patriarchs; two are the tablets of the Covenant; One is our God, in heaven and on earth.

שְׁנֵים עָשָׂר מִי יוֹדֵעַ, שְׁנֵים עָשָׂר אֲנִי יוֹדֵעַ, שְׁנֵים עָשָׂר שִׁבְטַיָּא, אַחַד עָשָׂר כּוֹכְבַיָּא, עֲשָׂרָה דִבְּרַיָּא, תִּשְׁעָה יַרְחֵי לֵידָה, שְׁמוֹנָה יְמֵי מִילָה, שִׁבְעָה יְמֵי שַׁבַּתָּא, שִׁשָּׁה סִדְרֵי מִשְׁנָה, חֲמִשָּׁה חוּמְשֵׁי תוֹרָה, אַרְבַּע אִמָּהוֹת, שְׁלֹשָׁה אָבוֹת, שְׁנֵי לוּחוֹת הַבְּרִית, אֶחָד אֱלֹהֵינוּ שֶׁבַּשָּׁמַיִם וּבָאָרֶץ.

שְׁלֹשָׁה עָשָׂר מִי יוֹדֵעַ, שְׁלֹשָׁה עָשָׂר אֲנִי יוֹדֵעַ, שְׁלֹשָׁה עָשָׂר מִדַּיָּא, שְׁנֵים עָשָׂר שִׁבְטַיָּא, אַחַד עָשָׂר כּוֹכְבַיָּא, עֲשָׂרָה דִבְּרַיָּא, תִּשְׁעָה יַרְחֵי לֵידָה, שְׁמוֹנָה יְמֵי מִילָה, שִׁבְעָה יְמֵי שַׁבַּתָּא, שִׁשָּׁה סִדְרֵי מִשְׁנָה, חֲמִשָּׁה חוּמְשֵׁי תוֹרָה, אַרְבַּע אִמָּהוֹת, שְׁלֹשָׁה אָבוֹת, שְׁנֵי לוּחוֹת הַבְּרִית, אֶחָד אֱלֹהֵינוּ שֶׁבַּשָּׁמַיִם וּבָאָרֶץ.

חַד גַּדְיָא, חַד גַּדְיָא, דְּזַבִּין אַבָּא בִּתְרֵי זוּזֵי. חַד גַּדְיָא, חַד גַּדְיָא.

וְאָתָא שׁוּנְרָא, וְאָכְלָה לְגַדְיָא, דְּזַבִּין אַבָּא בִּתְרֵי זוּזֵי. חַד גַּדְיָא, חַד גַּדְיָא.

וְאָתָא כַלְבָּא, וְנָשַׁךְ לְשׁוּנְרָא, דְּאָכְלָה לְגַדְיָא, דְּזַבִּין אַבָּא בִּתְרֵי זוּזֵי. חַד גַּדְיָא, חַד גַּדְיָא.

וְאָתָא חוּטְרָא, וְהִכָּה לְכַלְבָּא, דְּנָשַׁךְ לְשׁוּנְרָא, דְּאָכְלָה לְגַדְיָא, דְּזַבִּין אַבָּא בִּתְרֵי זוּזֵי. חַד גַּדְיָא, חַד גַּדְיָא.

וְאָתָא נוּרָא, וְשָׂרַף לְחוּטְרָא, דְּהִכָּה לְכַלְבָּא, דְּנָשַׁךְ לְשׁוּנְרָא, דְּאָכְלָה לְגַדְיָא, דְּזַבִּין אַבָּא בִּתְרֵי זוּזֵי. חַד גַּדְיָא, חַד גַּדְיָא.

וְאָתָא מַיָּא, וְכָבָה לְנוּרָא, דְּשָׂרַף לְחוּטְרָא, דְּהִכָּה לְכַלְבָּא, דְּנָשַׁךְ לְשׁוּנְרָא, דְּאָכְלָה לְגַדְיָא, דְּזַבִּין אַבָּא בִּתְרֵי זוּזֵי. חַד גַּדְיָא, חַד גַּדְיָא.

Who knows twelve? I know twelve!

Twelve are the tribes of Israel; eleven are the stars (of Joseph's dream); ten are the Commandments; nine are the months of pregnancy; eight are the days until circumcision; seven are the days of the week; six are the volumes of the Mishnah; five are the books of the Torah; four are the matriarchs; three are the patriarchs; two are the tablets of the Covenant; One is our God, in heaven and on earth.

Who knows thirteen? I know thirteen!

Thirteen are God's attributes of mercy; twelve are the tribes of Israel; eleven are the stars (of Joseph's dream); ten are the Commandments; nine are the months of pregnancy; eight are the days until circumcision; seven are the days of the week; six are the volumes of the Mishnah; five are the books of the Torah; four are the matriarchs; three are the patriarchs; two are the tablets of the Covenant; One is our God, in heaven and on earth.

One kid, one kid - that my father bought for two *zuzim*.

One kid, one kid.

Along came a cat and ate the kid - that my father bought for two *zuzim*.

One kid, one kid.

Along came a dog and bit the cat that ate the kid - that my father bought for two *zuzim*.

One kid, one kid.

Along came a stick and hit the dog that bit the cat that ate the kid - that my father bought for two *zuzim*.

One kid, one kid.

Along came a fire and burnt the stick that hit the dog that bit the cat that ate the kid - that my father bought for two *zuzim*.

One kid, one kid.

Along came water and extinguished the fire that burnt the stick that hit the dog that bit the cat that ate the kid - that my father bought for two *zuzim*.

One kid, one kid.

וְאָתָא תוֹרָא, וְשָׁתָה לְמַיָּא, דְּכָבָה לְנוּרָא, דְּשָׂרַף לְחוּטְרָא, דְּהִכָּה לְכַלְבָּא, דְּנָשַׁךְ לְשׁוּנְרָא, דְּאָכְלָה לְגַדְיָא, דְּזַבִּין אַבָּא בִּתְרֵי זוּזֵי. חַד גַּדְיָא, חַד גַּדְיָא.

Along came an ox and drank the water that extinguished the fire that burnt the stick that hit the dog that bit the cat that ate the kid – that my father bought for two *zuzim*.

One kid, one kid.

וְאָתָא הַשּׁוֹחֵט, וְשָׁחַט לְתוֹרָא, דְּשָׁתָה לְמַיָּא, דְּכָבָה לְנוּרָא, דְּשָׂרַף לְחוּטְרָא, דְּהִכָּה לְכַלְבָּא, דְּנָשַׁךְ לְשׁוּנְרָא, דְּאָכְלָה לְגַדְיָא, דְּזַבִּין אַבָּא בִּתְרֵי זוּזֵי. חַד גַּדְיָא, חַד גַּדְיָא.

Along came a slaughterer and slaughtered the ox that drank the water that extinguished the fire that burnt the stick that hit the dog that bit the cat that ate the kid – that my father bought for two *zuzim*.

One kid, one kid.

וְאָתָא מַלְאַךְ הַמָּוֶת, וְשָׁחַט לְשׁוֹחֵט, דְּשָׁחַט לְתוֹרָא, דְּשָׁתָה לְמַיָּא, דְּכָבָה לְנוּרָא, דְּשָׂרַף לְחוּטְרָא, דְּהִכָּה לְכַלְבָּא, דְּנָשַׁךְ לְשׁוּנְרָא, דְּאָכְלָה לְגַדְיָא, דְּזַבִּין אַבָּא בִּתְרֵי זוּזֵי. חַד גַּדְיָא, חַד גַּדְיָא.

Along came the angel of death and killed the slaughterer who slaughtered the ox that drank the water that extinguished the fire that burnt the stick that hit the dog that bit the cat that ate the kid – that my father bought for two *zuzim*.

One kid, one kid.

וְאָתָא הַקָּדוֹשׁ בָּרוּךְ הוּא, וְשָׁחַט לְמַלְאַךְ הַמָּוֶת, דְּשָׁחַט לְשׁוֹחֵט, דְּשָׁחַט לְתוֹרָא, דְּשָׁתָה לְמַיָּא, דְּכָבָה לְנוּרָא, דְּשָׂרַף לְחוּטְרָא, דְּהִכָּה לְכַלְבָּא, דְּנָשַׁךְ לְשׁוּנְרָא, דְּאָכְלָה לְגַדְיָא, דְּזַבִּין אַבָּא בִּתְרֵי זוּזֵי. חַד גַּדְיָא, חַד גַּדְיָא.

Then God came and killed the angel of death who killed the slaughterer who slaughtered the ox that drank the water that extinguished the fire that burnt the stick that hit the dog that bit the cat that ate the kid – that my father bought for two *zuzim*.

One kid, one kid.

This is the end of the Haggadah, but each person should, to the best of his ability, follow the dictum of the Sages that "whoever expands upon the recounting of the story of the Exodus from Egypt is praiseworthy." Some have the custom of reciting *Shir Hashirim* after the Seder.

ENDNOTES

Maggid Section Introductions

1. *Tehillim* 119:97. See also the question of the *tam*, מה זאת, to possibly be read this way. See note 46 in The Pure Son endnotes.

2. *Mishlei* 22:6.

3. See *Rashi*, *Bereishis* 14:14, ד"ה וירק את חניכיו.

4. *Bereishis* 15:13–14.

5. *Shemos* 12:40–41.

6. See *Rashi*, *Bereishis* 15:13; 42:2, *Shemos*, 6:18; 12:40, from *Midrash Tanchuma*, *Bereishis* §8.

7. The expression לעקור את הכל is perhaps used because the word עקר as in *Vayikra* 25:47 refers to descendants; Lavan wanted to assure that Yaakov would have no descendants. See note 90 in The Pure Son endnotes.)

8. The Mishnah, *Pesachim* 10:4, tells us at this point of the Haggadah to expound from *Arami Oved Avi* "עד שיגמור כל הפרשה כולה—until the entire *parashah* is completed." We can derive from this that, at a much earlier time, before Rav and Shmuel argued over how to fulfill מתחיל בגנות ומסיים בשבח (see *Avadim Hayinu* and *Mitchilah Ovedei Avodah Zarah*; Maggid Sections 3 and 9), there was a version of the Haggadah somewhat akin to what follows here. See *Sifri*, *Devarim* §301. See also *Midrash Lekach Tov*, *Devarim* 26:5–7, *Midrash Tannaim* p. 172, and *Yalkut Shimoni*, *Devarim* §938, for parallel passages.

9. See *Bamidbar* 20:14–16, *Yehoshua* 24:5–8, *Shmuel I* 12:6–8, and *Tehillim* 105:23–27.

10. See *Torah Temimah* to *Shemos* 6:6 where he points out that these redemptive words are not לשונות של גאולה. The language of the *Yerushalmi* is that they are גאולות — separate and distinct redemptions. See note 85 in The Pure Son endnotes.

11. *Shemos* 1:12.

12. Ibid., 1:22.

13. See *Tehillim* 105:25, "הפך לבם לשנא עמו להתנכל בעבדיו — He changed their heart to hate His people to plot against His servants." See also *Tehillim* 106:10, "ויושיעם מיד שונא — He delivered them from the hater."

14. *Shemos* 3:9.

15. See *Rashi*, *Shemos* 12:23.

16. The second proof text which obligates every man to regard himself as if he left Egypt, refers to the purpose of the Exodus, which was the immediate entry into the Land of Israel. This question asks how this obligation is meant to apply to those who are not in Israel, and is posed by *Abarbanel* in his Haggadah.

17. Our Sages frowned upon the protracted or elongated praise of God, as a limitation of the infinite. See *Talmud Bavli*, *Berachos* 33b and *Tosafos* 12a, ד"ה אמת.

The Wise Son

1. According to *Rambam*'s version of the Haggadah, *Ha Lachma Anya* is not said at the time the *korban Pesach* is brought in the Temple in Jerusalem, when we no longer eat the bread of affliction (and we no longer need to pray to be free and in Israel). Rav Menachem Kasher's *Haggadah Sheleimah* (p. 5) lists four versions of the Haggadah in which the opening words of *Ha Lachma Anya* are "כהא לחמא עניא – this is like the bread of

affliction," as if we have already achieved some manner of emancipation.

2. The Torah commands us to rejoice on *Yom Tov*, and this command is codified as one of the 613 mitzvos (*Rambam*, Positive Commandment §54, *Sefer HaChinuch*, mitzvah 488). On Shavuos we are told to rejoice (*Devarim* 16:11) and on Sukkos we are told twice to rejoice (*Devarim* 16:14–15), but no such command appears on Pesach. Rav David Tzvi Hoffman explains that since we gained our freedom on Pesach, the Torah didn't have to command rejoicing for it would come more naturally than on other festivals. The Codes warn us to refrain from selfish rejoicing known as שמחת כריסו, the joy of one's own stomach. See *Rambam, Mishneh Torah, Hilchos Yom Tov* 6:18, *Tur Shulchan Aruch, Orach Chaim* 529. The true spirit of the festival is to share with others, as *Ha Lachma Anya* (Maggid Section 1) indicates.

3. *Rashbam, Pesachim* 99b, points to *Kesubos* 50a, where a dispensation is given on any positive commandment that takes us beyond twenty percent of our assets. It would appear that to perform a mitzvah with communal funds as the Mishnah bids us to do, exceeds this dictum. *Rashbam* explains this exception as a function of the fact that these mitzvos involve food and of course poor people are to be fed from communal funds.

4. In Talmudic times, each person dined before an individual table and the entire table was removed and replaced at various intervals. Since by medieval times everyone sat at one large table, the removal of the table came to be accomplished by covering or removing the *Seder* plate. See *Pesachim* 115b, *Rashbam*, ואין עוקר את השלחן ד"ה.

5. See *Tosafos, Pesachim* 115b, כדי ד"ה.

6. Originally the child asked about the way the *korban Pesach* was prepared and omitted the question about reclining. This reflects a time when the *korban Pesach* was eaten, or memorialized by all foods at the *Seder* being eaten *only* roasted – see *Talmud Bavli, Pesachim* 53a. This was also a time when everyone reclined throughout the year, so the child saw nothing unusual in the reclining at the *Seder*.

7. One of the overarching themes of the Haggadah is מתחיל בגנות ומסים בשבח, that we begin the night with disparagement and conclude it with praise. The first two questions represent the גנות and the last two questions represent the שבח.

8. *Talmud Bavli, Pesachim* 116a.

9. In *Mitchilah Ovedei Avodah Zarah*, (Maggid Section 9) we deal with the question of why *Avadim Hayinu* is placed earlier in the Haggadah than *Mitchilah Ovedei Avodah Zarah*, which clearly precedes it chronologically.

Disputes between Rav and Shmuel that are not related to monetary issues generally side with Rav. We will pursue this matter as well – namely, if the reference to *Avadim Hayinu* here is an indication that the Haggadah sides with Shmuel over Rav.

10. *Devarim* 6:21.

11. See *Shemos* 3:19.

12. We will elaborate on this in Maggid Section 5; *Amar Rabbi Elazar ben Azaryah*.

13. *Shemos* 20:2.

14. The end of *Krias Shema* makes reference to *yetzias Mitzrayim* as do the subsequent blessings in both *Shacharis* and *Maariv*. See *Shulchan Aruch, Orach Chaim* 67, *Magen Avraham* §1, *Rabbi Akiva Eiger, Chasam Sofer*, and *Mishnah Berurah* §3, regarding whether we can fulfill this requirement with *Az Yashir* said at the end of *Pesukei D'Zimra*. See also *Talmud Bavli, Berachos* 13b, and *Shaagas Aryeh* §10, for other ways of possibly fulfilling the daily mitzvah of *zechiras yetzias Mitzrayim*.

15. See *Malbim*.

16. *Shemos* 2:11–12.

17. *Talmud Bavli, Pesachim* 108a.

18. *Sanhedrin* 32b.

19. *Shulchan Aruch, Orach Chaim* 472:5.

20. At the time of this story there was no Temple and the *korban Pesach* was no longer brought, but we are careful today to eat its symbolic replacement – the *afikoman* – by midnight to fulfill Rabbi Elazar's opinion. It is possible that Rabbi Akiva may agree with a Rabbinic stringency to curtail the time for eating, and agree in practice with Rabbi Elazar. The first Mishnah in *Maseches Berachos* lists a few examples of mitzvos that may be performed all night according to Torah law, but the Sages restricted the time of observance until midnight. The Mishnah does not list *korban Pesach* and is in line with another Mishnah, *Megillah* 21b, that also seems to follow Rabbi Akiva's position. The Mishnah says דבר שמצותו בלילה כשר כל הלילה; whichever mitzvah is performed at night may be performed all night. There are two additional *Mishnayos*, however, that side with Rabbi Elazar and they are in two tractates more closely related to *korban Pesach* than *Berachos* and *Megillah*. *Zevachim* 56b and *Pesachim* 120b unequivocally side with Rabbi Elazar. See *Tosafos, Megillah* 21b, ד"ה לאתויי, *Tosafos, Pesachim* 120b, ד"ה אמר רבא. See *Shulchan Aruch, Orach Chaim* 477:1, *Biur Halachah* ד"ה ויהא.

21. *Talmud Bavli, Sukkah* 28a.

22. Ibid., *Shabbos* 11a.

23. See *Tosefta Beitzah* 2:15.

24. *Targum Yonasan* to כובע, in *Shmuel I* 17:5, is קולס.

25. See *Talmud Bavli, Pesachim* 53a–b, regarding customs of eating the meal at the *Seder* today. See *Shulchan Aruch, Orach Chaim* 476. The general Ashkenazic custom is not to eat any roasted meat at the *Seder* to avoid any resemblance to the *korban Pesach*, which could only be roasted (*Shemos* 12:8–9).

26. *Chidah.*

27. *Abarbanel.*

28. *Talmud Bavli, Berachos* 12b.

29. Ibid., 27b–28a.

30. See *Tosafos, Berachos* 4b, ד"ה אמר ר' יוחן, for a connection between the two themes of *zechiras yetzias Mitzrayim* at night and *tefillas Arvis reshus*.

31. *Shemos* 12:41,51, and *Bamidbar* 33:3.

32. See *Talmud Bavli, Megillah* 20b, for a list of mitzvos performed only by day based on the appearance of the word יום in any form in connection with that mitzvah, such as יום תרועה for shofar, or ביום השמיני for circumcision. In fact, the Haggadah itself suggests that the section of the *Seder*, Maggid, takes place by day since the Torah says "והגדת לבנך ביום ההוא – You shall relate to your son on that **day**" (See *Yachol MeiRosh Chodesh*; Maggid Section 8). If not for the intrinsic connection between the matzah and the maror with the mitzvah of *sippur yetzias Mitzrayim*, we might have concluded that Maggid is by day; see *Tosafos, Megillah* 21a, ד"ה לאתויי.

33. The *Vilna Gaon* explains that in the phrase כל ימי חייך, the word כל includes כל היום, that is, the entire twenty-four-hour day of the days of our lives, as opposed to the general rule of mitzvos where the word יום appears. See previous note.

34. *Yirmiyahu* 23:7–8.

35. The literal meaning of the prophecy was meant to be realized with the return to Zion after the seventy-year Babylonian exile. Indeed, Chazal (*Sotah* 36a) indicate that the return of that exile should have been accompanied by miracles similar to those of the Egyptian redemption, if not for our sinful ways, שגרם החטא. See note 24 in The Pure Son endnotes.

36. *Rambam, Mishneh Torah, Hilchos Krias Shema* 1:3. This might explain why *Rambam* fails to include the daily mitzvah of *zechiras yetzias Mitzrayim* among his list of 613 mitzvos. If the halachah sides with Rabbi Elazar ben Azariah, then *zechiras yetzias Mitzrayim* will not be performed in the Messianic age as we do now. *Rambam* introduces his list of mitzvos with general rules of inclusion, the third of which states that any mitzvah that will change in any way in the Messianic era will not

37. be included. See Rav Joseph B. Soloveitchik, *Shiurim L'Zecher Aba Mori*, vol. I, ch. 1.

37. When Yaakov was in flight from his brother Eisav, he found comfort in approaching God as "המקום," in *Bereishis* 28:11. *Talmud Bavli, Berachos* 26b considers this verse to be the source of Yaakov instituting the nighttime prayer. Similar expositions are made of the word מקום in *Esther* 4:14 and *Melachim II* 5:11.

38. *Shemos* 3:12.

39. Rav Menachem Kasher cites five such versions in his *Haggadah Sheleimah*, p. 22.

40. See the *Maharal's* Haggadah.

41. P. 133.

42. Today that means that we don't eat anything after the *afikoman*, which means the last thing we eat at the *Seder* is *matzah*. See *Shulchan Aruch, Orach Chaim* 478 for the contemporary custom.

43. *Talmud Bavli, Pesachim* 116b.

44. The *Talmud Yerushalmi* and *Mechilta's* versions of the verse is אותו. Perhaps this change is a function of his wisdom. The Septuagint's version is also אותו. It would appear that the emendation was made with an eye to the Haggadah's treatment of the *rasha's* question.

45. *Shibbolei HaLeket, Maharal.*

46. See *Talmud Bavli, Megillah* 32a.

47. By way of comparison, see the relative sizes in pages of the following Talmudic tractates as well as the dedicated sections of *Shulchan Aruch* for each holiday. *Maseches Rosh Hashanah* has 35 pages, *Yoma* (Yom Kippur) has 88, *Sukkah* has 56, and *Pesachim* has 121. In the *Shulchan Aruch, Hilchos Rosh Hashanah* is 23 chapters (§581–§603), *Hilchos Yom Kippur* is 21 chapters (§604–§624), *Hilchos Sukkos* has 45 (§425–§469), and *Hilchos Pesach* contains 63 chapters (§429–§491). Shavuos has no specific tractate in the Mishnah and has one chapter of *Shulchan Aruch*, §494.

48. *Shemos* 12:2.

49. *Shibbolei HaLeket.* Some have the custom of reciting parts of Maggid on *Shabbos HaGadol* (*Shulchan Aruch, Orach Chaim* 430). The *Vilna Gaon* was against this minhag because of the Haggadah's statement that the mitzvah of *sippur yetzias Mitzrayim* does not apply before the Seder night, in *Yachol MeiRosh Chodesh* (Maggid Section 8).

50. See Mishnah, *Megillah* 20b, and the ensuing Gemara.

51. See above, introduction on the structure of *Maaseh B'Rabbi Eliezer* (Maggid Section 4).

52. See the answer to the *tam* in *Mah Nishtanah* (Maggid Section 2).

53. See the Haggadah of the *Shelah*.

54. *Pesachim* 116a.

55. Bottom of *Pesachim* 116a.

56. Rav Nachman's decision to follow Shmuel is problematic in view of the Talmudic principle that the halachah in non-monetary disputes between Rav and Shmuel is always in accordance with Rav. *Avudraham* cites this dispute in the names of Rava and Abaye with Rav Nachman siding according to Rava to begin with *Avadim Hayinu*.

57. *Avadim Hayinu* is actually the Torah's answer to the *chacham*'s question in *Devarim* 6:21.

58. Avraham is criticized by the Gemara for drafting *talmidei chachamim* into military service in the battle raging in Canaan at the time; מפני מה נענש אברהם אבינו ונשתעבדו בניו למצרים מאתים ועשר שנים, מפני שעשה אנגרייא בתלמידי חכמים. See *Talmud Bavli, Nedarim* 32a.

59. See *Ramban, Bereishis* 12:10.

60. See *Abarbanel*, introduction to his Haggadah, and especially his explanation of karpas.

61. See *Talmud Bavli, Yoma* 9a.

62. See Ruth Wisse's article in *Commentary* magazine, "How Not to Remember and How Not to Forget," January, 2008.

63. *Talmud Bavli, Berachos* 48b.

64. *Shibbolei HaLeket*.

65. The four hundred years do not begin with the birth of Avraham's eldest son Yishmael because, for the purpose of Avraham's destiny, God told him כי ביצחק יקרא לך זרע – for only **through Yitzchak** will offspring be continued for you." (*Bereishis* 21:12). As such, the fulfillment of "גר יהיה זרעך – your descendants will be strangers" begins with Yitzchak's birth.

66. Yitzchak was 60 when Yaakov was born (*Bereishis* 25:26), and Yaakov was 130 when he arrived in Egypt (*Bereishis* 47:9). These amounts added to 210 (see *Bereishis Rabbah* 91:2 and sources cited by Rav Menachem Kasher's *Torah Sheleimah, Bereishis* 42:2, note 18) – the years our tradition teaches us we spent in Egypt – add up to 400.

67. For a Talmudic example of סירום המקרא, see *Talmud Bavli, Bava Basra* 119b.

68. *Bereishis* 23.

69. Ibid., 33:19.

70. Ibid., 26:15–21.

71. See *Talmud Bavli, Maseches Avodah Zarah* 53b, and *Talmud Bavli, Maseches Bava Basra* 117b, where Chazal posit that Avraham did indeed take possession of the land. See *Bereishis Rabbah* 41:5, cited by *Rashi, Bereishis* 13:7, ד"ה ויהי ריב, that Lot considered Avraham to be the proper owner of the land, while Avraham himself at that time disagreed. We can perhaps reconcile these positions by noticing a grammatical inconsistency in the prediction of servitude. The decree begins, גר יהיה זרעך, which is singular, and continues בארץ לא להם, which is plural. Accordingly, these last three words refer to כנען who was destined to be in servitude of Shem's descendants (*Bereishis* 9:25–27). Therefore, this land would really belong to Shem's descendants, thus explaining the position of the two Talmudic sources above. See *Talmud Bavli, Sanhedrin* 91a.

72. *Talmud Bavli, Nedarim* 32a.

73. *Rashi*, in his Torah commentary, *Bereishis* 15:6 explains how Avraham did not demonstrate a breach in faith with these words. He was merely asking how he could be sure that he and his descendants would always merit the inheritance of God's beneficence. It is interesting to note that *Rashi* in *Yeshayahu* 43:27, ד"ה אביך הראשון חטא does consider Avraham's question to be a breach of faith.

74. *Yirmiyahu* 25:9.

75. See ibid., 50–51.

76. *Yeshayahu* 10.

77. *Melachim II* 19:35–37.

78. *Zechariah* 1:15, translation of new JPS Tanach.

79. *Shemos* 11:12.

80. *Talmud Bavli, Berachos* 9a. Actually, the word נא can mean "please," or it can mean "now." When Onkelos translates it as "כען," it means "now." When he translates it as "בבעו," it means "please." See Onkelos to *Bamidbar* 12:13, on the words נא רפא נא לה. The first נא is translated as "please," and the second נא is translated as "now." In our verse, Onkelos translates נא as כען – now."

81. *Bereishis* 15:14.

82. *Avudraham, Abarbanel*.

83. *Bereishis* 15:12.

84. See *Bereishis Rabbah* 44:17.

85. *Talmud Bavli, Megillah* 14a.

86. *Bereishis* 29:15.

87. *Talmud Yerushalmi, Pesachim* 10:1, cited by *Rashi* and *Rashbam* to *Talmud Bavli, Pesachim* 99b. See *Torah Temimah, Shemos* 6:6, §5. The four cups correspond to four separate redemptions. The four expressions upon which the four cups are based are not synonymous expressions of the same theme but are four separate and distinct levels of redemption. As such, the *Torah Temimah* prefers to refer to ארבעה לשונות של גאולה and not to ארבע גאולות.

88. See introduction of *Malbim* to his Haggadah, referenced in our general introduction above.

89. While it is true that in Midrash, Nimrod threatened Avraham (*Bereishis Rabbah* 38:13 cited by *Rashi*, *Bereishis* 11:28) and Yishmael threatened Yitzchak (*Bereishis Rabbah* 53:11 cited by *Rashi*, *Bereishis* 21:9), Lavan's threat included Yaakov's entire family.

90. See Rav Menachem Kasher's *Haggadah Sheleimah* pp. 32–33 for an exhaustive list of references. The Talmud often states תא שמע which means "come and listen." צא ולמד implies a necessity to leave the source of study to shed light on the subject. Rav Kasher's examples all seem to fit this paradigm, but it is beyond our scope to analyze them in depth.

91. *Bereishis* 31:13.

92. The *parashah* itself is called פרשת ויצא.

93. See *Rashi*, *Shemos* 14:5, ד"ה כי ברח העם.

94. See *Bereishis* 30:35.

95. *Shemos* 1:9–10.

96. *Bereishis* 30:27–30.

97. This is why the Egyptians became enamored of us right after the Plague of Darkness, in *Shemos* 11:3; they realized that the original accusation against us was a lie all along.

98. Balak speaks of a similar threat in *Bamidbar* 22:2–4. It is interesting to note that the *Targum Yonasan ben Uziel* to *Bamidbar* 22:5 associates Bilaam with Lavan!

99. See *Bereishis* 31:24, 29, 43.

100. See *Shemos* 12:3,16–17, and *Shemos* 6:6–8.

101. Ibid., 3:12.

102. See *Melachim I* 6:1.

103. See *Talmud Bavli*, *Zevachim* 116b.

104. This would appear to be the point of *Dayeinu* as well. See below, Maggid Section 15a.

105. *Shemos* 5:2.

106. See *Bereishis* 1:2, ורוח אלקים מרחפת על פני המים.

107. *Shemos* 7:17.

108. Ibid., 8:18–19.

109. Ibid., 9:4.

110. Ibid., 8:18.

111. Ibid., 9:19–20.

112. Ibid., 9:28. Avraham's status as a prophet (*Bereishis* 20:7) also comes in the context of praying for a king who had wronged him.

113. Ibid., 8:4.

114. Ibid., 9:27.

115. See *Leil Shimurim*, the Haggadah of the *Aruch HaShulchan*, where he explains Rabbi Yehudah's mnemonic in light of these three points. This breakdown is found there, as well as in the Haggadah of the *Ritva*, both of whom explain Rabbi Yehudah's mnemonic in light of these three points.

116. See below, Maggid Section 15; *Kamah Maalos Tovos/ Dayeinu*.

117. Note that the paragraphs of the holidays in *Devarim* chapter 16 refer to rejoicing for Shavuos and Sukkos but not for Pesach. *Meshech Chochmah* explains this omission as a function of this issue.

118. Seven on Shabbos (not including *maftir*, which repeats part of the seventh *aliyah*) as well as three on each of Shabbos afternoon, Monday, and Thursday.

119. See also *Klei Yakar*, *Shemos* 25:13, ד"ה ועשית בדי עצי שיטים. The *Aron* represents Torah, and the word בדי with the numerical value of sixteen connects to these sixteen *aliyos* of the week.

120. *Shemos* 12:11.

121. *Shmuel II* 4:4.

122. Genesis Jerusalem Press, 1991.

123. Part II, ch. 2.

124. Bear in mind as well that during the recent Plague of Darkness, the Israelites, who could see (*Shemos* 10:23), did not harm the blind Egyptians who were stuck in their tracks (ibid.). It must have been then that the Egyptians realized that the original canard accusing the Israelites of being a "fifth column" waiting for the opportunity to overrun Egypt (*Shemos* 1:9–10) was a cruel lie. We had that opportunity during three days of darkness. This is also when the Egyptians became enamored of us (*Shemos* 11:3). They realized the lie told to them about us, which was originally meant to elicit hatred against our people (*Shemos* 1:12). This is a scenario that has repeated itself time and again in our history.

125. *Shemos* 12:21.

126. *Mechilta D'Pischa* ibid. The *Torah Temimah* explains this in light of *Rambam's* explanation that the sacrificial order was meant to wean us off of the idolatrous ways of the ancient pagans. *Abarbanel* makes this point throughout his commentary to his Haggadah *Zevach Pesach*.

127. *Bamidbar* 9:11.

128. *Shemos* 12:8.

129. *Talmud Bavli*, *Pesachim* 39a.

130. See *Sefer HaRokeach*, *Hilchos Pesach*. See *Mishlei* 15:17, טוב **ארוחת** ירק ואהבה שם משור אבוס ושנאה בו. The numerical

value of ארוחת is the same as חזרת. See notes to this verse in the *Rokeach's* commentary to *Mishlei*, 2014, HaDaf Typesetting, note 73.

131. See the suggestion of this second reason in *Ibn Ezra*, to *Shemos* 12:8.

132. *Bereishis* 15:13.

133. See *Rashi*, *Shemos* 12:41, and above, in *Baruch Shomer Havtachaso L'Yisrael* (Maggid Section 10), question 1.

134. See above, *Baruch Shomer Havtachaso L'Yisrael* (Maggid Section 10), question 2.

135. *Tehillim* 106:44.

136. *Talmud Bavli, Berachos* 54b.

137. This is the order of the four groups in *Tehillim* 107. The Talmudic order is crossing the sea, crossing the desert, general threat to life, and leaving incarceration. See *Tosafos* ibid., ד"ה ארבעה.

138. *Tehillim* 118:5 reads, "מן המצר קראתי י-ה," and the word מצר is similar to the key word in וירא בצר להם. these words are phonetically close to מצרים, the paradigm of all these troubles.

139. *Vayikra* 25:33.

140. *Rus* 3:13. The process of acquiring Rus in marriage is referred again as גאולה in 4:6 and the text itself later in 4:10 describes this גאולה as an act of acquisition; "לי אשה **קניתי – I have acquired** this woman."

141. See *Talmud Bavli, Pesachim* 87b. The Israelites are one of four קנינים – acquisitions – of God. In *Az Yashir*, our nation is referred to as עם זו קנית (*Shemos* 15:16). The prophet, Hoshea (*Hoshea* 3:2) expresses his disappointment with Israel's rebelliousness in light of all that God had done for us. He expresses this in a cryptic manner "ואכרה לי בחמשה עשר כסף – I purchased her for me with fifteen *shekels* of silver." *Targum Yonasan* renders this number as a reference to the fifteenth of Nissan. We were not only *redeemed* by God on the fifteenth of Nissan, we were *acquired* as well. See also *Yirmiyahu* 32:7 for an additional juxtaposition of גאולה and קנין.

142. Perhaps the reason why להלל should be omitted is because *Lefichach* (Maggid Section 18) moves right into *Hallel* itself. Regarding לקלס, see Rav Baruch Halevi Epstein's *Haggadah Baruch She'amar*, where he calls for an omission of this word not only in the Haggadah but also at the end of the Shabbos morning *Pesukei D'Zimra*, because in Tanach the word is *not* used for praise, but derision. See *Melachim II* 2:23, *Yechezkel* 22:4–5, *Yirmiyahu* 20:8, and *Tehillim* 44:14.

143. The first of the Decalogue, the source of our faith, connects to the redemption from Egypt, *Shemos* 20:2.

144. The Haggadah expounds "אני ה' – I am God," *Shemos* 6:2.

145. As was declared to Moshe at the Burning Bush, *Shemos* 3:7.

146. This is abundantly clear throughout the Plagues, as the wicked of Egypt are punished and the Israelites are spared.

147. This is seen in the humbling of the mighty Egyptians and their perceived gods.

148. The miracles point to a purposeful order to the events before us.

149. Moshe's predictions prove the tenet of faith of prophecy so that even were one to explain all the miracles of *Shemos* in a natural order, we would still point to the miracle of the prophecy that the event took place when predicted. See *Ibn Ezra, Shemos* 14:27.

150. *Vayikra* 25:10.

151. *Shemos* 21:2.

152. *Yeshayahu* 61:1, *Yirmiyahu* 34:8,15,17, and *Yechezkel* 46:17.

153. *Shemos* 32:16.

154. See *Avos* 6:2. See *Shemos* 32:16, *Torah Temimah* §30–32.

155. *Mishnah Berurah* 51:17.

156. *Shemos* 33:4. The connection to the forgiveness of the Golden Calf is found in the Haggadah of the Vilna Gaon and is cited by the *Malbim*. Based on the inclusion of our ignominious and idolatrous past, referenced earlier in the Haggadah, it does make sense to include an element of *teshuvah* as part of our Seder observance.

157. See Mishnah, *Taanis*, ch. 4, *Talmud Bavli, Taanis* 26b, "לא היו ימים טובים לישראל כחמשה עשר באב וכיום הכיפורים – There were no joyful days for Israel on the level of the fifteenth of Av and Yom Kippur." The Gemara explains the joy of Yom Kippur as a function of our forgiveness. *Rashi* (ibid., 30b, ד"ה שניתנו בו לוחות אחרונות) shows at great length that this forgiveness refers first to the actual atonement for the Golden Calf. The Mishnah thus refers to that atonement as a יום טוב, and in this way connects to the third phrase, מאכל ליום טוב.

158. This historical connection is made by the Vilna Gaon and quoted by *Malbim*. The Haggadah is interested in teaching the lessons of history and this explanation fits that agenda.

159. *Shemos* 33:20.

160. Human judges are called אלהים, in *Shemos* 22:7–9.

161. See *Ibn Ezra, Bereishis* 1:1, ד"ה בראשית ברא אלקים. That the *gematria* of אלהים, which is the same as "הטבע – the nature," is noted often to this effect by the *Shelah* and others. *Baal HaTurim* to אספה לי שבעים איש, *Bamidbar* 11:16, refers to over one hundred Biblical descriptions of God's Name and Eminence.

162. See *Shemos* 5:22–6:7.

163. *Tehillim* 136:13.

164. *Shemos* 14:21.

165. The word appears as a noun in the form of a coin. It is a half-*shekel* and is so named because it is split in two. See *Shemos* 38:26.

166. *Bereishis* 7:11.

167. *Bamidbar* 16:31.

168. *Shemos Rabbah* 21:8.

169. *Bereishis Rabbah* 58:8, based on *Berieshis* 22:3; "בזכות אברהם אני בוקע להם את הים בעבור מה שעשה שנאמר ויבקע עצי עולה ואומר ויבקעו המים – In the merit of Avraham I will split the Sea for them because of what he did, as it says, 'And he split the wood of the *Olah*,' and it says, 'And He split the water.'"

170. We recreate this connection to God every day by inserting the recitation of the *Akeidah*, followed by a prayer that asks God to recognize that just as Avraham went against His grain to perform His Will, so too should God go against His grain to judge us favorably even when we don't deserve it.

171. *Talmud Bavli, Arachin* 10b.

172. *Yeshayahu* 30:29.

173. See *Midrash Tehillim* 113 and *Rashi, Yeshayahu* 30:29.

174. *Talmud Bavli, Pesachim* 95b. See *Korban Ha'Eidah, Yerushalmi Shekalim* 3:2, ד"ה בהלל.

175. Rav Joseph B. Soloveitchik's *Shiurim L'Zecher Aba Mori*, vol. I, p. 3.

176. See *Ohr Zarua, Hilchos Krias Shema*, §43, see also *Aruch HaShulchan, Orach Chaim* 473:26. For a collection of opinions on this issue, see Rav Moshe Shternbach's *Moadim U'Zemanim*, vol. 7, Maggid §179.

177. This has been discussed in *Yachol MeiRosh Chodesh* (Maggid Section 8), and in *Rabban Gamliel Hayah Omer* (Maggid Section 16).

178. *Talmud Bavli, Pesachim* 116b.

179. B. Yeushson, Jerusalem, 1977.

180. See *Rambam, Hilchos Melachim* 11:2.

181. Presently the blessing recognizes that the extent of our mitzvos of eating is limited to matzah and maror. This is consistent with *Rabban Gamliel Hayah Omer* (Maggid Section 16) which refers to our pointing at the matzah and maror that we eat now when saying מצה זו and מרור זה, but when we refer to the *korban Pesach*, we don't point and we simply refer to what our ancestors ate in Temple times. Similarly, *Yachol MeiRosh Chodesh* (Maggid Section 8) refers to "לא אמרתי בעבור זה אלא בשעה שיש מצה ומרור מונחים לפניך – 'For the sake of this' refers to the matzah and maror placed before you," omitting any reference to פסח. We additionally omit reference to the question in the Mishnah *Pesachim* 116a that mentions *korban Pesach*. At a time when we are not eating *korban Pesach*, a child will not notice anything unusual about it. Additionally, Rabbenu Tam is cited by *Machzor Vitry*, and *Sefer Hamanhig*, chapter 72, to omit the words, כל דצריר ייתי ויפסח, whoever needs, come and eat the korban Pesach. Rav Shlomo Zaalman Auerbach would interrupt these words by saying that we only say them as a remembrance of the korban Pesach. See his Haggadah page 128.

182. *Tosafos, Pesachim* 116b, ד"ה ונאמר.

183. *Talmud Bavli, Pesachim* 70a.

184. *Talmud Yerushalmi, Pesachim* 6:4.

185. *Shemos* 12:47.

186. *Pesachim* 38b.

187. *Talmud Bavli, Pesachim* 66a.

188. Mishnah, *Chagigah* 1:2. Mishnah, *Pesachim*, chapter 6.

189. See *Rambam, Mishneh Torah , Hilchos Korban Pesach* 8:3, *Hilchos Chametz U'Matzah* 8:7.

190. *Berachos* 13a derives this point from *Yirmiyahu* 23:7–8. (See also ibid., 16:14–15.) Our Sages state that such miracles would have occurred with the ingathering of the exiles from Babylonia if not for our sinful ways. See *Talmud Bavli, Sotah* 36a. For a full discussion on this issue, see above Maggid Section 5, answer to the wise son.

191. Chapters 37–38.

192. Chapter 14.

193. See *Mechilta, Beshalach, Maseches D'Shirah* §1.

194. See *Tosafos, Pesachim* 116b, ד"ה ונאמר.

The Cynical Son

1. This point is made by *Shibbolei HaLeket*. See also *Meshech Chochmah* to *Bereishis* 48:22, explaining בחרבי ובקשתי. See also *Shulchan Aruch, Yoreh Deah* 335:5, *Taz* §4, *Shach* §3; *Shulchan Aruch, Orach Chaim* 101:4, based on *Talmud Bavli, Shabbos* 12a.

2. *Devarim* 16:2.

3. *Avudraham*.

4. Rav David Tzvi Hoffman, *Devarim* 16:11, points out that on Shavuos and Sukkos, the Torah lists a number of people who must be supported for the festival, namely

the stranger, orphan, widow, and Leivi. Rav Hoffman notes that no such exhortation or list appears regarding Pesach. He explains that no such list is necessary. It is obvious that a holiday which celebrates our deliverance from the deprivations of Egypt should require such inclusions, which *Ha Lachma Anya* makes clear. See also *Talmud Bavli, Moed Katan* 28a, for examples of times when Jews of all stations assume a common denominator of the poor to level all participants.

5. *Abarbanel, Zevach Pesach.*

6. *Bava Metzia* 59b.

7. *Amos* 9:7.

8. See L. Rabinowitz, *From out of the Depths*, "*Parashas Kedoshim.*" The book was written in South Africa in 1946 and is critical of the treatment of Blacks in that country. It invokes these words of Amos for the Jews to rise up to take the lead in establishing equal rights for all.

9. *Shemos Rabbah* 5:16.

10. *Talmud Bavli, Kiddushin* 71a.

11. *Talmud Yerushalmi, Yevamos* 1:6.

12. Mishnah, *Maaser Sheini* 5:9, *Talmud Bavli, Arachin* 11b.

13. Rabbi Eliezer ben Horkanos was descended from the Hasmonean line of Kohanim. See *Korban Ha'Eidah, Sotah* 3:4 (14b).

14. *Talmud Bavli, Sanhedrin* 96b.

15. See *Chidah, Simchas HaRegel.*

16. See *Rasha*, above.

17. See Cecil Roth in his Haggadah, where he posits that this meeting was a secret gathering to determine how to react to the Hadrianic persecutions. This theory is widely quoted and it has many detractors. See the Jonathan Sacks Haggadah, p. 107, "The Sages in B'nei Brak."

18. *Rambam, Hilchos Melachim* 11:3.

19. See *Talmud Bavli, Gittin* 56 a–b. *Talmud Bavli, Yevamos* 62b, refers to thousands of Rabbi Akiva's students who died during the *Omer* because they showed no respect for one another. Perhaps this is a veiled reference to the fact that Rabbi Akiva sent them to battle against the Hadrianic persecutions of the day and his students, not being trained soldiers, had no respect for the chain of command and the discipline of battle. The censor might understandably change this version of events to the one that appears.

20. The same point is made in *Yirmiyahu* 31:20–21.

21. Rav Soloveitchik chose to name his book on the Jewish aspiration for redemption after this *Shir HaShirim* narrative, *Kol Dodi Dofek.*

22. *Shibbolei HaLeket.*

23. *Talmud Bavli, Nedarim* 81a, *Bava Metzia* 85a.

24. *Nedarim* ibid. See *Igros Moshe, Orach Chaim* I:20.

25. See *Talmud Bavli, Bava Basra* 12a, discussing the verse ונביא לבב חכמה – "The prophet has a heart of wisdom," (*Tehillim* 90:12). See also *Rashi, Shabbos* 119b, ד"ה ובנביאי, *Rambam, Moreh Nevuchim* 2:38.

26. *Talmud Bavli, Kiddushin* 40a.

27. *Yeshayahu* 3:11.

28. *Shemos* 13:14.

29. This type of assumption is common in Chazal. Chizkiyahu profusely thanked God for an additional fifteen years of life after he was told he would soon die (*Yeshayahu* 38:9–20). The absence of similar thanksgiving upon the salvation of Jerusalem induced Chazal to explain that Chizkiyahu did not thank God for that and was punished for it. (See *Sanhedrin* 94a.)

30. This story was told to me by Rav Yosef Kahaneman of the Ponevezh Yeshiva.

31. See *Rashi*, Rav Shimshon Raphael Hirsch, *Bereishis* 25:27, quoted above in the Introduction, footnote 12.

32. *Shemos* 13:5.

33. *Chizkuni*, quoting *Sefer HaRokeach.*

34. *Shemos* 12:43.

35. See *Ha Lachma Anya* (Maggid Section 1), answer to the Pure Son.

36. *Talmud Bavli, Chullin* 5a.

37. See *Ibn Ezra*'s quote of Rav Yehudah HaLeivi, in *Shemos* 20:1. This may be an additional reason why *Rambam* omits *zechiras yetzias Mitzrayim* as a daily mitzvah, as it's already a mitzvah subsumed by the first of the *Aseres HaDibros*. See above, *Amar Rabbi Elazar ben Azaryah*, note 36 in The Wise Son endnotes.

38. *Talmud Bavli, Gittin* 56b.

39. *Shibbolei HaLeket*, as cited by J.D. Eisenstein's *Otzar Peirushim* (New York, 1920) p. 153.

40. See *Shibolei Haleket* and the *Aruch HaShulchan*'s *Haggadah Leil Shimurim*. The philosophical discussions of *Talmud Bavli, Sotah* 49a, seem to also move in this direction. Notice the usages of the word הקהה a few times on that *amud*.

41. See *Talmud Bavli, Shabbos* 104a, for a demonstration of the barrier placed between the holiness of the letter ק (קדוש) and the wickedness of the letter ר (רשע). The ק of הקהה is surrounded by the letter ה which has the numerical value of 5, and the letter appears three times for a full value of 15. See Maggid Section 15a, for the significance of the number 15 at the *Seder*. The three

letters ה protect the ק from the next letter ר, which is indicative of the *rasha*.

42. *Tehillim* 127:4.

43. *Talmud Bavli, Moed Katan* 28a; חיי בני ומזוני לא בזכותא תליא מילתא אלא במזלא תליא מילתא.

44. *Shemos* 13:4.

45. *Devarim* 16:1. See also *Shemos* 23:15, 34:18.

46. *Ritva*. See also *Netziv* to *Shemos* 34:18, ד"ה בחודש האביב.

47. Recall that of all the sons, the *rasha*'s statement is the only one not connected to a specific day, of ביום ההוא or מחר.

48. See Schiffman, Lawrence H., *From Text to Tradition* (KTAV, 1991) pp. 18–19.

49. See *Shemos* 20:8–11, *Devarim* 5:12–15.

50. See *Talmud Bavli, Yoma* 22b, that we do not appoint a leader of the community unless he has a "can of worms" hanging from his neck so that if he lords it over others, we will tell him to step back. This is part of a Talmudic discussion which considers Shaul Hamelech to have naturally had moral inclinations superior to David HaMelech. However, because Shaul considered himself so inherently innocent, he was not able to admit his guilt, something David did more readily. See *Sifra, Parashas Vayikra* §5, cited by *Rashi* to *Vayikra* 4:22.

51. See *Sanhedrin* 98a – Mashiach is among the sick and suffering.

52. See Rav Shimshon Raphael Hirsch, *Bereishis* 12:6.

53. *Talmud Bavli, Pesachim* 116a.

54. See *Rabbeinu Bechaya, Shemos* 12:2.

55. *Shemos* 12:43,48.

56. See *Shibbolei HaLeket*.

57. *Abarbanel*.

58. The years of Leivi; *Shemos* 6:16.

59. The years of Kehas, ibid., 18.

60. The years of Amram, ibid., 20.

61. See *Shadal, Shemos* 12:40.

62. This is the formulation of *Rambam, Hilchos Teshuvah* 6:5.

63. *Devarim* 23:8. God told Moshe that when we would leave Egypt, ונצלתם את מצרים (*Shemos* 3:22), that we would despoil Egypt by taking gifts from them. In light of the mitzvah not to hate Egyptians, (*Devarim* 23:8), perhaps we can translate this as "We would save Egypt." As a result of the good will fostered by these gifts, we would be able to move on from the bitter memories of slavery and remove hatred and grudges from our hearts to fulfill the mitzvah of *Devarim* 23:8.

64. See *Esther Rabbah* §7. See also, *Talmud Bavli, Sanhedrin* 91b.

65. See *Talmud Bavli, Shabbos* 87a, הר סני – הר שירד ממנו שנאה לישראל. The Talmud suggests a linguistic *derash* to expound the name of the mountain upon which we received the Torah, connecting the word Sinai with the phonetically similar word for hatred, "*sinah*."

66. See *Esther* 3:8. See also *Rashi, Eichah* 1:21, ד"ה כי אתה עשית, quoted in the next question.

67. See *Tanchuma Yashan, Shemos* §6, expounding *Shemos* 1:7, that "ותמלא הארץ אותם – בטיאטרות ובקירקסאות – the land was filled with them; in the theaters and circuses."

68. *Bereishis* 31:24.

69. Ibid., 31:3.

70. See *Bereishis* 31:36–42. Even the way Yaakov speaks in verse 42 seems to be aware of some kind of fulfillment of how *Bereishis* 15:14 is understood by *Shemos* 3:21. See also *Bereishis* 31:7.

71. *Bereishis* 15:13.

72. Ibid., 30:43.

73. The departure from the simple meaning of a text uses a similar verb, of אין מקרא יוצא מידי פשוטו; צא ולמד thus bids us to depart from the פשט reading, to realize what Lavan did to us.

74. See *Torah Sheleimah*, vol. 9, pp. 243–244.

75. See *Rashbam, Devarim* 26:5. Avraham was from Aram and the verse quickly turns to refer to Yaakov and his sons.

76. *Ibn Ezra*, ibid. Yaakov is referred to as an Aramean because of all the years he spent there.

77. See *Targum Onkelos*, ibid. See also Nechama Leibowitz, Studies in *Devarim, Ki Tavo*, ch. 1, regarding the use of the word אבד as a verb as opposed to as an adjective.

78. *Bereishis* 30:27, 31:24, 42.

79. See *Avadim Hayinu* (Maggid Section 3), in the answer to the wise son.

80. Yaakov, according to tradition, felt the need to point this out to Eisav, in a comment that appears in some versions of *Rashi* to *Bereishis* 32:5, ד"ה גרתי. The comment expounds on the extraneous words of "עם לבן גרתי ואחר עד עתה – I resided with Lavan and remained until now." The verse could either have read, עם לבן גרתי עד עתה or עם לבן אחרתי עד עתה. The extraneous word גרתי is expounded to point out that this word's numerical value corresponds to the number of Torah commandments, 613. Yaakov tells Eisav, "עם לבן גרתי ותרי"ג מצוות שמרתי ולא למדתי ממעשיו הרעים – I resided with Lavan and I observed the 613 mitzvos, and I did not learn from his evil deeds." Yaakov had to always remain on guard to maintain his moral compass.

81. See end of *Sefer Yoel* and *Sefer Amos* who make this same point regarding tending to the fruits of Israel.

82. *Shemos* 12:12. See also *Bamidbar* 33:4.

83. *Shemos* 7:24.

84. Ibid., 8:8.

85. See *Rashi, Shemos* 8:17.

86. E.A. Wallis Budge, *Studies in Egyptian Mythology* (1904), vol. 2, p. 378. See also Robert A. Armour, *Gods and Myths of Ancient Egypt* (2001), p. 116.

87. See *Shemos* 8:22.

88. Ibid., 10:10.

89. Ibid., 10:15.

90. Bear in mind that the two verses cited above in note 82 in this section, regarding judgments against Egyptian gods, are both stated in the context of references to the tenth plague.

91. Recall that after the plague of *Arov*, Pharaoh suggested to Moshe to offer sacrifices to God in Egypt. Moshe told Pharaoh that the Egyptian people would never stand for that (*Shemos* 8:22). In the end, the Egyptians were subdued to such a level as to be incapable of responding to all our preparations and activities surrounding the *korban Pesach*.

92. Some translators believe that Ipuwer's admonitions are predictions of the future, if the king fails to heed his words, akin to the prophecies of Yirmiyahu and Yechezkel. However, Gardiner argued in his introductory remarks to his translation that the descriptive passages were too detailed to be considered predictions. Predictions of this sort would tend to be more general than what follows here. Ipuwer describes the events as if they are before his own eyes and he begs the king to take immediate action to end them. He also places the blame for the misery on the king himself. See *Shemos* 10:7.

93. Recall that at the Burning Bush, Moshe was told to take water from the Nile and pour it on the ground where it would turn to blood (*Shemos* 4:9).

94. Hail fell with fire flashing in its midst (*Shemos* 9:24).

95. The locusts devoured whatever grew from the fields (*Shemos* 10:15).

96. *Shemos* 12:35.

97. Ibid., 12:38.

98. Ibid., 13:21.

99. See Rav Ovadiah Yosef, *Yabia Omer* 1:41, regarding Chanukah and Purim, which also involved the death of others.

100. *Mishlei* 24:17.

101. *Avudraham*. See also *Beis Yosef, Orach Chaim* 490, ד"ה כל הימים, *Shulchan Aruch, Orach Chaim* 490:4, *Taz* §3, *Mishnah Berurah* §7.

102. See *Talmud Bavli, Menachos* 96; ד"ה זז ד יה ז". Rabbi Yehudah listed the mnemonic this way, in the Mishnah's words, so that he would not err.

103. *Iyov* 33:29.

104. See *Seforno, Shemos* 8:12.

105. *Melachim I* 18:21.

106. *Shemos* 12:26–27.

107. See these and other differences between the *rasha* and the other three sons; above, *Arbah Banim* (Maggid Section 7a–7d.)

108. Based on a *sichah* given by Rav Lichtenstein, adapted by Shaul Barth and translated by Kaeren Fish.

109. *Shemos* 12:27.

110. This is the same reference as in the *Aleinu LeShabei'ach* prayer.

111. See *Talmud Bavli, Zevachim* 91a, that sacrificial meat should be eaten in the finest style possible.

112. See *Rashi, Shemos* 12:2, ד"ה בארץ מצרים.

113. *Talmud Bavli, Bava Metzia* 59b.

114. *Shemos* 20:1.

115. *Amos* 9:7 makes the point that other nations have also been delivered from great travail, but only Israel had been redeemed through our revelation of a code of morality. Amos' point is to ask how we are any better than those nations if we are not living up to our moral standard.

116. As our redemption continued, we were faced with a mortal threat from the vengeful Egyptians with our backs to Yam Suf. Responding to the dread expressed by the Israelites, Moshe told them, "ה' ילחם לכם ואתם תחרישון – God will fight for you and you will hold your peace" (*Shemos* 13:14.) This can also homiletically be translated, "God will make bread for you but you must first plow." In this way we are partners with God in our own redemption, as well as in our daily sustenance.

117. *Tehillim* 113.

118. *Maharal* connects *Lefichach* (Maggid Section 18) to *Talmud Bavli, Pesachim* 117a. The ten words for praise mentioned in the Gemara are synonyms, and are ניצוח, ניגון, משכיל, מזמור, שיר, אשרי, תהילה, תפילה, הודאה, and הללויה.

119. See *Talmud Bavli, Berachos* 33b, where Rabbi Chanina rebukes a student for praising God with ten words. Once we use ten words perhaps we should continue ad infinitum! Therefore, we curtail ourselves to the minimal references used in the Torah. Our passage

refers to verbs, not adjectives, so technically we are not in violation of Rabbi Chanina's rebuke. See also *Tosafos, Berachos* 12a, ד"ה אמת.

120. See *Rambam, Hilchos Yesodei HaTorah*, chapter 8.

121. See *Ramban, Shemos* 1:10, ד"ה נתחכמה לו.

122. For this reason our first mitzvah as a free nation was to establish a calendar, where *we* could begin to be the masters of our own time.

123. *Shemos* 5:1.

124. *Avudraham.* See *Midrash Tanchuma, Devarim* §6; see also *Rashi, Devarim* 8:1, ד"ה כל המצוה; *Radak, Yehoshua* 24:32, ד"ה אשר העלו בני ישראל.

125. See *Aruch HaShulchan, Orach Chaim* 473:26.

126. *Talmud Bavli, Berachos* 54a.

127. See above *Bechol Dor VaDor* (Maggid Section 17), Answer 1 to the Wise Son. See also *Lefichach* (Maggid Section 18), Question 1 to the Wise Son.

128. *Shemos* 15:1.

The Pure Son

1. *Eichah* 1:3.

2. *Bereishis* 15:13. See below, *Baruch Shomer Havtachaso L'Yisrael* (Maggid Section 10).

3. See *Talmud Bavli, Sanhedrin* 92b, based on *Divrei HaYamim I* 7:21 and *Tehillim* 78:9. See also *Targum* to *Shir HaShirim* 3:5.

4. *Yirmiyahu* 28.

5. See Rav Yaakov Emden's Haggadah on this part of Maggid. His commentary has been cited regarding the question of inviting gentiles to the *Seder* today. Besides the obvious practical issues of their touching kosher wine, and of any chametz they may have with them, we have the issue of שמא ירבה בשבילים, lest we add more food for them, since the Torah only allows cooking on *Yom Tov* for Jews, as the verse says "אך אשר יאכל לכם לכל נפש – Only what every person is to eat, that alone may be prepared **for you** (*Shemos* 12:16). See *Shulchan Aruch, Orach Chaim* 512, and commentaries.

6. See *Shulchan Aruch, Orach Chaim* 101:4, *Mishnah Berurah* §13, and *Biur Halachah* ד"ה יכול.

7. See *Sefer HaChinuch*, mitzvah 3, *Gid Hanasheh*, in which Yaakov's all-night struggle with the angel is a harbinger for our own struggles in the exile. The morning dawn at the end of the struggle is likened to the redemption that will end the exile. See also *Ramban, Bereishis* 32:26.

8. *Bereishis* 15:13.

9. See *Talmud Bavli, Sanhedrin* 92a based on *Divrei HaYamim I* 7:20–22. See also *Targum* to *Tehillim* 78:9, *Targum* to *Shir HaShirim* 2:7, *Rashi, Shemos* 16:14, ד"ה יושבי פלשת.

10. *Yirmiyahu* 25:12; 29:10.

11. Ibid., 28:3.

12. Ibid., 28:17.

13. *Talmud Bavli, Sanhedrin* 98a.

14. *Yeshayahu* 22:11–12.

15. Such as *shofar* (יום תרועה), or *bris milah* (יום השמיני). See Mishnah, *Megillah* 20b.

16. *Shemos* 12:8.

17. The *Vilna Gaon* made this point with the word לילה itself, because it looks like a feminine word, which connotes the feminine exemption of time-bound mitzvos. This is what nighttime is – a time of general exemption from time-bound mitzvos. But in reality, לילה is a masculine word, for on this night, time-bound mitzvos are incumbent upon us, and upon women as well. See also *Iyov* 3:3 and *Talmud Bavli, Niddah* 16b, regarding the angel overseeing conception named לילה.

18. *Vayikra* 25:42.

19. The *korban todah* is *kodashim kalim*, which means that among other leniencies compared to *kodashei kodashim* such as the *chatas* and *asham*, a *todah* should be able to be eaten for two days. Yet the Torah (*Vayikra* 7:15) only allows one day for its consumption. This is so that the one who offers it will have to invite many family members and friends to join him so as not to waste so much meat. During this time, one of these guests would be sure to ask him why he was bringing this offering. And even if no one asked, he would be moved himself to explain and tell the story of his personal salvation to the entire group. It emerges that the *Seder* can be compared to a meal of a *korban todah*, for *korban Pesach* is the only example of a *kodashim kalim* that has an even *shorter* time period of consumption than the *korban todah*.

20. *Talmud Bavli, Berachos* 54b.

21. This is the order in *Tehillim* 107 based on the level of threat to life. The Talmud's list (ibid.) is 4, 1, 3, 2, which according to *Tosafos* (ibid., ד"ה ארבעה) is the order of the more common events. See *Shulchan Aruch, Orach Chaim* 219:1 for another order, based on the liturgy of our daily *Amidah*; "וכל החיים יודוך סלה – Everyone **alive** will gratefully acknowledge you." The word חיים is an acronym for חבוש (incarceration), יסורים (general threat to life), ים (crossing a body of water), and מדבר (crossing a desert). This is also chronologically the order of events in our redemption story.

22. To further draw the connection between *korban todah*, *korban Pesach*, and *Birchas HaGomel*, note the unusual nature of this blessing, that it is *only* recited in the presence of a *minyan* and it involves a communal response.

23. The recitation of *Mizmor L'Sodah* follows the same schedule as days when we can possibly offer and eat the *korban todah*, to the exclusion of Shabbos, Yom Tov, Erev Pesach, Chol HaMoed Pesach, and Erev Yom Kippur.

24. Yeshayahu, when referring to future redemption (chapters 7–10), uses *yetzias Mitzrayim* as a paradigm, even referring to the drying up of bodies of water so that more can readily return to Israel (perhaps a hint to air travel?). Yirmiyahu goes so far as to proclaim (chapters 16, 23) that the future redemption will outdo *yetzias Mitzrayim* in scope and measure. This prophecy is used by Ben Zoma in *Amar Rabbi Elazar ben Azaryah* (Maggid Section 5) to bolster his opinion of how we will perform the mitzvah of *zechiras yetzias Mitzrayim* in the Messianic age. Chazal maintain that the return to the Second Commonwealth under the Persians should have been accompanied by miracles along the lines of *yetzias Mitzrayim*, but these failed to materialize because שגרם החטא, our sins prevented it (*Talmud Bavli, Sotah* 36a).

25. *Talmud Bavli, Sukkah* 27b.

26. Ibid., *Sanhedrin* 32b.

27. *Margoliyos Hayam*, ibid.

28. *Tosefta Pesachim* 10:8.

29. See *Shulchan Aruch, Orach Chaim* 476, *Hagahos HaGra*, ד"ה וישן מיד, *Mishnah Berurah* §7.

30. לבקר means to discern between similar items in an effort to clarify their differences. The root is used this way in *Vayikra* 13:36; 27:33. See also *Yechezkel* 34:12.

31. לערב means to mix. An ערוביא is a mixture, as the plague of ערוב was a mixture of animals.

32. See *Klei Yakar, Bereishis* 1:6, ד"ה ויהי ערב ויהי בקר, on the confluence of the forces of the day and night as well as good and evil.

33. *Tehillim* 92:3.

34. *Talmud Bavli, Berachos* 12a.

35. This is known as a remembrance of מדת יום בלילה ומדת לילה ביום (*Berachos* 11b), whereby the nighttime *Shema* blessings reference the elements of daytime, while the daytime *Shema* blessings reference the elements of nighttime.

36. In the liturgy of *Kedushah*, we say, "משרתיו שואלים זה לזה איה מקום כבודו – God's ministering angels ask each other, 'Where is the place of His glory?'"

37. *Yeshayahu* 6:3.

38. Similarly, we ask the rhetorical "מי כאלוקינו – Who is like our God," the answer of which would require a comparative religion course to comprehend, but only if we are already steeped in the conviction that "אין כאלוקינו – There is *none* like our God." This is an aspect of *yiras Shamayim* preceding *chochmah*, as in *Pirkei Avos* 3:9.

39. *Talmud Yerushalmi, Pesachim* 10:4, *Rashi, Shemos*, 13:14, *Rambam, Hilchos Chametz U'Matzah* 7:2 all refer to the one asking this question as a טיפש.

40. *Bereishis* 25:27.

41. *Bereishis* 4:3–4. To be consistent with what Hevel brought, Kayin should have offered מראשית פרי האדמה, from the first (choicest) of his fruits.

42. *Shemos* 13:2, ד"ה קדש לי כל בכור.

43. *Klei Yakar, Shemos* 13:14, ד"ה והיה כי ישאלך בנך מחר לאמר מה זאת.

44. *Shemos* 5:22–23.

45. Note the connection between "בחוזק יד הוציאנו ה' – With a strong hand did God take us out," and wearing *tefillin* on the weaker hand. *Kedushas bechor* teaches that we reserve our best for God, while *tefillin* reminds us how weak we are without Him. This is to say, with God we have everything and without Him we have nothing.

46. Consider also that מה זאת is a statement of wonderment at the events of the Exodus. See the end of the introduction in *Mah Nishtanah* (Maggid Section 2).

47. See *Torah Temimah, Shemos* 6:6, note §5. He notes the source of the cups at the *Seder* from redemptive stages. He prefers to refer to these stages as גאולות and not לשונות של גאולה the latter implying that these words are synonymous expressions for redemption. Rather, they are separate events leading finally to the Promised Land.

48. *Ramban, Shemos* 1:10, demonstrates how Pharaoh dealt with his Jewish problem in stages. Although he may have always intended for their full subjugation, he started with incremental denial of rights and liberties, moving ultimately to murder and open genocide. These five stages of subjugation correspond to the five stages of redemption. They are in *Shemos* chapter 1 and include (1) taskmasters (v. 11), (2) backbreaking labor (v. 13), (3) embittered existence (v. 14), (4) hidden murder (v. 15–19), and (5) open genocide (v. 22).

49. *Avudraham, Malbim*, and *Ohr HaChaim, Shemos* 12:8, each have lists of twelve mitzvos and none are the same. A sample list gleaned from all three includes (1–4) four cups of wine, (5) karpas, (6) washing the hands, (7) matzah, (8) maror, (9) *charoses*, (10) *korech*, (11) *sippur yetzias Mitzrayim*, and (12) *Hallel*.

50. *Bereishis Rabbah* ch. 42 expounds "העברי אברם" (*Bereishis* 14:13) as "אחד מעבר והוא אחד מעבר כולו העולם כל", that Avraham "was on a different side from the rest of the world." This is not to say that Avraham was literally on the other side of a river, but on the other side of a moral plane with the rest of the world.

51. *Tehillim* 146:10.

52. As in *Shemos* 21:6 לעולם ועבדו, *Shmuel I* 1:22 עד שם וישב עולם, and *Melachim I* 1:33 לעולם דוד המלך אדני יחי..

53. Ibid.

54. See also *Rashi* and *Targum Onkelos*, *Bereishis* 14:18. It would appear that this would be a better claim to the land in the eyes of the nations than the source *Rashi* cites in his very first comment to the Torah. That source is for *Avraham*'s descendants to justify their place in their land, as the proof text from *Tehillim* 111:6 seems to say; גוים נחלת להם לתת לעמו הגיד מעשיו כח – He revealed to **His people** His powerful works by giving them the heritage of nations."

55. See also *Tosafos* (*Berachos* 4a, בניהו ד"ה, and *Sanhedrin* 16b, ואחרי ד"ה) regarding a similar phenomenon.

56. See Lavan's words in *Bereishis* 31:53. In *Bereishis* 48:16, Yaakov bids his descendants to name their offspring after him, his father, and his grandfather, but we do not find a single *Tanach* personality bearing the names of any of the Patriarchs.

57. See *Devarim* 22:13 and *Talmud Bavli*, *Kiddushin* 2a.

58. *Bereishis* 13:17.

59. *Talmud Bavli*, *Bava Basra* 119b.

60. *Bereishis* 12:6.

61. See *Talmud Bavli*, *Nedarim* 32a. See also *Rambam*, *Hilchos Avodah Zarah* 1:3, and *Hagahos Maimonis* §2. See also *Ramban*, *Bereishis* 2:3, לעשות אלוקים ברא אשר ד"ה, especially his comment on השלישי ביום.

62. *Bereishis* 21:12.

63. Ibid., 28:4.

64. Ibid., 25:5–6. See *Talmud Bavli*, *Sanhedrin* 91a.

65. Ibid., 27:36. We can also contrast the order of Avraham's sons who bury him; in *Bereishis* 25:9 Yitzchak precedes Yishmael, but Eisav precedes Yaakov in *Bereishis* 35:29.

66. *Shemos* 4:22.

67. The verse refers to King David as a בכור, even though he was the youngest in the family.

68. *Shelah*.

69. See Shemos 12:6 — למשמרת לכם והיה; 12:17 — הזה היום את וכי הזה הדבר את ושמרתם; 12:24 — המצות; 12:42 — הוא שמורים ליל; 12:25 — הזאת העבודה את ושמרתם; 13:10 — לה'; וכי שמורים לכל בני ישראל ושמרתם את החוקה הזאת

70. See *Tiferes Yisrael*, Mishnah *Pesachim* 10:5.

71. Ibid.

72. See *Shir HaShirim Rabbah* 2:8, which says מביט אינו בחשבונותיכם, that the exile was supposed to last longer but God couldn't wait for us. This applies to the future in a Rabbinic discourse in *Talmud Bavli*, *Sanhedrin* 98a, based on *Yeshayahu* 60:22, that our exile can be shortened by our good deeds.

73. *Ramban*, Torah Commentary, *Bereishis* 12:10.

74. *Torah Commentary*, *Bereishis* 15:14.

75. *Talmud Bavli*, *Bava Basra* 119a.

76. Moshe would later use this defense for Israel in the aftermath of the golden Calf. Had God not "begged" him with the word נא to get the gold of Egypt, B'nei Yisrael would not have had the material to make the Golden Calf. צחות בדרך, this is what Moshe meant when he told God, "If you don't forgive them, 'מספרך נא מחני – erase me from Your Book,'" (*Shemos* 32:32). In this vein we read Moshe saying, "God, you must forgive them, for if not, then you should have erased for me the נא from Your Book, back in *Shemos* 11:2, and I wouldn't have gotten the gold in the first place!" See also *Talmud Bavli*, *Berachos* 32a, מעלה כלפי דברים הטיח משה.

77. *Bereishis Rabbah* 44:14. See also *Targum Yonasan* to *Bereishis* 15:10.

78. Midrash *Tehillim* 68:8. See also *Ramban* and *Radak* to *Bereishis* 15:9, and *Tosafos*, *Shabbos* 49a, כנפיה ד"ה.

79. See *Shemos* 32:11–13. *Bamidbar* 14:13–19.

80. See *Shmuel I* 5:1–2.

81. *Yeshayahu* 10:7–11.

82. *Devarim* 32:29–35.

83. See *Yirmiyahu* 7:11.

84. See *Shoftim* 2:20–23; 3:1–2.

85. In a similar vein, such verses as *Yirmiyahu* 5:10,18, 30:11, and 46:28 can be expounded.

86. *Tehillim* 116:13.

87. Ibid., 104:15.

88. *Shulchan Aruch HaRav* (*Orach Chaim* 473:44) draws this connection between salvation and holding the cup. See also *Aruch HaShulchan* (*Orach Chaim* 473:23).

89. *Shemos* 14:13. See also *Divrei HaYamim II* 20:17.

90. See *Bereishis* 31:24. God appeared to Lavan the Aramean in a dream by night and said to him, "Beware of attempting anything with Yaakov, good or bad."

91. See *Rashi*, *Eichah* 1:21, עשית אתה כי אתה ד"ה, that "גרמת אתה בם ומתחתן וממשתכם ממאכלם שהבדלתני אותי שונאים שהם לי ובנותיהם בנותי ועל מרחמים היו בהם נתחתני אם. – You brought

this upon me, that they hate me, because you have set me apart from their food and drink and from marrying them. If I had married among them, they would pity me and their grandchildren." We see that as a result of God's intervention, Lavan did demonstrate pity for his grandchildren even as Yaakov was always made to feel like an outsider. In fact, Yaakov went to Lavan in the first place because he was family (*Bereishis* 27:43), something that Lavan himself noted (ibid., 29:14–15). If even in such an environment Yaakov was made to feel like a stranger, how much more so in other countries.

92. See *Maharal*'s Haggadah where he suggests that Eisav is not included in this paradigm even though it seemed to Yaakov at least that he too wanted to uproot everything, because the paradigm of hatred here is the one who has baseless hatred for Yaakov. Eisav's hatred was rooted in the blessing Yaakov took from him, *Bereishis* 27:41.

93. *Bereishis* 35:2.

94. *Rashi*. See also *Targum Yonasan ben Uziel*.

95. *Bereishis* 31:19. See *Rashi* from *Bereishis Rabbah* 74:5. We discover from Lavan's own words in 31:30 that these were idolatrous objects. See also *Radak, Shmuel I* 19:13.

96. *Shemos* 4:22.

97. Consider other such mitzvos such as the first of our animals (*Shemos* 13:2), the first of our dough (*Bamidbar* 15:20), the first of our shearings (*Devarim* 18:4), and the first of our crops (*Devarim* 18:4).

98. See *Rashi, Shemos* 6:3–4.

99. See *Bereishis* 15:14.

100. See *Avos* 5:1.

101. Chapters 78, 105, 106.

102. The firstborn establishes his forebears as parents. Our mission as a people is to establish the Creator as the Redeemer. For this reason, Moshe's opening words to Pharaoh established that Israel is God's *bechor; Shemos* 4:22.

103. See note 101 in The Cynical Son endnotes. See also *Talmud Bavli, Arachin* 10a, as well as *Teshuvos HaRashba* 1:231.

104. *Talmud Bavli, Sukkah* 55b.

105. *Shemos* 10:14.

106. *Yoel* 2:2.

107. See *Netziv, Shemos* 10:14, for an additional novel way to explain *Radak*'s question on *Rashi*.

108. *Talmud Bavli, Bava Kama* 60a. See also *Rashi, Shemos* 12:22.

109. See *Ramban, Shemos* 12:22.

110. The word הציל in conjunction with בתינו is unusual. The parallel to בנגפו את מצרים should be ואותנו הציל. See *Rashi, Bereishis* 31:16, ד"ה הציל. The meaning of הציל is not "He saved." Rather, הציל in this context is לשון הפרשה, an expression denoting separation.

111. *Shemos* 5:2.

112. Ibid., 8:22.

113. Ibid., 12:39.

114. *Yirmiyahu* 2:2. See *Rashi* to *Shemos* 12:39, as well as to *Yirmiyahu* 2:2.

115. *Vayikra* 2:11.

116. *Moreh Nevuchim* 3:30.

117. I, 27:7.

118. *Shemos* 20:2, אנכי ה' אלקיך אשר הוצאתיך מארץ מצרים. *Hilchos Yesodei Hatorah* 1:1, *Minyan Hamitzvos* #1.

119. See *Torah Temimah* to *Shemos* 6:6, §5.

120. *Shemos* 13:2.

121. Ibid., 13:14.

122. The root פדה, not גאל, is used regarding this mitzvah, and the two words are synonymous. They are used as parallel terms in our liturgy, taken from *Yirmiyahu* 31:10, "כי פדה ה' את יעקב וגאלו מיד חזק ממנו – For God will **ransom** Yaakov and **redeem** him from one too strong for him."

123. See *Baruch Shomer Havtachaso L'Yisrael* (Maggid Section 10), Question 5.

124. See how *Shemos* 10:2 connects to the mitzvah of *sippur yetzias Mitzrayim*. One who experiences a miracle will tell the story of the event to others.

125. *Shemos* 20:2.

126. In the first blessing after *Krias Shema* of *Maariv, V'Emunah Kol Zos*.

127. *Chazal* refer to two types of *Hallel* in *Tehillim*. Chapter 136, which is included in the *Hallel*, at the end of the *Seder*, is known as *Hallel HaGadol* (the Great *Hallel*) because of the repetition of the phrase "כי לעולם חסדו – His *chessed* is eternal" twenty-six times, according to the *gematria* of God's Name. Our Sages especially considered verse 25, "נותן לחם לכל בשר – He gives nourishment to all flesh," to define the greatness of this chapter. (See *Talmud Bavli, Berachos* 4b). Chapters 113–118, which we call *Hallel*, is known as *Hallel HaMitzri* (the Egyptian *Hallel*) because of its connection to *yetzias Mitzrayim* in chapter 114, and our Sages explain that prophets at the time of the Exodus established it. See *Talmud Bavli, Pesachim* 113b.

128. See *Talmud Bavli, Sotah* 36b from *Bereishis* 39:11. See also *Torah Temimah*, §5.

129. *Bereishis* 39:12.

130. See *Midrash Tanchuma, Naso* §30; "הים ראה וינס מה ראה ראה ששמר יוסף כל עשרת הדברות – The Sea saw and split. What did it see? It saw that Yosef observed the *Aseres HaDibros*." This source explains why Yosef's descendant, the Prince of Ephraim, brought his offering on Shabbos, because Yosef especially refused to violate the seventh of the *Aseres HaDibros*, "לא תנאף – You shall not commit adultery." For this his descendants would merit the Sea going against its nature on the seventh day after the Exodus.

131. *Talmud Bavli, Pesachim* 118a. See *Abarbanel*.

132. See above *Baruch HaMakom*, in the answer to the Cynical Son.

133. *Vayikra* 26:13.

The Withdrawn Son

1. See *Vayikra Rabbah, Emor* §32. See also *Targum Yonasan* to *Amos* 6:1.

2. See *Shemos* 5:6–11.

3. See *Bereishis* 19:2–3; *Shmuel I* 28:22–24.

4. *Netziv, Shemos* 12:4, ד"ה ושכנו, stresses the communal aspect of the *korban Pesach*.

5. *Tehillim* 104:24.

6. *Bereishis* 28:17.

7. *Bamidbar* 24:5.

8. *Avos* 6:2.

9. See *Talmud Bavli, Kiddushin* 31a–b, and *Sefer HaChinuch*, mitzvah 33.

10. *Shemos* 12:42.

11. *Talmud Bavli, Pesachim* 112b.

12. See ibid., *Shabbos* 24b.

13. *Shulchan Aruch, Orach Chaim* 487:1.

14. *Talmud Bavli, Berachos* 5a.

15. *Rama, Orach Chaim* 481:2.

16. See *Magen Avraham*, introduction to §494. See also *Klei Yakar, Shemos* 15:22, ד"ה וילכו שלשת ימים.

17. See note 29 in The Pure Son endnotes.

18. *Talmud Bavli, Moed Katan* 28a.

19. *Shemos* 12:30–31.

20. *Devarim* 16:1.

21. *Talmud Bavli, Berachos* 9a, *Rashi* ibid., ד"ה לילה: Did we not leave by day as is stated, on the *morning* after the *korban Pesach* the People of Israel went out (*Bamidbar* 33:3)? However, since at night Pharaoh gave them permission to leave...the verse says "night."

22. See H. Tawil, *An Akkadian Lexicographical Comparison for Biblical Hebrew*, (KTAV: New Jersey, 2009), root שמר, pp. 412–413. See also *Yirmiyahu* 3:5 for the words "שמר – guarding" and "נטר – bearing a grudge," used in a parallel structure.

23. Consider, that to say the word for mother – אם – a child need not use any teeth, only lips, but to recognize the word for father – אב – the child needs to be older, for he needs to use his teeth to say this word.

24. *Talmud Bavli, Pesachim* 3b; לעולם ישנה אדם לתלמידו דרך קצרה, a person should always teach his students in a succinct manner.

25. See *Talmud Bavli, Berachos* 48b, and *Kiddushin* 49b.

26. *Talmud Bavli, Pesachim* 116b, ד"ה ונאמר.

27. See Rav Baruch Halevi Epstein's *Haggadah Baruch She'amar*.

28. This is the source of the name of the "Ptach" program for program for children with difficulties in learning.

29. This answer is the text of what appears later in the Haggadah in answer to the question, "פסח שהיו אבותינו אוכלים בזמן שבית המקדש היה קים על שום מה – the *korban Pesach* that our forefathers ate at the time the Temple stood, for what reason?"

30. The text of the *Mechilta* actually has the response to the *rasha* in second person. The *Talmud Yerushalmi*'s version, like the Haggadah's, though, responds in third person.

31. See the *Maharal*'s Haggadah for a development of this theme.

32. See *Rashi, Vayikra* 16:1.

33. These occasions include the characteristics of the moon on *Rosh Chodesh* (החודש הזה לכם, *Shemos* 12:2), the half-shekel (זה יתנו, *Shemos* 30:13), and the signs of pure and impure animals (זאת החיה אשר תאכלו, *Vayikra* 11:2, 4, 9, 21, 29). See Introduction, "The Structure of Maggid," footnote 24, for a more exhaustive list.

34. The extraneous מונחים לפניך, **placed** before you, might add another dimension. The matzah and maror are not simply before us, they are *placed* deliberately before us for the sake of *sippur yetzias Mitzrayim*.

35. Our Sages point to the root אמר as a word that connotes a soft voice, of acceptance and compassion. See *Rashi Shemos*, 19:3, ד"ה לבית יעקב. This is underscored by the fact that in the active voice the word only appears in בנין קל (פעל), and never in בנין כבד (פיעל).

36. See also *Netziv* to *Vayikra* 1:1, ד"ה וידבר וגו' לאמר, and 1:2, ד"ה דבר.

37. See Foer, Joshua, *Moonwalking With Einstein: The Art and Science of Remembering Everything* (New York: Penguin Books, 2011), ch. 5, "The Memory Palace." Chazal have already pictured such learning in *Talmud Bavli, Eruvin* 53a: "בני יהודה דדייקי לישנא ומתנחי להו סימנים נתקיימה תורתם בידן – Because the people of Yehudah were precise on matters of language and assigned symbols to their teachings, their Torah succeeded."

38. See Introduction.

39. *Bereishis* chapter 45.

40. Ibid., 48:8–20.

41. *Shemos* 4:18. The majority of *Sefer Bereishis* runs through generations of brothers who do not get along, but concludes with stories of brotherly resolution. This trend continues into *Sefer Shemos*, where Moshe and Aharon work in tandem, with none of the competetive spirit between brothers that pervades *Sefer Bereishis*.

42. *Rus* 4:6.

43. *Malbim*. See *Rashi, Shemos* 6:18.

44. See *Yechezkel* chap. 20, comparing the contemporary moral depravity of his people, with that of the Jews in Egypt.

45. Chapter 1.

46. See *Rashi, Shemos* 12:40, ד"ה שלושים שנה וארבע מאות שנה. See also *Rashi* to *Bereishis* 15:13 and 42:2, and to *Talmud Bavli, Megillah* 9a, ד"ה ובשאר ארצות.

47. See *Rashi* to *Bereishis* 4:1 and 21:1 for other examples.

48. *Shemos* 12:40.

49. *Talmud Bavli, Megillah* 9a; *Sofrim* 1:8.

50. There is still a problem though because according to this answer, *Shemos* 12:40 refers to the sojourning of Avraham and Yitzchak in the reckoning of "B'nei Yisrael." Rabbi Yitzchak Mirsky (in the translated *Hegyonei Halachah Haggadah* pp. 88–89) explains that Avraham's anguish at the news of the ultimate exile was tantamount to an exile that he himself experienced. It is therefore appropriate to consider that he was part of the Diaspora experience of "B'nei Yisrael."

51. *Talmud Bavli, Bava Metzia* 59b.

52. *Shemos* 7:3.

53. See *Talmud Bavli, Sanhedrin* 90a. God punishes people according to their own deeds and measure.

54. *Bereishis Rabbah* 40:8.

55. See *Ramban, Bereishis* 12:6,10. Avraham descended to Egypt in time of famine to survive there temporarily. The Egyptians oppressed him and took his wife. God avenged this wrong by afflicting the Egyptians with great plagues until finally, Pharaoh sent Avraham from his land with great riches. So too, Yaakov descended to Egypt in time of famine to survive there temporarily. The Egyptians oppressed his descendants, killing the males so that they could assimilate the females for themselves. God avenged this with great plagues until Pharaoh sent the Israelites from the land with great riches.

56. *Bereishis* 12:16.

57. Ibid., 14:23.

58. *Devarim* 15:13. The expression "לא תשלחנו **ריקם** – Do not send him **empty-handed**" mirrors the promise God made to Moshe that the Israelites would not leave Egypt empty-handed "והיה כי תלכון לא תלכו **ריקם** – When they leave, they will not leave **empty-handed**," in *Shemos* 3:21, Yaakov complained with this same language about the way Lavan would send him away after twenty years of servitude: "כי אתה **ריקם** שלחתני – You would have sent me away **empty-handed**," in *Bereishis* 31:42.

59. Chazal contrast Moshe's gathering of Yosef's bones with Israel's gathering of the riches of Egypt (*Talmud Bavli, Sotah* 13a). *Mishlei* 10:8 is cited to describe Moshe's behavior; "חכם לב יקח מצות – He whose heart is wise accepts commandments."

60. *Vayikra* 26:44. This interpretation of the promise appears in the *Malbim*'s Haggadah.

61. *Talmud Bavli, Avodah Zarah* 29b.

62. Ibid., *Megillah* 13b.

63. See *Avos* 3:2, based on *Yirmiyahu* 29.

64. *Bereishis* 31:41.

65. Sephardim read *Hoshea* 11:17–12:14, and Ashkenazim read *Hoshea* 12:13 to the end of the *Sefer*.

66. See answer 1 above to the Withdrawn Child in this section of Maggid and contrast Lavan's name with that of Eisav, also known as Edom, red. Like the colors themselves, Lavan's intentions are harder to read and recognize than are Edom's. See *V'Hee She'Amdah* (Maggid Section 11), answer to question 3 to the Wise Son.

67. *Bereishis* 27:43–45.

68. Yaakov is bolstered by God's assurance, see *Bereishis* 31:3, yet also relies on additional strategies in meeting Eisav, as we read in *Bereishis* 32.

69. See *Ramban, Bereishis* 41:54. Of course, Yaakov descended to Egypt because that is where the food was and that was part of God's plan all along, but it would appear that he had other choices.

70. See above Maggid Section 13l; "וירא את ענינו – זו פרישות דרך

ארץ – He saw our afflictions – This refers to disruption of marital relations."

71. See *Shemos* 4:22–23. The plague of the Firstborn is considered above and beyond the other nine plagues, insofar as it was preordained from the outset of Moshe's mission. Consider that *Dayeinu* lists this plague separately from the other שפטים, judgements, as if it is the purpose of the other nine plagues. See *Shemos* 9:14–16, and *Rashi* to 9:14.

72. *Shemos* 7:22, 8:3, and 8:14.

73. Ibid., 8:15.

74. The forefinger is called אצבע. The other fingers have specific names, (Like forefinger, thumb, etc.), and while all five fingers can refer to אצבע in Tanach, and are pluralized together often as אצבעות, only one is specifically called אצבע, the forefinger. The finger that dips the wine should therefore be the forefinger.

75. This is so even though the word היא, as is usually the case in the Torah, is spelled הוא.

76. *Shemos* 5:2.

77. *Shibbolei HaLeket*. Numerical values are considered acceptable even when off by one, since Yaakov said אפרים ומנשה כראובן ושמעון, which literally means, אפרים and מנשה are like ראובן and שמעון. The first numerical value is 731 and the second is 732, and Yaakov said they are similar.

78. *Yeshayahu* 31:5.

79. A function of this is the omission of prayers whose purpose is to guard and protect, specifically the prayers that accompany the nighttime *Birchas Hamapil* and *Shema*, as well as *Magen Avos* when the *Seder* night coincides with Friday night. See *Shulchan Aruch* and *Rama*, *Orach Chaim* 481:2, and *Mishnah Berurah* §4. See also *Orach Chaim* 487:1.

80. *Bereishis* Chapter 19. At the beginning of the story, Lot serves *matzos* to his guests as this passage continues to describe.

81. *Bamidbar* 11:4–5. The rabble that was among them cultivated a craving, and the children of Israel also wept and said, "Who will feed us meat? We remember the fish that we ate in Egypt free of charge, the cucumbers, melons, leeks, onions and garlic."

82. See ibid., 11–15, and *Rashi*, *Bamidbar* 20:12.

83. *Bereishis* 19:3.

84. *Shmuel I* 28:24.

85. *Yeshayahu* 52:12. See a wondrous Midrashic explanation of the difference between the original redemption and the future redemption in *Klei Yakar*, *Parashas Vayigash*, ד"ה אנכי ארד עמך מצרימה.

86. See *Seforno*, *Shemos* 14:5.

87. See *Nechemiah* 7:72–8:1, and *Rama*, *Orach Chaim* 583:2.

88. *Talmud Bavli*, *Bava Metzia* 59b.

89. See *Ha Lachma Anya* (Maggid Section 1).

90. *Talmud Bavli*, *Pesachim* 39a.

91. This is also the *Targum Onkelos* to the verb ופסח, in "ופסח ה' על הפתח – God will pass over the wall," (*Shemos* 12:23). The *Targum* renders ופסח as וייחום.

92. *Talmud Bavli*, *Rosh Hashanah* 31a.

93. See *Ramban*, *Shemos* 20:8.

94. Interestingly, the only *Yom Tov* we don't say *Yizkor* is Rosh Hashanah, which is called *Yom Hazikaron*. Since the essence of the day is remembrance, *Yizkor* would be superfluous.

95. *Shemos* 12:42.

96. See H. Tawil, *An Akkadian Lexical Companion for Biblical Hebrew* (Ktav Publishing, 2009), p. 412.

97. See *Talmud Bavli*, *Yevamos* 62b. See *Shulchan Aruch*, *Orach Chaim* 493.

98. See *Shulchan Aruch*, *Orach Chaim* 218:1.

99. לקלם is omitted.

100. *Tehillim* 113–118 is known as *Hallel HaMitzri* (the Egyptian *Hallel*) because of chapter 114. It is the only chapter of the six chapters of *Hallel* that directly relates to *yetzias Mitzrayim*.

101. *Tehillim* 115 begins with a long description of the folly of idolatry followed by a long litany of blessings. Our redemption took us from the desperation of an idol worshipping despot with no sense of morality to the joy of God's blessings. See *Yerushalmi Berachos* 1:1, cited by *Torah Temimah*, *Bereishis* 2:3, §5 for the connection between *berachah* and *simchah*. The two parts of *Tehillim* 115 exemplify מיגון לשמחה by beginning with the depravity of idolatry and concluding with the blessing and joy of God's service. This is another manifestation of מתחיל בגנות ומסיים בשבח, that we begin with disparagement and end with praise. See Maggid Sections 3 and 9.

102. *Tehillim* 116:3–4. The entire chapter moves from despair to salvation and joy.

103. *Tehillim* 118:14.

104. Ibid., 15.

105. Ibid.

106. Ibid.

107. *Talmud Bavli*, *Megillah* 31a.

108. *Shemos* 12:22; "ואתם אל תצאו איש מפתח ביתו עד בקר – None of you shall go outside the door of his house until morning."

109. See *Bereishis Rabbah* 50:12. *Rashi Bereishis* 19:3, ד"ה ומצות אפה.

110. *Bereishis* 19:17; "אל תביט אחריך – Do not look behind you."

111. *Talmud Bavli, Arachin* 10b.

112. The number of bulls brought on each day of *Sukkos* decreases by one with each passing day, initially from thirteen, eventually down to seven; *Bamidbar* 29:12–34.

113. *Shibbolei HaLeket Hilchos Sukkah, Beis Yosef, Orach Chaim* 490, *Taz* §3, and *Mishnah Berurah* §7.

114. *Talmud Bavli, Sukkah* 55b.

115. *Zechariah* 14:16–21.

116. *Tefillas Maariv, Birchas Hashkiveinu.*

117. See *Talmud Bavli, Maseches Avodah Zarah* 3a.

118. *Shemos* 12:43.

119. Ibid., verse 48.

120. *Michah* 7:15.

121. *Haggadas Yaavetz*, p. 41.

122. *Yirmiyahu* 31:20.

123. This fits very well with the beginning of the verse in which God asks us how much longer we will continue to disappear from before Him.

124. This is an allegory used often in *Tanach*, especially in *Yirmiyahu* (see chapters 2, 3, and 31) and *Hoshea* (see chapters 1–2) and of course *Shir HaShirim*. See also above, *Amar Rabbi Elazar ben Azaryah* (Maggid Section 5), response to the cynical son.

125. *Yirmiyahu* 31:21, ד"ה נקבה תסובב גבר.

126. This fits very well with the verse's declaration that the new thing presenting itself will be "בארץ – in the Land."

127. *Bereishis* 2:21–22. This refers to God fashioning Chavah from Adam's rib.

128. See *Bereishis Rabbah* 17:13.

129. See *Reflections of the Rav*, Rabbi A. Besdin (1979), ch. 11, "The Singularity of the Lord of Israel," where the connection between the People of Israel and the Land of Israel is likened unto a marriage.

The Four Sons

1. See *Talmud Bavli, Chullin* 5b, על פי הדבור שאני, *Bereishis Rabbah* 61:4, ד"ה על פי הדבור נשיאה, and ibid., 82:11, ד"ה על פי הדבור קברתיה.

2. *Bereishis* 26:2.

3. Ibid., 26:33.

4. Ibid., 46:1.

5. Ibid., 46:2–3.

6. See *Talmud Bavli, Shabbos* 89b, that Yaakov could have descended to Egypt in the chains of slavery, but through his merit this decree was canceled.

7. *Machzor Vitri, Ritva*. See also *Talmud Bavli, Sotah* 10a, וירד שמשון תמנתה. The word וירד here could actually be used because Egypt is south of where Yaakov was at the time. Chazal often cite *Yirmiyahu* 23:8 as a proof text that Israel is higher than other lands. Yirmiyahu speaks of bringing up B'nei Yisrael from lands to the North, back to Israel. Even coming from the North is an *aliyah*. (There are some cases, however, where וירד could appear to delineate some kind of descension, voluntary or otherwise. See *Shoftim* 11:37, *Shmuel II* 11:8–11, and *Yonah* 1:3–5).

8. *Bereishis* 12:6.

9. This is not conclusive, for we see several instances of the root of ויגר used to describe Patriarchal residence in Canaan. See *Bereishis* 26:3, 37:1, 47:9.

10. *Malbim*.

11. This additionally makes a subliminal reference to the *Bris Bein HaBesarim* in *Bereishis* chapter 15 with the reference to the stars (verse 5). There will be an additional number of such references in these expositions. (I am grateful to Rabbi Menachem Liebtag for pointing this out to me.)

12. See *Yirmiyahu* 31:20 cited by *Rashi, Devarim* 11:18.

13. *Mechilta, Parashas Bo* §5.

14. *Netziv* points out this difference between the words גוי and עם. Pharaoh was the first person to refer to us as עם, *Shemos* 1:9. Chazal understood this word as a perjorative. See *Sifri* and *Rashi, Bamidbar* 11:1, ויהי העם כמתאוננים. See also, *Igra D'Kalla, Shemos* 13:17, פן ינחם העם. Although today the word גוי tends to be used as a pejorative, *Netziv* in a number of places points to it as an exalted reference. See *Bereishis* 35:11; 46:3, *Devarim* 26:5; 32:8.

15. *Shemos* 1:7

16. According to the cantillation, the pause is on the word גדול. According to the exposition of the Haggadah, the pause is on לגוי.

17. See *Rashbam, Shemos* 1:7.

18. *Shemos* 11:3.

19. *Yeshayahu* 11:1.

20. *Yirmiyahu* 23:5.

21. Chapter 36.

22. *Zechariah* 3:9.

23. These words are found across the facade of the front of Yad Vashem in Jerusalem.

24. See *Mechilta*, *Pischa* §5.

25. *Abarbanel* and *Netziv*.

26. *Ramban* points out that שרי מסים, while often translated as "taskmasters," actually means "tax-masters." The "tax" due to the country took on the form of physical labor.

27. Indeed, Chazal (*Talmud Bavli*, *Sotah* 11b) say that Pharaoh had such meetings.

28. *Ohr HaChaim* elaborates on this, in *Shemos* 2:23.

29. See *Shemos Rabbah* 21:5. The parable implies that B'nei Yisrael did not pray before this time.

30. The same two reasons may apply as well to the stories of *Sefer Shoftim* when B'nei Yisrael were afflicted by enemies. See Rav Menachem Kasher's *Torah Shleimah* to *Shemos* 2:23, for *midrashim* which give both sides, namely, that B'nei Yisrael cried from affliction or that they cried in repentance.

31. See Nechama Leibowitz, Studies in *Shemos*, *Parshas Shemos*, Essay 5.

32. See *Rashi*, *Shemos* 3:2, ד"ה מתוך הסנה, bolstered by *Tehillim* 91:15, "עמו אנכי בצרה – I am with him in pain." *Yeshayahu* 63:9 makes the same point; "בכל צרותם לא צר – in all their pain He has pain." The word לו is spelled לא according to the *mesorah* to indicate that even when it appears that God is aloof of our suffering, He nonetheless feels the pain with us.

33. *Bereishis* 26:2–5.

34. Ibid., 28:13–15.

35. *Abarbanel*.

36. It seems from Chazal that this separation was voluntary and was led by Moshe's own father Amram. See *Talmud Bavli*, *Sotah* 12a and *Rashi*, *Shemos* 2:1 *Abarbanel* also explains that this separation was voluntary. *Malbim* differs, and explains the separation was forced upon them by the Egyptians. It would appear that the use of עינו would connote an involuntary situation.

The question at hand though is another one: Once the Egyptians were no longer committing infanticide, why would they separate the men and the women if by then, they were interested in a greater population of slaves? Usually slave owners are happy with the promiscuity of their slaves. Our tradition tells us, though, that everyone in Israel knew their specific lineage, as we are told, "על משפחותם לבית אבותם ויתילדו – They declared their pedigrees according to their families," (*Bamidbar* 1:18). The exception to this is given special reference

in *Vayikra* 24:10–23, indicating that the Israelites were not promiscuous.

37. It would appear that Amram's establishment of divorce and his remarriage as an official act, in light of what *Rambam* says of pre-Sinaitic marriage in *Hilchos Ishus* 1:1, may explain an otherwise puzzling reference to Amram in *Hilchos Melachim* 9:1.

38. See *Talmud Bavli*, *Yoma* 77b, and *Nedarim* 81b.

39. See *Bereishis* 4:25, *Shmuel I* 1:19. *Machzor Vitri* makes this connection.

40. 65:23.

41. *Iyov* 5:7. This point is also the main focus of *Tehillim* chapters 49 and 144. Also, notice the preponderance of the root עמל in *Koheles* 5:12 through 6:7, in reference to childbearing and childrearing.

42. See *Ramban*, *Bereishis* 12:6.

43. *Yeshayahu* 30:20.

44. *Bamidbar* 22:25.

45. *Tehillim* 106:42.

46. *Shoftim* 2:18. *Metzudas Tziyon* sees those two words in *Shoftim* as parallel and repetitive, while *Malbim* suggests a difference between the two words.

47. *Seforno*. This would appear to be the simple reading of *Shemos* 12:23.

48. *Abarbanel*.

49. See verses such as *Bereishis* 22:15, *Bereishis* 32:29, *Shemos* 3:2–4, and *Rashbam* to *Bereishis* 18:2, where man experiences the Shechinah through an angel. This is why Manoach, in *Shoftim* 13:22, feared for his life after seeing an angel, saying, "כי אלקים ראינו – for we saw God."

50. See *Talmud Bavli*, *Bava Basra* 15a, הוא שטן הוא יצר הרע הוא מלאך המות.

51. *Vilna Gaon*.

52. *Shemos* 12:30.

53. *Shemos Rabbah* 18:3. This has ramifications for firstborn women and the fast of *Erev Pesach*. See *Rama*, *Orach Chaim* 470:1, *Mishnah Berurah* §3. See also Rav Ovadiah Yosef, *Teshuvot Yechaveh Daat* 3:25. See also Rabbi Yehudah HaChassid to *Shemos* 12:29, regarding the Midrash's statement that when God's Name is preceded by the letter ו, His Heavenly Court is included as well. See *Bereishis Rabbah* 51:2, *Rashi*, *Bereishis* 19:24, ד"ה וה' המטיר. This is relevant to our discussion since the Tenth Plague begins וה' הכה. See *Rashi*, *Shemos* 12:29, as well.

54. *Teshuvot Yechaveh Daat* 3:25.

55. *Shemos Rabbah* 10:2, *Midrash Tehillim* 78:16.

56. *Shemos* 9:16. In the verse just before this, God tells

Moshe to tell Pharaoh "עתה שלחתי את ידי ואך אותך ואת עמך **בדבר** – I could have stretched forth my hand and stricken you and your people **with Dever**."

57. Shemos 5:3.

58. Ibid.

59. See Rashi, Shemos 7:3, and the answer to the Withdrawn Son to the fourth question in Baruch Shomer Havtachaso L'Yisrael (Maggid Section 10).

60. The sword described in this verse is one of three choices of punishment that were offered to King David for his sin of haughtiness in counting the Israelites in Shmuel II chapter 24. David's choice was preceded by a statement of tribulation, "ויאמר דוד אל גד צר לי מאד נפלה נא **ביד ה' כי רבים רחמיו וביד אדם אל אפולה** – David said to Gad, 'I am in great distress. Let us fall into the hands of the Lord, for His compassion is great, **and let me not fall into the hands of man**.'" See Radak to Shmuel II 24:14, for an explanation as to how David's choice of pestilence put him in God's merciful hands more than the other two choices. In any event, this story connects to our previous theme of God's sole action – even as we have a reference to an angel – a reminder to the משחית in the Tenth Plague. The חרב in Shmuel II as well as in the Tenth Plague, came directly from God.

61. Malbim.

62. The problem is that Moshe and Aharon showed B'nei Yisrael the miracles *before* they appeared to Pharaoh (Shemos 5:30). As such, they exhausted their vehicle of proving to B'nei Yisrael that God indeed had sent them. See my article on Parashas V'Eschanan in Mitoch Ha'Ohel, Yeshiva University Press, 2010, pp. 423–427.

63. The Yoel citation is not a proof text that "מופתים" refers to דם. If that were so, the Haggadah would here read שנאמר, and not כמה שנאמר (Malbim).

64. Malbim contrasts these two words similarly, in Shemos 7:3 and Yeshayahu 8:18.

65. Malbim.

66. Kuzari.

67. The Tenth Plague alone is the exception to this, as we see from Shemos 12:29. Perhaps only a captive from another nation in Egypt would suffer this fate as he had become a quasi-resident of Egypt. A foreigner who happened to be passing through Egypt at the time may not have suffered such a fate.

68. Shemos 15:26.

69. Vilna Gaon.

70. See Seforno, Shemos 14:30.

71. Shemos 14:31.

72. See the commentaries of Chasam Sofer and Rabbi Akiva Eiger to this verse, as well as Magen Avraham, in his comments to the end of Orach Chaim §67.

73. See Bava Basra 116a for a similar exposition of יד.

74. Shibbolei HaLeket.

75. See Ramban, Shemos 1:10, לו. ד"ה הבה נתחכמה The stages of subjugation were (1) שרי מסים – tax-masters, (2) עבודת – backbreaking work, (3) וימררו את חייהם – embittered lives, (4) העבריות מילדות – the decree on the Jewish midwives (to secretly kill the boys), and (5) השלכת הבנים ביאור – openly drowning the boys.
These five stages of subjugation are undone by five stages of redemption. These include (1) והוצאתי, (2) והצלתי, (3) וגאלתי, (4) ולקחתי, and (5) והבאתי. These expressions are known as לשונות של גאולה, expressions of redemptions. See Torah Temimah, Shemos 6:6, note §5, who suggests referring to these terms as "stages of redemption," rather than "expressions of redemption."

76. Talmud Bavli, Berachos 54b. This takes the form of Birchas HaGomel today, and in Temple times a korban todah, thanksgiving offering, would be brought.

77. Notice the juxtaposition of Tehillim 107 which is the source of this law (see Berachos 54b), and the chapter just before it, which reviews the redemption from Egypt. Both chapters refer to God responding to the Israelites, "בצר להם – in their tribulations" (see 106:44, 107:6,13,19,28), as if to connect yetzias Mitzrayim with personal travails.

78. See Mishnah, Zevachim 5:6.

79. To Vayikra 7:15, 22, and 29.

80. The korban Pesach has even less time for consumption than the korban todah. See Mishnah, Zevachim 5:8.

81. Tehillim 92:2.

82. This is an exposition of the word עלינו. The simple meaning of this passage describes what God did for **us**, and this exposition understands what is incumbent upon us. See Klei Yakar, Devarim 17:14, עלי. ד"ה אשימה

83. Mishnah, Middos 2:5.

84. Horeb, Vayikra 23:4.

85. Shemos Rabbah 15:26. See also Rabbeinu Bachaya to Bereshis 38:30 and to Shemos 12:2.

86. These generations run through the tribe of Yehudah based on Rus 4:18–22. They are (1) Avraham, (2) Yitzchak, (3) Yaakov, (4) Yehudah, (5) Peretz, (6) Chetzron, (7) Ram, (8) Aminadav, (9) Nachshon, (10) Salmon, (11) Boaz, (12) Oved, (13) Yishai, (14) David, and (15) Shlomo.

87. The Temple was built in Shlomo's fourth year as king (Melachim I 6:1), and Rechavam was born before Shlomo assumed the throne. We know this because Shlomo

ruled for forty years (ibid., 11:42), and Rechavam became king at the age of forty-one (ibid., 14:21).

88. The list of kings who ruled following Shlomo until the *Churban* differs between *Shemos Rabbah* 15:26 and *Rabbeinu Bachaya* (*Bereishis* 38:30). (1) Rechavam, (2) Aviah, (3) Asa, (4) Yehoshafat, (5) Yehoram, (6) Achazyahu, (7) Yoash, (8) Amatziah, (9) Uziah, (10) Yosam, (11) Achaz, (12) Yechezkiah, (13) Menasheh, (14) Amon, and (15) Yehoyakim.

89. See also *Yalkut Me'am Lo'ez, Shmuel II* 7:1 (p. 92). See also the liturgy of *Kiddush Levanah*, which cites an explanation of *Yeshayahu* 60:20, that when the moon will be in a constant state of fullness, the verse reads "וירחך לא יאסף –your moon shall not wane." This is obviously not a cosmological designation, and in light of the comparison here, refers to a time when we will fall no more.

90. For the additional references to the number fifteen as it relates to our deliverance from Egypt, see the answer to the wise son below, in *Bechol Dor VaDor* (Maggid Section 17).

91. *Sifsei Chachamim* to *Bamidbar* 33:3. See note 71 in *The Withdrawn Son* endnotes to explain why *Makkas Bechoros* is given a separate entry in addition to the general "שפטים" used to refer to the other Plagues.

92. *Bereishis* 15:14.

93. Ibid., 12:16.

94. Ibid., 14:23.

95. See *Ramban, Bereishis* 12:10.

96. See Nechama Leibowitz, Studies in *Bereishis, Parashas Bereishis*, essay 5, on the three things Kayin and Hevel fought over, pp. 38–39.

97. See *Rashbam, Shemos* 13:21.

98. *Shemos* 14:21, and the same root appears in *Tehillim* 78:13 and *Nechemiah* 9:11. When Yehoshua splits the *Yarden*, the word "יכרתון – cut," is used; *Yehoshua* 3:13. When Eliyahu and Elisha split the *Yarden*, "ויחצו – divided" is used; *Melachim II* 2:8,14. This seems to be akin with *Tehillim* 136:13 where we find the poetic "לגזר ים סוף לגזרים – who cut the Yam Suf into pieces." This is the source of the midrashic explanation that the Yam Suf was cut into twelve sections, one for each tribe. See *Talmud Bavli, Arachin* 15a.

99. *Shemos* 14:16,22, *Nechemiah* 9:11. *Tehillim* 106:9 refers to the sea bed as totally dry; ויחרב.

100. See *Torah Sheleimah, Shemos* 14:22, note 143, as well as an abundance of sources cited in Ginzberg, Louis, *The Legends of the Jews*, vol I, pp. 555–558, "The Passage through the Red Sea."

101. *Tehillim* 106:9.

102. *Rashbam, Shemos* 14:21.

103. *Shemos* 14:30–31.

104. See *Seforno, Shemos* 14:30.

105. See *Devarim* 8:15–16.

106. *Talmud Bavli, Bava Metzia* 86b.

107. *Bereishis* 18:5, "ואקחה פת לחם – I will take bread."

108. *Shemos* 16:4; "הנני ממטיר לכם לחם מן השמים – I will rain bread for you from the heavens."

109. *Bereishis* 18:4; "יוקח נא מעט מים – Let a little water be brought."

110. *Shemos* 16:23.

111. *Bereishis* 2:1–3.

112. See *Shir HaShirim Rabbah* 1:28.

113. Shemos 19:2 describes how the Israelites arrived at the mountain to receive the Torah, and begins with three plural verbs; ויסעו,ויבאו, and ויחנו. The fourth, describing how they camped there, is in singular, ויחן, hence the *derash* that they were all united in their focus of receiving the Torah.

114. *Shemos* 3:12.

115. See *Shemos* 3:17.

116. In this way God said, "והוצאתי אתכם מתחת סבלות מצרים – I will bring you out from under the burdens of Egypt." We do, however, see the causative used in *Shemos* 12:42 and 51. These words mean that God caused us to be brought out.

117. See *Rashi, Sukkah* 41a, ד"ה אי נמי, and *Rashi, Shemos* 15:17, ד"ה מקדש ה' כוננו ידיך.

118. See end of *Ha Lachma Anya* (Maggid Section 1).

119. See *Kamah Maalos Tovos/Dayeinu* (Maggid Section 15a). See also Mishnah *Middos* 2:5.

120. *Shoftim* 5:4–5, *Tehillim* 68:8–9 and *Chavakuk* 3:3 are all veiled references to *Matan Torah*. The latter sourse is read as part of the *Haftarah* for the second day of Shavuos in the Diaspora.

121. See *Rambam, Peirush HaMishnah Sanhedrin, Perek Cheilek, yesod* 9.

122. See the last Mishnah in the first chapter of *Maseches Berachos*, quoted earlier in the Haggadah, in *Amar Rabbi Elazar ben Azaryah* (Maggid Section 5). Ben Zoma cites *Yirmiyahu* Chapters 16 and 23 to bolster his position that *yetzias Mitzrayim* will be eclipsed by the scope of the future return to Israel by the exiles from numerous lands. Yirmiyahu's words are the following: "הנה ימים באים נאום ה' ולא יאמרו עוד חי ה' אשר העלה את בני ישראל מארץ מצרים כי אם חי ה' אשר העלה ואשר הביא את זרע בית ישראל מארץ

צפונה ומכל הארצות אשר הדחתם שם וישבו על אדמתם – A time is coming, says the Lord, when it shall no longer be said 'As the Lord lives who brought the Israelites out of the Land of Egypt,' but rather 'As the Lord lives who brought out and led the offspring of the House of Israel from the northland and from all the lands to which I have banished them,' and they shall dwell upon their own land" (*Yirmiyahu* 16:14–15; 23:7–8). The end of *Yeshyahu* 11 also uses the Egyptian redemption as a paradigm for future exiles. He refers to the return to Israel through dried up bodies of water, to facilitate an easy return. Perhaps Yeshayahu is referring to air travel.

123. See *Shnei Luchos HaBris, Meseches Pesachim, Matzah Shemurah*, p. 20.

124. See *Avos* 6:4. See also *Tanna D'Bei Eliyahu Zuta* §17.

125. See *Yalkut Me'am Loez, Shmuel II* 5:4.

126. For example, see *Mechilta, B'Chodesh* §2, and *Rashi* to *Shemos* 19:3, that אמר only appears in the בנין קל and never in בנין כבד, as opposed to דבר which almost exclusively appears in בנין כבד and hardly ever in בנין קל.

127. *Talmud Bavli, Pesachim* 116a.

128. See also Rav Ovadiah Bartenura to *Avos* 1:2, הוא היה אומר.

129. *Pesachim* 116b, ד"ה ואמרתם.

130. See *Shemos* 12:8, *Bamidbar* 9:11.

131. See *Talmud Bavli, Rosh Hashanah* 28a, ד"ה כפאו ואכל מצה יצא, *Rambam Hilchos Chometz U'Matzah* 6:3, *Shulchan Aruch, Orach Chaim* 475:4.

132. *Talmud Bavli, Zevachim* 2a.

133. See *Devarim* 6:20–23, *Shemos* 13:14.

134. Consider the last two steps of *Dayeinu*, which are entry into Israel and building the Beis Hamikdash.

135. *Shemos* 3:8.

136. Although Miriam's role in the Torah seems to be limited to her leading a troupe of women with musical instruments after *Krias Yam Suf* (*Shemos* 15:20–21), Chazal explain that she took on an active role in our redemption. To say the least, saving Moshe's life in the beginning of the story, *Shemos* 2:4–9, should certainly be considered a significant redemptive role. She continued to lead throughout the forty years in the desert, and the Well of water that miraculously followed us in the desert did so in her merit. See *Talmud Bavli, Taanis* 9a, שלשה פרנסים טובים עמדו לישראל אלו הן משה ואהרן ומרים. Although some Biblical references to our redemptive leadership at the time of the Exodus mention only Moshe and Aharon, such as *Yehoshua* 24:5 and *Tehillim* 77:21, Michah's reference and certainly the Rabbinic statement above suffices to make our point.

137. *Michah* 6:14.

138. See the source cited by *Yalkut Shimoni, Beha'aloscha* §737.

139. *Bamidbar* 15:1–16.

140. Ibid., 17–21.

141. Ibid., 37–41.

142. See *Yechezkel* 44:30.

143. *Shemos* 12:23.

144. See *Midrash Vayosha* §3.

145. Perhaps, after naming her first child Miriam, Yocheved bemoaned the fact that she was pregnant again a few years later and named the child אהרן, as if to say, "Woe is to my pregnancy." After this Chazal indicate that Amram and Yocheved separated to avoid bringing more children to experience their misery. See *Talmud Bavli, Sotah* 13a.

ABOUT MOSAICA PRESS

MOSAICA PRESS is an independent publisher of Jewish books. Our authors include some of the most profound, interesting, and entertaining thinkers and writers in the Jewish community today. There is a great demand for high-quality Jewish works dealing with issues of the day — and Mosaica Press is helping fill that need. Our books are available around the world. Please visit us at **www.mosaicapress.com** or contact us at **info@mosaicapress.com**. We will be glad to hear from you.

ABOUT THE AUTHOR

RABBI ALLEN SCHWARTZ has served the Upper West Side of Manhattan since 1985 and has been the rabbi of the historic Congregation Ohab Zedek for the past thirty-one years. He has taught over 3,000 students at Yeshiva University since 1983 and currently teaches at Ramaz High School and Manhattan Day School as well. His Bible curriculum is widely used in day schools and high schools in the New York area, and he has also served as camp rabbi and educational director at Camp Morasha and Camp Mesorah for many summers. He is the author of numerous articles on Biblical and Rabbinic themes and recently published the commentary of Rabbi Elazar Rokeach to *Sefer Mishlei* (The Book of Proverbs).